THE GOOD CIDER GUIDE

From the publishers of the **GOOD BEER GUIDE**

David Kitton

IN ASSOCIATION WITH
THE CAMPAIGN FOR REAL ALE

Author: **David Kitton**
Design: **Opus**
Illustrations: **Phil Evans**
Typeset and printed by: Cambridge University Press
ISBN **1–85249–104–3**
Published by **Alma Books Ltd.,** *a wholly-owned subsidiary of the Campaign for Real Ale Ltd., 34 Alma Road, St Albans, Herts.*

Alma Books would like to thank Rick Zaple of APPLE for his help in producing this guide.

CONTENTS

HOW TO USE THE GUIDE

COUNTY GUIDE
This lists every cider outlet in separate county sections, with a location map at the start of each. Refer to this if you are travelling and looking for general information on the availability of cider in the vicinity.

MAKERS' GUIDE
This describes each maker, large and small, his products and where they may be obtained. Use this section if you are seeking details of a particular cider. Directions for finding cider makers who sell direct from their premises are also given.

OUTLETS

(P) Pubs, hotels, restaurants and clubs having a licence for the consumption of cider or perry on the premises.
(OL) Premises at which cider or perry may only be purchased to take away.
▲ Makers from which cider or perry may be purchased to take away only.
(D) Distributors.

PUB FACILITIES

Snacks:
sandwiches; rolls; pies and pasties sufficient to keep the wolf from the door.

Meals:
at least one hot and/or cold dish with vegetables: often a full three courses.

Restaurant:
a separate dining area apart from the bar.

Childrens' room:
a room or space within the pub which children may occupy if accompanied by an adult: many pubs do not permit children under 14 in the bar area, though this may be varied if a full meal is being taken. In some cases pubs also provide a separate play room for children – parents are then free to leave the little darlings and enjoy a quiet drink!

Accommodation:
the standard and facilities offered varies widely, as does the price: you are advised to telephone first to ensure satisfaction. Often the small pub with one or two bedrooms gives better value for money than the large town hotel with massive overheads.

Garden:
can range from a small patch by the car park to several acres of lawn: it may be assumed that children accompanied by an adult are permitted.

Outdoor drinking space:
the urban equivalent of "garden" – often more cramped, and less likely to provide relaxed and comfortable eating or drinking conditions, with notable exceptions.

Games:
universal games such as darts are not included, only those which are not so usually found.

Access for disabled:
usually to at least one bar and toilets, unless otherwise stated. In some cases old pubs may have hazards such as thresholds, but it is assumed that assistance will be given if required and sought.

Camping facilities:
for individual tents overnight, not for an invasion of caravans or long stay.

Near BR station:
normally within ½ mile: services may be intermittent, especially at weekends, and you should check before using the route that you will be able to get back – otherwise see "Camping facilities"!

TELEPHONE NUMBER

Use this to establish if the particular cider you are seeking is "on", rather than travelling hundreds of miles on a wasted journey (yes we've all done it!) Use it too if requiring a meal, especially at weekends, when it is always wise to book, and also for booking accommodation in advance. If possible please respect the proprietor's privacy, and only phone during opening hours.

OPENING HOURS

Under Government legislation introduced in 1988, these are now flexible within certain limits, and details are included where the establishments have given them. Where no information is shown, it is wise to assume the worst, and take it that the old hours still apply. In some cases longer hours than shown may be in force during the summer months. If in any doubt, once again phone first.

METHODS OF DISPENSE

(B) Bottle (BB) Bag in box (CK) Carry keg (DJ) glass demijohn (E) Cask and electric pump (F) Flagon (H) Cask and hand pump (J) glass jar (PC) polycask (PL) plastic container (PP) polypin (W) wooden cask

KEY TO MAPS

- ⊕ town or village with one or more real cider or perry outlets
- ▲ location of cider or perry maker selling direct to public from premises

CATEGORIES

***Category A**
Indicated against individual makers in the Makers' Section of the Guide: a definition agreed by APPLE to denote the very best of cider and perry, with nothing added or taken away. (see separate box for details)

Category B
A more liberal definition of real cider and perry, covering firms in the Makers' Section of the Guide not indicated as Category A: more commercial brands, but with nothing to affect the taste and character of the drink (see separate box for details).

CATEGORIES OF CIDER AND PERRY AS RECOGNISED BY APPLE

Category A – must:

- not be pasteurised before or after fermentation
- not be filtered
- not receive enzyme treatment
- not contain preservatives or colouring
- not have the natural yeast replaced by a cultured yeast
- not have a nitrogen source added unless essential to start fermentation
- not be diluted
- only contain sweeteners if labelled "Medium" or "Sweet", and then only if they are shown to be safe and do not affect the taste
- be produced from only freshly-pressed fruit, and
- not contain concentrate
- not contain extraneous carbon dioxide

While the above Category covers the majority of the makers in the Guide, it accounts for only a small proportion of the total gallonage. Most "real" ciders made in large quantities differ from the definition in some degree, but are sufficiently authentic to qualify as good ciders, the taste and character of the drink being unimpaired. These are covered by the definition below

CATEGORY B – must:

not be entirely made from concentrate
not contain extraneous carbon dioxide

WHAT **IS** GOOD CIDER?

Basically *natural* cider – the fermented juice of the apple, with nothing added and nothing taken away. A hundred years ago you would not have needed to ask that question: almost all cider then conformed to that simple definition. In those days a glass of cider would have been strong, still, and a flavoursome reflection of the complex varieties of fruit from which it was blended.

Today 90 percent of "cider" is a fizzy, frozen concoction of limited strength, owing more to the skills of the chemist than the cider maker: mostly made from imported apple concentrate, which as Anthony Gibson points out in his article, is now essential to meet demand, and actually costs less than using home-grown supplies. Most commercial cider is chock full of artificial colourings, sweeteners, and preservatives, is filtered to appeal to the

eye rather than the palate, is pasteurised to render it inert, and kept and served under carbon dioxide pressure.

But for those in the know, there is a natural alternative, unadulterated and unaltered over the years, which still offers you the pure taste of English apples. With the trend away from processed and artificial food and drink fast becoming a stampede, natural cider is coming centre stage, as the drink you can trust. This is the cider you will find in the Good Cider Guide – and perry too, for the same criteria apply: there are many small firms, selling direct from the farm; but even the "Big Three" – Bulmer, Taunton, and Showerings – are featured, for besides their millions of gallons of keg they also produce the real thing.

CAMRA CAMPAIGNS FOR YOUR CHOICE

You will hear and see much more of the "real thing" from now on, with the recent entry of the Campaign for Real Ale into the cider ring. Labelled "the most successful consumer movement in Europe" for bringing real beers back into the pubs, CAMRA is intent on doing the same for natural ciders and perry. Its sub committee, APPLE, has defined degrees of excellence, detailed in this Guide: Category A – the best and most natural products; Category B – the more commercial brands which still conform in taste and appearance to traditional standards. The full resources and experience of CAMRA and its 24,000 strong membership are now directed to the growth and prosperity of these drinks, on your behalf.

As you will read, there are massive problems to overcome. The number of orchards is declining – an occurrence not confined to this country – and foreign fruit and apple concentrate is flooding in to fill the growing gap, a circumstance which does little for our balance of trade. One wonders just how safe some of these supplies are: other countries such as Malawi, and Eastern Europe, may not have such stringent rules on poisonous chemical sprays as ourselves; what too of the water supplies used here to reconstitute the concentrate to its "original" form? Many of the apples that we *do* grow in this country – only 10 percent of those needed for the whole cider industry – will be found in the ciders featured in this Guide.

Jon Hallam's account of the similar plight of perry pears makes grim reading. But though we may regret the bubbly nature of "Babycham", it would be churlish not to mention that its makers, Showerings, have invested in hundreds of acres of perry pears since the late 1950s, and currently grow a range of 17 or more celebrated old varieties, which are fruiting well. For perry pears at least, Somerset is not all doom and gloom.

The recently launched campaign by the conservation group Common Ground to save our orchards is another encouraging step, not just to ensure future supplies of apples and pears, but also for the future appearance and well-being of our countryside: environmentalists and cider consumers must unite behind this welcome initiative.

WHAT'S IN A NAME?

We have to tackle the problem of name and image. When I first began my then lone campaign for natural cider in the early 1980s, I soon came face to face with this: cider makers appeared uneasy with "scrumpy", or "real cider". The first, they claimed, gave the wrong message to their customers, a bumpkin image they were trying hard to lose: landlords too reacted violently to the word – I have been thrown out of more than one pub for daring to utter it! As to "real cider", the makers argued that "all cider is real, so what does it mean?"

I was firmly persuaded to use the work "traditional", as that was universally acknowledged by the industry as the description for natural cider. Some years on, it is interesting to see how attitudes have changed. One of the firms which earlier echewed "scrumpy" now uses it widely on its products; and so too do many others! Though the word "traditional" is still in common use, especially by the large makers to differentiate the still from the fizzy, it is in fact *this* word which is now being devalued by misuse. Indeed the very firm that urged me to use "traditional" in 1984, today labels its *keg* brand as "Traditional Draught Cider". Even carbonated bottled brands now add "traditional" to their name. Some makers also claim carbonation is traditional – "after all it was used in Queen Victoria's day!"

And the word "draught" is being misappropriated. I have before me a letter from a reader: "I wish there were some legislation that would allow only proper draught cider to be described as such. I am sick of the sweet fizzy drink that is served up in pubs being described as "draught". A few weeks ago my husband and I went into a pub in Weymouth, where we saw a wooden barrel with "cider" marked on it, behind the bar. I asked the barmaid if they sold draught cider – she replied they did. On the strength of this we ordered and paid for our meals. Imagine my disappointment at then being told by the barmaid that "the barrel is only for decoration", and being offered a weak fizzy alternative!"

Even if the aforementioned keg version was not in evidence, it would have done my correspondent no good instead asking for "traditional cider" – I have tried this many times, only to be greeted by blank stares. Had she mentioned "scrumpy" she could easily have finished up in Weymouth Harbour! "Proper cider" would only have made matters worse – implying criticism of the landlord's other products. "Natural cider" would have fared little better, probably resulting in a bottle of Taunton "Natch". "Original" – now that must fit the bill. But no, it has of course been adopted by Bulmers for their far from original keg brand. "Olde", especially with that last letter, should imply authenticity, but I doubt that William Gaymer would recognise the brand that bears his name as his 1770 introduction!

THE CAMPAIGN FOR *REAL CIDER*

The public are now utterly confused about what is being sold, the publicans about what is being asked for. Are there any words left to clarify the situation? I am convinced the answer lies in CAMRA's word for traditional beer – "real". "Real ale" is now recognised and included in the Supplement to the Oxford English Dictionary (Vol 3): the public knows what it stands for; even the dullest bar staff have some inkling. APPLE has thrashed out a comparable definition for cider – so let us all ask for, nay demand, REAL CIDER.

If "real cider" drinkers in the past were guilty of using the wrong words, cider producers now seem set deliberately to create the wrong image. For serving beer or cider, the hand pump has always been regarded as guarantee of a "real" product. But now several cider makers sport a "hand pump" on the bar which dispenses carbonated cider. When pressed – a process I should enjoy applying personally to some of them – they have their answers off pat: "Our product is made from such wonderful English cider apples, and is so pure and wholesome, that we needed a hand pump to put that message across"; "We are appealing to the mature cider drinker, and he expects a quality product to be on a hand pump" – and so on.

We have been down this road before with the brewers, and caused them to withdraw their deceptive fake beer engines: we shall do the same with the cider makers. As with words, so with images, both customers and landlords are being misled. Were Symonds, for instance, to retitle their pump clip "Scrumpy Fake" we should all know where we stood!

THE REAL CIDER REVIVAL STARTS HERE

We stand on the brink of a real cider renaissance. The discerning public are daily becoming "greener" in their eating and drinking choices, and increasingly seeking out the pure, wholesome and organic. Real cider and perry is – literally – made for this fast emerging market: a high quality drink, of infinite variety to suit all tastes and occasions; the only ingredient, first class English fruit (those who do not use chemical sprays or fertilisers on their supplies step forward for an extra cheer!)

Real cider makers must act fast to respond to this new demand for quality. Given that much of the existing paltry apple and pear crop goes into the real segment of the market, and supplies are still shrinking, they must urgently replant old orchards, and create many new ones. It is high time to make good the ravages of those who grubbed up trees like there was no tomorrow, and produced unwanted grain mountains. There is a bright tomorrow, and with the Government sold on taking agricultural land "out of production", growers and makers must unite and use "set aside" positively – designate much of this surplus land for orchards, and press for Government grants to re-establish a self-sufficient apple and pear supply for this county's future needs.

We need too many more makers. Anthony Gibson refers to the dwindling ranks: there are though new faces appearing on the scene, as witness firms included in the Guide for the first time – but this trickle must become a flood. To earn and retain an increased market share in pub and off licence, real cider must rid itself of all that has jeopardised it for so long. A new name "real cider", will help shake off the bumpkin image. But behind the bar old prejudices die hard: the drink will need to be priced to reflect its strength and quality. On purely economic grounds, put yourself in the landlord's shoes – which would you rather sell to a customer: three pints of beer at 120p each, or two pints of real cider at 120p each? The customer drinks less of the stronger product, and the bar receipts benefit less from his visit. That is why many publicans, on taking over a "cider pub", have thrown ou cider – and it is still happening.

With real cider at a premium price, the customer will for the first tin come to realise the potency of his drink, and treat it with the respect deserves. Real cider can be twice the strength of an average pint of beer – dare I suggest the price should be pro rata? A realistic pricing policy would, at a stroke, deter the undesirables, and win back the support of the licensed trade, thus ensuring real cider in our pubs. It would equally importantly benefit the long suffering man at the start of the chain – the grower, who reaps so little reward that he might be better advised to sell his trees for firewood. If we are to encourage investment in new orchards, an essential pre-requisite for the cider revival, there must be sufficient financial incentive.

Up to now, real cider has always amazed me by its cheapness – it is the only exception to the rule "you get what you pay for". In the topsy-turvy world of apples and presses the best ciders have always been the least costly. Small wonder that orchard after orchard, and cider maker after cider maker, have swirled down the economic plug hole. Sensible prices, at the bar – and thus in the orchard, are the only way of ensuring real cider and perry capture their fair share of the new market.

CAMRA believes in the future of real cider and perry. It will campaign for a fair deal for growers, makers, and consumers. It will support new initiatives, publicise the "real" segment of the market, and act as a shop window for the many brands. It will also encourage the commercial firms, including the Big Three, to continue to make and distribute their real products as widely as possible.

Chief among CAMRA's promotion of course is the Good Cider Guide, which will continue to feature all known real ciders and perries in pubs and off licences – and at the farm gate, for many firms will continue to sell direct, and the best bargains will still be found down muddy tracks in remote parts: we shall make sure you hear of them. The Good Cider Guide is the Bible for everyone who cares about what he or she drinks: perhaps in time caring friends will arrange for it to be placed in every hotel bedroom but till then please buy your own, and a copy for each of your friends too!

EPILOGUE

There is a rumour going round the orchards at the moment that the great green Goddess of the apple trees – Pomona – has lately become so disheartened by what she has seen that she has taken to signing herself "Pomme Moaner". Let us hope that, with CAMRA's help, the events of the next few years will cheer the old girl up!

DAVID KITTON

ACKNOWLEDGEMENTS

I should like to thank yet again all those who have assisted in any way in the compilation of this Guide: the cider makers and brokers for details of their products and their outlets; the many landlords and proprietors who took the time to fill in my irritating little forms; individual members and branches of the Campaign for Real Ale for survey forms and information on local outlets; users of the last Guide for updates and corrections; my contributors for their articles; and members of APPLE for their support – especially after a few jars.

DK.

FARM PERRY GETS PARED AWAY

Jon Hallam

It vies with mead and metheglyn for the title of "Britain's most neglected drink": in the minds of many drinkers it is equated with "Babycham", or even mistaken for "Perrier Water"; yet, somehow, farmhouse perry survives with us into the bitter dawn of the 1990s.

Let me define my object. I consider it a personal crusade to ensure the continued availability of real perry. I trust these few lines will convince you that this battle is far from won. Perry is fermented pear juice, analogous to cider, produced from the milling and pressing of dedicated varieties of pears. While many ciders, particularly those of the tradition of Eastern England, utilise culinary and dessert varieties, this is untenable for a decent perry. The word "perry" has long been in common usage. Originally meaning a place where pear trees grew, the name soon became associated entirely with the fermented product, and the former definition became archaic.

Perry was once made throughout a wide area: I have seen the remains of perry pear orchards way outside the "perry heartlands" – in Berkshire and even Cambridgeshire. There are even a few perry pear trees in the Ormskirk area of Lancashire. Such exotic geography has, sadly, passed away: it is to the perry heartlands that we must now journey. Today's epicentre of farm perry is North Gloucestershire; makers are still found throughout this county, and in Herefordshire to the north, Worcestershire to the north east, and Avon to the south. This, though, represents virtually the sum total of the genuine farm house perry seen today. Yet the largest amount of perry by far is made outside this area – by Showerings of Shepton Mallet in Somerset, a subsidiary of Allied Lyons. Sadly none of their production appears in still traditional form, but as a fizzy filtered drink known to millions as "Babycham". Let us speak no more of this factory conditioned drink, and return to the form of perry of our collective youth.

The contraction in farm perry making areas is mirrored in the decline of the traditional orchards of the old varieties of the fruit. Huge acreages have been grubbed up and set to the plough, sounding the death knell for scores of the ancient names. What of Stouton Squash, Clusters, Green Horse, or Winnal's Longden – does even one of these illustrious trees exist today?

The loss of orchards has not only affected perry pears of course – cider apples, even traditional cherries, continue to be lost – but none has suffered the decline of the perry pear. At least half the surviving traditional orchards now contain only aged specimens, many well over 200 years old, whose yield diminishes year by year. Replanting has not taken place, save in the case of one or two far sighted farmers, and with a 50 year gap between planting and a worthwhile yield the future is as bleak as a nuclear winter.

If only there was sufficient fruit, the dozen or so surviving makers would be joined by several more. Even amid this grim epistle there are a few rays of light – new farm perries are being produced in Gloucestershire, Berkshire and the Black Country; but their quantities are severely limited, only a few hundred gallons in all. Today's commercial and semi-commercial farm house perry makers are shown in this Guide: but the merest glance through the County Sections will be enough to show you that there are in this country virtually no regular pub outlets for farm house perry.

This lack of outlets is slightly compensated for by the welcome shown to customers by the individual makers. You may visit the farms at most reasonable times – details are shown in the Guide – and purchase direct. This is a meagre crumb of comfort if you happen to live in say the North East, or in Scotland. Fortunately, however, few parts of the country are entirely remote from CAMRA-organised beer festivals, most of which now include a farm cider and perry bar.

At the time of writing we awaited any changes that the Monopoly and Mergers Commission might institute, but it was hard to see how it would improve the lot of farm perry. To ensure the continued availability of the drink we need to ask for it at every opportunity – nagging your local landlord may have some effect. It will though, never, again I fear be a drink for the masses. Are we then resigned to witnessing the death of farm perry in our lifetime? I say not; CAMRA says not; **you** should say not! It is hardly an original exhortation, but "use it or lose it" is as applicable to farm house perry as to any other threatened portion of our culture.

Jon Hallam is a committee member of the Apple and Pear Produce Liason Executive of CAMRA, and regional contact for Southern England: he is a wholesale distributor of farm ciders and perries.

INTRODUCING APPLE – THE NO PRESSURE GROUP

Mick Lewis

For many years local CAMRA Beer Festivals have sold traditional cider and perry as well as real ale. Very often though it was only one or two brands, with the cider dotted about among the beers. Now all that is changing – more and more festivals are serving a whole range of ciders and perries. Often they are sold on a separate Cider Bar, and at the bigger festivals you may expect to find up to 20 different ciders, and perhaps two or three perries. In this way people can discover that cider has the same variety of flavours as beer: no two ciders taste the same.

These local beer festivals are a valuable source of information to customers and staff alike: a lot of drinkers will be trying cider for the first time, and be asking how and where it is made, where they can buy it locally, and so on. Customers also tell the staff of new cider makers they have come across, and outlets they have found. This exchange of information is very important: it is extremely difficult to keep track of the world of cider – with beer it is easy; there are no breweries hidden away in barns in the middle of nowhere, selling by word of mouth to a handful of villagers: every brewery is well known, and changes can be monitored. But cider is a different story: there are still cider makers all over the West Country who are unheard of outside their own village, and it is a never ending task trying to keep pace with what is happening.

With all this information floating about, mostly in people's heads, it seemed strange that there was no official group within CAMRA to collate what was already known, let alone monitor the situation. Thus in May 1988 a national cider committee was formed within CAMRA; the quaintly named APPLE – the Apple and Pear Produce Liaison Executive.

APPLE has numerous objectives. The most important is to promote cider to a public which has for too long been brought up on fizzy concoctions that have more in common with Tizer than traditional cider. Cider's present position is very similar to that of real ale some 15 years ago – without help, traditional cider will soon vanish. An obvious demand is being ignored by the "Big Three": Bulmer's, Taunton and Showerings. Almost monthly it seems a new keg cider is being launched, to the exclusion of existing traditional products, which are elbowed aside by the advertising men in their quest for yet more "designer" drinks. You will see for example in the Guide the diminishing number of outlets outside the West Country for Taunton Traditional Cider: this is a trend that must not be allowed to continue.

Even more urgent is the plight of perry. This drink is in very serious danger of disappearing in our own lifetime. In the pub, the mainstay of the British drinking public, perry is virtually unknown. Babycham, a drink made from perry pears, is the most extreme example of a relatively new product forcing the original into oblivion. There must be positive action before it is too late.

APPLE aims to publicise cider and perry as much as possible. To this end we have instituted a Cider and Perry of the Festival Award at the Great British Beer Festival every year. Such promotion has given cider and perry national and local media coverage, and brought home to people that the traditional versions of these drinks do still exist. In addition, letting the public know about the more dubious practices of the cider industry is equally important. For example, Symonds' "Scrumpy Jack" is available in both traditional and keg form: but Symonds' practice nowadays is to use a fake hand pump to dispense the fizzy version – this deceives the drinker, who naturally associates a hand pump with something "real". Similarly Addlestones is served by a fake hand pump, with the added nastiness of gas pressure. These practices must be stopped: these firms must not be allowed to get away with it.

APPLE also offers technical support. Since the committee was formed, we have encouraged a number of people to start producing cider and perry for the first time. These even include new ciders in non-cider making areas such as Berkshire and the Black Country. With cider makers retiring and leaving the industry all the time, new blood must be encouraged, and given all possible help.

The point of sale – the public house – is another area where education is urgently needed. Landlords must be told that there is still a market for traditional cider. Unfortunately, with brewery owned pubs, it is often brewery policy that forces the landlord to sell only keg cider. Breweries must be forced to sell the public what they want to drink, not force us to drink what they decree.

As you can see, there is a lot to be done. If you are interested in helping us to promote traditional cider and perry, and ensure its survival, join CAMRA – and get involved!

Mick Lewis is Secretary of the Apple and Pear Produce Liaison Executive of CAMRA, and regional contact for London and the South East.

THE TALE OF TWO CIDERS

ADDLESTONES: THE RISE AND FALL OF A "REAL" CIDER

It was the best of times, it was the worst of times...when Showerings went "traditional". Under their Coates brand they already were of course: selling a very acceptable Farmhouse dry and medium cider. But the firm's commitment to traditional cider had always been less than that of the other two members of the "Big Three", Bulmer and Taunton. Then, in 1986, Showerings awoke to the growing interest in real cider, and decided to aim for "the serious cider drinker".

The spring of hope

Instead of developing their existing Farmhouse brand, Showerings introduced an entirely new cider – Addlestones. It was heralded as "a product that behaves in every way like a real ale. . . . fermented in the barrel and pulled up by hand pump. . . . .with no induced CO2 blankets or pasteurisation to inhibit the naturalness of a unique drink". It was Showerings response to the long established brands of its competitors – Bulmer's Traditional, and Taunton Traditional. Admittedly a touch of modern technology was evident, in the form of two one-way valves allowing the cider to breathe in the cask, but in a world largely dominated by fizzy keg ciders this was a minor quibble. Addlestones was marketed in about 100 pubs, selected for the excellence of their cellars and the expertise of their staff, for "it's important that licensees and cellarmen understand the craft involved in serving a live drink as opposed to pressurised cider".

The cider found general approval: the number of outlets for a commercial traditional cider, especially in parts of the country hitherto uncidered, looked set to increase. In answer to CAMRA's anxious enquiries, the company also pledged its continuing commitment to the Farmhouse brand: good news all round for the "serious cider drinker".

The winter of despair

But all did not go well with Addlestones, and soon the bouncing baby became a sickly child. There were, it appeared, problems with the secondary fermentation in the cask causing unacceptable fobbing on dispense. What was to be done – pasteurise the cider, as was done in another place? Showerings felt that was untraditional, and instead opted for placing the cider in 11 gallon stainless steel kegs, but only filling to 10 gallons. Carbon dioxide would then be introduced into the cask, to keep the naturally produced CO2 in suspension during dispense: the amount of such blanket pressure would, it was understood, be minimal, and not noticeable to the consumer.

When this reformulated version appeared, it was again warmly welcomed; cider enthusiasts drank and enjoyed it. Some, at least, knew of the blanket pressure, but it did not affect the drink, and in many places such as Wales and North-west England, it brought a traditional cider, on a par with Bulmer's or Taunton Traditional, where up to then nothing had existed. Though the blanket pressure put it strictly outside Category A or B of APPLE's code, it seemed fair to condone this mavarick, and include pubs selling it in the Good Cider Guide, while at the same time clearly drawing attention to its shortcomings.

But soon there were disturbing rumours – there were reports of "fizzy pints" in certain pubs. The concern grew when publicans stocking Addlestones revealed the documents they had received introducing the brand and containing instructions for handling it: these spoke of CO2 pressure of up to 10 psi, sufficient to force the cider out of the keg and up the pipes to the bar. They also described the hand pump, a "Keating Simulated Cider Engine", known to the initiated as a fake hand pump. Further reading of these papers showed top pressure and dummy hand pumps to be part of Showerings' policy. This "unique dispense system" it was claimed had been decided upon as "the ideal system to suit both product and consumer imagery". The hand pump, the literature went on, "to the consumer, looks like any conventional 'real ale' system – the handle looks and works just like a traditional beer (sic) pump, but to account for specific product requirement, it is dispensed by CO2 top pressure". In fact the "hand pump" was a tap!

All this was a far cry from those heady days of 1986, and "the craft involved in serving a live drink as opposed to pressurised cider"! Perestroika *without* the glasnost? In the light of these revelations, APPLE decided it could not support the misleading practices being perpetrated by the company, and thus you will not find any pubs selling Addlestones in the County Section of this Guide. It has not been possible, in the time available, to establish individual landlords' attitudes to the gas dispense: some are clearly abusing it, hence the "fizzy pints"; some we believe are not using it, and are serving Addlestones as a perfectly straight cask conditioned cider *pulled* by hand pump – which seems to indicate that all the paraphernalia is uncalled for. Some landlords though, as many customers, may still be regarding the "hand pump" as proof of authenticity.

If Showerings *really* want to produce, as they claim they do, the "best possible" real traditional cider, we shall be with them all the way. At the moment, by CAMRA's definition they do *not* appear so to do. Only "pressure" from all of us can convince them: we ask *you* to take the battle to the pubs which stock Addlestones, and seek to persuade publicans, and through them the company, to come clean with the public, and change their ways. We publish below a list of those pubs known to date to be selling Addlestones – though the number is constantly growing. This is where our campaign must be waged.

With your concerted effort, the next edition of the Guide will be able to welcome them all back into the fold, serving cask conditioned Addlestones as nature intended – we need your *pressure* to end *theirs*!

AVON
Avonmouth: Royal Table
Bristol: Cumberland
Old England
Red Lion
Royal (Clifton)
Nailsea: Queens Head

BEDFORDSHIRE
Leighton Buzzard: Eagle

CHESHIRE
Nantwich: Malbank Hotel

DERBYSHIRE
Annwell Place: Mother Hubbards
Chesterfield: Derby Tup

DEVON
Brixham: Blue Anchor
Chagford: Ring of Bells
Drewsteignton: Anglers Rest
Exeter: Cowley Bridge Inn
Mill on the Exe
University Ram Bar
Kingsbridge: Seven Stars
Newton St. Cyres: Beer Engine
Plymouth: Star of the West
Woodside
Tedburn St. Mary: Kings Arms

DURHAM
Durham: St. Cuthberts Society

ESSEX
Dunmow: Queen Victoria

GLOUCESTERSHIRE
Gloucester: County Arms

HAMPSHIRE
Horndean: George
Liphook: Railway
Petersfield: Old Drum
Portsmouth: Eastney Cellars
Stampshaw
Southsea: Florence Arms

HERTFORDSHIRE
Amwell: Elephants Head

KENT
Hook Green: Elephants Head
Sandgate: Ship Inn

LANCASHIRE
Ormskirk: Buck

LEICESTERSHIRE
Frisby on the Wreake: Bell Inn

LINCOLNSHIRE
Waddingham: Cider Centre

GREATER LONDON
EC1: Crown

GREATER MANCHESTER
Bolton: Ainsworth Arms
Hare & Hounds
Howcroft Inn
Sally Upstairs
Stags Head
Farnworth: Market
Wigan: Raven Hotel

MERSEYSIDE
Liverpool: Coffee House
Masonic
Oakfield
Old Ship
Priory
Richmond Arms
Rose & Crown
Victoria (Waterloo)
Waldeck
Willowbank
Lydiate: Running Horses

WEST MIDLANDS
Birmingham: College of Food
University
Bloxwich: Spread Eagle
Handsworth Wood: Village Inn

NORFOLK
Banham: Ye Olde Cider House
Norwich: Take 5 Co-op

NORTHAMPTONSHIRE
Cosgrove: Navigation Inn

NORTHUMBERLAND, TYNE & WEAR
Newcastle: Cooperage
Forth Hotel
Rosies
North Shields: Wooden Doll

NOTTINGHAMSHIRE
Nottingham: Polytechnic

SHROPSHIRE
Broseley: Foresters Arms

STAFFORDSHIRE
Keele: University
Stoke on Trent: New Bull & Bush
Stoke Inn

SOMERSET
Brean: Leisure Centre
Shepton Mallet: Kings Arms

SURREY
Farnham: Farnham College Grapes Club
Mickleham: Running Horses
Westcott: Crown

EAST SUSSEX
Brighton: Queens Head
Lewes: Dorset Arms

WEST SUSSEX
Amberley: Black Horse
Angmering: Lamb Inn
Billingshurst: Limeburners
Bognor: Friary Arms
Chichester: Rainbow Tavern
Eastergate: Wilkes Head
East Lavant: Royal Oak
East Preston: Three Crowns
Ferring: Tudor Close
Selsey: Neptune
Singleton: Horse & Groom
Wisborough Green: Three Crowns

WILTSHIRE
Biddlestone: Crown

YORKSHIRE
Keighley: Boons Arms
Leeds: Fenton
Pack Horse
University
Long Sutton: Travellers Rest
Ossett: Boons End
Sheffield: Beehive
Broom Hall Tavern
Hadfield
Mail Coach
Porter Cottage
West End

WAKEFIELD: Henry Boons

WALES: DYFED
Fishguard: Old Coach House
Tenby: Lamb Inn
Tiers Cross: Welcome Traveller
Haverfordwest: County Hotel

GLAMORGAN
Cardiff: University

GWYNEDD
Deganwy: Farmers Arms
Llandudno: Gresham
Kings Arms
Penmaenmaur: Legend Inn

CIDER THROUGH THE AGES

Sara Hicks

As elephants will become drunk on fermenting juice, so must some of the ancient inhabitants of these islands, when they first experienced the over-ripe fruit of the wild crab apple tree. They obviously enjoyed it enough to repeat it – for cider is still with us today.

Apples have long been grown in Britain. The apple tree was nurtured by the Druids as a host of mistletoe, and perhaps they too drank cider. Certainly the wassailing ceremonies, still sometimes seen today, are of pagan origin.

The first planted apple trees were "wildings" – wild crab apple trees taken into cultivation. Presumably those with sweeter fruit, or heavier cropping, were chosen for this purpose – the start of selective breeding.

The Roman invasion brought more apple trees. The cider apple Pomme d'apis is thought to be of Roman origin. The name cider itself may derive from the Latin "sicera" (cf Greek "sikera", Old English "seider") meaning an alcoholic drink. Indeed the Romans differentiated between "seider" and "verjuice"; the first being the fermented juice of cultivated apples, and the latter that of wild crab apples. The Romans were, indirectly, credited with the introduction of cider to Brittany: many people fled there because of the invasion, and took their apple trees and cider making knowledge with them.

Cider also reached Normandy from Britain. St. Teilo of Wales visited Bishop Sampson there in the 6th century; he took cider apple trees with him, and together the two men planted a great orchard – "Arboretum Teliavi et Samsonis". The site of this orchard was still known, and famed, in the 12th century. The first recorded named cider apple was the Permain, mentioned as used for cider making in Norfolk in 1204. At that time the monasteries were in their heyday, and were very enthusiastic cider producers. In 1230 Jocelin, Bishop of Bath, received a grant for the purchase of cider presses. In 1282, when records were beginning to be kept, cider was known to be made in Yorkshire, Kent, Surrey, Sussex, Suffolk, and Bedfordshire, as well as the West Country.

The French connection continued: in 1500 Henry VIII sent his fruiterer, Robert Harris, to Normandy in search of apples for introduction to Britain. Harris returned with a whole collection of Pippins, suitable for both cider and dessert purposes. In 1611 the famous plant collector, John Tradescant, visited Holland, Belgium and France in search of fruit trees, including apples. Following this tradition, John, first Viscount Scudamore, of Holme Lacy, Herefordshire, spent four years in France as English Ambassador. During his time there he visited many Normandy orchards, and was responsible for introducing the "Norman" apples, such as Sherrington Norman, White Norman, Strawberry Norman, and so on. Many of this group of apples are still grown today, and newer varieties have subsequently been introduced, such as Bulmers Norman. On his return to Herefordshire this splendid cider maker did not retire, but devoted his remaining years to improving apples and cider making methods. He built a special Repository for the maturation of vintage ciders and perries. The renowned Hereford Redstreak was a "wilding" collected by him.

This achievement won him mention in the remarkable contemporary poem "Cyder", by John Philips, who died in 1703:

> Yet let here to the Redstreak yield that once
> Was of the Sylvan kind, unciviliz'd
> Of no regard, till Scudamore's skilful hand
> Improved her, and by courtly discipline
> Taught her the savage nature to forget.

This poem is an amazing blend of patriotism and bibolatry: it promotes cider over every other alcoholic drink, attacks the people and alcoholic beverages of many other countries, with religious fervour. It is also one of the first widely published works on cider, and contains descriptions of cider making and cider apples: apart from the Redstreak it lists Pearmain, Pippin, Moyle, Treacle and Woodcock, and concludes:

. . . . Where're the British spread
Triumphant banners, or their fame has reach'd
Diffusive, to the utmost bounds of this
Wide universe, Silurian cyder borne
Shall please all tastes and triumph o'er the vine.

Another important work was John Evelyn's "Pomona" published in 1664, and one of the first giving detailed information on cider apples. Following this comes the excellent, and often amusing, "Vinetum Brittanicum or a Treatise of Cider", by J. Worlidge, Gentleman, inventor of the modern apple mill. He was very knowledgeable and enthusiastic on his subject, claiming that "cider of the fruit of the apple tree and perry of the pear are of more use and advantage in these Northern regions than the Blood of the Grape." Worlidge gives much information on cider making (made by ciderists!), the choosing of rootstocks, grafting, and orchard management. But he had some odd ideas on additives, recommending sugar, eggs, mustard seed, wood chips, and isinglass as remedies for "sick cider". He opines on the amount drunk by other nations: he considered the Germans the worst, closely followed by the Dutch and the Poles. He then relates the tale of eight men in a Morris side, who danced regularly, and whose combined ages exceeded 800 years – these men were of course all "constant cider drinkers".

Another drink mentioned in Vinetum Brittanicum is "ciderkin", or "watercider", made by pressing the apple pulp a second time using water, and fermenting the result. This would be the cider equivalent of small beer, and the second rate cider which farm labourers drank in such staggering quantities at that time.

At the time Worlidge was writing there was no duty paid on cider and perry, which encouraged its production, as it was relatively cheap compared with beer or wine. But this all changed in 1763, when a tax of four shillings a hogshead was imposed, and gave excisemen the right, for the first time, to enter a person's home. There was a huge outcry over this, and in 1766 the tax was relaxed to exclude "home brewed" cider. But this duty, along with cheap gin, led to the decline of cider in the 18th century, halted only by the Napoleonic Wars, which slowed the imports of French wines and spirits.

In 1811 the "Pomona Herefordiensis" was published. Written by Thomas

Andrew Knight, it contained detailed colour engravings of cider apples and perry pears. Knight's book was followed by the "Herefordshire Pomona", published in seven parts between 1876 and 1885. This contained pomological descriptions and colour illustrations of nearly 400 cider apples and perry pears. It was the work of the Woolhope Naturalists Field Club, a society of local amateur enthusiasts with an interest in orchard fruits. As a result of their orchard visits they "became strongly impressed with the necessity of some great effort to restore Herefordshire to its true fruit growing supremacy; to call the attention of the growers to the best varieties of fruit for the table and the press; to improve the methods followed in the manufacture of cider and perry, and the quality of these products; and thus to improve in every way the marketable value of its orchard products".

The named authors of this Herefordshire Pomona were Dr. H. G. Bull, a local man, and Dr. Robert Hogg, secretary of the Royal Horticultural Society, and also author of the Fruit Manual. The Woolhope Club set up a Pomona Committee, and distributed young apple and pear trees grafted from old vintage varieties: they were instrumental in saving several from extinction – eg. the Taunton Squash pear. Another great campaigner in Herefordshire at this time was C. W. Radcliffe-Cooke, the local MP, whose enthusiasm earned him the nickname in the Commons of the "Member for Cider". He was one of the founders of the National Fruit and Cider Institute, which came into being in 1903. This was at Butleigh Court, where another enthusiast, R. Neville Grenville, had been experimenting with cider making. The Institute later moved to Long Ashton, near Bristol, and became part of the Government Research Station there. It continued to do marvellous work on tree growing and cider and perry making until a few years ago, when the Government cut off all fruit research there. In 1989 the cider and perry business was sold off privately.

What is the state of cider today? Pretty grim really. Over 90 percent of all British cider is made by just three companies – H. P. Bulmer, Showerings, and Taunton Cider Company. The policy of these "Big Three" seems to be the introduction of trendy "designer cider" It is keg, of course, including a PINK cider for women. There is heavy promotion of established keg brands on television. Keg ciders are now even being sold through fake hand pumps, deliberately designed to appear "traditional".

The small cider maker was hit hard by the imposition of tax on all cider production over 1,500 gallons, brought in the 1970s, and now some of the larger cider makers are lobbying for tax on *all* cider produced. APPLE and CAMRA will have their work cut out to save the small individual "ciderist" from the ravages of the Big Three. The time is ripe for new champions of cider and perry, in the mould of Messrs. Philips and Worlidge, and the splendid members of the Woolhope Naturalists Field Club.

Sara Hicks is a Committee member of the Apple and Pear Produce Liaison Executive of CAMRA, and regional contact for South West England.

STATE OF THE APPLE

Anthony Gibson

It is a rotten time for cider in the West Country. 1989 was an "off year", when the trees cropped lightly – a natural tendency which was of course exaggerated by the drought. In such years any apples the trees vouchsafe are small and hard as ping pong balls. They make good cider, mind you, but not much of it.

Worst of all, though, the established trends of rock bottom prices for apples, the use of imported apple concentrates by the Big Three, the disappearance of small cider makers, and the grubbing up of orchards, are all becoming still more deeply entrenched. The National Association of Cider Makers would doubtless beg to differ from this gloomy assessment. They would point to "bouyant" cider sales during the heatwave (they might have been even better had Somerset's cricket team been rather more successful!) and to their "declaration of intent" to use more home-grown fruit.

For several years now, the cider apple growers, in the shape of the National Farmers' Union, have been trying to persuade the cider makers to agree to the latest French standards: among other things, these insist that to be called "cider", a beverage must be made from at least 50 percent recognised cider varieties of whole apples. Given the present situation, in which the total acreage of cider fruit in Britain is sufficient to supply barely 10 percent of annual cider production, the NFU was prepared to wait until the turn of the century for even this limited objective to be reached.

But the NACM would have none of it. After months of prevarication, they eventually came up with their "declaration", which pledged that members would "endeavour" to source more of their apples from within the EEC or EFTA – that has the advantage of including Switzerland, a popular source of concentrate. Big deal!

Cider apple prices, even in these times of shortage, reflect the major manufacturers' utter indifference to what their product is made from. For a ton of apples, which will yield perhaps 175 gallons of cider, with a retail value of over £1,000, the grower will receive as little as £62. If he is lucky enough to be one of Taunton Cider Company's contract growers he could get £108. But concentrates are even cheaper than that, and you don't have the fag of having to press the fruit. Even if the price of apples were to be doubled tomorrow, it would not add – or at least *should* not add – more than 1p to the price of cider in the pub.

Against this background, it is hardly surprising that the acreage of cider orchards has been halved in the past 15 years. Cider production over the same period has doubled, incidentally! The NFU has warned that "the long process of attrition in reducing the cider apple area could turn into a dramatic fall". But there is just a glimmer of light at the end of the long dark tunnel. Julian Temperley's "Somerset Royale", the West Country's answer to Calvados, looks set to be a roaring success.

"We can use every single high quality late cider apple grown in Somerset for our distillery, and we'll pay a good price for them," bubbled the ebullient Mr. Temperley. "This is the single most exciting development in the cider industry in the last 50 years". But Julian will now have to buy in the apples for his own Burrow Hill Cider from Hereford, as most of his own 30 acres will go to make cider for his distillery.

All of which is splendid news for cider apple growers, and indeed those wine buffs who can afford to spend £14 on a bottle of Somerset Royale. But what about those of us who prefer to take our cider undistilled? Once again,

Anthony Gibson (left) discussing cider making at Bulmer's

I fear, the news is bad – unless you happen to be a collector of cider bygones. Because hardly a month goes by, it seems, without one of the dwindling band of now aging traditional high quality cider makers handing in his sample mug, if not to the Great Presser in the sky, at least to his local auctioneer. Recently we have lost Williams Bros. of Nailsea, whose cider was perhaps the finest in the West. Stan Stone sold up in the autumn of 1989; Ken Duck of Kingsbury Episcopi has gone. Symonds is now owned by Bulmer's, and Inch is no longer an independent family firm. Even the great John Dix – "Dixie" – scourge of the Big Three; poet and philanthropist; maker of "Cripplecock" – has been forced by bankruptcy to seek his fortune elsewhere.

True there are other small cider makers – the Temperleys, Langdons, Perrys, Sheppys, Thatchers and Richs of this world – whose businesses are ticking over very nicely, thank you, despite the gloom and doom. Thanks not least to the publication of the Good Cider Guide, theirs and similar delights are sought after more than ever. But to imagine, as some idealists may, that CAMRA can do for cider what it has done for beer is just so much pomace in the sky! Factory cider is now so different a product to the traditional article, its manufacture so profitable, and its image so down market, that it would be idle to pretend that the Big Three will ever experience a conversion experience on the road to Fizzville. The only hope of even slowing down the trend, let alone reversing it, would be legislation – requiring that a product that purports to hail from Somerset or the West Country should contain a set minimum of local raw material: unless the EEC somehow becomes involved, such a development must remain a pious wish.

We must accept that real cider will remain a minority product, catering for a "niche market". For the connoisseur, in search of his nectar, that will mean more forays into deepest Somerset or Devon, more anxious enquiries at the village post office and the pub, and more nervous entrances, cider jug in hand, to apparently deserted and seemingly hostile farms.

But then seeking out good cider always was half the fun of drinking it: and there is still no shortage of the real thing – if you know where to look.

Anthony Gibson is Senior Policy Adviser to the South West Region of the National Farmers' Union.

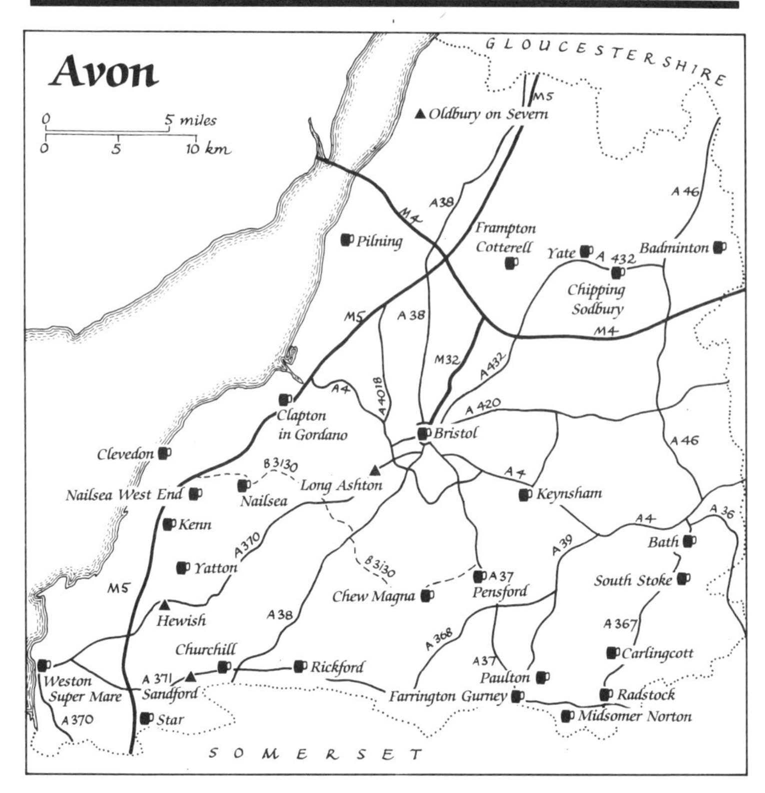

Badminton

Village Club (P)
High Street
☎ (045421) 234
Weston (PC)

Bath

Weekdays: 11–11, Sunday: 12–3; 7–10.30

Beehive Inn (P)
3 Belvedere, Lansdown
☎ (0225) 20274
Taunton (H)
A sturdy stone built pub on the hillside, well worth the climb. An enthusiastic cider outlet, and friendly local. Snacks

Monday–Thursday, Saturday: 11–3; 5–11, Friday: 11–11: Sunday: 7–10.30.

Ram (P)
20 Claverton Buildings, Widcombe
☎ (0225) 421938
Bulmer (H)
Near first lock on Kennet and Avon Canal. Meals and snacks lunchtime; evenings only by prior arrangement. Near Bath Spa BR station.

Monday–Friday, 10.30–2.30; 5–11, Saturday: 11–11

Rose & Crown (P)
6 Brougham Place,
St. Saviour's Road, Larkhall (400 yards northwest of junction of A4 and A46)
☎ (0225) 25700
Thatcher (H)
Old fashioned local in Larkhall village centre. Worth seeking out. Pool table.

Stogdens Wine & Fine Food Co (OL)
14 Chatham Row
☎ (0225) 462034
Dymock Farmhouse (B)

Weekdays: 11–3; 5–11, Saturday: 11–11, Sunday: 12–3; 7–10.30.

White Horse (P)
4 Northampton Street
☎ (0225) 425944
Taunton (H)
A friendly local in a Bath stone terrace. Home cooked bar snacks – the only pub in Bath which serves "home made chips" and home made pasties; shove ha'penny; impressive modern pool room skilfully added at rear.

Bristol

Albert (P)
155 Church Road, Redfield (A420)
Richards (PC) (PP)
Near Lawrence Hill BR station.

Weekdays: 10.30–11.

Apple Tree (P)
27 Philip Street, Bedminster
☎ (0270) 667097
Taunton (H)
Probably the smallest pub in Bristol; unchanged cider house of much character. Meals and snacks lunchtime and evening.

Weekdays: 10–2; 4–10, Sunday and Bank Holidays: 12–1.30; 7–10

Berkeley Arms Off Licence (OL)

286 Lodge Causeway
☏ (0272) 653833
Richards (PC)
Taunton (PC)

Monday–Friday: 10–2.15; 5–10, Saturday–Sunday: 10–10.

Britannia Off Licence (OL)
93 Nags Head Hill, St. George
☏ (0272) 61985
Richards (PC)

Weekdays: 9–1.30; 3.30–9.30.

BJ's Stores (OL)
30 Bedminster Road, Bedminster
☏ (0272) 661906
Broad Oak (PC)

Brown Jug (OL)
77 Garnet Street, Bedminster
☏ (0272) 635145
Langdon (PC)
Near Parson Street BR station.

9–10.30 all week.

Carpenters (OL)
387 Gloucester Road, Horfield
☏ (0272) 424283
Thatcher (E) (PL)

Monday, Wednesday–Saturday: 9–6; Tuesday, 9–3.

Clifton Cellars (OL)
22 The Mall, Clifton
☏ (0272) 730287
Long Ashton (B)
Original cellars of Georgian assembly rooms, dating from 1792. Near Clifton Down BR station.

Coronation Tap (P)
8 Sion Place, Clifton
☏ (0272) 739617
Bulmer (W)
Bristol's most famous cider pub in a pleasant, parkland location near north end of Clifton Suspension Bridge. Traditional in character with no juke box. Meals and snacks lunchtimes.

Weekdays: 12–11.

Cotham Porter Stores (P)
15 Cotham Road South, Cotham
☏ (0272) 249198
Taunton (PC)
One bar cider house full of atmosphere, also selling draught Courage Bitter.

Earl Russell (P)
143 Lawrence Hill (on A420)
☏ (0272) 558710
Bulmer (H)
Large pub with contrasting bars on busy main road and overlooking Lawrence Hill Railway Station. Snacks weekday lunchtimes

Monday–Friday: 10–1; 6–10, Saturday: 10–10, Sunday: 12–2; 7–10.

Elstons (OL)
509 Wells Road, Hengrove
☏ (0272) 775957
Broad Oak (PC) (B)

Weekdays: 10–1; 4–10.

Empire Wines (OL)
327 Southmead Road
☏ (0272) 502954
Broad Oak (PC) (B)
Cripple Cock

Monday–Friday: 11–11, Saturday: 11–3; 5.30–11, Sunday: 12–2.30; 7–10.30.

Essex Arms (P)
237 Two Mile Hill, Kingswood
☏ (0272) 674161
Taunton (H)
A noted cider house. Snacks; garden.

10–2; 6–10.30 all week.

Friendship (OL)
77 Hill Street, Kingswood
☏ (0272) 67088
Richards (PC)

Weekdays: 9–1.30; 6–10.

Gillmore (OL)
2 Birchwood Road, St. Annes
☏ (0272) 716906
Richards (PC)

Monday–Saturday: all day; closed Sunday.

Horse & Groom (P)
St Georges Road, Bristol 1 (rear of Council House and College Green)
☏ (0272) 273641
Taunton (H)
Close to Cathedral, Brandon Hill, and Cabot Tower. Meals and snacks lunchtime; small outdoor drinking area.

Weekdays: 12–2; 4.30–10.30.

Humpers Off Licence (OL)
26 Soundwell Road, Staple Hill
☏ (0272) 565525
Richards (PC)

Kings Arms (P)
51 Stokes Croft
☏ (0272) 249589
Taunton (H)
High-ceilinged, split-level, no-nonsense, honest boozers with tropical electric fans. Snacks.

Monday–Saturday: 11–4; 6–11, Sunday 12–3; 7–10.30.

Mardyke (P)
128 Hotwell Road, Hotwells
☏ (0272) 20475
Coates (H)
Bohemian flavoured pub on main road near Cumberland Basin. Lunchtime meals.

Weekdays: 11–11, Sunday: 12–3; 7–10.30.

Old Gloucester Tavern (P)
69 Gloucester Road, Bishopston
☏ (0272) 241501
Taunton (H)
Old established Victorian cider pub, recently refurbished and enlarged. Bar snacks 11–3; meals 12–2.

Weekdays: 11–3; 5.30–11, Sunday 12–3; 7–10.30.

Orchard (P)
Hanover Place, Cumberland Road
Taunton (H)
Unspoilt one room local, one of the city's last genuine cider houses: near SS Great Britain. Meals and snacks lunchtimes and evenings: outdoor drinking area.

Redland Mini Market (OL)
Redland
Long Ashton (B)

St. Georges Wines (OL)
355 Church Road, St. George (on A420 near junction with A431)
☏ (0272) 540604
Thatcher (PP)

Weekdays: 6.30am–10pm.

T.T. Superstore (OL)
29–37 West Street, Old Market
☏ (0272) 550734
Broad Oak (PC)

Weekdays: 11–3; 6–11, Sunday: 12–3; 7–10.30.

Volunteer Tavern (P)
9 New Street, St. Judes
☏ (0272) 557982
Taunton (H)
Cider drinkers' local, built at time of Queen Anne. Live music.

Weekdays: 11–11, Sunday: 12–3; 7–10.30.

White Horse (P)
166 West Street, Bedminster
☏ (0272) 663223
Taunton (PC) (H)
Bar snacks all times; children's room; outdoor drinking area/garden. Near Parson Street BR station.

Weekdays: 11–11.

White Swan (P)
70 North Street, Downend
☏ (0272) 560261
Taunton (PC)
Good home made meals and snacks always available; children welcome.

Carlingcott

Monday–Friday: 11–3; 6–11, Saturday 12–11, Sunday: 12–3; 7–10.30.

Beehive (P)
☏ (0761) 34442
Bulmer (H)
Pleasant village local with panoramic views. Collection of oil lamps in public bar. Snacks. Garden. Skittles.

Chew Magna

Weekdays: 12–2.30; 7–11.

Pony & Trap (P)
Newtown
☏ (0272) 332627
Bulmers West Country (H)
Traditional black and white locals' pub. Rolls 12–2; children's room; garden.

Chipping Sodbury

Monday–Thursday: 11–3; 5–11, Friday and Saturday: 11–11, Sunday: 12–3; 7–10.30.

Portcullis Hotel (P)
Horse Street
☏ (0454) 312004
Taunton (H)
Friendly locals' pub. Meals lunchtime and evening every day; accommodation.

Clapton in Gordano

Weekdays: 11–2.30; 6–11, Sunday: 12–2.30; 7–10.30.

Black Horse (P)
Clevedon Lane
☏ (0272) 842105
Taunton (H)
Unspoilt country pub with original stone floor. Children's room; garden.

Clevedon

Weekdays: 11–11, Sunday: 12–3; 7–10.30.

Reading House (P)
Alexandra Road
☏ (0272) 873545
Taunton (H)
Three bar Victorian pub. Full meals 12–2; bar snacks all times; restaurant; children's room.

Farrington Gurney

Monday–Thursday: 11–3; 7–11, Friday–Saturday: 11–11.

Miners Arms (P)
Main Street (A362)
☏ (0761) 52158
Taunton (H)
Lively village local. Snacks; garden; skittles.

Frampton Cotterell

Weekdays: 8–9.

Country Stores (OL)
149 Church Road
☏ (0454) 776905
Sheppy (J)
Old world village store and off licence. Near Bristol Parkway BR station.

Live & Let Live (P)
Clyde Road
☏ (0454) 772254
Taunton (PC)
Village local with two comfortable lounge bars. Meals and snacks lunchtime and evenings; garden.

Hewish

CROSSMAN'S PRIME FARM-HOUSE CIDER ▲
Mayfield Farm (on A370)
☏ (0934) 833174

LANGDON'S WEST COUNTRY CIDER ▲
The Cider Mill (off A370)
☏ (0934) 833433

Kenn

Weekdays: 11–3; 7–11.

Drum & Monkey (P)
Kenn Road (B3133 Yatton to Clevedon road)
☏ (0272) 873433
Taunton (H)
Friendly country local. Reasonably priced meals at lunchtimes and some evenings (phone to check). Garden. Disabled access.

Keynsham

Weekdays: 8.30–5.30, Sunday: 9.30–12.30; 7–9.

Gater's Off Licence (OL)
71 Queens Road
☏ (0272) 862623
Broad Oak (PC) (B)

Weekdays: 10–2.30; 5.30–11.

Trout Tavern (P)
46 Temple Street
☏ (0272) 862754
Taunton (H) (PC)
18th century former coaching inn, the cider centre of the town. Snacks; live music.

Long Ashton

Little Tipple (OL)
50 Weston Road
☏ (0272) 392508
Long Ashton (B)

LONG ASHTON CIDER ▲
Long Ashton Research Station
☏ (0272) 392181

Weekdays: 11.30–3; 6.30–11, Sunday: 12–3; 7–10.30.

Robin Hoods Retreat (P)
Providence Lane
☏ (0272) 394195
Taunton (PC)
Wood panelled bar with atmosphere. Snacks; garden.

Midsomer Norton

Weekdays: 10.30–2.30; 6–11.

White Hart (P)
The Island (off B3355)
☏ (0761) 412957
Taunton (PC)
Victorian pub with many rooms. Meals lunchtime; children's room; access for disabled.

Nailsea

Butchers Arms (P)
1 Union Street
☏ (0272) 852741
Taunton (PC)

Avon

Friendship Inn (P)
Stockway North
Bulmer (PC)
Old pub with stone floor. Snacks available.

Weekdays: 7–11.30.

Nailsea Comrades Club (P)
15 Chapel Barton
☏ (0272) 853006
Long Ashton (DJ)
Taunton (PC)
Club allowing visitors; garden; regular skittles, snooker, pool and darts; live entertainment Saturdays; bingo Sundays.

Nailsea Wine Merchants (OL)
67 High Street
☏ (0272) 855641
Long Ashton

Nailsea West End

Monday–Saturday: 11–3; 5.30–11, Sunday: 12–3; 7–10.

Blue Flame (P)
☏ (0272) 856910
Bulmer (PC)
Country pub 1 mile west of Nailsea. Snacks; large garden; family room; open fires.

Oldbury on Severn

COWHILL CIDER ▲
Fishermans Cottage, Cowhill
☏ (0454) 412157

Paulton

Monday–Thursday: 11–3, Friday–Saturday: 11–11, Sunday: 12–3; 7–10.30.

Lamb (P)
Park Road
☏ (0761) 412878
Taunton (H)
Happy family village pub. Hot and cold food; pool and all other pub games.

Monday–Thursday: 12–2.30; 6–11, Friday–Saturday: 12–3; 6–11, Sunday: 12–3; 7–10.30.

Somerset Inn (P)
Bath Road
☏ (0761) 412828
Taunton (H)
Traditional country pub with superb views: no fruit machines or juke box. Meals lunchtime and evenings all week; garden.

Pensford

Weekdays: 11.30–2.30; 7–11, Sunday: 12–2.30; 7–10.30.

Rising Sun (P)
Church Street
☏ (07618) 402
Bulmer (H)
Pub food lunchtimes Monday–Saturday, and evenings Tuesday–Saturday; traditional roast lunch on Sundays; riverside garden in very attractive setting; club room available for modest functions.

Pilning

Weekdays: 11–2.30; 6.30–11, Sunday: 12–3; 7–10.30.

Plough Inn (P)
☏ (04545) 2556
Bulmer (PC)
Just outside the village, convenient for the industrial companies, but still a country pub. Meals lunchtime Monday–Friday; skittle alley.

Radstock

Monday–Thursday: 11–2.30; 7–11, Friday–Saturday: 11–11, Sunday: 12–3; 7–10.30.

Railway (P)
Welton Road
☏ (0761) 35100
Taunton (H)
Though you cannot catch a train from Radstock, the pub keeps the theme going, with railway carriage seating and memorabilia. Snacks; patio garden and play area.

Rickford

Weekdays: 10–3; 5–11.

Plume of Feathers (P)
Off A368
☏ (0761) 62682
Taunton (PC)
In small village at foot of Mendips, popular with ramblers and potholers. Garden; accommodation.

Sandford

THATCHER'S CIDER ▲
Myrtle Farm, Station Road
☏ (0934) 822862

Star

Monday–Friday: 11–2.30; 6–11, Saturday: 11–2.30; 7–11, Sunday: 12–2; 7–10.30.

Star Inn (P)
On A38 near Shipham
☏ (0934) 842569
Bulmer (E)
Meals and snacks lunchtime to 1.45; Friday evening meals 7–8 only; garden.

South Stoke

Monday–Friday: 11–3; 6–11, Saturday: 11–11, Sunday: 12–3; 7–10.30.

Packhorse (P)
Off B3110
☏ (0225) 832060
Taunton (PC)
Unspoilt 15th century village pub. Snacks; garden.

Weston Super Mare

Peter Dominic (OL)
207 Milton Road
☏ (0934) 624031
Long Ashton

Yate

Codrington Arms (P)
North Road
☏ (045422) 581
Bulmer (H)
Traditional locals' pub. Lunchtime meals. Garden. Camping facilities nearby.

Yatton

Butchers Arms (P)
31 High Street (B3133 at east end of town)
☏ (0934) 833377
Bulmer (PC)
17th century inn. Snacks lunchtime; garden. Half a mile from Yatton BR station.

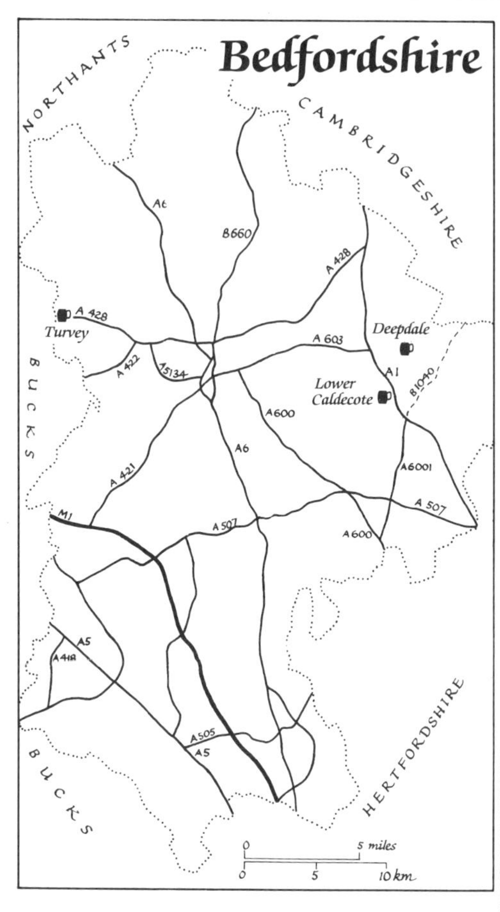

Deepdale

Locomotive (P)

On B1042
☎ (0767) 260365
Bulmer (H)
Warm and lively pub at bottom of Sandy television mast. Meals and snacks lunchtimes and evenings. Garden.

Lower Caldecote

Kings Head (P)

Great North Road (northbound side)
☎ (0767) 312323
Weston (H)

Turvey

Weekdays: 11.30–3; 5.30–11, Sunday: 12–3; 7–10.30.

Ye Three Fyshes Inn (P)

Bridge Street (on A428)
☎ (023064) 264
Guest Ciders (PC)
Riverside pub on border of Bedfordshire and Bucks. Meals and snacks; children's room; garden.

Berkshire

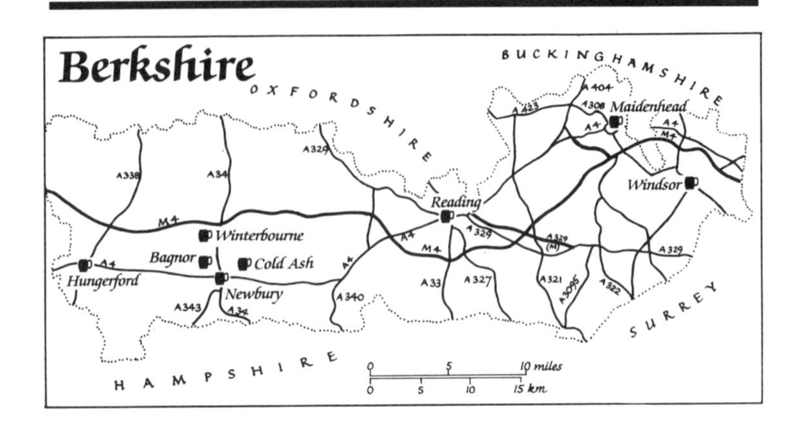

Bagnor

Watermill Theatre (P)
Mill House
☎ (0635) 46044
Bulmer (PC)
Theatre and restaurant in converted 19th century mill.

Cold Ash

Weekdays: 8–1; 2–5.30.

Cold Ash PO Stores (OL)
Cold Ash Hill
☎ (0635) 62440
James White (J)

Hungerford

Littlecote House (OL)
To west of town
☎ (0488) 84000
Country Fayre
Sheppy
An unspoilt Tudor manor with authentic Roman excavations.

Weekdays: 11–3; 6–11.

Railway Tavern (P)
1 Station Road
☎ (0488) 83100
Bulmer (H)
Local's pub. Near Hungerford BR station

Sun Inn (P)
36 Charnham Street
(A4 Bath road)
☎ (0488) 82162
Bulmer (PC)
Homely local where visitors are made particularly welcome. Bar snacks 12–2; outdoor drinking area/garden; pool table; solitaire table.

Maidenhead

Weekdays: 10–8.30.

David Alexander (OL)
60 Queen Street
☎ (0628) 30295
Dunkerton (B)

Newbury

Weekdays: 9–5.30.

Sunstore (OL)
Marsh Lane
☎ (0635) 30825
Weston – full range of cider and perry
Somerset Farmhouse cider

Reading

Grog Shop (OL)
11 London Road
☎ (0635) 35171
Weston (H)

Windsor

JON HALLAM, COMPOUNDER OF SPIRITS (D)
34 Devereux Road
☎ (0753) 852609

Winterbourne

New Inn (P)
Near B4494
Bulmer (H)
Free house, noted for its gardens

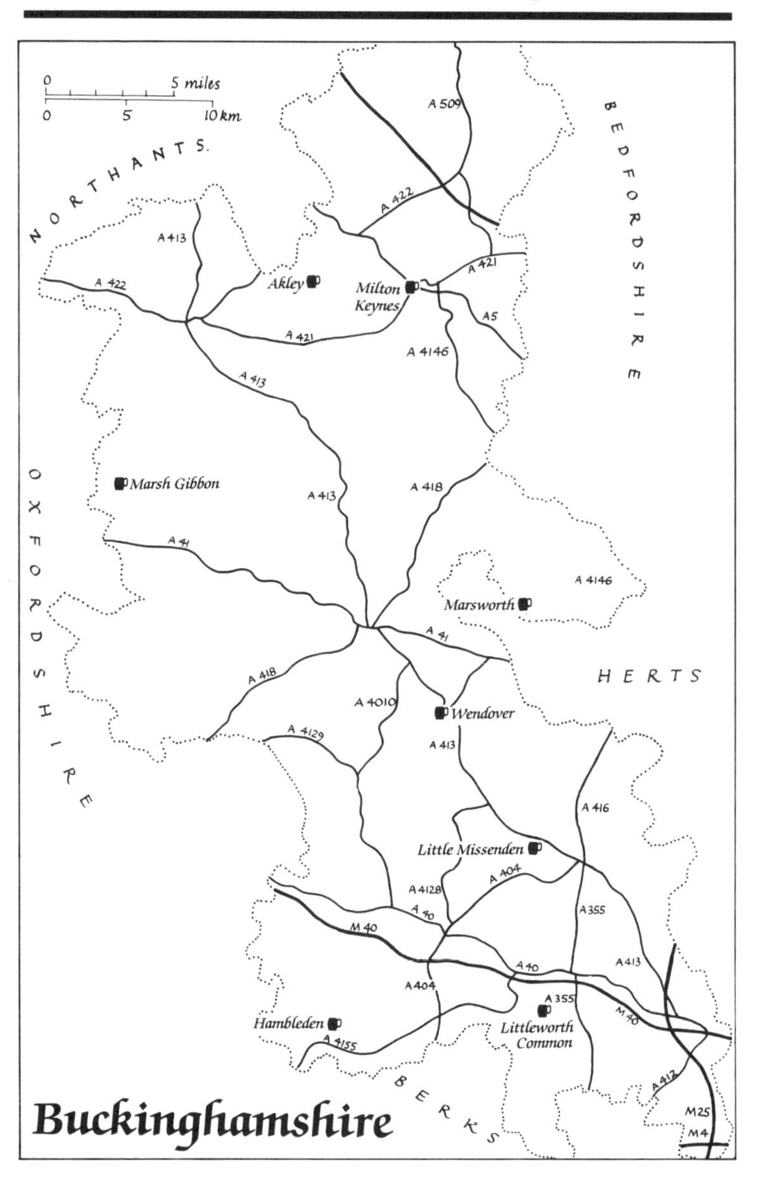

Akeley

Monday–Friday: 12–2.30; 6–11, Saturday: 12–3; 6–11, Sunday: 12–3; 7–10.30.

Bull & Butcher (P)
The Square (A413)
☎ (02806) 257
Bulmer (H)
In the centre of the village. Meals lunchtime except Sunday, and evenings except Sunday and Monday; restaurant; garden.

Hambleden

Weekdays: 11–2.30; 6–11.

Stag & Huntsman (P)
3 miles north east of Henley off A4155
☎ (0491) 571227
Bulmer (H)
Unspoilt pub in picturesque brick and flint National Trust village. Meals and snacks lunchtime, and evenings except Sunday; garden; accommodation; access for disabled.

Little Missenden

Weekdays: 11–2.30; 6–11, Sunday: 12–2.30; 7–10.30.

Crown (P)
Off A413
☎ (02406) 2571

Bulmer (PC)
Excellent village inn which has been in the same family since 1923. Snacks available lunchtimes. Games include shove ha'penny and shut-the-box.

Littleworth Common

Blackwood Arms (P)
Common Lane
☎ (02814) 2169
Various (PC)
Country pub on edge of Burnham Beeches. Meals lunchtime and evenings; garden; access for disabled.

Marsh Gibbon

Weekdays: 11–2.30 (3.30 Saturday), 6–11.

Plough (P)
Church Street
☎ (08697) 305
Westons Old Rosie (PP)
Pleasant 16th century pub for all ages. Meals lunchtime and evening; separate dining room; garden; camping facilities nearby.

Marsworth

Weekdays: 11–3; 6–11, Sunday: 12–3; 7–10.30.

Red Lion (P)
90 Vicarage Road
☎ (0296) 668366
Weston (PC)
Improved but unspoilt pub, near Grand Union Canal, and Tring nature reserve. Meals and snacks except on Sundays; garden.

Milton Keynes

Monday–Friday: 11–9.15, Saturday: 10–8, Sunday 12–2; 7–9.

Eldergate Wines (OL)
Station Square
☎ (0908) 607885
Dunkerton (B) range
Inch (J)
Product finder service. Adjoins Milton Keynes Central BR station.

Wendover

Red Lion Hotel (P)
High Street (A413)
☎ (0296) 622266
Bromell (PC)
Town centre hotel. Snacks 12–2.30; 6–10.30; meals 12–2.30; 7–9.30; restaurant; accommodation.

Vinetum Britannicum:
OR A
TREATISE
OF
CIDER,
And other Wines and Drinks extracted from Fruits Growing in this Kingdom.
With the Method of Propagating all ſorts of Vinous FRUIT-TREES.
And a DESCRIPTION of the New-Invented INGENIO or MILL, For the more expeditious making of *CIDER*.
And alſo the right way of making METHEGLIN and BIRCH-WINE.

The Second Impreſſion, much Enlarged.

To which is added, A Diſcourſe teaching the beſt way of Improving BEES.

With Copper Plates.

By *J. Worlidge*. Gent.

LONDON,
Printed for *Thomas Dring*, over againſt the Inner-Temple-gate; and *Thomas Burrel*, at the Golden-ball under St *Dunſtan's* Church in *Fleet-ſtreet*. 1678.

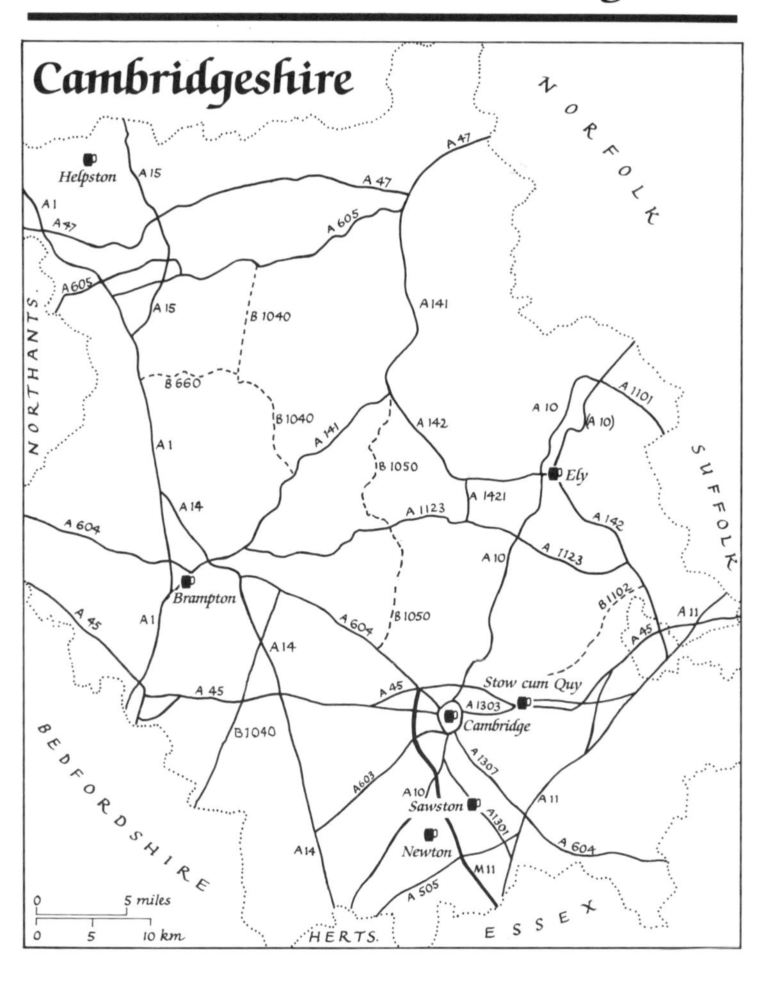

Brampton

Old Mill (P)
Bromholme Lane
☎ (0480) 218754
Weston (H)
Bar and restaurant.

Cambridge

Weekdays: 11–2.30; 6–11

Alma Brewery (P)
26 Russell Court
☎ (0223) 64965
Taunton (H)
Comfortable pub with snacks at lunchtimes

Barwell & Jones (OL)
70 Trumpington Road
☎ (0223) 354431
James White (J)

Cambridge Blue (P)
85 Gwydir Street (off Mill Road)
☎ (0223) 61382
James White (PP)
Busy, friendly little pub with no-smoking bar and snug. Petanque and barbecues in the garden. Meals and snacks at lunchtimes and summer evenings.

Weekdays: Monday–Friday: 11–2.30; 6–11, Saturday: 11–3; 6–11

Dobblers Inn (P)
184 Sturton Street (off East Road, opposite Grafton Centre)
☎ (0223) 356092
James White (H)
Back street pub with local flavour. Meals lunchtime; garden; access for disabled.

Weekdays: Monday–Thursday: 10.30–9.30, Friday: 10–2; 2.30–10, Saturday: 10–10, Sunday: 12–2; 7–9

Jug & Firkin (OL)
90 Mill Road
☎ (0223) 315034
James White (B)
French cider and perry (B)

Let & Let Live (P)
40 Mawson Road
☎ (0223) 354602
James White (H)
Pleasant local.

St. Radaghund (P)
King Street/Short Street
☎ (0223) 311794
James White (H)

Cambridgeshire

Weekdays: 11–3; 5.30–11

Salisbury Arms (P)
Tenison Road
☎ (0223) 60363
Taunton (H)
Unusually renovated side street pub near railway station. Lunchtime bar food.

Ely

Peter Dominic (OL)
49 High Street
☎ (0353) 662172
James White (J)

Helpston

Weekdays: 11–2.30; 6–11

Bluebell Inn (P)
10 Woodgate
☎ (0733) 252394
Bulmer (H)
Next to poet John Clare's cottage. Snacks any time; garden; accommodation.

Newton

Weekdays: Monday–Friday: 11.30–2.30; 6–11, Saturday: 11–2.40; 6–11, Sunday: 12–2; 7–10.30

Queens Head (P)
Off B1368
☎ (0223) 870436
Bulmer (PC)
Ancient pub, cellar dates from 1450, remainder from 1680. Snacks all sessions; no garden, but customers may sit outside, or on the green opposite; children's room.

Peterborough

Weekdays: Monday–Friday: 11–3; 6–11, Saturday: 11–11, Sunday: 12 noon–3; 7–10.30

Gladstone Arms (P)
124–128 Gladstone Street
☎ (0733) 44388
Symonds (PC)
Symonds Perry (PC)

Sawston

Weekdays: Monday–Thursday: 12–2.30; 6–11, Friday–Saturday: 12–2.30; 5–11

University Arms (P)
84 London Road (south end of village)
☎ (0223) 832165
Various (PC) – summer only
Emphasis on good food. Live music most weekends. Garden. Access for disabled.

Stow cum Quy

Prince Albert (P)
Newmarket Road
☎ (0223) 811294
James White (J)
Lively, friendly wayside tavern with 30-seat restaurant (no food Mon evening) Children's play area in barn.

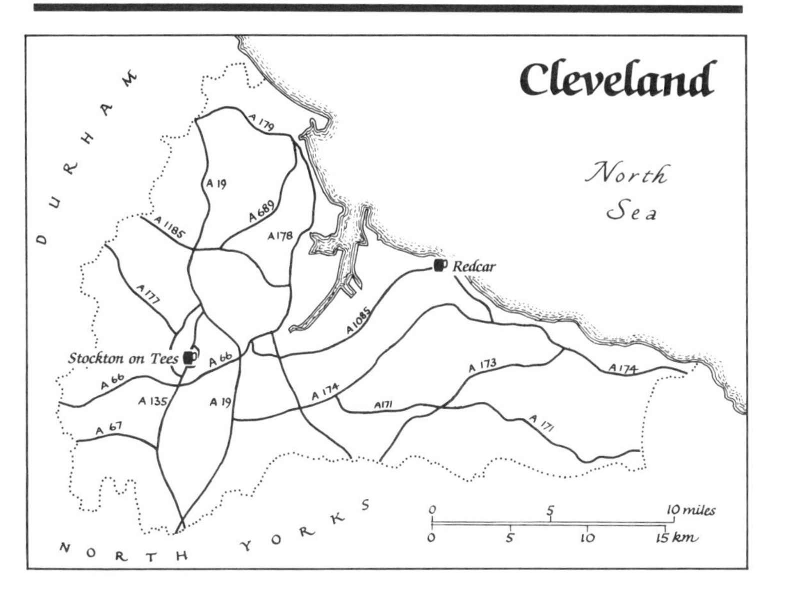

Redcar

Weekdays: 12–11, Sunday: 12–3; 7–10.30

Newbigging Hotel (P)

Queen Street/Turner Street
☎ (0642) 482059
Scrumpy (PC)
Choice of one cider, changed monthly. Meals and snacks Monday–Saturday 12–2; children welcome; outdoor drinking area; accommodation.

Stockton on Tees

Weekdays: Monday–Thursday: 11.30–4; 5.30–11, Friday: 11–5; 5.30–11, Saturday: 11–3; 7–11

Cricketers (P)

Portrack Lane
☎ (0642) 675468
Bulmer (H)
Comfortable and friendly one-room pub with separate games area. Set amid housing estates but not far from town centre. Meals lunchtime. Access for disabled.

METHODS OF DISPENSE
(B) Bottle (BB) Bag in box (CK) Carry keg (DJ) glass demijohn (E) Cask and electric pump (F) Flagon (H) Cask and hand pump (J) glass jar (PC) polycask (PL) plastic container (PP) polypin (W) wooden cask

KEY TO MAPS
🍺 town or village with one or more real cider or perry outlets
▲ location of cider or perry maker selling direct to public from premises

Cornwall

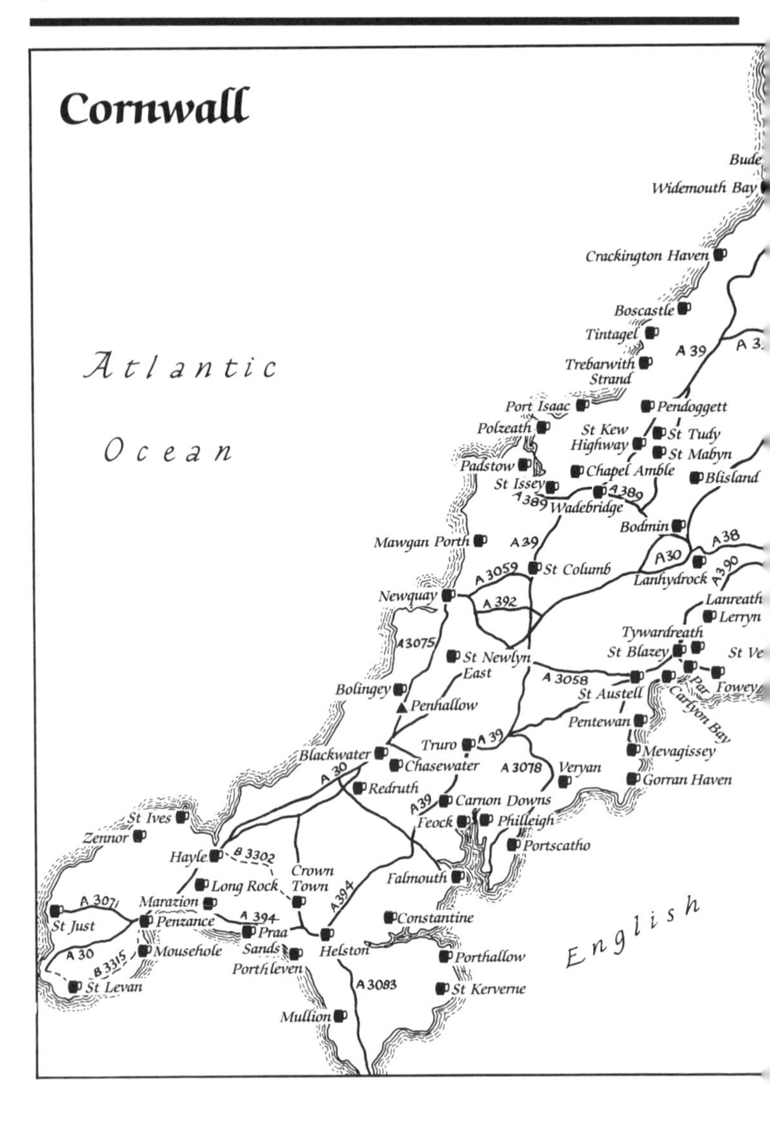

Albaston

Weekdays: Monday–Friday: 11–2.30; 6–11, Saturday: 11–3; 6–11, Sunday: 12–3; 7–10.30

Queens Head (P)

Off A390, south of Gunnislake
☎ (0822) 832482
Taunton (PC)
Lively local in old mining area. Snacks. Near Gunnislake BR station, on scenic route from Plymouth.

Blackwater

Blackwater Stores (OL)

☎ (0872) 560320
Apple Blossom (B)

Blisland

Weekdays: 11–3; 6–11

Royal Oak (P)

Near Bodmin ($1\frac{1}{2}$ miles north of A30)
☎ (0208) 050739
Inch (H)
In only Cornish village with a green; close to Bodmin Moor. Meals lunchtime and evening except Sunday night; children's room; patio; access for disabled; camping nearby.

Bodmin

Garland Ox (P)

65 Higher Bore Street
☎ (0208) 75372
Taunton (PC) (H)

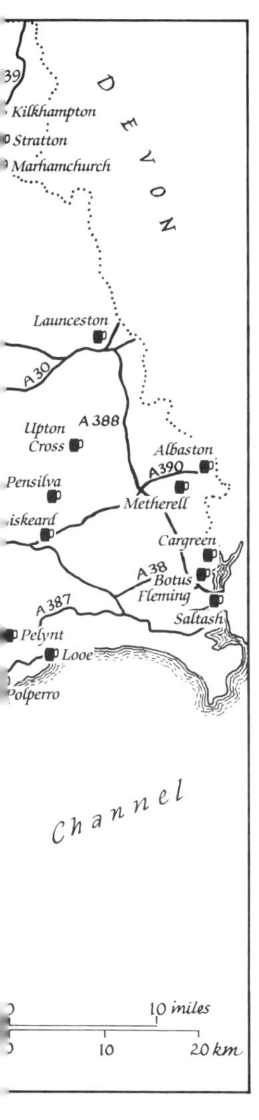

A friendly, welcoming local pub with garden. Meals lunchtimes and evenings. Families welcome.

REALLY FOWL CORNISH CIDER (D)
Really Fowl Cider Company
☏ (020882) 431

White Hart Inn (P)
Pool Street
☏ (0208) 2597
Haye Farm (E)
Town centre pub. Meals and snacks; outdoor drinking area.

Bolingey

Weekdays: 11–3; 6–11

Bolingey Inn (P)
Near Perranporth
(off B3284)
☏ (0872) 572794
Bulmer West Country (PC)
An oasis from the holiday oriented coastal pubs. Meals lunchtime and evening; children's room; garden access for disabled; camping facilities nearby.

Boscastle

Weekdays: 11–11

Cobweb Inn (P)
Bude Road
☏ (08405) 278
Inch (PC)
300 year old wine and spirit cellar where cobwebs insulated the roof, and spiders kept other bugs at bay. Meals and snacks 11.30–3; 6–10; restaurant; children's room; outside seating.

Monday–Friday: 11–3; 5.30–11, Saturday and Bank Holidays: 11–11

Wellington Hotel (P)
The Harbour
☏ (08405) 203
Inch (BB) (PP)
Historic listed 16th century coaching inn in area of outstanding natural beauty by Elizabethan harbour. Nearby National Trust walks. Snacks 12–2; 6.30–9.30; full meals 7.30–9.30; restaurant; children's room; garden; accommodation; pets welcome.

Botus Fleming

Weekdays: 12–3; 6–11

Rising Sun (P)
½ mile off A388 close to village church
☏ (0752) 842792
Inch (PC)
Country pub with 12th century origins in quiet village near Saltash. Garden.

Bude

Weekdays: 9 am–10 pm, Sunday: 12–1.30; 7–9

Bevill House Wines (OL)
22 Lansdown Road
☏ (0288) 2320
Cripple Cock

Weekdays: 9 am–9.30 pm

Grosvenor Wines (OL)
22b Belle Vue
☏ (0288) 4304
Apple Blossom (J) (PL)
Inch (PC) (BB) (DJ) (J)

Jersey Cow (OL)
5 Belle Vue
☏ (0288) 55130
Gray

WONNACOTT'S CIDER ▲
Lansdown Yard
☏ (0288) 3105

Cargreen

Weekdays: 11–3; 6–11, Sunday: 12–3; 7–10.30

Spaniards Inn (P)
Fore Street (off A388)
☏ (0752) 842830
Local Cider (PC)
Riverside inn set in beautiful Tamar Valley. Meals lunchtime and evenings; children's room; garden; accommodation; access for disabled.

Carlyon Bay

Weekdays: 8–7, Sunday: 9.30–2

Terry's (OL)
12 Beach Road
☏ (072681) 7988
Cornish Scrumpy (J) (PL) (S)
Independent supermarket half a mile from the beach on the approach road.

Carnon Downs

Ringwell Holiday Park (OL)
Bissoe Road
☏ (0872) 862194
Cornish Scrumpy (PL)

Chapel Amble

Monday–Saturdays: 11–2.30; 6–11, Sunday: 12–3; 7–10.30

Maltsters Arms (P)
☏ (020881) 2473
Cornish Scrumpy (PC)
16th century inn situated in middle of village, with 3ft thick walls, slate floors and

ancient ship's timbers, overlooking village green. Comprehensive menu during opening hours; garden; holiday flats and caravan sites nearby; facilities for disabled.

Chasewater

Leverton Place Caravan & Camping Park (OL)
Greenbottom, Three Mile Cross
☏ (0872) 560462
Cornish Scrumpy – range

Constantine

Weekdays: 11–3; 6–11, Sunday: 12–3; 7–10.30

Trengilly Wartha Inn (P)
Nancenoy (near head of Helford River)
☏ (0326) 40332
Really Fowl (PL)
Beautifully sited in extensive grounds near river, in wooded valley. Bar snacks 12.30–2.30; 6.30–9.30; meals in restaurant 7.30–9.30; children's room; garden; accommodation.

Crackington Haven

Weekdays: 11–3; 5.30–11

Coombe Barton Inn (P)
☏ (08403) 345
Cornish Scrumpy (PC)
Sheppy (PC)
By the beach in a beautiful Cornish bay. Full meals and snacks every day 11–2.30; 6.30–9.30; restaurant; garden; accommodation.

Crowntown

Crown (P)
On B3303
☏ (0326) 572660
Bulmer (H)
Pleasant village inn. Meals and snacks lunchtime and evenings; garden.

Falmouth

Weekdays: 9–9, Sunday: 12–2; 7–9

Peter Dominic (OL)
52 Church Street
☏ (0326) 312157
Inch (B) (BB) (PL) (J)

Weekdays: 8.30 am–9 pm, Sunday: 12–3; 7–9

Victoria Wine (OL)
7a Killigrew Street
☏ (0326) 311839
Cornish Scrumpy (B) (PL) (S)

Feock

11–6 (April–October)

Trelissick Gardens (P)
On both sides of B3289 above King Harry Ferry
☏ (0872) 862090
Apple Blossom (PC)
Extensive park and gardens beside River Fal with rare plants and shrubs; National Trust property. Restaurant.

Fowey

Fowey Foods (OL)
2 South Street
Cornish Scrumpy (B) (PL)

Park Road Stores (OL)
21 Park Road
☏ (0726) 832560
Cornish Scrumpy (PL)

Gorran Haven

Weekdays: 11.30–3; 6.30–11 (summer): 12–2.30; 7–11 (other times)

Llawnroc Inn (P)
Chute Lane
☏ (0726) 843461
Bulmer (PC)
Near Coastal Path, overlooking fishing village and harbour. Meals and snacks 12–2; 7–9; children's room; outdoor drinking area; large terraced lawns; accommodation; access for disabled; camping facilities nearby.

Hayle

Weekdays: 8–5.30

Anns Minimarket (OL)
16 Riviere Towans
☏ (0736) 754332
Cornish Scrumpy (PC) (PP) (PL)
Beach shop. Near Hayle BR station.

Copperhouse Gift Shop (OL)
57 Fore Street, Copperhouse
☏ (0736) 752470
Cornish Scrumpy – range

Excaliburs Meadery Restaurant (P)
24 Foundry Square
☏ (0736) 756595
Cornish Scrumpy (F)
Open Wednesday to Saturday from 6.30 pm.

St. Ives Bay Holiday Park (OL)
73 Loggans Road, Upton Towans
☏ (0736) 752274
Cornish Scrumpy – range

Helston

Spar Shop (OL)
Fore Street
☏ (0326) 562345
Cornish Scrumpy (PL)

Triggs Fruit Shop (OL)
2 Meneage Street
☏ (0326) 572867
Cornish Scrumpy – range

Kilkhampton

Monday–Fridays: 11–2.30; 6–11, Saturday: 11–11 (summer): 11–2.30; 6–11 (other times): Sunday: 12–3; 7–10.30

London Inn (P)
On A39 5 miles north of Bude
☏ (028882) 205 and 343
Gray (PC)
Old coaching inn. Meals and snacks 12–2; 7–9.30; restaurant; children's room; garden; camping facilities nearby.

Lanhydrock

11–6 (April–October); garden only for rest of year

Lanhydrock House (P)
2½ miles south east of Bodmin – signed from A38 and B3268
☏ (0208) 3320
Apple Blossom (PC)
Victorian reconstruction of 17th century manor house, with fine gardens, owned by National Trust. Restaurant.

Lanreath

Weekdays: 11–3; 6–11, Sunday: 12–3

Punch Bowl Inn (P)
½ mile off B3359, 5 miles north of Polperro
☏ (0503) 20218

Haye Farm (PC) – summer only
400 year old inn. Meals lunchtime and evenings; restaurant; children's room; garden; accommodation; access for disabled.

Launceston

Weekdays: 11–11

White Horse (P)
14 Newport Square (on A388 down hill from Castle)
☏ (0566) 2084
Bulmer (PC) (H)
18th century coaching inn. Meals and snacks lunchtime and evenings; children's room; outdoor drinking area; accommodation; access for disabled.

Lerryn

Weekdays: 11–2.30; 6–11, Sunday: 12–2.30; 7–10.30

Ship (P)
In centre of village near river
☏ (0208) 872374
Haye Farm (W)
Old pub in delightful Fowey valley, at the head of the River Lerryn. Meals and snacks lunchtime and evenings; garden.

Liskeard

Monday–Tuesdays 9.30–1; 2–8, Wednesday: 9.30–1; 5–8, Thursday–Saturdays: 9.30–8, Sunday: 12–2; 7–8

Baileys Wine Store (OL)
2 Lower Lux Street
☏ (0579) 45151
Countryman (B) (PL) (S)
Inch (PL) (J)

Godfrey's Stores (OL)
Barn Street
☏ (0579) 42506
Haymaker (B) (PL)
On road from Liskeard BR station into town.

HAYMAKER'S SCRUMPY
Haymakers Cider Mill, Taphouse Commercial Units, East Taphouse
☏ (0579) 45910

Monday–Thursdays: 9–9, Friday–Saturday: 9–10, Sunday: 12–2; 7–9

Peter Dominic (OL)
3 Bay Tree Hill
☏ (0579) 42318
Cripple Cock (B) (PL) (S)

Weekdays: 11–11

White Horse Inn (P)
The Parade
☏ (0579) 45954
Cornish Scrumpy (BB)
16th century town centre inn. Bar snacks all day; meals 12–3; 6–9; children's area; outdoor drinking area/garden; camping facilities nearby. Within half a mile of Liskeard BR station.

Long Rock

Mounts Bay Vineyard (OL)
Tolver Water
☏ (0736) 60774
Cornish Scrumpy (PL)

Looe

Spar Shop (OL)
Princess Square
☏ (05036) 2408
Cornish Scrumpy (PL)

Trelawne Manor Tourist Park (OL)
West of town, off A387
☏ (0503) 72151
Cornish Scrumpy (PL)

Trebel B Holiday Centre (OL)
☏ (05036) 2425
Cornish Scrumpy (PL)

Marazion

Weekdays: 9–6.30

Baden House Pharmacy (OL)
The Square
☏ (0736) 710206
Apple Blossom (B) (PL)
To be taken three times daily during and after meals.

Bone Valley Caravan Park (OL)
Heamoor
☏ (0736) 60313
Cornish Scrumpy (PL)

Eastern Green Caravan Park Shop (OL)
Eastern Green
☏ (0736) 65765
Cornish Scrumpy (PL)

Weekdays: 10.30–5.30

Sail Loft Restaurant (P)
St. Michaels Mount
☏ (0736) 710748
Cornish Scrumpy (PC)
A National Trust property, on an off shore rock containing a castle and a 14th century chapel: tidal causeway, and ferry at high tide.

Marhamchurch

Bullers Arms (P)
☏ (028885) 277
Sheppy (PC)
In completely unspoilt hilltop village 2 miles from the sea. Meals lunchtime and evenings; garden; accommodation.

Mawgan Porth

Surfside Stores (OL)
☏ (0637) 860302
Cornish Scrumpy (PL) (PET) (S)
Countryman (B) (PET)

Metherell

Weekdays: 12–2.30; 7–11

Carpenters Arms (P)
☏ (0579) 50242
Countryman (PP)
15th century inn close to National Trust House and holiday village. Snacks 11–1.30; full meals 12–1.30; 7–9.30; garden.

Mevagissey

Boyle Chemist (OL)
3 Fore Street
☏ (0726) 842349
Cornish Scrumpy (PL)

Weekdays: 11–11, Sunday: 12–3; 7–10.30

Cellar Bar (P)
2a St. Georges Square
☏ (0726) 842951
Haye Farm (PC)
Meals and snacks 12–4; 6–9.30; children allowed inside within main eating/dining area; outdoor drinking area; charcoal barbecue in summer season.

Weekdays: 11.30–11 (summer): 11–3; 6–11 (winter)

Fountain Inn (P)
Cliff Street (centre of town, opposite war memorial)
☏ (072684) 2326
Bulmers West Country (PC)
Cosy pub near harbour. Meals and snacks lunchtime

and evenings; children's room; outside drinking area; accommodation, access for disabled; camping facilities nearby.

Somerby Wines (OL)
18 Fore Street
☎ (0726) 843865
Apple Blossom (PL)

Mousehole

Central Stores (OL)
Fore Street (by harbour)
☎ (0736) 62411
Cornish Scrumpy (B) (PL) (S)
Also sells groceries and home cooked ham.

Mullion

Mullion Holiday Park Shop (OL)
Ruan Minor
☎ (0326) 240428
Cornish Scrumpy – range

Newquay

Cornish Goodies (OL)
Cliff Road
Apple Blossom (PL) (S)
Cripple Cock (B) (PL) (S)

Country Goodness Shop (OL)
29 Bank Street
☎ (0637) 874870
Apple Blossom (PL)

Forbuoys (OL)
36 Cliff Road
☎ (0637) 873208
Cornish Scrumpy (B) (PL) (S)
Haymakers (PET)

Gillian Barrow (OL)
2 Cliff Road
☎ (0637) 872957
Scrumpy (S)

Hendra Tourist Park (OL)
☎ office: (0637) 875778
☎ shop: (0637) 875996
Cornish Scrumpy

7–11
Porth Minimarket (OL)
Alexandra Road, Porth
☎ (0637) 872026
Cripple Cock (PC) (PP) (H) (J) (PL)
About half a mile from Newquay BR station.

Padstow

Weekdays: 9 am–10 pm (summer): 9–5 (other times)
Corner House (OL)
1 Lanadwell Street
☎ (0841) 532257
Apple Blossom (J) (PL)
Cripple Cock (J) (PL)
Cornish Scrumpy (J) (PL)
Countryman (J) (PL)
Off licence and bakery.

Henwoods (OL)
Strand
☎ (0841) 532325
Apple Blossom (B) (PL)
Cripple Cock (PL)

Lamorrick General Stores (OL)
New Street
Haymakers (PET)

Par

Cornish Arms (P)
5 Par Green
☎ (072681) 2013
Bulmer (PC)
Within easy reach of Par Sands. Bar snacks and meals lunchtime and evenings. Five minutes walk on footpath south from Par BR station.

Weekdays: (June 1st–September 30th) 11–11
Par Inn (P)
2 Harbour Road
☎ (072681) 3961
Bulmer (PC)
Close to the docks. Snacks and meals lunchtime and evenings – real Cornish pasties made on the premises; accommodation. Within half a mile of Par Sands and Par BR station.

Pelynt

Post Office Stores (OL)
On B3359
☎ (0503) 20239
Cornish Scrumpy – range

Pendoggett

Weekdays: 11–11, Sunday: 12–3; 7–10.30
Cornish Arms (P)
On B3314
☎ (020880) 263
Bulmer (PC)
Countryman (PC)
17th century inn, popular with holiday makers from nearby beaches and coves, and locals. Meals lunchtime and evenings; restaurant; children's room lunchtime; accommodation.

Penhallow

CORNISH SCRUMPY ▲
Cornish Scrumpy Company Ltd., Callestock Cider Farm
☎ (0872) 573356

Pensilva

Pensilva Stores (OL)
Plymouth House
☎ (0579) 62547
Cornish Scrumpy (PL)

Pentewan

Weekdays: 11–11 (summer): 11–3; 6–11 (other times)
Ship Inn (P)
West End
☎ (0726) 842855
Bulmer (PC)
1 minute walk from beach, overlooking the old harbour. Meals and snacks 12–2; 6.30–9.30; restaurant; accommodation; camping and caravan park nearby.

Penzance

Little Shop (OL)
Alverton Terrace
☎ (0736) 62208
Cornish Scrumpy (PL)

Mounts Bay Wine Co (OL)
19a Bread Street
☎ (0736) 64118
Cornish Scrumpy (PL)

Weekdays: 9–9, Sunday: 12–2; 7–9
Peter Dominic (OL)
Green Market
Cripple Cock (B) (PL) (S)
Inch (BB)

Monday–Thursdays: 9–7, Friday–Saturday: 9–9
Peter Dominic (OL)
91 Market Jew Street
☎ (0736) 67098
Cripple Cock (B) (PL) (S)

Weekdays: 9–9, Sunday: 12–3; 7–9
Victoria Wine (OL)
Market Jew Street
☎ (0736) 63126
Cornish Scrumpy (B) (PL) (S)

Philleigh

Weekdays: 11.30–2.30; 6–11

Roseland Inn (P)
Off A3078 on King Harry Ferry road
☎ (087258) 254
Bulmer West Country (PC) – summer only
17th century pub close to King Harry Ferry, with cob walls, low ceilings, and wooden seats. Meals and snacks (no chips) lunchtime, and evenings in summer; terrace.

Polperro

Blue Peter (P)
Quay Road
☎ (0503) 72743
Haye Farm (CH)
Smallest pub in Polperro, beside the harbour. Lots of atmosphere and good food.

Weekdays: 10–8 (summer): 10–12.30; 3–5 (winter

Chy an Gwyn (OL)
☎ (0503) 77241
Cornish Scrumpy

Weekdays: 11–11 (summer): 11–3; 6–11 (winter)

Crumplehorn Mill (P)
☎ (0503) 72348
Churchward (PC) – May–October
16th century building, once a corn mill and counting house for privateering: now skilfully converted into a complex of luxury self catering flats, hotel, restaurant and inn. Half a mile from Polperro harbour. Meals lunchtime and evenings; garden; accommodation (send for brochure).

Weekdays: 11–11

Three Pilchards (P)
Lansallos Street, The Quay
☎ (0503) 72233
Haye Farm (PC)
15th century pub on quay of fishing village, popular with locals and visitors. Meals – with no chips – lunchtime and evenings; outdoor drinking area; access for disabled.

Yaxleys (OL)
Rock House
☎ (0503) 72227
Dead Dick (PL)

Polzeath

The Supermarket (OL)
☎ (020886) 2556
Cripple Cock (PL) (S)

Porthallow

Weekdays: 12–3; 6.30–11

Five Pilchards Inn (P)
St. Keverne, Helston
☎ (0326) 280256
Cornish Scrumpy (BB) (B) – draught only in summer months, bottles to take away all year.
Small village pub adjacent to beach. Meals lunchtime; garden; accommodation – self contained flat for six; access for disabled.

Porthlevan

Cliff Road Stores (OL)
Cliff Road
☎ (0326) 572504
Cornish Scrumpy (PL)

Port Isaac

Stanley House (OL)
Fore Street
☎ (0208) 880314
Cripple Cock (PL) (S)

Portscatho

Plume of Feathers (P)
The Square (off A3078)
☎ (087258) 321
Bulmer (H)
Old granite smugglers pub in picturesque harbour village. Meals and snacks lunchtime and evenings; children's room; garden; camping facilities nearby.

Praa Sands

Weekdays: 11–1

Welloe Rock Inn (P)
☎ (073676) 3516
Cornish Scrumpy
Situated on the beach. Meals and snacks lunchtime and evenings; a la carte restaurant; children's room; outdoor drinking area; camping facilities nearby; large disco bar at weekends.

Redruth

Wine Mine (OL)
60 Fore Street
☎ (0209) 215147
Cornish Scrumpy (B) (PL)

Wineshaft (OL)
12 Penryn Street
☎ (0209) 211025
Cornish Scrumpy
Countryman
Inch

St. Agnes

Churchtown Stores (OL)
5 Churchtown
☎ (087255) 2459
Apple Blossom (B)

St. Austell

Fine Wines (OL)
2a East Hill
☎ (0726) 67307
Countryman (S)
Really Fowl (PL)
Near St. Austell BR station.

Penhaven Tourist Park (OL)
☎ (0726) 843687 or 843870
Cornish Scrumpy (PL)

Pentewan Sands Holiday Park (OL)
☎ (0726) 843896
Cornish Scrumpy – range

Victoria Wine (OL)
10 Fore Street
☎ (0726) 65693
Cornish Scrumpy (B) (PET) (PL) (S)

St. Blazey

Cornish Arms (P)
Church Street (A390) adjoining church
☎ (072681) 3001
Bulmers West Country (PC)
Hotel with two bars, pool room and garden. Families welcome. Bar snacks.

St. Columb

CRIPPLE COCK FARMYARD SCRUMPY
Business Centre, Barn Lane
☎ (0637) 880992

St. Issey

Weekdays: 10–5 (April–October): reduced opening rest of year.

Cornish Shire Horse Centre (OL) (P)

On A39 north of St. Columb
☎ (0841) 540276
Cornish Scrumpy (PC) (J)
120 acres of farm and woodland, with 36 shire horses, blacksmith, cart rides, museum, displays, and play area: gift shop and scrumpy tasting; restaurant; outdoor eating and drinking area; access for disabled.

St. Ives

Ayr Stores (OL)

Ventnor Terrace
☎ (0736) 795805
Cornish Scrumpy (PL)

Weekdays: 9–10, Sunday: 12–3; 7–10

Johns Off Licence (OL)

75 Fore Street (near harbour)
☎ (0736) 795797
Cornish Scrumpy (B) (PL) (S)
Comprehensive nourishment – cooked meats; cheeses, dairy produce; pasties; pies.

Weekdays: 8.15–9.45 all week

Milk Churn (OL)

Tregenna Hill
☎ (0736) 798168
Cornish Scrumpy (B) (PL)
Cripple Cock (B) (PL) (S)
Near St. Ives BR station.

Nangivey Stores (OL)

Stennack Gardens
☎ (0736) 797232
Cornish Scrumpy (PL)

Polmantor Farm Campsite (OL)

Halestown (1 mile south of town)
☎ (0736) 795640
Cornish Scrumpy – range

Spar Shop (OL)

St. Ives Road, Carbis Bay
☎ (0736) 796208
Cornish Scrumpy (PL)

St. Just

Commercial Hotel Shop (OL)

Market Square
☎ (0736) 788455
Cornish Scrumpy – range

St. Kerverne

Spar Stores (OL)

Commercial Road
☎ (0326) 280216
Cornish Scrumpy – range

St. Kew Highway

Red Lion (P)

☎ (020884) 271
Inch (PC)
17th century village inn with cosy beamed front bar and spacious back bar/games room. Accommodation. Families welcome.

St. Levan

PK Stores (OL)

St. Levan Post Office
☎ (0736) 810227
Cornish Scrumpy (PL)

St. Mabyn

St. Mabyn Inn (P)

Off B3266
☎ (020884) 266
Bulmer (PC)
Unspoilt 15th century village local next to the church

St. Newlyn East

Weekdays: 11–6 (April–October)

Trerice House (P)

From Newquay via A3058, turn off at Kestle Mill
☎ (0637) 35404
Apple Blossom (PC)
Small manor house rebuilt in 1571, small museum tracing history of the lawn mower: owned by National Trust. Restaurant in Elizabethan barn. One and three-quarter miles from Quintrel Downs BR station.

St. Tudy

Cornish Arms (P)

Near B3266
☎ (0209) 850656
Inch (PC)
Attractive village inn

St. Veep

HAYE FARM CIDER ▲

Haye Farm (between Wooda Cross and St. Veep)
☎ (0208) 872250

PENPOL CIDER ▲

Middle Penpol Farm (½ mile south of village)
☎ (0208) 872017

Saltash

Weekdays: 11–11

Two Bridges (P)

13 Albert Road
☎ (0752) 848952
Taunton (PC)
Situated between the two bridges across the Tamar. Splendid views from garden. Opposite Saltash BR station (limited service)

Stratton

Weekdays: 11.30–3; 6.30–11

Tree House (P)

Fore Street
☎ (0288) 2038 and 2931
Inch (PL)
Historic scheduled building, home of the last of the Cornish giants, Anthony Payne, 7ft 4 inches tall, and weighing 38 stone! Snacks 11–2; 7–10; meals 12–1.45; 7–10; restaurant; children's room; garden; accommodation; games room; folk evenings every Friday.

Tintagel

Cornishman (P)

Fore Street
☎ (0840) 770238
Countryman (PC) summer only
14th century building has been a pub since 1979. Previously a pottery. Children's room and garden; camping facilities nearby. Meals and snacks lunchtimes and evenings.

Freemans Stores (OL)

☎ (0840) 770801
Cornish Scrumpy

Monday–Thursday: 10.30–11, Friday–Saturday: 10.30–midnight: Sunday: 12–10.30

King Arthurs Arms (P)

Fore Street
☎ (0840) 770831
Countryman (PC)
14th century building with 2ft thick walls. Meals and

snacks lunchtime and evenings; children's room; garden; camping facilities nearby.

Weekdays: 8.30–10

Tintagel Supermarket (OL)
Bossiney Road
☎ (0840) 770323
Wonnacott (PC)

Trebarwith Strand

Weekdays: 11–11 (summer): 12–3; 7–11 (winter

Port William (P)
☎ (0840) 770230
Countryman (H) – summer only
Beachside pub, once the harbour master's house and stables. Meals and snacks all sessions; children's room; terrace; self catering accommodation.

Truro

APPLE BLOSSOM CIDER
The Cornish Cider Company, Trevean Farm, Coombe Kea
☎ (0872) 77177

Weekdays: 11–11

Barley Sheaf (P)
Old Bridge Street
☎ (0872) 42383
Bulmer (H)
Next to Truro Cathedral, boasts longest bar in Cornwall. Meals and snacks 12–2.30; outdoor drinking area. Half a mile from Truro BR station.

Cheese Board (OL)
Creation Centre, Lemon Quay
☎ (0872) 70813
Apple Blossom (B)
Haymaker (B) (PL)

Weekdays: 11–11

City Inn (P)
Pydar Street (on Perranporth road)
☎ (0872) 72623
Taunton (H)
Sympathetically restored local with a profusion of brassware, jugs and old photos of Truro. Genuinely friendly. Separate large pool room and outdoor drinking area. Meals lunchtimes and evenings.

Weekdays: 7–6, Sunday: 8 am–1 pm

City News (OL)
St. Clement Street
☎ (0872) 72091
Inch (PP) (H) (DJ) (J)

Weekdays: 9.30–5

Pottles (OL)
Pannier Market, Back Quay
☎ (0872) 71384
Cornish Scrumpy (PL) (B)

Weekdays: 8.30–9.30 (closed Sunday)

Victoria Wine (OL)
27a Boscawen Street
☎ (0872) 72644
Cornish Scrumpy (PC) (DJ) (PL)
Half a mile from Truro BR station.

Walter Hicks (OL)
4 River Street
☎ (0872) 72100
Cornish Scrumpy

Tywardreath

New Inn (P)
Off A3082, in centre of village
☎ (072681) 390
Bulmer (PC)
On hill behind the beach at Par sands: an oasis from the holiday makers. Meals lunchtime except Sunday; garden; accommodation; camping facilities nearby.

Veryan

Weekdays: 11–2.30; 6–10.30 (11 in summer)

New Inn (P)
Off A3028
☎ (0872) 501362
Bulmer (PC) – summer only
18th century pub in beautiful countryside near beaches: village contains number of round houses to prevent the devil hiding in a corner. Meals lunchtime and evening; garden; accommodation; camping facilities nearby.

Upton Cross

Weekdays: 11–3; 5.30–11, Sunday: 12–3; 7–10.30

Caradon Inn (P)
Near Liskeard, on B3254
☎ (0579) 62391
Farmhouse Cider (Haye Farm) (PC)
Delightful and welcoming 17th century country inn popular with both locals and holidaymakers. Pool and bar billiards. Garden. Snacks 12–2; 6.30–9.45

Wadebridge

Weekdays: 9–6

Wadebridge Wines (OL)
The Old Foundry, Polmorla Road
☎ (020881) 2692
Apple Blossom (B)

Widemouth Bay

Weekdays: 11–3; 5.30–11

Widemouth Manor (P)
Near Bude
☎ (0288) 85263
Countryman (PC)
Inch (PC) (BB)
Bustling pub and hotel with late night discos. Meals and snacks all sessions; restaurant; children's room; outdoor drinking area; accommodation.

Zennor

Tinners Arms (P)
On B3306 St. Ives to Lands End coast road
☎ (0736) 796927
Inch (PL)
Thornton (PL)
An old church house, originally housing masons working on the splendid local church; converted into a pub in the 14th century, "modernised" in the 17th century. Beware of the Mermaid of Zennor, who lures local lads to their doom – stick to the cider! Meals and snacks lunchtime and evenings; children's room; garden; camping facilities nearby.

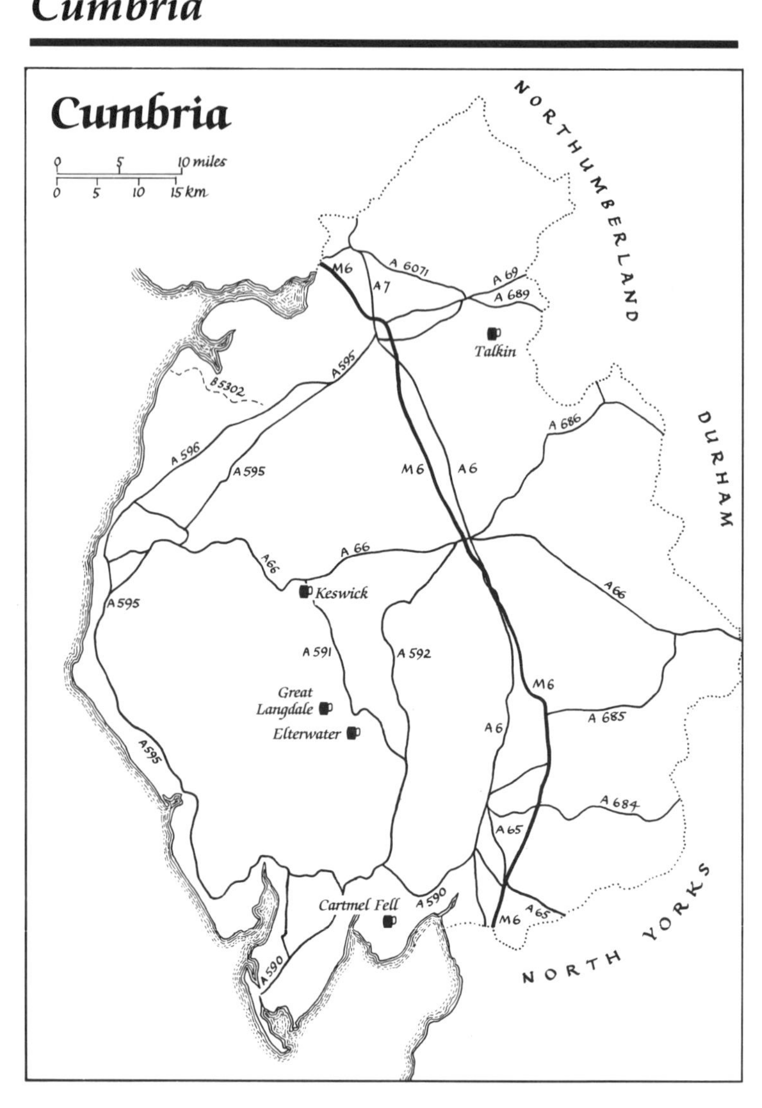

Cartmel Fell

Weekdays: 11.30–3; 6–11

Masons Arms (P)

Strawberry Bank
(Off A5074)
☎ (04488) 486
Long Ashton (B)
James White (B) (H)
Scrumpy (PC)
Perry (PC)
An award winning pub set in a remote valley: a good selection of guest ciders and perrys are available on a rotation basis. Meals and snacks 12–1.45; 6–8.45 (7–8.45 on Sunday); childrens' room; garden; accommodation. Stay a few weeks and go through the whole cider cycle!

Elterwater

Weekdays: 11–11, Sunday: 12–3; 7–10.30

Britannia Inn (P)

Near Ambleside (off B5343)
☎ (09667) 210 or 382
Bulmer (H)
400 year old traditional village inn, with log fires: a good centre for fell walkers. Bar meals 12–2; 6.30–9; light snacks and afternoon teas 2–5.30; restaurant 7.30; garden; accommodation – 10 bedrooms; facilities for camping 2 miles up the valley.

Great Langdale

Weekdays: 11–11, Sunday: 12–3; 7–10.30

Old Dungeon Ghyll (P)

Head of Langdale valley, 100 yards off B5343
☎ (09667) 272
Bulmer West Country (H)
Ideally situated for walkers and climbers. Meals lunchtime and evenings; garden; accommodation;

camping on National Trust site nearby

Keswick

Open All Hours (OL)
13 St. John Street
☏ (07687) 72128
Cornish Scrumpy – range

Talkin

Weekdays: 7–11: Lunchtimes: 12–2.30 only on Saturdays, Bank Holidays, and Monday–Friday in July and August

Hare & Hounds (P)
From B6413 take village turning, not Tarn
☏ (06977) 3456/7
Bulmer (H)
In the heart of the fells: once used by monks as a stop over on the way from Armathwaite to Lanercost Priory; excellent walking and fishing country. Lunchtime meals till 1.30; evening meals till 9 (childrens' menu also); childrens' room; garden; access for disabled; accommodation; camping facilities nearby.

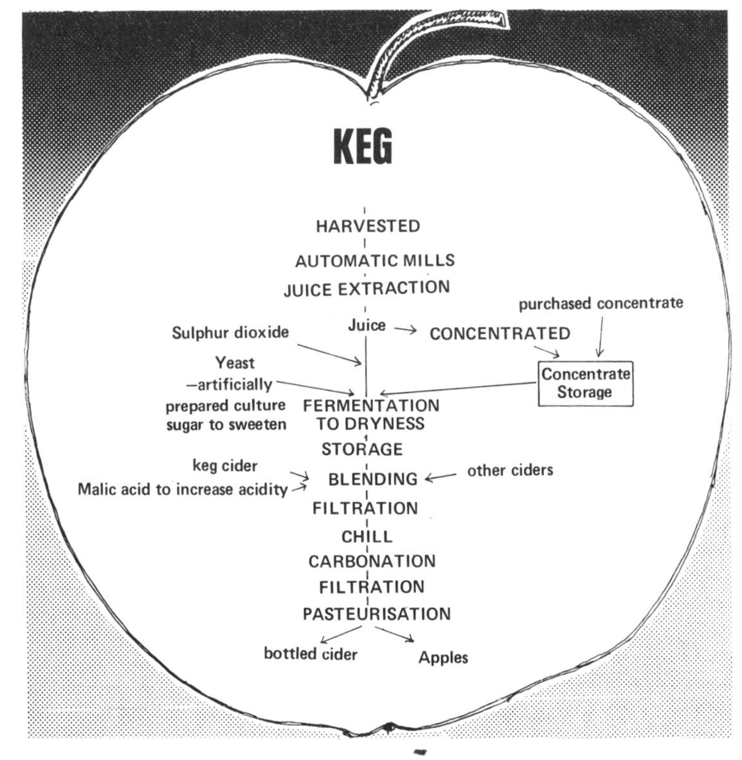

Now turn to page 47 to see what you *should* be drinking

Derbyshire

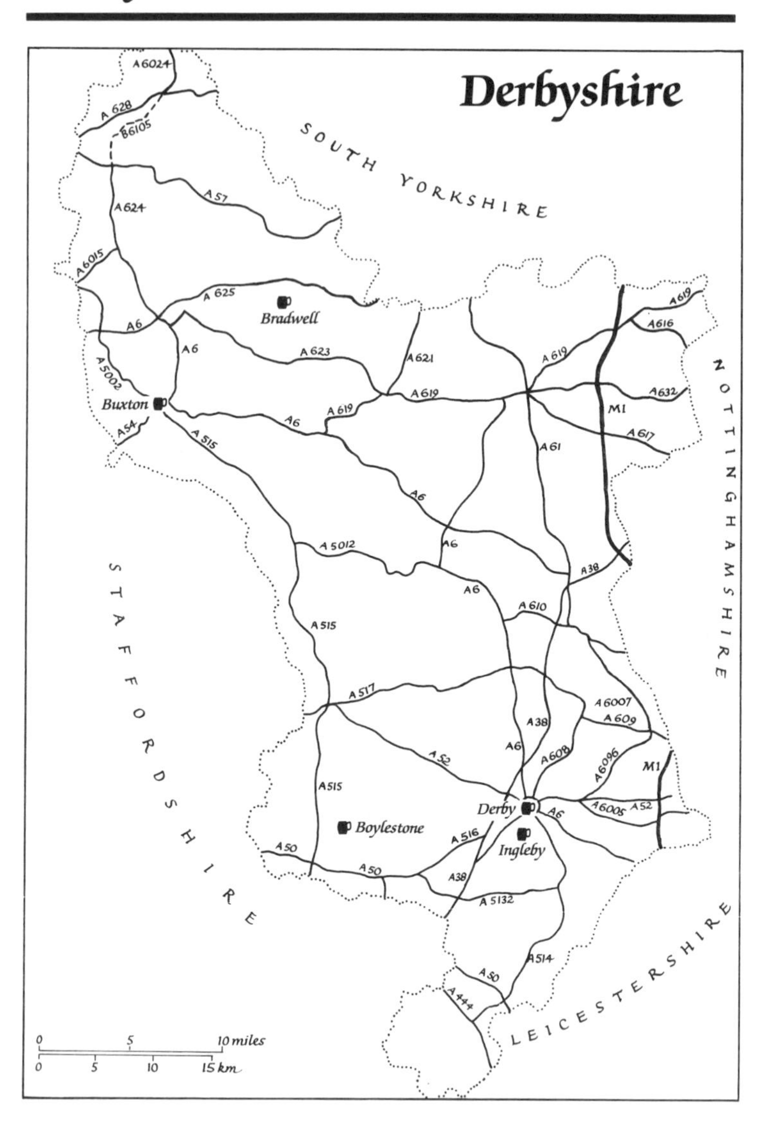

Boylestone

Weekdays: 11–3; 7–11 (closed Tuesday)

Rose & Crown (P)
Off A515 west of village
☎ (033523) 518
Bulmer (PC)
Small whitewashed pub in pleasant setting. Two small low-ceilinged rooms. Garden.

Bradwell

Weekdays: 12–3; 7–11.30

Travellers Rest (P)
Brough Lane Head (on main road $\frac{1}{4}$ mile east of Hope BR station)
☎ (0433) 20463
Bulmer (H)
Meals and snacks lunchtime and 7–8.30 evenings; large garden with children's facilities.

Buxton

Weekdays: 11–11; Sunday: 12–2.30; 7–10.30

White Lion (P)
Spring Gardens
☎ (0298) 23099
Bulmer (PC)
Bar snacks all times; outdoor drinking area; access for disabled. Buxton BR station 600 yards.

Derby

Weekdays: 11–11

Brunswick Inn (P)
1 Railway Terrace
☎ (0332) 290677
Westons Farm Brand
Westons Old Rosie

The oldest purpose built railway pub in the world: stone flagged floor. Meals lunchtime; children's room; access for disabled. Near Derby BR station. CAMRA East Midlands pub of the year 1989.

Ingleby

LLOYD'S COUNTRY BEERS (D)
John Thompson Brewery
☎ (0332) 863426

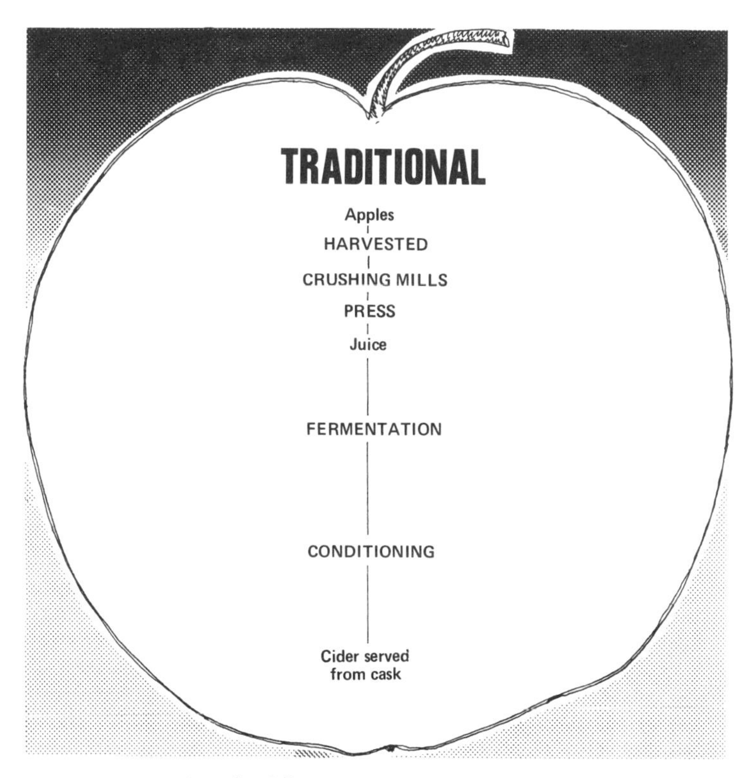

Spot the difference? – turn back to page 45

Devon

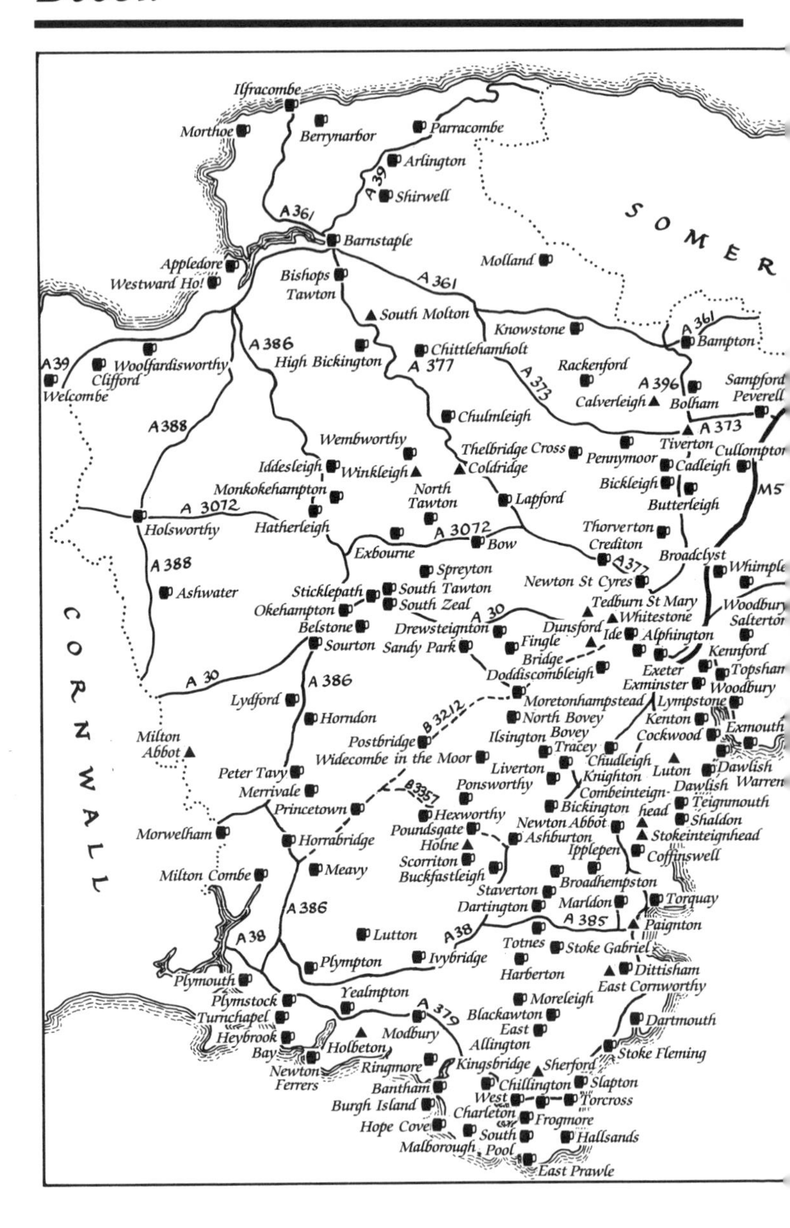

Alphington

Admiral Vernon (P)
Alphington Street
☎ (0392) 76990
Bulmer (H)

Wine Rack (OL)
Yearlstone (F)

Appledore

Weekdays: 11–3; 6–11

Bell Inn (P)
New Quay Street
☎ (02372) 74769
Inch (H)
Slipway to the Torridge estuary, and seating on the sea wall. Snacks 11–2.30; children's room; outdoor drinking area.

Arlington

April–October: 11–6; November–March gardens only: daylight hours

Arlington Court (P)
On A39 8 miles north east of Barnstaple

Devon

0 5 10 miles
0 15 km

S E T

Holcombe Rogus
Luppitt
A30
Stockland
Broadhembury
Cotleigh
Honiton
Membury
Feniton
A35
Axminster
Ottery St Mary
Musbury
Newton Poppleford
Colyton
A3052
Beer
Axmouth
Sidford
Seaton
Sidmouth
Branscombe
Otterton
Budleigh Salterton

☏ (027182) 296
Bromell (PC)
National Trust house in beautiful wooded country west of Exmoor; contains fascinating collection of various objects d'art and horse drawn vehicles. Licensed restaurant 11–5.30.

Ashburton

Monday–Thursday: 11–3; 5–11, Friday–Saturday: 11–11

Bay Horse (P)
North Street
☏ (0364) 52838
Inch (PL)
Luscombe (PC)
A well kept local with a children's room and garden. Snacks until 8 pm.

Weekdays only: 8–7

The Fords (OL)
12 North Street
☏ (0364) 53546
Luscombe

Weekdays: 11–11, Sunday: 12–3; 7–10.30

Golden Lion Hotel (P)
East Street
☏ (0364) 52205
Inch (PC)
Old town centre hotel with ground floor opened up into open plan lounge bar. Local HQ of Monster Raving Loony Party. Meals. Outdoor drinking area.

Restaurant and residential licence: 11–2.30; 6.30–10.30

Holne Chase Hotel (P)
Two Bridges Road (3 miles off A38 towards Tavistock)
☏ (03643) 471
Dartmoor Tinners Cider (PC)
A country house in a secluded position in the Dartmoor National Park, overlooking River Dart: open fires. Lunch and light meals 12–1.45; dinner 7.15–9; restaurant; accommodation; salmon fishing.

Weekdays: 11–2.30; 5–11

London Inn (P)
West Street
☏ (0364) 52478
Sheppy (PC)
Comfortable coaching house with enormous meandering lounge and its own brewery. Lunchtime and evening meals.

Ashwater

Manor Inn (P)
☏ (040921) 357
Inch (PC)
Sheppy (PC)
Pleasant village inn with a family room with children's games and a garden. Meals. Pool.

Axminster

ABBEYGATE CIDER

Abbeygate Farm (on A358)
☏ (0297) 33541

Axminster Inn (P)
Silver Street
☏ (0297) 33282
Taunton (PC)
Small back street local behind church. Pool room. Near Axminster BR station.

Weekdays: 7.30 am–11 pm

New Commercial (P)
Trinity Square
☏ (0297) 33225
Taunton (H)
Comfortable town centre local. Snacks 10.30–2.30; 6–10; meals 7.30–5 in separate restaurant; coffee shop.

6.30 am–9 pm all week

VG Late Shop (OL)
3 Western Parade, West Street
☏ (0297) 34415
Inch (BB) (J)

Wine Shop (OL)
Trinity Square, near Axminster BR station.
Farmer John (B) (J)
Inch (BB)

Axmouth

Weekdays: 11–2.30; 6–11

Harbour Inn (P)
☏ (0297) 20371
Perrys Cider (PC)
800 year old thatched inn with many rooms. Meals; accommodation.

Monday–Friday: 11–2; 6–11, Saturday: 10.30–2.30; 5.30–11

Ship (P)
1 mile north of coast to east of Seaton
☏ (0297) 21838
Taunton (PC) – summer only
Village inn with collection of dolls. Meals and snacks lunchtime and evenings (no evening food Fridays in winter); garden; access for disabled; camping facilities nearby.

Devon

Bampton

Bampton General Stores (OL)
39 Brook Street
☏ (0398) 31403
Sheppy

Weekdays: 11–2.30; 5.30–11

Bridge House Hotel (P)
24 Luke Street
☏ (0398) 31298
Hancock (F)

Exeter Inn (P)
Tiverton Road (A396)
☏ (0398) 31345
Hancock (PC)
Pleasant busy roadside pub. Meals; children's room, garden; accommodation.

Sewards Stores (OL)
Newton Square
☏ (0398) 31200
Sheppy

Bantham

Weekdays: 11–2.30; 6–11; 7–10.30 in winter

Sloop Inn (P)
Near A379, at top of village
☏ (0548) 560489
Churchward (PC)
16th century inn 300 yards from beach; excellent surfing. Meals and snacks lunchtime and evenings; separate restaurant; garden; accommodation; camping facilities nearby.

Barnstaple

TheDeli (OL)
Butchers Row
Yearlstone (F)

Union Inn (P)
Princess Street (off Vicarage Street)
☏ (0271) 42863
Taunton (E)
Snacks; children's room; pool table.

Beer

Weekdays: 11–2.30; 5.30–11, Sundays: 12–2.30; 7–10.30

Anchor Inn (P)
Fore Street
☏ (0297) 20386
Taunton (H) – summer only
Sea views from the garden. Friendly staff and atmosphere. Good fresh fish and varied cuisine to suit every purse.

Belstone

Weekdays: 11–2.30; 6–11, Sundays: 12–3; 7–10.30

Tors Hotel (P)
☏ (0837) 840689
Gray (PC)
Solid Victorian hotel on edge of Dartmoor. Meals and snacks 12–2, 7–9.30; restaurant; children's room; accommodation; garden; riding and pony trekking available – just phone to book.

Berrynarbor

Weekdays: 8.30–9 (July–Sept), 8.30–6 rest of year

Manor Stores & Off Licence (OL)
near Ilfracombe
☏ (0271) 882447
Hancock (B)

Bickington

Toby Jug (P)
On old A38
☏ (062682) 278
Tinminers (PC)
Well-run, clean, friendly and atmospheric 16th century inn with garden. Food includes unusual home-made specials.

Bickleigh

Daily 10–6 (Easter–Christmas): Weekend only 10–5 (Christmas–Easter)

Bickleigh Mill Farm Shop (OL) Restaurant (P)
Bickleigh Bridge (A396)
☏ (08845) 419
Bromell (PL)
Farmer John (B)
Inch (B) (BB) (J)
Knee Cracker (B) (PL) (S)
Yearlstone (F)
Craft and farm centre. Meals and snacks all times; restaurant; children's room; garden; access for disabled; camping facilities nearby.

Weekdays: 11–2.30; 6–11

Trout Inn (P)
On A396
Clarke (PC)
17th century thatched inn. Meals lunchtime and evenings; accommodation.

Bishops Tawton

Chichester Arms (P)
☏ (0271) 43945
Bulmer (PC)
Pleasant village local.

Blackawton

Weekdays: 10.30–2.30; 5.30–11.

Normandy Arms (P)
2 miles south of B3207
☏ (080421) 316
Stancombe (PC)
15th century village pub, named after the Normandy landings – the British troops did their pre-invasion training nearby. Meals and snacks lunchtime and evenings; restaurant; children's room; garden; accommodation.

Bolham

April–October; garden 11–5.30; house 1.30–5.30; restaurant (separate entrance) 11–6.

Knighthayes Court (P)
Turn right off Tiverton – Bampton road (A396)
☏ (0884) 254665
Bromell (PC)
Victorian mansion in large garden on east side of River Exe valley overlooking Tiverton; fine art collection; owned by National Trust.

Bovey Tracey

Dolphin Hotel (P)
On B3344
☏ (0626) 832413
Tinminers (PC)
Plush hotel bar. Meals; accommodation.

Spar Stores (OL)
Dead Dick (PL)

Bow

Weekdays: 11–3; 7–11.

White Hart (P)
On A3072
☏ (03633) 240
Inch (PC)
16th century listed building. Meals and snacks; restaurant; children's room; garden; accommodation; skittles; pool room.

Branscombe

Weekdays: 11–2.30; 6.30–11 (summer): 11–2; 6.30–10.30 (other times)

Fountain Head (P)
Near A3052
☏ (029780) 359
Taunton (PP)
14th century inn with original slate floor: forge bar a converted blacksmith's shop still with original central chimney. Meals and snacks 12–2; 7–9.30; children's rooms; outdoor drinking area; camping facilities nearby.

Weekdays: 11–2.30; 6–11

Masons Arms (P)
Near A3052
☏ (029780) 300
Inch (PC)
Old attractive inn. Meals; garden; accommodation.

Weekdays: 11–11 (July–September): 11–3; 6–11 (other times)

Three Horseshoes (P)
On A3052 outside village
☏ (029780) 251
Local Cider (H)
Meals lunchtime and evenings; children's room; garden; accommodation; camping facilities nearby.

Broadclyst

Weekdays: April–October: 11–6: garden all daylight hours throughout year.

Killerton House (P)
On west of B3181 (old A38)
☏ (0392) 881345
Bromell (PC)
National Trust property, rebuilt in 1778, housing collection of costumes in period settings; 15 acres of hillside gardens, with fine views of Clyst and Culm valleys; delightful walks. Restaurant (entrance from garden) 11–5.30.

Open all week

Young Hayes Farm (OL)
On A30 Exeter to Honiton road, 1 mile Honiton side of airport
☏ (0404) 822201
Gray (PL)
Sheppy (PL)
Full range of local produce. No cider sold on Sundays.

Broadhembury

Weekdays: 11–2.30; 6–11

Drewe Arms (P)
Off A373, in centre of village
☏ (040484) 267
Bulmers West Country (PC)
Ancient thatched pub in picture book village. Meals and snacks lunchtime and evenings; children's room; garden; accommodation.

Broadhempston

Monday: 6.30–11, Tuesday–Saturday: 12–2.30; 6.30–11, Sunday: 12–2.30; 7–10.30

Monks Retreat (P)
The Square
☏ (0803) 812203
Luscombe (PC)
Monks Retreat (PC)
Small 15th century pub, with friendly resident ghost! Better than average bar snacks (except Mondays). The Monks Retreat cider is made from Broadhempston apples only.

Buckfastleigh

Monday–Tuesday, Thursday–Friday: 10.30–9, Wednesday: 10.30–1, Saturday: 10–9, Sunday: 12–2; 7–9

Buckfastleigh Wines (OL)
3–4 Fore Street
☏ (0364) 43790
Churchward (PP)
Farmer John (B)
Inch (BB) (PP)
Tin Miners (PP) – summer only

DEAD DICKS SCRUMPY (D)
The Smugglers Lair, 32a Fore Street
☏ (0364) 43095

Weekdays: 11–11, Sunday: 12–3; 7–10.30

Globe Inn (P)
Corner of Plymouth Road and Chapel Street
☏ (0364) 42223
Luscombe (PC)
17th century stone built coaching inn. Meals and snacks lunchtime and evenings; garden; accommodation.

LUSCOMBE CIDER

Luscombe Farm
☏ (0364) 42373

Watermans Arms (P)
Market Street
☏ (0364) 43200
Tinminers (PC)
13th century coaching inn. Meals and snacks.

Weekdays: 11–3; 6–11

White Hart (P)
3 Plymouth Road
☏ (0364) 42336
Churchward (PC)
Luscombe (PC)
Town centre pub. Children's room; garden; accommodation.

Budleigh Salterton

Monday–Friday: 9–9, Saturday: 9–8, Sunday: 10–9

Creamery (OL)
34–36 Fore Street
☏ (03954) 2064
Dead Dick (PL)
Inch (BB) (J)

Feathers Hotel (P)
High Street (A376)
☏ (03954) 2042
Bulmer (H)
Town centre hotel. Meals and snacks; outdoor drinking area; accommodation.

Weekdays: 9–6

Peter Dominic (OL)
13 High Street
☏ (03954) 2034
Inch

Burgh Island

Weekdays: 11–2.30; 7–11

Pilchard Inn (P)
600 yards off the coast at Bigbury on Sea
☏ (0548) 810304
Bulmer West Country (H)
Built in 1336, and possesses a smuggler's ghost: the island can only be reached on foot at low tide – at other times you travel on the world's only giant sea tractor! Meals and snacks lunchtime and evening in summer only; children's room; garden.

Butterleigh

Monday–Thursday: 11–2.30; 6–11, Friday: 11–2.30; 5–11, Saturday: 11–2.30; 6–11

Butterleigh Inn (P)
3 miles west of Cullompton
☎ (08845) 407
Black Hand (PC)
Friendly, long established, multi-roomed village inn with stained glass porch. Popular for food. Garden. Occasional live jazz on Sundays.

Cadleigh

Cadleigh Arms (P)
Near A3072
☎ (08845) 238
Clark (PC)
Country pub with good views. Children's room. Meals.

Calverleigh

PALMERHAYES CIDER ▲
On B3221 Tiverton to Rackenford Road
☎ (0884) 25479

Chillington

Weekdays: 12–2.30; 6–11

Chillington Inn (P)
On A379
☎ (0548) 580244
Stancombe (PC)
Village inn with good local atmosphere. Two small bars, garden and restaurant (Tuesday–Saturday evenings) with good home cooking. Comfortable accommodation.

Union Inn (P)
On A379
☎ (0548) 580241
Stancombe (PC)
A very individual pub. Meals; garden.

Chittlehamholt

Weekdays: 11.30–2.30; 6–11, Sunday: 12–3; 7–10.30

Exeter Inn (P)
Near Umberleigh
☎ (07694) 281
Hancock (W)
Taunton (H)

Chudleigh Knighton

Weekdays: 11–3; 6–11

Claycutters Arms (P)
Old Bovey Tracey Road
☎ (0626) 853345
Taunton (BB) (PL)
Thatched country pub, built in 1606, with open log fires. Meals and snacks 12–2.30; 7–10.30; restaurant; garden; accommodation; camping facilities nearby.

Chulmleigh

Weekdays: 10.30 am–11 pm, Sunday 12–3

Barnstaple Inn (P)
South Molton Street
☎ (0769) 80388
Inch (PC)
Basic market town pub with friendly welcome and proper pubby atmosphere. Former coaching inn. Lunchtime and evening meals, children's room and accommodation.

Cockwood

Weekdays: 11–11, Sunday: 12–3; 7–10.30

Anchor Inn (P)
☎ (0626) 890203
Taunton (H)
16th century inn overlooking small harbour between Dawlish Warren and Starcross: log fires and beams. Meals and snacks 11.30–2; 6–10; also afternoon teas; fresh seafoods daily; restaurant; outdoor drinking area.

Coffinswell

Weekdays: 11–2.30; 6–11

Linney (P)
Off A380
☎ (08047) 3192
Churchward (PC)
14th century thatched former farmhouse with low beams and antique furniture. Popular food pub.

Coldridge

YEARLSTONE CYDER ▲
Yearlstone Vineyard, Chilverton (just south of B3220)
☎ (0363) 83302

Colyton

Weekdays: 11–3; 6–11

Bear Inn (P)
King Street
☎ (0297) 52256
Sheppy (PC)
Owned by family since 1852, on banks of River Coly. Snacks and full meals – no chips or anything fried – all opening hours; Devonshire clotted cream teas 11–12; 2–3; children's room; garden; camping facilities nearby.

Kingfisher (P)
Dolphin Street
☎ (0297) 52476
Farmer John (H)
Plain, modern pub with bags of atmosphere. Children's room and garden. Pub food.

Combeinteignhead

HOME HOUSE CIDER ▲
Home House
☎ (0626) 872591

Cotleigh

WOOLACOTT'S CIDER ▲
Bull Farm
☎ (040483) 255

Crediton

Weekdays: 9–6

Lee's Wine Store (OL)
21 High Street
☎ (03632) 2561
Inch (PL)
Yearlstone (F)

Cullompton

Monday–Friday: 11–2.30; 6–11, Saturday 11–11, Sunday: 12–3; 7–10.30

Market House Inn (P)
High Street
☎ (0884) 32339
Bulmer West Country (H)
Traditional market town pub. Bar snacks 12–2; 7–9.30; outdoor drinking area; accommodation; camping facilities nearby.

Weekdays: 11–2.30 (3.30 Saturdays), Sunday: 12–3; 7–10.30

Pony & Trap (P)
10 Exeter Hill
☎ (0884) 33254
Bulmer (H)
Pleasant, one-bar pub.

Dartington

Weekdays: 10–5

Cider Press Centre (OL)

Shinners Bridge (A384)
☎ (0803) 864171
Various (B) (PL) (J)
Once a cider press, now a complex of craft shops and restaurants: annual cider festival in August, with free tastings. Restaurant; outdoor eating area; traditional Devon farm foods on sale.

Dartmouth

Dartmouth Vintners (OL)

The Butterwalk, Duke Street
☎ (08043) 2602
Several West Country Ciders (PL)

Dawlish

Monday–Friday: 11–3; 5–11, Saturday: 11–11

Exeter Inn (P)

2 Beach Street
☎ (0626) 865677
Taunton (PC)
In small alley off main street near station. Meals and snacks lunchtime; children's room; pool table.

Weekdays: 8–5, Sunday: 9–5

Gays Creamery (OL)

20 Brunswick Place
☎ (0626) 863341
Cripplecock (PL)
Dead Dick (PL)
Home made cooking to take away; Devon clotted cream, also by post; groceries. Near Dawlish BR station.

Dawlish

Weekdays: 8.30–5.30

Lansdowne Stores (OL)

4 Park Road
☎ (0626) 863891
Gray (PC)
Also a selection of about 30 cheeses to go with the cider!

Railway Inn (P)

Beach Street
☎ (0626) 863226
Bulmer (PC)
A back street local near the station. Children's room. Snacks.

Weekdays: 11–2.30; 5–11

Swan Inn (P)

94 Old Town Street
☎ (0626) 863677
Bulmer (E)
A friendly town local with a garden. Snacks until half an hour before closing time.

Dawlish Warren

Welcome Holiday Park (OL)

☎ (0626) 862070
Bromell (PL)

Dittisham

Red Lion (P)

☎ (080422) 235
Tinminers (PC)
Lovely old country pub overlooking River Dart. Meals and snacks; restaurant; terrace and garden.

Doddiscombsleigh

Weekdays: 12–2.30; 6–11 (summer): 12–2.30; 7–10.30 (other times)

Nobody Inn (P)

Near B3193
☎ (0647) 52394
Gray (PL)
16th century old world country inn, with beams, inglenook fireplaces and brasses. Bar snacks all opening times; meals 7–9 except Sunday and Monday; restaurant; outdoor drinking area/garden; accommodation.

Drewsteignton

April–October: 11–6

Castle Drogo (P)

1 mile south of old A30 from Crockernwell; or off A382 at Sandy Park
☎ (06473) 3306
Bromell (PC)
National Trust property: a twentieth century castle, designed by Sir Edwin Lutyens for Julius Drewe, a grocery magnate who made a fortune out of Home and Colonial Stores, and spent it here: overlooks a wooded gorge of the River Teign, with fine views of Dartmoor. Restaurant 11–5.30.

Weekdays: 10.30–2.30; 6–11, Sunday: 12–2; 7–10.30

Drewe Arms (P)

The Square (off A30/A382)
Bulmer (PC)
Ancient pub of great character, which achieved fame by possessing the oldest, and longest serving landlady in Britain, Aunt Mabel.

Dunsford

BRIMBLECOMBE'S DEVON FARM-HOUSE CIDER ▲

Farrants Farm
☎ (039281) 456

Weekdays: 9–10.30; 4.30–5.30 (Easter–October)

Clifford Bridge Caravan Park (OL)

2 miles west on Drewsteignton road
☎ (064 724) 226
Brimblecombe (PL)
Small shop serving camp site.

Post Office Stores (OL)

☎ (0647) 52330
Brimblecombe (PL)

Steps Bridge Inn (P)

Steps Bridge
☎ (0647) 52313
Gray (PL)
Restaurant and bar at edge of Dartmoor National Park; over looking weir and bridge. Meals 10.30–5.30; 7.30–10.30; snacks 7.30–10.30; cream teas; garden; accommodation; camping facilities in grounds; nature walks.

East Allington

Weekdays: 12–2; 6.30–11

Fortescue Arms (P)

Near Totnes
☎ (054852) 215
Stancombe (PP) – summer only
Hearty village pub in an attractive port of the South Hams. Big on food and accommodation offering breaks all year round. Some nice quality ingredients. Garden. Camping nearby.

East Cornworthy

WHITESTONE FARM TRADITIONAL CIDER ▲
Whitestone Farm
☎ (080422) 400

East Prawle

Piglet Stores (OL)
Stancombe (PL)

Exbourne

Weekdays: 12–3; 7–11

Red Lion Inn (P)
High Street
☎ (083785) 683
Inch (BB)
An Exe Valley village local. Snacks all sessions; evening meals; restaurant; garden; accommodation.

Exeter

Canns Food Market (OL)
Little John Cross, Dunsford Hill
☎ (0392) 56441
Brimblecombe (PL)

Continental Food Store (OL)
120 Old Tiverton Road
☎ (0392) 58633
Bromell (PL)

Crossways Stores (OL)
92 Cowick Street
☎ (0392) 72842
Gray (PL)
Near Exeter St. Thomas BR station.

Weekdays: 11–11, Sunday: 12–3; 7–10.30

Double Locks Hotel (P)
Canal Bank
☎ (0392) 56947
Gray (PC)
Successful, slightly eccentric canalside pub about one mile from City Centre. Two rooms suitable for families and large outdoor drinking area. Good value food – barbecues in Summer. Frequent live music. Guest ciders. CAMRA South West England Pub of the Year 1989.

Exwick Stores (OL)
29 Exwick Villas
☎ (0392) 55737
Bromell (PL)
Dead Dick (PL)

H. A. Kasba (OL)
5 Well Street
☎ (0392) 34323
Bromell (PL)

Lion Holt Off Licence (OL)
Well Street
☎ (0392) 55179
Bromell (PL)

Weekdays: 11–11, Sunday: 12–3; 7–10.30

Locomotive Inn (P)
New North Road
☎ (0392) 75840
Churchward (H)
Coates (H)
Taunton (H)
Excellent cider pub just off City Centre, with cosmopolitan clientele. Meals and snacks. Near Exeter Central BR station.

Red Cow (P)
St. Davids
☎ (0392) 72318
Taunton (PC)
Plain, atmospheric two-bar pub with split level public bar and an outdoor drinking area. Wide range of customers including university students and passengers from St. Davids Railway Station 100 yards away.

Weekdays: 9–6

Victoria Wine (OL)
20 Guildhall
☎ (0392) 436512
Cornish Scrumpy (J) (PL) (S)
Inch (PC) (J) (PL)
Near Exeter Central and Exeter St. Davids BR stations.

Monday–Thursday: 11–3; 5–11, Friday–Saturday: 11–11, Sunday: 12–3; 7–10.30

Whipton Inn (P)
54 Whipton Village Road
☎ (0392) 66736 and 67615
Churchward (H)
Taunton (H)
Good cider pub just east of the city. Meals and snacks lunchtime and early evening; family garden; accommodation; skittle alley; pool table; function room.

Exminster

Royal Oak (P)
On old main road
Bulmer West Country (PC)
Friendly village pub. Family room. Garden.

Weekdays: 11–2.30; 6–11, Sunday: 12–3; 7–10.30

Turf Hotel (P)
On towpath at entrance to Exeter Canal
☎ (0392) 833128
Inch (PC)
On the Exe estuary, approached by track from Exminster or towpath from Exeter. The Turf runs its own canal boat, the Water Mongoose, from Countess Weir to the pub – please phone for details. Bar snacks all sessions; full meals also during winter months; children's room; garden; accommodation.

Exmouth

Albion (P)
Albion Street
☎ (0395) 272960
Bulmer (H)

Monday–Friday: 11–2.30, 5–11, Saturday: 11–11, Sunday: 12–3; 7–10.30

Country House Inn (P)
176 Withycombe Village Road, Withycombe
☎ (0395) 263444
Taunton (H)
Popular and modernised. Snacks all sessions; barbecues most weekends; large garden with aviary.

Weekdays: 11–11

Pilot Inn (P)
Chapel Inn
☎ (0395) 263382
Taunton (H)
Traditional town local. Bar lunches (except Sundays)

Pines Road Stores (OL)
Pines Road
☎ (0392) 263905
Dead Dick (PL)

Weekdays: 11–11, Sunday: 12–3; 7–10.30

South Western (P)
The Parade
☎ (0395) 263649
Taunton (H) (PC)

Railway atmosphere next to the station. Snacks 12–2; 6–10, full meals 12–2.

Victoria Wine (OL)
Unit 13, New Shopping Precinct
☎ (0395) 274275
Cornish Scrumpy – range

Feniton
Weekdays: 11–3; 6–11

Nog Inn (P)
Ottery Road (opposite Feniton station)
☎ (0404) 850210
Lane (PC)
Cheerful pub with squash court and possessive cat. Adjoins railway station. Provides lunches and overnight accommodation.

Fingle Bridge

Anglers Rest (P)
☎ (064721) 2287
Bromell (PC)
Bar cum restaurant on edge of Dartmoor, by wellknown beauty spot, popular with fishermen and ramblers. Limited winter opening. Riverside terraces; children welcome.

Frogmore
Weekdays: 11–2.30; 5.30–11 (6.30–11 in winter)

Globe Inn (P)
On A379
☎ (054853) 351
Luscombe (PC)
Lively modern-style roadside lounge with large rooms and good family facilities. Lunchtime and evening food, garden and overnight accommodation.

Hallsands
Weekdays: 11–11 (high season): 11–3; 6–11 (low season)

Hallsands Hotel (P)
☎ (054851) 264
Stancombe (PC)
One of the few remaining buildings in a village most of which was washed away by tempestuous seas during a storm early this century. Lunchtime and evening snacks and full evening meals in restaurant. Garden. Compressed air for divers. Hotel accommodation.

Harberton
Weekdays: 11–2.30; 6–11

Church House (P)
just off village centre by church
☎ (0803) 863707
Inch (PC)
Enormous heavily-beamed lounge and well equipped family room. Some real antique furnishings and lots of real food.

Hatherleigh
Weekdays: 11–11, Sunday: 12–3; 7–10.30

George Hotel (P)
Market Street (A386)
☎ (0837) 810454
Inch (BB) (PL)
15th century cob and thatched coaching inn, with cobbled courtyard. Monday and Tuesday market days. Bar meals all sessions; restaurant, closed Sundays; accommodation with 4 poster beds; outdoor unheated swimming pool.

Weekdays: 11–2.30; 6–11

Tally Ho Inn (P)
14 Market Street
☎ (0837) 810306
Inch (PC)
Ancient market town pub, beautifully demodernised with accent on Italian home cooking (fresh pasta). Garden and elegant en suite accommodation.

Hexworthy

Forest Inn (P)
☎ (03643) 211
Tinminers (PC)
Small hotel high up in the West Dart valley about half a mile off the cross Dartmoor road from Ashburton to Tavistock. Interesting collection of franking stamps from Dartmoor postboxes. Meals. Garden.

Heybrook Bay

Eddystone Inn (P)
☎ (0752) 862356
Farmer John (PC)
Remote situation on a headland, panoramic sea views. Snacks and meals lunchtime and evenings; garden and sun patio; accommodation.

High Bickington
Winter weekdays: 12–3; 6.30–11, flexible opening in summer

Old George (P)
Near Umberleigh; off B3217, in centre of village, near church
☎ (0769) 60513
Inch (PC) – summer only
Meals lunchtime and evening; children's room; accommodation. 2 mile walk from Umberleigh BR station. Pleasant main bar and comfy back room.

Holbeton

Dartmoor Union Inn (P)
Fore Street
☎ (075530) 288
Symons (PC)
18th century building, once a workhouse. Meals; children's room.

Mildmay Colours (P)
☎ (075530) 248
Symons (H)
Welcoming pub with front patio overlooking village and a garden containing a mini aviary. Wide ranging menu and a noted carvery restaurant.

SYMONS FARM CIDER ▲
Borough Farm
☎ (075530) 247

Holcombe Rogus
Weekdays: 11.30–3; 6.30–11

Prince of Wales (P)
Off A38
☎ (0823) 672070
Bulmer (H)
Excellent, old fashioned and welcoming village local set back from road in village centre. Lunchtime and evening meals; restaurant.

Holne
Weekdays: 11.30–2.30; 6.30–11, Sunday: 12–2.30; 7–10.30

Church House Inn (P)
☎ (03643) 208
Tinminers Cider (PC)
14th century inn in centre of village: listed building, said to have housed Oliver Cromwell during the

fighting at Totnes: old oak beams and screen date from 1530: in Dartmoor National Park. Bar meals 12–2; 7.30–9; dinners 7.30–9; Sunday lunches 12–2 in restaurant; accommodation, including ensuite facilities, open all year.

TINMINERS CIDER

▲

The Dartmoor Cider Company, Mitchelcombe Farm
☏ (03643) 491

Holsworthy

Weekdays: 9–1; 2–5.30

Cross & Herbert (OL)

3 The Square
☏ (0409) 253461
Inch (BB) (J)

Honiton

Monday–Friday: 10.30–2.30; 6.30–11, Saturday: 10.30–3; 6.30–11, Sunday: 12–3; 7–10.30

Red Cow (P)

High Street
☏ (0404) 42579
Taunton (H)
Popular town centre pub. Snacks lunchtime.

Weekdays: 11–2.30; 6.30–11

Volunteer (P)

177 High Street
☏ (0404) 42125
Lane (PC)
Very friendly old fashioned pub at edge of town centre. Snacks 11–2; 6.30–9.30; children's room; table skittles. Half a mile from Honiton BR station.

World Wines (OL)

High Street
Yearlstone (PL) (F)

Hope Cove

Weekdays: 11–11 (summer): 11–2.30; 6–11 (winter)

Hope & Anchor (P)

Outer Hope (on the cove)
☏ (0548) 561294
Inch (PC)
Near sandy beaches. Meals and snacks lunchtime and evenings; children's room; garden; accommodation, camping facilities nearby.

Weekdays: 8.30–5.30

Hope Cove Post Office & Stores (OL)

☏ (0548) 561249
Churchward (BB) (PL)
Hot and cold snacks and locally made pasties.

Horndon

Elephants Nest (P)

Near Mary Tavy
☏ (082281) 273
Countryman (PC)
Views across the Moors. The name derives from the physical appearance of a previous landlord! Meals 11.30–2; 7–10 every day; 6 specials, at least 3 vegetarian dishes; garden.

Horrabridge

Round the Bend Shop (OL)

Whitestone Farm (PL)

Iddesleigh

Weekdays: 11.30–4; 6.30–11

Duke of York (P)

just off B3217
☏ (0837) 810253
Inch (H)
Thatched, whitewashed village inn noted for brilliant home cooking (not Monday) – on the high calorie side. Popular despite being off beaten track. Garden. Accommodation.

Ide

Weekdays: 11–3; 5.30–11, Sunday: 12–3; 7–10.30

Huntsman (P)

2 High Street (in village centre, just off A30)
☏ (0392) 72779
Bulmer (H)
Ancient thatched village pub, with the longest inn sign in Devon across its end wall. Meals and snacks lunchtime and evenings except Sundays; garden; bar billiards.

Ilfracombe

10–10

Grapevine (OL)

138 High Street
☏ (0271) 63697
Inch (BB) (J)
Many different traditional and local ciders available.

Ilsington

Weekdays: 11–2.30; 6–11

Carpenters Arms (P)

Near Bovey Tracey; 2 miles west of A382
☏ (03646) 215
Churchward (PC)
Timeless one-bar village pub on the edge of Dartmoor, the haunt of serious darts players. Garden.

Ipplepen

Pick & Park (OL)

Park Hill Farm
☏ (0803) 812613
Sheppy

Ivybridge

Monday–Saturday: 10–2; 4.30–9.30, Sunday: 12–2; 7–9.30

Westerley Wines (OL)

Clare Street
☏ (0752) 896998
Inch

Kennford

Post Office Stores (OL)

High Street (off A38)
☏ (0392) 832201
Gray

Kenton

Weekdays: 11–2.30; 5–11

Devon Arms (P)

On A379
☏ (0626) 890213
Bulmer (H)
18th century inn. Snacks all sessions; meals Tuesday—Saturday evenings; restaurant; children's room; garden; pets' corner; accommodation.

Kingsbridge

Avon Farmers (OL)

Wallingford Road
☏ (0548) 7321
Inch

Grays Delicatessen (OL)

Fore Street
☏ (0548) 3625
Whitestone Farm (PL)

Weekdays: 11–2.30; 5.30–11

Hermitage Inn (P)

8 Mill Street
☏ (0548) 3234

Bulmer (H)
Town pub with unique carved woodwork. Meals lunchtime and evenings during summer; accommodation.

Kingsbridge Creamery (OL)
28a Fore Street
☎ (0548) 2456
Whitestone Farm (PL)

Victoria Wine (OL)
33 Fore Street
☎ (0548) 2087
Cornish Scrumpy – range

Knowstone

Weekdays: 11–3; 5.30–11 (summer): 11–3; 7–11 (winter): Sunday: 12–3; 7–10.40

Masons Arms (P)
Near A361, in centre of village
☎ (03984) 231
Reed (PL) – summer only
Delightful, thatched 13th century inn just south of Exmoor. Children's room; garden; exceptional food and romantic accommodation. Camping facilities close by.

Lapford

Weekdays: 11–2.30; 7–11

Old Malt Scoop (P)
½ mile off A377 in village centre
☎ (03635) 330
Inch (PC)
16th century pub, once a brewery. Meals and snacks lunchtime and evenings; children's room; garden; accommodation; access for disabled; camping facilities nearby. Half a mile from Lapford BR station.

Liverton

Weekdays: 11–2.30; 6–11, Sunday: 12–2.30; 7–10.30

Star Inn (P)
☎ (0626) 821376
Taunton (PC)
Old unspoilt pub of character. Meals 11–2; 6–9, Sunday: 12–2; 7–9; large children's area – climbing frame, swings, and giant amusement centre.

Luppitt

Luppitt Inn (P)
3 miles north west of A30 at Monkton
Coates (PC)
Devon's simplest pub in ancient village three miles into the Blackdown Hills off the A35. Main bar seats about half a dozen people. A rare surviving example of the authentic village local pub style. Closed Sundays.

Luton

REDDAWAY'S FARM CIDER ▲
Lower Rixdale
☎ (06267) 75218

Lutton

Weekdays: 11–3; 6–11

Mountain Inn (P)
Near Ivybridge: north of A38 – at eastern end of village
☎ (075537) 247
Farmer Johns (PC)
Cosy public bar, elegant quiet lounge. Recent family room suitable for older children. Patio garden. Meals. Car park requires good manners!

Lydford (P)

Weekdays: 11–3; 6–11

Castle Inn (P)
In village, next to old stannary prison
☎ (082282) 242
Inch (PC)
16th century stone pub with massive fireplace and bread oven. Meals and snacks lunchtime and evenings; small children's room; large garden and play area; accommodation.

Weekdays: 11–3; 6–11, Sunday: 12–3; 7–10.30

Dartmoor Inn (P)
On A386
☎ (082282) 221
Bulmer (PC)
Countryman (PC)
16th century inn on west side of Dartmoor: low ceilings, wood panelling, and massive fireplaces. Extensive bar meal and restaurant menus: 12–2; 7–10; garden; accommodation. The Countryman cider is also sold in 2½ litre containers to take away.

Lympstone

Weekdays: 11–3; 6–11, Sunday: 12–3; 7–10.30

Globe Inn (P)
The Strand
☎ (0395) 263166
Taunton (PC)
Old pub in centre of small fishing village. Famous for seafood: meals Monday–-Saturday 12–2 (1.45 in lounge); Sunday 12–1.15. Near Lympstone BR station on Exeter to Exmouth line.

Weekdays: 11.30–2.30; 6–11, Sunday: 12–2; 7–10.30

Redwing Inn (P)
Church Road
☎ (0395) 271656
Bulmer (H)
Meals and snacks all sessions; restaurant; children permitted. Near Lympstone BR station.

Monday–Thursday: 11–2.30; 5.30–11, Friday–Saturday: 11–11, Sunday: 12–3; 7–10.30

Swan Inn (P)
The Strand
☎ (0395) 272284
Bulmer (H)
Snacks 12–1.45; 7–9.30. Adjacent to Lympstone BR station on Exeter to Exmouth line. 19th century two-bar local adjacent to railway station. Garden and overnight accommodation.

Malborough

Royal Oak (P)
Off A381
☎ (0548) 561481
Luscombe (PC)
Meals and snacks all sessions; patio; children's room; camping facilities nearby; accommodation; pool table; traditional folk evenings every Wednesday.

Marldon

Weekdays: 11–2.30; 5.30–11

Church House Inn (P)
☎ (0803) 558279
Taunton (H)
Out of the way local in old part of suburban village. Odd windows! Children's room and garden.

Meavy

Weekdays: 11–3; 6–11

Royal Oak (P)
☎ (0822) 852944
Inch (PC)
15th century local owned by parish council. Lovely slate-floored public bar with large fireplace. Stands next to ancient oak on village green. Garden.

Membury

Longbridge Inn (P)
☎ (040488) 366
Reed (PL)
Village local. Food served.

Merrivale

Weekdays: 11–3; 6–11

Dartmoor Inn (P)
On B3347, 4 miles from Tavistock
☎ (082289) 340
Countryman (PC)
Set amid the Dartmoor tors, overlooking the Walkham Valley. Meals lunchtime and evenings; large outdoor seating area; accommodation; camping facilities nearby.

Milton Abbot

COUNTRYMAN CIDER ▲
Felldownhead
☎ (082287) 226

Weekdays: 11–3; 6–11

Edgcombe Arms (P)
On A384
☎ (082287) 229
Countryman (PC)
Superb moorland views, in good touring area. Bar snacks lunchtime and evenings; garden.

Milton Combe

Weekdays: 11–2.30; 6–11

Who'd Have Thought It (P)
in village centre near A386
☎ (0822) 853313
Bulmer (H)
16th century pub with low beams in small village in steeply wooded valley. Meals lunchtime and evenings; garden; level access front and rear for disabled.

Modbury

Mackgills (OL)
Church Street
☎ (0548) 830860
Symons (PL)

Molland

Weekdays: varies depending on demand, Saturday: 11–11

London Inn (P)
between South Molton and Dulverton, north of A361
☎ (07697) 269
Hancock (PC)
Traditional Devon inn on edge of Exmoor Meals lunchtime and evening; children's room; garden; facilities for camping nearby.

Monkokehampton

Weekdays: 11–2.30; 6–11, Sunday: 12–2; 7–10.30

Olde Swan (P)
On B3217
☎ (083785) 313
Inch (PC)
Comfortable village pub. Meals; children's room; garden; accommodation.

Moreleigh

Weekdays: 12–2; 6.30–11

New Inn (P)
Between Totnes and Kingsbridge, on B3207
☎ (054882) 326
Churchward (PC)
Traditional village local maintaining good all-year trade although off the beaten tourist track. Lunchtime and evening meals.

Moretonhampstead

Manor House Hotel (P)
☎ (0647) 40355
Bromell (F)
Country house hotel, noted for its food just off the Two Bridges road on the edge of the Moor.

Weekdays: 11–3.30; 6–11

White Hart (P)
The Square
☎ (0647) 40406
Coates (PC)
Georgian coaching house, more a hotel than a pub but with a pleasantly furnished, friendly bar at the back. Restaurant. Seating in courtyard.

Mortehoe

Winter weekdays: 11–2; 6–11, may vary in summer

Ship Aground (P)
Near Ilfracombe
☎ (0271) 870856
Hancock (PC)
Modern style lounge bar with attractive furnishings. Children's room and small, pleasant patio. Meals lunchtime and evening.

Morwelham

Morwelham Quay (OL)
☎ (0822) 832766
Whitestone Farm (PL)
Historic port and copper mine, a popular holiday venue.

Musbury

Weekdays: 11–2.30; 6–11

Golden Hind (P)
The Street
☎ (0297) 52413
Taunton (PC)
Traditional style country pub. Bar snacks all times; outdoor drinking area; camping facilities nearby.

Newton Abbot

Weekdays: 11–11

Dartmouth Inn (P)
61 East Street
☎ (0626) 53451
Coates (PC)
Tinminers (PC)
Thriving town local on main road on edge of central area.

Devon Arms (P)
67 East Street
☎ (0626) 68725
Churchward (PC)
Attractive exterior and cosy, traditional interior.

Weekdays: 10–10

Queen Street Stores (OL)
103 Queen Street (near War Memorial)
☎ (0626) 65373
Haymaker
Inch (BB) (B)
Dead Dick

Saracens Head (P)
Fairfield Terrace
☎ (0626) 65430

Bulmer (E)
Comfortable side street pub. Meals and snacks. Near Newton Abbot BR station.

Swan (P)
4 Highweek Street
☏ (0626) 65056
Tinminers (PC)
Snacks; pool table. Unremarkable local at edge of shopping area, convenient for the market.

Weekdays: 8.30–6
Victoria Wine Co (OL)
14 Market Walk
☏ (0626) 60421
Cornish Scrumpy (J) (PL)
Inch (J) (PL)
Within half a mile of Newton Abbot BR station.

Tuesday–Friday: 10–10, Monday, Saturday: 9–10, Sunday: 12–2; 7–9
Vine & Video (OL)
17 Bank Street
☏ (0626) 69413
Countryman (S)
Inch (B) (BB) (J)

Monday–Thursday: 11–2.30; 5–11, Friday–Saturday: 11–11, Sunday: 12–3; 7–10.30
Olde Cider Bar (P)
99 East Street
☏ (0626) 54221
Bromell (W)
Hunt (W)
Inch (H)
Richards cider (PC)
Richards perry (PC)
An experience not to be missed – a genuine cider house, selling a comprehensive range of vintage, draught farmhouse, and bottled ciders: the draught is dispensed from 40 gallon wooden barrels: also a range of fruit and grape wines. Substantial bar snacks all sessions; children's room; outdoor drinking area.

Newton Ferrers

Weekdays: 11–3; 6–11
Dolphin (P)
Riverside Road East (bottom of the main street)
☏ (0752) 872007
Symmonds (PC)
Pub on small sailing creek, on estuary of River Yealm. Meals lunchtime and evenings; children's room till 9; sunny south facing garden overlooking river.

Newton Poppleford

Weekdays: 11–2.30; 6.30–11
Cannon Inn (P)
High Street (A3052)
☏ (0395) 68266
Taunton (PP)
Meals and snacks 12–2; 7–9; outdoor drinking area/garden; accommodation; camping facilities nearby.

Exeter Inn (P)
On A3052
Taunton (PC)
Meals and snacks lunchtime and evenings; separate restaurant.

FARMER JOHN'S DEVONSHIRE FARMHOUSE CIDER ▲
Parsons Farm
☏ (0395) 68152

Newton St. Cyres

Weekdays: 11–2.30; 6–11
Crown & Sceptre (P)
On A377
☏ (0392) 851278
Inch (PC)
Meals and snacks lunchtime and evenings; children allowed into part of lounge; large garden with play facilities for children. Near Newton St. Cyres BR station (limited service).

North Bovey

Ring of Bells (P)
By village green
☏ (0647) 40375
Gray (PC)
13th century pub on the Moors, with thatched roof and low ceilings. Snacks lunchtime and evenings; meals evenings; restaurant; children's room; garden with moorland views; accommodation.

North Tawton

Weekdays: 11–3.30; 6.30–11 and restaurant licence
Copper Key Inn (P)
Fore Street
☏ (083782) 357
Bromell (PC)
Tastefully restored inn dating back to 1520, with thatched roof, open fires, lots of atmosphere. Bar snacks; a la carte restaurant menu; children's room; garden; access for disabled; accommodation.

Monday–Friday: 11–2.30; 5.30–11, Saturday: 11–11
Fountain Inn (P)
3 Exeter Street
☏ (0837) 82551
Bulmer West Country (H)
Fine old coaching inn with warm friendly local character. Bar snacks all opening hours; children's room; outdoor drinking area.

Weekdays: 12–2.30; 6–11
Railway (P)
The Station, Whiddon Down Road
☏ (083782) 789
Inch (BB)
The station, on the line to Okehampton, has long since closed, but the pub has plenty of railway atmosphere. Meals and snacks 12–2; 6–10.30; restaurant; children's room; garden; accommodation.

Okehampton

Weekdays: 10.30–11, Sunday: 12–3; 7–10.30
Kings Arms (P)
St. James Street
☏ (0837) 2809
Bulmer (H)
Hotel with comfortable lounge, basic bar and garden. Bar snacks lunchtimes.

Weekdays: 10.30–11, but may vary
Plume of Feathers (P)
38 Fore Street
☏ (0837) 2815
Taunton (PC)
Busy town centre pub. Meals lunchtime; evening meals for residents only; accommodations; access for disabled.

Weekdays: 10.30–11, Sunday: 12–3; 7–10.30
White Hart (P)
Fore Street
☏ (0837) 2730
Inch (PC)
Large town centre hotel. Meals; accommodation.

Otterton

Weekdays: 7.30 am–1 pm; 2 pm–5 pm

Kingsway (OL)
☎ (0395) 68267
Bromell (PL)

Ottery St. Mary

Monday–Friday: 10.30–2.30; 5.30–11, Saturday: 10.30–11

London Hotel (P)
Gold Street
☎ (040481) 4763 or 4755
Inch (PC)
Modernised hotel with a restaurant, children's room, patio, skittles alley and pool room.

Weekdays: 10.30–3; 5.30–11

Plume of Feathers (P)
Yonder Street
☎ (040481) 2395
Taunton (PC)
Lively local. Snacks available at lunchtimes.

Victoria Wine (OL)
17 Broad Street
☎ (040481) 2643
Cornish Scrumpy – range

Paignton

CHURCHWARD'S CIDER ▲
Yalberton Farm
☎ (0803) 55817

Grange Court Shop (OL)
Grange Court Holiday Centre, Grange Road, Goodrington
☎ (0803) 558010
Dead Dick (PL)

HUNT'S DEVON CIDER ▲
Higher Yalberton Farm, Collaton St. Mary
☎ (0803) 557694

Three Beaches Wines (OL)
101 Dartmouth Road
☎ (0803) 554917
Dead Dick (PL)

Parracombe

Weekdays: 11–11 (April–November): 11–3; 7–11 (November–April)

Hunters Inn (P)
Heddons Mouth (off A39)
☎ (05983) 230
Hancock (W)
Beautiful gardens with ponds, peacocks and ducks: walks around coast and down to beach. Snacks 12–2; 6–9.30; meals 7–8; restaurant; children's room; accommodation; function room.

Pennymore

Cruwys Arms (P)
1 mile south of A373
☎ (03636) 347
Clark (PC)
16th century village pub with cobbled courtyard giving views of Dartmoor during clear weather. Lounge has a splendid inglenook and home-prepared meals are served in a separate dining area.

Peter Tavy

Weekdays: 11.30–2.30; 6.30–11, Sunday: 12–3; 7–10.30

Peter Tavy Inn (P)
☎ (082287) 348
Taunton (PP)
Small low ceilinged 15th century inn on edge of Dartmoor. Meals and snacks 12–2; 7–9.30; children's room; garden; camping facilities nearby.

Plymouth

Weekdays: 10.30–1; 3–9

Leos (OL)
252 Old Laira Road, Laira
☎ (0752) 667542
Bromell (PL)

Monday–Thursdays: 10 am–10.30 pm, Friday–Saturday: 10 am–11 pm, Sunday: 10–3; 7–10.30

Lipson Wine Stores (OL)
8 Ladysmith Road, Lipson
☎ (0752) 228866
Local cider

Weekdays: 10–10; Sunday 12–2, 7–10

Punch Bowl Off Licence (OL)
15 Wolseley Road, Milehouse
☎ (0752) 569300
Dead Dick
Haymaker
Inch

Weekdays: 11–3; 6–11

Pym Arms (P)
16 Pym Street, Devonport (off Albert Road, between Stoke village and Dockyard)
☎ (0752) 561823
Symmons (PC)
Refurbished one-bar pub where young clientele create a brash and breezy atmosphere. Plymouth's premier beer pub but cider not forgotten. Snacks. Near Devonport Railway Station.

Weekdays: 11–11

Star of the West (P)
7 Brownlow Street, Stonehouse
☎ (0752) 221125
Coates (PC)
Taunton (H)
Bar snacks.

Victoria Wine (OL)
58 Eastlake Walk, Drake Circus
☎ (0752) 220789
Cornish Scrumpy – range

Weekdays: 9–9, Sunday: 12–2; 7–9

Victoria Wine (OL)
76 Hyde Park Road, Mutley
☎ (0752) 660766
Cornish Scrumpy (J) (PL)
Inch (J) (PL)
Half a mile from Plymouth BR station.

Weekdays: 11–3; 5.30–11, Sunday: 12–3; 7–10.30

Woodside (P)
12 Gasking Street
☎ (0752) 669700
Coates (PC)

Weekdays: 9.30–5.30

Wren Pottery (OL)
House that Jack Built, Barbican
☎ (0752) 220655
Gasping Goose Scrumpy (PL)

Plympton

Langage Farm Shop (OL)
Higher Langage Farm
☎ (0752) 337723
Symons (PL)

April–October: 12.30–6 (Tuesday–Sunday): gardens every day during year in daylight hours.

Saltram House (P)
Between A38 and A379
☎ (0752) 336546
Bromell (PC)

National Trust property: remarkable survival of George II mansion and original contents; garden with orangery, rare shrubs and trees and 18th century octagonal summerhouse; landscaped park. Restaurant in house Tuesday–Sunday and Bank Holiday Monday: 11–5.30

Plymstock

Victoria Wine (OL)
35 The Broadway
☏ (0752) 401220
Cornish Scrumpy – range

Ponsworthy

Sunday–Fridays: 8–6

Post Office & Stores (OL)
☏ (03643) 234
Gray (PL)
Small village stores selling everything from brandy to bootlaces.

Postbridge

East Dart Hotel (P)
On B3212
☏ (0822) 88213
Gray (PC)
Popular stopping place in the middle of Dartmoor with 30 miles of fishing. Meals.

Postbridge

Weekdays: 11–11 (summer): 11–2.30; 5.30–11 (other times): Sunday: 12–3; 7–10.30

Warren House Inn (P)
☏ (0822) 88208
Gray (PC)
Remote moorland inn, third highest in England: originally a tinminers' pub: the open log fire has been burning for 144 years! Meals and snacks 12–2.30; 5.30–9; children's room; garden.

Poundsgate

Weekdays: 11–11 (Easter to end of September): 11–3; 5.30–11.30 (other times)

Tavistock Inn (P)
On B3352
Ashburton – Tavistock road
☏ (03643) 251
Taunton (PC)
Old traditional granite moorland pub. Meals lunchtime and evenings; children's room; garden.

Princetown

Plume of Feathers Inn (P)
On B3212
☏ (082289) 240
Taunton (PC)
Princetown's oldest building – established 1785. As well as its own campsite it offers an Alpine style bunkhouse; a mecca for Dartmoor walkers. Meals, children's room and garden.

Two Bridges Hotel (P)
Tinminers (PC)
Small hotel in West Dart Valley to north east of town, where the two cross-Dartmoor roads intersect. Good value bar food.

Rackenford

Weekdays: 12–3; 6–11, Sunday: 12–3; 7–10.30

Stag Inn (P)
Just off B3221 in village centre
☏ (088488) 369
Inch (PC)
Reputedly Devon's oldest pub, dating from 1237. Meals and snacks lunchtime and evenings; children's room (games room); garden; accommodation; camping facilities nearby.

Ringmore

Weekdays: 11–2.30; 6–11

Journeys End Inn (P)
At bottom of village – walk down from car park
☏ (0548) 510205
Inch (PC)
Stancombe (PC)
14th century building which used to act as overnight lodging for pack horse teams; in seaside village. R. C. Sherriff wrote his play "Journeys End" here, and the name has stuck. Meals and snacks lunchtime and evenings; children's room; garden; accommodation.

Weekdays: 9–7

Ringmore Country Fayre (OL)
☏ (0548) 810217
Countryman (J) (PL)
Inch (BB) (J) (PL)
Stancombe (PC) (PL)
14th century village shop of outstanding Devon character. Accommodation; camping facilities nearby.

Sampford Peverell

Weekdays: Tuesday–Saturday: 9–5.30

Little Turberfield Farm Shop (OL)
On approach road to Tiverton Parkway BR station
☏ (0884) 820908
Inch (PP) (PL)
Palmershayes (PP) (PL)
Sheppy (PP) (PL)
Also sells home produced meat and vegetables.

Sandy Park

Weekdays: 11.30–11

Sandy Park Inn (P)
Near Chagford. On A382 between Whiddon Down and Moretonhampstead
☏ (06473) 3538
Farmer Johns (PC) – summer only
Classic crossroads inn on edge of Dartmoor, with stone floor and rustic furniture. Cobwebs over ancient wine bottles. Tiny dining room (being extended) serves good home-cooked food. Accommodation and disabled access.

Scorriton

Tradesmans Arms (P)
☏ (03643) 206
Tinminers (PC)
Basic one bar pub overlooking beautiful, secluded valley on eastern edge of Dartmoor.

Seaton

PIPPINFIELD CIDER ▲
'Pippinfield', Harepath Hill
☏ (0297) 20597

Weekdays: 9.30–9

Seaton Wine Company (OL)
50 Queen Street
☏ (0297) 22134
Cornish Scrumpy (B) (PL)
Cripplecock (PL) (B)

Devon

Shaldon

Royal Standard Hotel (P)
Fore Street
☎ (0626) 872442
Taunton (H)
In centre of village at mouth of the River Teign. Meals and snacks lunchtime and evenings; family room; pool room; holiday flat.

Sherford

STANCOMBE CIDER ▲
Stancombe Farm
☎ (0548531) 634

Shirwell

Shirwell Stores (OL)
Off A39 north east of Barnstaple
☎ (027182) 362
Bromell (J) (PL)

Sidford

Weekdays: 10.30–2.30; 5.30–11

Blue Ball (P)
On A3052 at east side of village
☎ (0395) 514062
Taunton (H)
Flagstoned floor, inglenook fireplace. Meals and snacks lunchtime and evenings; children's room; garden; accommodation.

Rising Sun (P)
in village centre
Taunton (PC)
Meals and snacks; garden; accommodation.

SPILLER'S CIDER ▲
Burscombe Farm (off A3052 west of village, or off A375 half a mile to north)
☎ (03957) 267

Sidmouth

Anchor Inn (P)
Old Fore Street
☎ (03955) 4129
Bulmer (E)
Meals and snacks lunchtime and evening; family room; children's adventure playground; large garden; interesting collection of old cider jars.

Peter Dominic (OL)
4 Fore Street
☎ (03955) 283
Countryman (PL)
Taunton (BB)
Weston (J)

Radway Inn (P)
1 Radway Place (opposite cinema)
☎ (03955) 3444
Taunton (H)
Lively town pub with old iron scrolled pillar and large collection of beer bottles. Lunchtime snacks and evening meals.

Victoria Wine (OL)
Market Place
☎ (03955) 77358
Cornish Scrumpy – range

Slapton

Weekdays: 11.30–2.30; 6–11

Queens Arms (P)
Off A379
☎ (0548) 580800
Churchward (PC)
Westons Old Rosie (PC)
Traditional village local half a mile from Slapton Sands and the Ley.

Weekdays: 11.30–2.30; 6–11

Tower Inn (P)
In village centre
☎ (0548) 580216
Stancombe (PC)
14th century inn – part of old chantry. Meals and snacks 12–2; 7–10; restaurant; children's room; garden; accommodation; camping facilities nearby.

Sourton

Weekdays: 10–2; 6–10.30,
Sunday: 12–2; 7–10.30

Highwayman Inn (P)
On A386
☎ (083786) 243
Gray (PC)
Fantastically themed roadside pub offering snacks and overnight accommodation.

South Molton

Weekdays: 9.15–5.15

Beehive Wine Store (OL)
6 East Street
☎ (07695) 2644
Gray (PL)
Inch (BB) (J)

HANCOCK'S DEVON CIDER ▲
Clapworthy Mill
☎ (07695) 2678

South Pool

Weekdays: 11 am onwards to 11 pm according to tides

Millbrook Inn (P)
At head of Southpool creek (near Kingsbridge, sign-posted off A379)
☎ (0548) 531581
Churchward (PC)
14th century coaching inn, in very pretty village; on Salcombe estuary. Meals and snacks all opening hours; specialises in crab salads and sandwiches; the Millbrook Aylesbury ducks on the pub pond are *not* on the menu!; children's room; garden; camping facilities nearby; moorings for yachts and small boats.

South Tawton

Weekdays: 11–2.30; 6–11,
Sunday: 12–3; 7–10.30

Seven Stars Inn (P)
Off old A30
☎ (0837) 840292
Inch (H)
Stone built village pub. Meals and snacks till 9; restaurant; garden; accommodation.

South Zeal

Weekdays: 11.30–2.30; 6.30–11

Kings Arms (P)
☎ (0837) 840300
Inch (PC) (BB)
Thatched roofed old world country inn. Bar snacks all times; full meals for residents; outdoor drinking area/garden; accommodation; camping facilities nearby.

Weekdays: 11–2.30; 6–11

Oxenham Arms (P)
Off A30, in centre of village
☎ (0837) 840244
Gray (PC)
Ancient pub on edge of Dartmoor, once the dower house of the Oxenham family. Meals and snacks lunchtime and evenings; children's room; garden; accommodation; camping facilities half a mile.

Spreyton

Weekdays: 12–2.30; 6–11

Tom Cobley Inn (P)

4 miles north of A30
☏ (064723) 314
Inch (PC)
A militantly traditional local with a regulars' front bar and a plusher back bar. Excellent food and good value accommodation. Children's room and garden.

Staverton

Riverford Farm Shop (OL)
☏ (080426) 636
Yearlstone (F)

Sticklepath

Devonshire Inn (P)
On old A30
☏ (083784) 626
Gray (PC)
Thatched village inn with big log fire in beamed bar and a cosy lounge. Bar food and restaurant. Children's room.

Stockland

Kings Arms (P)
Village centre
☏ (040488) 361
Reed (PL)
Rambling old thatched country pub. Meals and snacks; garden; accommodation.

Stockland

REEDS CIDER ▲
Broadhayes, Sawmills
☏ (040488) 366

Stoke Fleming

Weekdays: 11–3; 6–11 (April–October); 12–2.30; 7–11 (winter)

London Inn (P)
☏ (0803) 770397
Local cider (PC)
Very close to Blackpool Sands. Snacks 12–2; full meals 12–2; 6–9.30; also children's menu: large selection of speciality seafood; children's room; garden.

Stokeinteignhead

Weekdays: 11–3; 6–11

Church House Inn (P)
nr. Newton Abbott
☏ (0626) 872475
Churchward (PC)
In centre of village. Meals and snacks 12–2 and 7–10; restaurant; garden; children's room; large collection of antique brass.

TEIGNHEAD FARM CIDER ▲
Higher Farm
☏ (0626) 873394

Stoke Gabriel

Church House Inn (P)
☏ (080428) 384
Taunton (PC)
Traditional two-bar pub in village which just manages to remain a village. Meals. Small patio for outdoor drinking.

Tedburn St. Mary

BROMELL'S DEVON FARM CIDER ▲
Lower Uppercott
☏ (06476) 294

GRAY'S FARM CIDER ▲
Halstow
☏ (0647) 61236

Kibbey's Stores (OL)
☏ (06476) 375
Bromell (PL)

Kings Arms (P)
On old A30
☏ (06476) 224
Bromell (PC)
Old coaching inn at centre of village. Long bar created from several rooms being knocked together. Meals; accommodation.

Log Cabin Restaurant (P)
Pathfinder Village
☏ (06476) 394
Bromell (PC)
Eating place in caravan site on edge of village.

Teignmouth

Kangaroo Off Licence (OL)
Teign Street
☏ (06267) 4661
Bromell (PL)
Attached to Kangaroo pub – but cider only on sale OL.

Weekdays: 11–11, Sunday: 12–3; 7–10.30

Kings Arms (P)
French Street
☏ (06267) 75268
Taunton (PC)
Pleasant pub close to railway station. Snacks all sessions.

Weekdays: 11–11, Sunday: 12–3; 7–10.30

Teign Brewery Inn (P)
20 Teign Street
☏ (0626) 772684
Taunton (H)
Traditional old style pub, small but friendly, near docks. Bar snacks all times; outdoor drinking area. Near Teignmouth BR station.

Teign Wines (OL)
Clarendon House,
19 Orchard Gardens
☏ (06267) 5651
Gray (PL)

Victoria Wine (OL)
21 Wellington Street
☏ (06267) 4116
Cornish Scrumpy – range

Thelbridge Cross

Weekdays: 11.30–3; 6.30–11, Sunday: 12–3; 7–10.30

Thelbridge Cross (P)
On B3042
☏ (0884) 860316
Clark (PL)
Inch (BB)
Old country inn overlooking Dartmoor at the front, and Exmoor at the rear. Meals and snacks all opening hours; restaurant; children's room; outdoor drinking area/garden; camping facilities nearby.

Thorveston

Weekdays: 11–3; 6–11

Exeter (P)
Bullen Street (village centre): near Exeter
☏ (0392) 860206
Taunton (H)
Enlarged village bar whose stone walls are adorned with interesting implements and bric-a-brac. Watch out for the well! Table tennis in family room. Garden; camping facilities nearby and access for disabled people.

Tiverton

Banner Wines (OL)
23 West Exe North
☎ (0884) 255644
Clark (PL)
Yearlstone (F)

Barley Mow (P)
Barrington Street
☎ (0884) 252028
Bulmer (H)
Town centre pub.

CLARKS FARMHOUSE CIDER ▲
Shortridge Hill, Seven Crosses
☎ (0884) 252632

Monday–Friday: 9–5.30, Saturday: 9–5
Country Cupboard (OL)
24a Bampton Street
☎ (0884) 257220
Clark (PL)
Farmer John (B) (PL)
Inch (BB) (J)
Yearlstone (B)
Yearlstone Wine (B)

Monday–Friday: 11–2.30; 5.30–11, Saturday: 11–11, Sunday: 12–3; 7–10.30
Hare & Hounds (P)
Chapel Street
☎ (0884) 252013
Taunton (H)
A spacious local. Bar snacks all sessions; garden; function room.

Weekdays: 11–11, Sunday: 12–3; 7–10.30
Racehorse (P)
Wellbrook Street
☎ (0884) 252606
Bulmer (H)
Popular local near town centre. Bar snacks 12–8; meals 12–2.30 (all home cooked food); covered patio; large garden with play equipment; access for disabled.

Topsham

Monday–Friday: 11–2.30; 6–11, Saturday: 11–11, Sunday: 12–3; 7–10.30
Exeter Inn (P)
68 High Street
☎ (039287) 3131
Taunton (H)
Meals lunchtime and evenings; accommodation. Near Topsham BR station, on Exeter to Exmouth line.

London & South Western (P)
14 Fore Street
☎ (039287) 3542
Taunton (H)
A good darts playing pub near station. Snacks lunchtimes and evenings.

Torcross

Weekdays: 11–2.30; 6.30–11
Village Inn (P)
☎ (0548) 580206
Inch (PC)
Village pub at southern end of Slapton Sands.

Torquay

Babbacombe Florist & Fruiterers (OL)
122 Reddenhill Road, Babbacombe
☎ (0803) 314069
Dead Dick (PL)

Weekdays: 11–11
Brunswick Inn (P)
217 Union Street, Torre
☎ (0803) 292518
Bulmer (H)
Small, narrow pub at top end of main shopping street.

Victoria Wine (OL)
Fleet Street
☎ (0803) 22325
Cornish Scrumpy – range

Totnes

Weekdays: 7–6
Happy Apple (OL)
60 High Street
☎ (0803) 866261
Whitestone Farm (PL)

Weekdays: 9–6 (closed Sunday)
Victoria Wine (OL)
28 High Street
☎ (0803) 862362
Cornish Scrumpy (J) (PL)
Inch (J) (PL)
Near Totnes BR station.

Watermans Arms (P)
Victoria Street
Bulmer (H)
Pleasant, quiet local in back street just off the Plains. Meals and snacks.

Turnchapel

Weekdays: 11–3; 6–11, Sunday: 12–3; 7–10.30
Boringdon Arms (P)
☎ (0752) 402053
Stancombe (H)
Meals and snacks 12–2.15; 7.15–10.15; children's room; outdoor drinking area/garden; accommodation; access for disabled; camping facilities nearby.

Welcombe

Weekdays: 11.30–2.30; 6–11
Old Smithy Inn (P)
2 miles west of A39 at Welcombe Cross
☎ (028883) 305
Bulmer (H)
13th century former blacksmith's home; heavily beamed ceilings. Bar snacks 12–2; meals 6.45–9.30; restaurant; children's room; garden; accommodation; camping facilities nearby.

Wembworthy

Weekdays: 11–3; 6–11
Lymington Arms (P)
2 miles east of B3220; 2 miles west of A377
☎ (0837) 83572
Inch (PC)
Lively village local. Bar snacks; lunches; evening meals – seven days a week; garden; pool table; shove hapenny; skittles. Parties catered for.

West Charleton

Weekdays: 11–2.30; 6–11
Ashburton Arms (P)
On A379
☎ (0548) 531242
Luscombe (PC)
Stancombe (PC)
Modernised old pub with nautical relics. Home cooked lunches and dinners, also bar snacks; bed and breakfast accommodation.

Westward Ho!

Grenville Arms (P)
Youngaton Road
☎ (02372) 77331
Bulmer (H)
Quiet and away from the beach.

Whimple

Weekdays: 11.30–2.30; 6.30–11
New Fountain (P)
☎ (0404) 822350
Bulmer West Country (H)

Built in 1640, and named after a water pump in the grounds. Meals lunchtime and evenings; garden. Near Whimple BR station (limited service).

Weekdays: 11–2.30; 6.30–11

Paddock (OL)

On A30, half mile from village
☏ (0404) 822356
Bromell (PC)
Although this is a fully fledged pub, it only sells cider to take away: this however is a very popular facility for those holiday makers returning home from the West Country. Whimple BR station half a mile (irregular service).

Thirsty Farmer (P)

Near railway station
☏ (0404) 822287
Bulmer (PC)
All thirsts are catered for! Snacks; garden.

Whitestone

SNELLS FARM CIDER ▲

Snell Bros., Styles Barton Farm (on Exeter road)
☏ (039281) 280

Widecombe in the Moor

Weekdays: 11–2.30; 6–11, Sunday: 12–3; 7–10.30

Old Inn (P)

Adjoining the church
☏ (03642) 207
Gray (PC)
Built in the 14th century; devasted by fire in the 1970s, but now restored – much of the original stonework and fireplaces remain. Haunted by *two* ghosts! Meals; garden.

Weekdays: 8.30–8 (summer): 8.30–5.30 (other times)

Post Office Stores (OL)

☏ (03642) 220
Gray (PC) (J) (PL)

Winkleigh

INCH'S CIDER ▲

Inch's Cider Company, Western Barn, Hatherleigh Road
☏ (083783) 263 and 560

Weekdays: 11–3; 6–11, Sunday: 12–3; 7–10.30

Winkleigh Hotel (P)

The Square
☏ (0837) 83247
Inch (PC)
A small village hotel serving home cooked food lunchtime and evenings. Garden; accommodation.

Woodbury

Weekdays: Monday–Friday: 11–2.30; 6–11, Saturday: 11–3; 6–11, Sunday: 12–2.30; 7–10.30

Maltsters Arms (P)

Off B3179 in centre of village
☏ (0395) 32218
Bulmer (PC)
A large and modernised pub with an outdoor terrace. Meals and snacks served. The cider is behind the scenes – ask for it!

Woodbury Salterton

Weekdays: 11–2.30; 6–11

Diggers Rest (P)

☏ (0395) 32375
Farmer John (PC)
Old world village pub with oak beams and open fires. Meals and snacks 12–1.45; 7–10, Sunday 12–1.30; 7–9.45; children's room; garden; skittle alley.

Woolfardisworthy

Weekdays: 12–2.30; 6–11

Farmers Arms (P)

Near Clovelly
☏ (02373) 467
Inch (PC)
14th century thatched pub in village pronounced, should you get lost and need to ask, as "Woolsery". Snacks 12–2; 7–9.30; meals 7.30–10; restaurant; children's room; garden.

Yealmpton

National Shire Horse Centre (P) (OL)

☏ (0752) 880268
Farmer John
Haymaker
Inch
Luscombe
Sheppy
Symons
One of the most popular attractions in the South West – a day out for the whole family. Meals and snacks 11–5; children's room, garden. Also on sale are country wines and mead.

Claycutters Arms, Chudleigh Knighton

Dorset

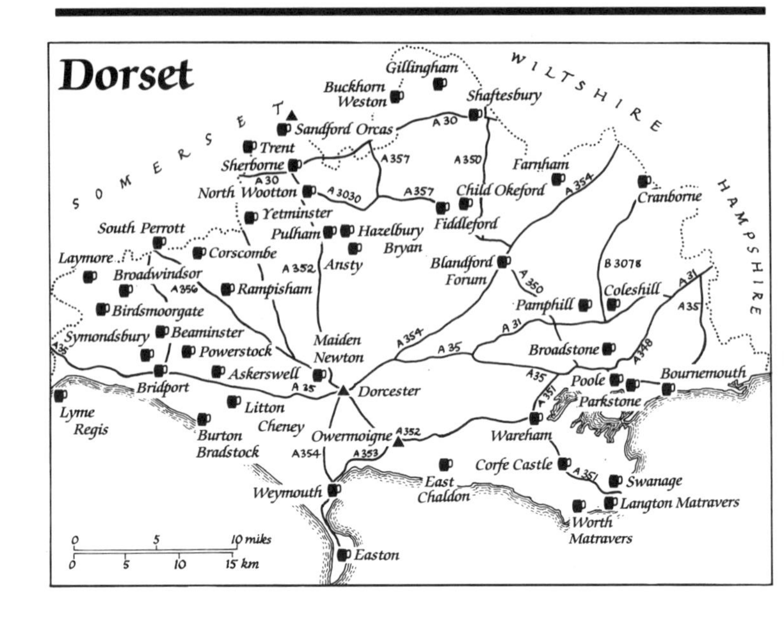

Ansty

Weekdays: 11–3; 6–11

Fox (P)
4 miles north of A354
☏ (0258) 880328
Wilkins (PC)
In Hardy country, far from the madding crowd: a solid brick and flint pub in an unspoilt farming village. The building dates from 1771, and was the original Woodhouse brewery and family home. Public bar has the largest collection of Toby jugs in England. Meals and snacks lunchtime and evenings; restaurant; children's room; garden; accommodation; access for disabled, including special toilet; skittles.

Askerswell

Weekdays: 11–11

Spyway Inn (P)
Off A35 on far side of village
☏ (030885) 250
Bulmer West Country (PC)
Country pub with marvellous views. Meals and snacks lunchtime and evenings; children's room; large garden; access for disabled.

Beaminster

Weekdays: 11–2; 7–11

Eight Bells (P)
Church Street
☏ (0308) 863241
Taunton
16th century village pub, catering for drinkers rather than food. Snacks lunchtime only; outdoor drinking area; accommodation; access for disabled.

Birdsmoorgate

Weekdays: 10–3; 6–11, Sunday: 12–3; 7–10.30

Rose & Crown (P)
On B3165 1 mile north of Marshwood
☏ (02977) 527
Perrys Cider (H)
Superb views over Marshwood Vale. Meals and snacks all times; restaurant; children's room; garden; camping facilities in grounds.

Blandford Forum

Weekdays: 11–11

Half Moon (P)
Whitecliff Mill Street (up from town centre towards Shaftesbury)
☏ (0258) 52318
Taunton (H)
Old fashioned one-bar pub with friendly public bar atmosphere. Folk music Saturday nights. Regular barbecues in summer. Lunchtime food. Garden and separate games room.

Bournemouth

Drinks on Tap (OL)
791 Christchurch Road
☏ (0202) 421805
Cornish Scrumpy – range

Bridport

Weekdays: Monday–Friday: 11–3; 7–11, Saturday 11–11, Sunday: 12–3; 7–10.30

Kings Arms (P)
North Allington (B3162)
☏ (0308) 22833
Taunton (PC)
Meals and snacks weekends only.

Weekdays: 10–11, Sunday: 12–3; 7–10.30

Lord Nelson Hotel (P)
52 East Street
☏ (0308) 22437
Taunton (PC)

Monday–Friday: 11–3; 5.45–11, Saturday: 11–11, Sunday: 12–3; 7–10.30

Oddfellows Arms (P)
172 North Allington (B3162 Chard road)

☏ (0308) 22665
Taunton (PC)
Little red bricked terraced boozer. Garden; accommodation. A keen cider outlet.

Broadstone

Vin Varies (Wholesale Supplier)
39 Lancaster Drive
☏ (0202) 602621
James White (B) range
Sells wholesale to trade and public: no premises open to the public.

Broadwindsor

Weekdays: 11–3; 6–11

White Lion (P)
The Square
☏ (0308) 68855
Taunton (PC)
Dark, old and friendly pub. Midly eccentric landlord with talkative parrot. Meals and snacks lunchtime and evenings; children's room, garden; accommodation; bar skittles.

Buckhorn Weston

Weekdays: 11.30–2.30; 6–11, Sunday 12–2.30; 7–10.30

Stapleton Arms (P)
In centre of village
☏ (0963) 70396
Lazy Daisy (PC)
Georgian country inn with good local following. Meals and snacks lunchtime and evenings; restaurant; outdoor drinking area/garden; accommodation; camping facilities in grounds. 3 mile level walk from Templecombe BR station.

Burton Bradstock

Anchor (P)
High Street
☏ (0308) 897228
Taunton (PC)
Village pub built in 1560. Meals lunchtime and evenings; families welcome; camping facilities nearby.

Child Okeford

Monday: 6.30–11 only; Tuesday–Saturday: 12–2; 6.30–11

Union Arms (P)
Station Road (north west of Shillingstone on A357)
☏ (2580) 860540
Taunton (H)
Small village local with real fire. Meals lunchtime and evening; separate restaurant; garden; facilities for camping nearby.

Coleshill

Weekdays: 10.30–2.30; 7–11

Horns Inn (P)
Burts Hill (1 mile north east of Walford Bridge, Wimborne)
☏ (0202) 883557
Taunton (H)
Meals and snacks lunchtime and evening; garden.

Corfe Castle

Weekdays: 9–5.30 (winter): 8.30–6 (summer), Sunday: 11–6

Coopers Stores (OL)
24 West Street
☏ (0929) 480223
Cornish Scrumpy

Corscombe

Weekdays: 12–2.30; 7–11

Fox (P)
☏ (093589) 330
Taunton (PP)
Thatched pub with inglenook and stone floor; not flashy! Meals and snacks 12–2; 7–10; children's room; garden; access for disabled; camping facilities nearby.

Cranborne

Weekdays: 10.30–3; 6–11

Fleur de Lys (P)
5 Wimborne Street
☏ (07254) 282
Taunton (H)
Meals and snacks lunchtime and evenings, including vegetarian dishes, all week; own bread baking; restaurant; garden; accommodation.

Dorchester

WOLFETON CIDER
▲
Wolfeton House
☏ (0305) 63500

East Chaldon

Weekdays: 11–2.30; 7–11

Sailors Return (P)
Off A352
☏ (0305) 853847
Taunton (PC)
18th century thatched country inn. Meals and snacks lunchtime and evenings; restaurant; garden; bar billiards.

Easton

Weekdays: 11–2.30; 6–11

Mermaid (P)
Wakeham (on road to Portland Bill)
☏ (0305) 821062
Bulmer (H)
At edge of town, near Portland Museum. Meals; skittle alley.

Weekdays: 11–11, Sunday: 12–3; 7–10.30

Punch Bowl (P)
46 Easton Street
☏ (0305) 820437
Bulmer (H)
In centre of main Isle of Portland town. Full meals and snacks; skittle alley.

Farnham

Weekdays: 11–11

Museum (P)
Near Blandford Forum (2 miles north of A354 at Cashmoor)
☏ (07256) 261
Taunton (PC)
Cooper's memorabilia in Lounge Bar. Meals lunchtime and evening; garden; accommodation.

Fiddleford

Weekdays: 11–3; 6–11

Fiddleford Inn (P)
On A357, two miles south west of Sturminster Newton
☏ (0258) 72489
Perry (PC)
Pub was once a brewery: close to ancient mill. Meals lunchtime and evening; garden; accommodation; bar billiards.

Gillingham

Weekdays: 11–2; 5–11, Sunday: 12–3; 7–10.30

Queens Head (P)
Queen Street
☏ (0747) 822689
Taunton (H)
Good cider pub in town centre. Meals and snacks all sessions; garden; pool table.

Dorset

Hazelbury Bryan

Weekdays: 10.30–3; 6–11

Antelope (P)
Off B3143
☏ (0258) 817295
Taunton (PC)
Snacks.

Langton Matravers

Weekdays: 11–2.30; 6.30–11

Kings Arms (P)
On B3069
☏ (0929) 422979
Bulmer (PC)
Village local in Purbeck style with many interconnecting rooms. Snacks lunchtime; family room; garden; camping facilities nearby.

Laymore

Weekdays: 11–2.30; 6–11

Squirrel (P)
Near Winsham (B3162)
☏ (0460) 30298
Vickery (PC)
Large unprepossessing brick pub with a friendly welcome. Excellent centre for exploring this remote part of the Dorset/Somerset border. Meals and snacks lunchtime and evenings; children's room; garden; accommodation; access for disabled; camping facilities nearby; bar skittles.

Litton Cheney

Weekdays: 11.30–2.30; 6.30–11, Sunday: 12–3; 7–10.30

White Horse (P)
☏ (03083) 539
Taunton (PC)
At Burton Bradstock end of village; local with Youth Hostel next door. Meals lunchtime and evenings; children's room; garden; access for disabled.

Lyme Regis

Weekdays: 11–2.30; 6.30–11

Angel (P)
Mill Green (down Coombe Street from Square)
☏ (02974) 3267
Taunton (PC)
Northern 1950s style locals' pub, plain but friendly. Children's room and accommodation.

Weekdays: 11–11 (summer): 11–2.30; 7–11 (other times)

Royal Standard (P)
The Cobb
☏ (02974) 2637
Taunton (PC)
Very old pub on sea front. Meals lunchtime and evenings; outdoor drinking area; access for disabled.

Maiden Newton

Weekdays: 11–2.30; 6.30–11

Chalk & Cheese (P)
53 Dorchester Road
☏ (0300) 20600
Bulmer (H)
Typical village pub (previously named Brewery Inn). Snacks 12–1.45; 7–9; garden. Near Maiden Newton BR station.

North Wootton

Three Elms (P)
On A3030
☏ (0935) 812881
Burrow Hill (PC)
Smart roadside pub. Meals and snacks lunchtime and evenings; garden.

Owermoigne

MILL HOUSE CIDER ▲
Millhouse Nurseries
☏ (0305) 852220

Pamphill

Weekdays: 11–2.30; 7–11

Vine Inn (P)
Vine Hill (off B3082) – take Cowgrove Road by hospital for ½ mile, and turn right)
☏ (0202) 882259
Bulmer (PC)
Smallest pub in East Dorset: village cricket in summer. Children's room; large garden with swings, climbing net, donkey and pony.

Parkstone

Weekdays: 11.30–2.30; 6.30–11

Bricklayers Arms (P)
Parr Street (north of Ashley Cross traffic lights on A35)
☏ (0202) 740304
Taunton (H)
Opposite St. Peter's Church. Bar snacks lunchtime; live music room.

Weekdays: 11.30–2.30; 6.30–11

Britannia (P)
20 Britannia Road, Lower Parkstone (south of Ashley Cross traffic lights on A35)
☏ (0202) 740046
Bulmer (PC)
Two bar local. Children's room; garden.

Weekdays: 11–1.30; 4.30–10.30

Happy Tippler (OL)
212 Ashley Road
☏ (0202) 748823
Purbeck Ruin (PC)
Near Branksome BR station.

Poole

Dorset Country Fare (OL)
Rowley House, The Quay
☏ (0202) 683319
Kneecracker (B)

King Charles II (P)
Thames Street (off the Quay)
☏ (0202) 674950
Bulmer (H)
15th century stone and timber Grand Hall (Kynges Hall). Meals and snacks lunchtime; children's room; outdoor drinking area; showers and victualling for boating fraternity. Half a mile from Poole BR station.

Off licence: 10–6 (later in summer): restaurant: 1–10

Potters (OL) (P)
The Quay
☏ (0202) 670867
Inch (full range) – off licence
Inch (PC) – restaurant

Swan Inn (P)
Laglands Street (next to Poole Pottery, at far end of Quay)
☏ (0202) 673825
Bulmer (H)
Meals and snacks lunchtime.

Monday–Friday: 11–2.30; 5.30–11, Saturday: 11–3; 6–11, Sunday: 12–3; 7–10.30

Sweet Home Inn (P)
25 Ringwood Road
☏ (0202) 676297
Taunton (H)
Locals' pub on main road into Poole from Ringwood. Bar snacks lunchtime, Monday–Saturday; large garden; access for disabled; live entertainment Saturday evening.

Weekdays: 10–5.30, Sunday: 12–2

Wine Lodge (OL)
84 High Street
☎ (0202) 686937
Countryman (B) (S)
Poole Scrumpy (B)
The Poole Scrumpy is specially made for the Wine Lodge. Half a mile from Poole BR station.

Powerstock

Weekdays: 11–2.30; 6–11

Three Horseshoes (P)
☎ (030885) 328
Taunton (PC)
At foot of Eggardon Hill; noted for its food. Meals lunchtime and evening; garden; access for disabled.

Pulham

Weekdays: 11–3; 6–11

Halsey Arms (P)
On B3143
☎ (0258) 817344
Taunton (H)
Village pub with good food. Meals lunchtime and evenings; children's play area and garden.

Rampisham

Weekdays: 11–3; 6.30–11, Sunday: 12–3; 7–10.30

Tigers Head (P)
On A356
☎ (0935) 8344
Perrys Cider (PC)
Old, real village pub in heart of countryside, leased from Rampisham Estate. Unusual and delicious food in both bar and restaurant. Comfortable family room. Garden and accommodation with four poster bed and brass bedsteads.

Sandford Orcas

Mitre (P)
In centre of village
☎ (096322) 271
Sandford (PC)
A pleasant 3 mile walk through quiet lanes from Sherborne. Meals and snacks lunchtime and evenings; range includes vegetarian dishes; separate restaurant (booking appreciated) garden.

SANDFORD CIDER
▲
Lower Farm House (at south end of village)
☎ (096322) 363

Shaftesbury

Weekdays: 8.30–5.30

Farmer Bailey's (OL)
54 High Street
☎ (0747) 53260
Rosies (BB) (PL)

Fountain Inn (P)
2 Breach Lane, Enmore Green
☎ (0747) 2062
Lazy Daisy (PC)

Monday–Wednesday: 10.30–2.30; 5–11, Thursday–Saturday: 10.30–11, Sunday: 12–3; 7–10.30

Kings Arms (P)
Bleke Street
☎ (0747) 52746
Taunton (H)
Highest pub in Dorset. Snacks Monday–Saturday lunchtime; outdoor drinking area; boule court.

LAZY DAISY QUALITY CIDER
Tumblefirkin, Umbers Hill
☎ (0747) 54890

Sherborne

Monday–Friday: 11–2.30; 6–11, Saturday: 11–11, Sunday: 12–3; 7–10.30

Britannia Inn (P)
Westbury Street
☎ (0935) 813300
Coates (PC)
18th century inn, once a school for wayward girls! Meals and snacks 12–2; 7–10; restaurant; accommodation.

Weekdays: 11–2.30; 5.30–11

Digby Tap (P)
Cooks Lane
☎ (0935) 813148
Taunton (H)
In side street close to Abbey; unspoilt town local. Full bar menu at lunchtime; outdoor drinking area. Near Sherborne BR station.

Greyhound (P)
Cheap Street
☎ (0935) 812785
Taunton (H)
Snacks; accommodation; pool room.

Monday–Wednesday: 10–2.30; 6–11, Thursday–Saturday: 10–11, Sunday: 12–3; 7–10.30

White Hart Inn (P)
2 Cheap Street
☎ (0935) 814903
Taunton (H)
Bar snacks and home made specials 12–2 daily; accommodation.

South Perrott

Weekdays: 11–3; 7–11

Coach & Horses (P)
☎ (093589) 270
Taunton (H)
Meals lunchtime, and evenings except Monday; children's room; garden; access for disabled; skittle alley.

Swanage

Weekdays: 11–3; 6–11

Anchor (P)
High Street
☎ (0929) 423020
Bulmer (PC)
One bar local. Meals and snacks lunchtime.

Bootleggers (OL)
28 Institute Road
☎ (0929) 424478
Purbeck Ruin (J)
Swanage Scrumpy (PET)

Durlston Castle (P)
Durlston Park
☎ (0929) 424693
Purbeck Ruin (PC)
19th century turreted "castle" with excellent views to the Isle of Wight. Children allowed in games room. Bar snacks.

PURBECK RUIN CIDER
122 High Street
☎ (0929) 426376

Weekdays: 10.30–3; 6–11

Red Lion (P)
63 High Street
☎ (0929) 423533
Bulmer (PC)
Town centre pub. Meals and snacks lunchtime and evenings; children's room; outdoor drinking area.

Weekdays: 10.30–3; 7–11

White Swan (P)
The Square
☎ (0929) 423615
Bulmer (PC)
Town centre pub with open plan bar. Snacks lunchtime and evenings; outdoor drinking area.

Dorset

Symondsbury

Weekdays: 11–2.30; 7–11, Sunday: 12–3; 7–10.30

Ilchester Arms (P)

Off A35
☎ (0308) 22600
Taunton (PC)
Charming 600 year old thatched country inn. Interesting meals and snacks all sessions; restaurant; garden; accommodation.

Trent

Weekdays: 12–2.30; 7–11

Rose & Crown (P)

☎ (0935) 850776
Rosies (BB)
Former farmhouse highly acclaimed for its restaurant food. Meals and snacks lunchtime and evening; garden.

Wareham

Weekdays: 10.30–11 (summer): 11–2.30; 6–11 (other times).

Quay Inn (P)

The Quay
☎ (0929) 552735
Bulmer (PC)
18th century riverside inn overlooking Purbeck hills; traditional old fashioned atmosphere. Meals and snacks 12–2.15; 6–9.30; restaurant; outdoor drinking area/walled garden; accommodation; camping facilities nearby. Half a mile from Wareham BR station.

Weymouth

Weekdays: 11–11, Sunday: 12–3; 7–10.30

Boot (P)

High Street West, North Quay
☎ (0305) 786793
Taunton (H)
Weymouth's oldest pub, overlooking inner harbour. Good range of meals 12–2; 6.30–10. Half a mile from Weymouth BR station.

Weekdays: 10–4.30; 7.30–11

Duke of Cornwall (P)

St. Edmunds Street
☎ (0305) 786593
Taunton (PC)
Meal lunchtime and evenings. Near Weymouth BR station.

Weekdays: 10–11, Sunday: 12–3; 7–10.30

Kings Arms (P)

Trinity Road
☎ (0305) 770055
Taunton (PC)
Quayside local. Lunchtime meals. The cider is not on show, so please ask for it by name. Half a mile from Weymouth BR station.

Rock Hotel (P)

41 Abbotsbury Road (corner of Newstead Road), Westham
☎ (0305) 784563
Taunton (H)
Enthusiastic basic cider pub. Pool room.

Wessex Wines (OL)

36 Crescent Street
☎ (0305) 774825
Broadoak (B)
Haymaker (B) (PL)
Kneecracker (PL) (S)
Very near Weymouth BR station and sea front.

Worth Matravers

Weekdays: 11–3; 6–11

Square & Compass (P)

south of B3069
☎ (092943) 229
Bulmer (PC)
Converted stone cottages, with superb sea views, set high in the Purbeck hills: building dates from 14th century. Children's room; garden; camping facilities nearby – please book.

Yetminster

Monday–Friday: 11–2.30; 7–11, Saturday: 11–2.30; 7–1 am

Railway Inn (P)

Station Approach
☎ (0935) 872622
Taunton (PC)
Meals and snacks all sessions, and to take away; children's room; garden. Adjacent to Yetminster BR station on Yeovil to Weymouth line (trains only stop on request).

NOW SHOWING AT THE REX

A look round a little known museum

The former Rex cinema at Chagford, on the edge of Dartmoor, is the unlikely setting for what may be largest collection of cider presses in the world. They have been brought together over the years by antique dealer John Meredith and his sister Avril, and what makes them remarkable is that they all come from Devon.

John found his first press in an old dark barn, and bought it, hoping to sell it at the shop. But having taken it to pieces, and admired the Victorian workmanship, he could not bear to part with it – short of running the shop from *inside* the press he had to find somewhere spacious to put it, and discovered the old cinema building, where he rebuilt it. From then John kept seeing other presses as he travelled round the county, and by now he was hooked: they joined the growing collection at the Rex. He found some too from advertisements in the local papers. He would be the first to admit to being one of those few lucky folk, mentioned by Tony Gibson, to have benefited from cider makers "handing in their mugs", though now he finds that prices for ancient equipment have hardened, and some farmers are also reluctant to part with what is almost one of the family, even if it has been pensioned off.

Not all the presses are, of course, the direct result of a cider maker packing up: some have been made redundant by the introduction of more modern machinery. The oldest exhibit dates from 1780, a wooden screw press, discovered under the fallen roof of an old cob barn. There are presses from many parts of Devon: Iddesleigh, Shaldon, Chagford, and Exmouth to name but a few. There are plenty of examples of the huge wood beam and vast iron screw types, operated by hand, with a timber base on which the "cheese" was built, and underneath a stone trough to catch the juice, up to 50 gallons at a time.

Some of the exhibits are, to all appearances, intact, and in working order, though there is no sign of oil or grease on the metal threads and moving parts. John prefers to keep them rusty, just as he found them. One problem that he has to address, however, is woodworm: all the timbers need to be sprayed regularly.

There are specimens, too, of the all essential equipment for crushing the apples in the first place, before they are ready for the press. Made almost exclusively of wood – apple juice and metal don't mix – some were hand turned, needing two men to move the huge wheel, others would have been horse powered. You would imagine that John might want to try some of his treasures out, just for the satisfaction of seeing them in operation. But though he is fascinated by the way cider used to be made, he does not drink it, so perhaps there is not much incentive.

In any case, it needs little imagination once you step into this world of vast beams, troughs and wheels, to picture the frantic action every autumn, as they faithfully delivered their harvest of juice. Methods now may be more efficient, but they lack the romance of these giants of the past.

John Meredith's museum is open to the public by appointment: you can contact him at his home, 41 New Street, Chagford, tel: Chagford (06473) 3405; or at his shop, at 36 The Square, Chagford, tel Chagford (06473) 3474. There is a nominal admission charge.

Essex

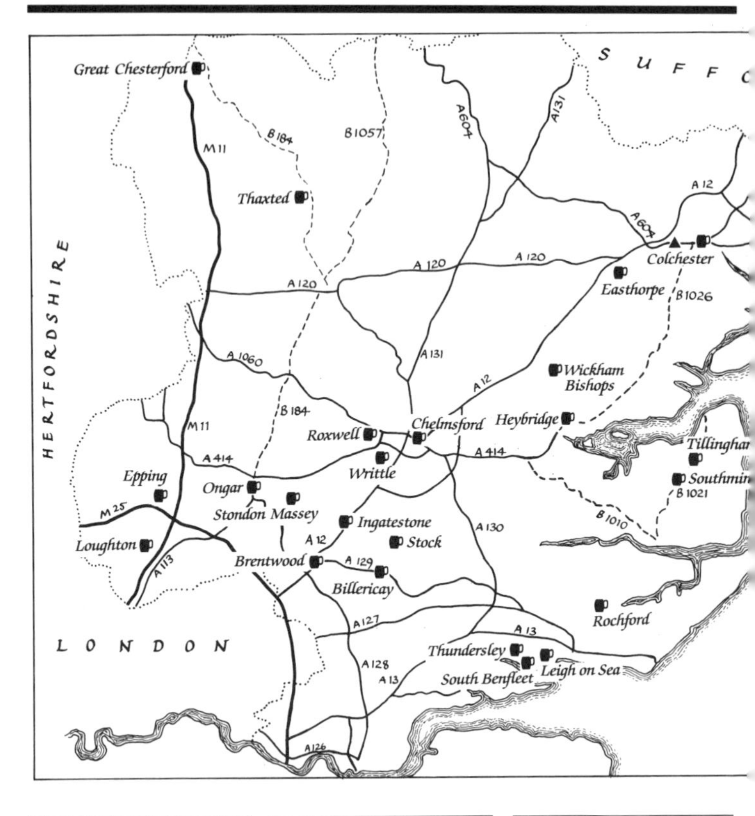

Billericay

Duke of York (P)
Southend Road
☏ (0277) 651403
James White (J)

Brentwood

Weekdays: 10–1; 6–10, Sunday: 12–2; 7–10.

Tony's Cellar (OL)
1 Waterloo Road
☏ (0277) 227400
Inch
James White (B)

Chelmsford

Odd Fellows (P)
195 Springfield Road (A1113)
☏ (0245) 490514
James White (J)
Popular town pub.

Peter Dominic (OL)
Unit 2, 35/37 Moulsham Street
☏ (0245) 287672
James White (J)

Weekdays: 11–11.

Prince of Orange (P)
7 Hall Street (near A130)
☏ (0245) 281695
Thatcher (PC)
Meals and snacks lunchtime; garden. Guest ciders also when available.

Clacton on Sea

Weekdays: 11–4; 7–11.

Imperial Hotel (P)
Rosemary Road
☏ (0255) 422778
Bulmer (H)
Meals lunchtime and evenings; children's room; garden; accommodation.

Peter Dominic (OL)
147 St. Osyth Road
☏ (0255) 425018
James White (J)

Colchester

Peter Dominic (OL)
18 Culver Street
☏ (0206) 571900
James White (J)

Monday–Thursday: 5.30–11, Friday: 11–2.30; 5.30–11, Saturday 11–2.30; 6–11, Sunday: 12–2; 7–10.30.

Odd One Out (P)
28 Mersea Road
☏ (0206) 578140
Really Fowl Cornish Cider (PP)
Victorian street corner local near St Botolphs Station, adapted into a unique free house. Public bar area has bare boards and wooden benches, saloon area has carpet and leather chairs.

OLIVERS ORCHARD CIDER ▲
Olivers Lane (near Colchester Zoo, off Gosbecks Road)
☏ (0206) 330208

Easthorpe

Weekdays: 10.30–3; 7–11.

House Without a Name (P)
Easthorpe Road ($1\frac{1}{2}$ miles off A12)

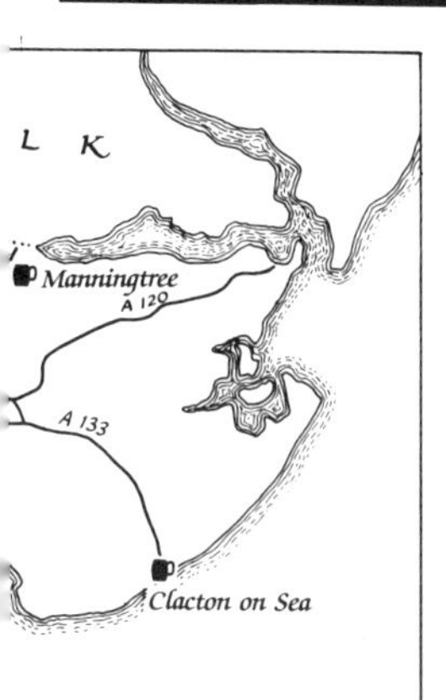

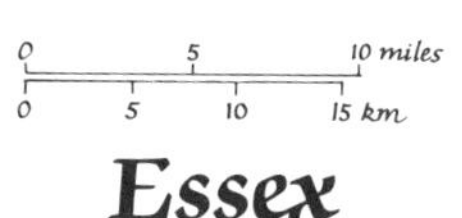

☎ (0206) 210455
Zum (PC)
16th century beamed local. Meals and snacks lunchtime; garden.

Epping

Monday–Friday: 10–2.30; 6–11, Saturday: 10–3.30; 6–11.

Forest Gate Inn (P)
Bell Common (off B1393)
☎ (0378) 72312
Bulmer (H)
Basic old free house on edge of Epping Forest. Snacks 12–2.15; 7–10.15; garden.

Great Chesterford

Monday-Friday: 7.30–5.30 (closed 1–2), Saturday: 7.30–1 (closed Sunday)

Lovedays (OL)
School Street
☎ (0799) 30201
Various Ciders (B)

Heybridge

Maltsters Arms (P)
Hall Road (near B1022)
James White (J)
Good no-frills boozer, dark and friendly.

Ingatestone

Star (P)
High Street (B1002)
☎ (0277) 3618
James White (J)
15th century pub with decor untouched for 40 years. Country and Western and folk music 2 or 3 evenings a week in a renovated bakehouse at the rear. Children's room.

Leigh on Sea

Essex Wine (OL)
223 Elmsleigh Drive
☎ (0702) 71334
James White (J)

Loughton

Peter Dominic (OL)
223 High Street
☎ (01) 508 3493
James White (J)

Manningtree

Stour Wines (OL)
23 High Street
☎ (0206) 39509
James White (B)

Ongar

Peter Dominic (OL)
Ye Olde Wine Shop,
162 High Street
☎ (0277) 362008
James White (J)

Rochford

Monday–Friday: 11–2.30; 5–11, Saturday and Bank Holidays 11–11

Golden Lion (P)
35 North Street
☎ (0702) 545487
Thatcher (PP)
Small popular free house in town centre: unusual stained glass panels. Meals lunchtime except Sunday. Near Rochford BR station.

Roxwell

Weekdays: 11–11, Sunday: 12–3; 7–10.30

Chequers Inn (P)
The Street
☎ (0245) 48240
Bulmer (H)
Meals and snacks lunchtime and evenings (except Sunday); outside seating at front.

Southminster

Monday–Friday: 11.30––3; 5–11, Saturday: 11.30–3; 6–11

Rose Inn (P)
Burnham Road (on B1021 ½ mile outside village)
☎ (0621) 772915
Guest ciders (PC)
Traditional roadside inn with real public bar. Normally one medium and one dry available: makes include Thatcher, Henry, Sheppy, and Symonds. Meals and snacks lunchtime and evenings; access for disabled.

South Benfleet

Weekdays: 11–2; 6.30–10

New Park Stores (OL)
224 London Road
Inch
James White

Stock

Weekdays: 11–11, Sunday: 12–3; 7–10.30

Hoop (P)
21 High Street (B1007)
☎ (0277) 841137
Rich (PC)
Small freehouse on village green. Meals and snacks all times; garden. Good bus service from Chelmsford and Billericay.

Stondon Massey

Bricklayers Arms (P)
Ongar Road
☎ (0277) 821152
James White (PP)
Atmospheric and friendly split-level pub with two moose heads in lounge.

Thaxted

Cuckoo Wine Bar (P)
36 Town Street
☎ (0371) 830482
Guest Ciders (PC) – summer only
Meals and snacks 12–2; 7–10 (10.45 Friday–Saturday); children welcome; dogs welcome, anything welcome!

Thundersley

Cheers (OL)
273 Kiln Road
☎ (0702) 556717
James White (J)

Tillingham

Weekdays: 11.30–3; 6–11; open all Saturday afternoon in summer.

Cap & Feathers (P)
South Street (village centre)
☎ (062187) 212
Thatcher (PC)
15th century village pub, no canned music or fruit machines. Meals lunchtime and evening; children welcome if supervised; garden; accommodation; access for disabled. CAMRA East Anglia Pub of the Year 1989.

Wickham Bishops

Weekdays: 11–3; 5.30–11, Sunday: 12–3; 7–10.30

Mitre (P)
9 The Street
☎ (0621) 891378
Bulmer (H)
Tastefully renovated old local. Meals lunchtime (except Sunday) and every evening; garden.

Writtle

Monday–Friday: 11–2.30; 5.30–11, Saturday 11–11

Wheatsheaf (P)
70 The Green (behind service station on junction of A414 and the Green)
☎ (0245) 420695
James White (PC)
Friendly local in pleasant village, popular with morris dancers.

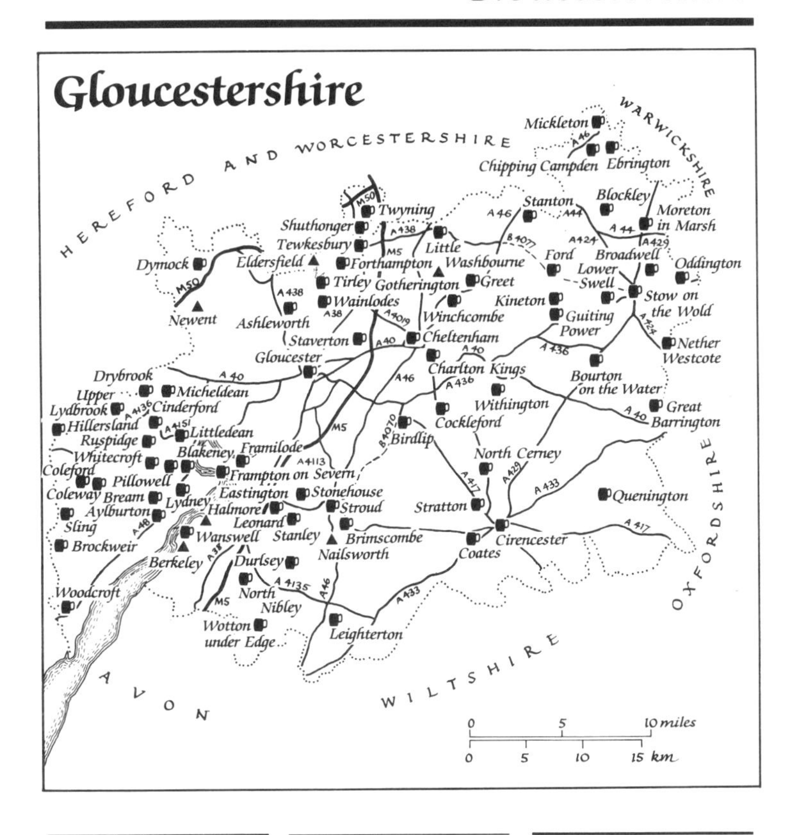

Ashleworth

Boat Inn (P)
The Quay (off A417)
☏ (045270) 272
Weston (PC)
Old fashioned pub on bank of River Severn, near ancient tithe barn. Garden.

Aylburton

Weekdays: 11–2.30; 5.30–11

Cross (P)
☏ (0594) 842823
Bulmer (H)
400 year old pub with traditional atmosphere. Meals and snacks; children's room; garden.

Berkeley

Bird in Hand (P)
On B4066
☏ (0453) 811101
Bulmer (H)
Three handpumps for the cider. Meals and snacks. Garden.

George (P)
Market Place
☏ (0453) 810257
Bulmer (E)
Two bar town local. Meals and snacks.

TONY CULLIMORE'S GENUINE FARMHOUSE CIDER ▲
Berkeley Heath Farm
☏ (0453) 810220

Birdlip

Weekdays: 12–2.30; 6–11

Golden Heart (P)
Nettleton Bottom, Coberley (A417)
☏ (024287) 261
Dunkerton (PC)
Weston (H)
Isolated old Cotswold inn. Meals and snacks lunchtime and evenings; restaurant; children's room; garden.

Blakeney

Yew Tree (P)
☏ (0594) 510400
Bulmer (H)
Snacks; garden.

Blockley

Great Western Arms (P)
On B4479
Bulmer (H)
One time blacksmith's house and shop, now much altered. Meals and snacks; children's room; garden.

Bourton on the Water

Weekdays: 11–2.30; 6–11

Coach & Horses (P)
Foss Way (A429)
☏ (0451) 21064
Bulmer (H)
Busy pub on Foss Way. Meals and snacks; garden.

Gloucestershire

Weekdays: 11–3; 6–11

Old New Inn (P)
High Street
☏ (0451) 20467
Bulmer (PC)
A substantial stone built inn, dating from 1709, on the River Windrush. Adjacent to model village and model railway. Meals and snacks; restaurant; children's room; garden; accommodation.

Bream

Monday–Friday: 11–3; 6.30–11, Saturday: 11–4; 6.30–11, Sunday: 12–3; 7–10.30

Cross Keys Inn (P)
High Street
☏ (0594) 562358
Bulmer (E)
Westons Old Rosie (H)
Bar snacks; large garden; live music every Saturday.

Weekdays: 11–3; 7–11

Rising Sun (P)
High Street
☏ (0594) 562374
Bulmer (H)
Well known Forest of Dean viewpoint. Snacks; garden; live music.

Brimscombe

Ship Inn (P)
Off A419
☏ (0453) 884388
Weston (PC)
Friendly pub just off main road. Snacks; garden.

Broadwell

Weekdays: 11–2.30; 6–11

Fox Inn (P)
½ mile east of A429
☏ (0451) 30212
Weston (H)
Overlooking village green. Meals except Sunday and Monday evening; snacks; restaurant; garden; caravan site and camping.

Rising Sun (P)
Poolway Road (near Coleford)
☏ (0594) 33428
Bulmer (H)
Large pub at road junction on edge of village. Meals and snacks; restaurant; children's fun area; garden.

Brockweir

Monday–Friday: 11.30–2.30; 7–11, Saturday: 11.30–3.30; 7–11

Brockweir Country Inn (P)
Off A466 over bridge 1 mile north of Tintern
☏ (0291) 689548
Bulmer (H)
Unspoilt 17th century inn on the bank of the River Severn in a small historic village. Bar meals lunchtime and evenings; garden; accommodation.

Charlton Kings

Weekdays: 11–3; 6.30–11

Merry Fellow (P)
2 School Road (off A40 and A435)
☏ (0242) 525883
Bulmer (H)
Welcoming old-style pub in original village centre. Snacks; garden; skittle alley.

Weekdays: 11–3; 6–11, Sunday: 12–3; 7–10.30

Reservoir Inn (P)
London Road (A40)
☏ (0242) 29671
Weston (H)
Lunchtime and evening menu; large play area for children and balcony.

Ryeworth Inn (P)
Ryeworth Road, Ryeworth
☏ (0242) 528692
Weston (H)
Comfortable village pub. Meals and snacks; garden.

Cheltenham

Monday–Friday: 11–3; 5–11, Saturday: 10.30–4; 5.30–11

Bayshill Inn (P)
St. Georges Place (near bus station)
☏ (0242) 524388
Bulmer (H)
Georgian building with old stables at rear, constantly under threat from road schemes. Lunchtime meals, evening snacks; outdoor drinking area; accommodation.

Rose Tree Fine Wine Co (OL)
15 Suffolk Parade
☏ (0242) 583732
Cotswold Cider (B)

Weekdays: 10–11, Sunday: 12–2; 7–10.30

Shakespeare Inn (P)
386 Lower High Street
☏ (0242) 513685
Bulmer (H)
Meals and snacks.

The Shambles (OL)
Montpellier Court, Montpellier Street
☏ (0242) 577548
Dunkerton (B)

Chipping Campden

Monday–Friday: 11–2.30; 6–11, Saturday: 11–11

Lygon Arms (P)
High Street
☏ (0386) 840318
Bulmer (PC)
Comfortable and friendly free house in one of the loveliest towns in the country. Meals and snacks; restaurant; accommodation; skittle alley.

Cinderford

Monday–Thursday: 12–3, Friday–Saturday: 11–11, Sunday: 12–3

Railway (P)
Station Street
☏ (0594) 22064
Bulmer (H)
Opposite the site of the old GWR station. Snacks.

Cirencester

Oddfellows Arms (P)
Chester Street
Bulmer (PC)
Quiet pub in residential area. Snacks; garden.

Coalway

Crown Inn (P)
Coalway Lane End, east of Coleford
☏ (0594) 36620
Bulmer (H)
Tiny, friendly pub. Snacks; garden; live music.

Coates

Weekdays: 11–3; 6–11

Tunnel House (P)
Off A433, up side road between Tarlton and Coates
☏ (0285) 770280
Bulmer (H)
At entrance to Sapperton canal tunnel, built in 1780 for the tunnel diggers.

Meals and snacks; children's room; garden; live music. Unusual pub animals!

Cockleford

Weekdays: 11–2.30; 6–11, Sunday 12–3; 7–10.30

Green Dragon Inn (P)

Off A435 (take Elkstone turning)
☏ (024287) 271
Bulmer (PC)
Surprisingly large pub just off main road with two comfortable bars and many side rooms. Varied menu offers vegetarian option. Trad jazz Mondays and folk on Wednesday evenings.

Coleford

Weekdays: 11–2.30; 6.30–11

Feathers (P)

Market Place
☏ (0594) 33497
Bulmer (H)
Friendly town centre pub. Meals and snacks; outdoor drinking area; live music; folk night first Friday of the month.

Weekdays: 11–11, Sunday: 12–2; 7–10.30

Masons Arms (P)

2 Boxbush Road
☏ (0594) 34633
Bulmer (PC)
Bar snacks; outdoor barbecue; garden; games room.

Drybrook

Bowketts Off Licence (OL)

Weston (PP)

Weekdays: 11–11

Rose in Hand (P)

Morse Lane
☏ (0594) 542788
Westons Old Rosie (PC)
Meals and snacks all opening hours; garden; pool table; nine pin skittles alley.

Dursley

Monday–Thursday: 9.30–1.30; 5.30–10, Friday–Saturday: 9.30–10, Sunday: 12–2; 7–10

The Brewery Stores (OL)

26a Silver Street
☏ (0453) 3918
Thatcher (PC)

Weekdays: 10–2.30; 7–11

Fox & Hounds (P)

Hill Road
☏ (0453) 2870
Bulmer (H)
Meals and snacks all times; restaurant; garden with birds, fish and guinea pigs; access for disabled; camping facilities nearby.

Dymock

Weekdays: 12–11

Beauchamp Arms (P)

☏ (053185) 266
Weston (H)
Old tastefully extended pub. Meals and snacks; children's room; garden; accommodation.

Eastington

Weekdays: 11–2.30; 6.30–11

Victoria Inn (P)

☏ (045382) 2892
Bulmer (H)
Lunchtime snacks except Sunday; garden.

Ebrington

Weekdays: 11–2.30; 6–11, Sunday: 12–3; 7–10.30

Ebrington Arms (P)

On B4035, 2 miles east of Chipping Campden
☏ (038678) 223
Bulmer (H)
Stone built pub in centre of village. Meals and snacks lunchtime and evenings; garden; accommodation.

Eldersfield

HARTLAND'S FARMHOUSE CIDER ▲

Flat Farm
☏ (045284) 213

Ford

Weekdays: 11–2.30; 6–11

Plough (P)

On B4077
☏ (038673) 215
Coates (PC)
Cellar used to be a jail! Meals and snacks lunchtime and evenings; garden; accommodation; access for disabled; camping facilities nearby.

Forthampton

Weekdays: 11–11, Sunday: 12–3; 7–10.30

Lower Lode Hotel (P)

On bank of River Severn south west of Tewkesbury
☏ (0684) 293224
Westons Old Rosie (PC)
15th century inn with $3\frac{1}{2}$ acres of grass river bank. Bar snacks 12–2.30; 6–9.30; garden; accommodation; camping facilities in grounds.

Framilode

Weekdays: 10 am–11 pm

Darell Arms (P)

Framilode Passage, Saul
☏ (0452) 740320
Bulmer (H)
Vantage point for watching Severn Bore. Hot and cold bar meals and snacks all sessions; children's room; garden; shove ha'penny; pool table; live music, country and western.

Weekdays: 11–3; 6–11

Ship Inn (P)

☏ (0452) 740260
Bulmer (PC)
Canalside pub. Meals and snacks; garden; live music.

Frampton on Severn

Weekdays: 11–2.30; 6–11

Bell Inn (P)

On B4071
Bulmer (H)
On edge of huge village green. Meals and snacks; Sunday lunch.

FRAMPTON VILLAGE CIDER COMPANY

Bridge Road
☏ (0452) 741094

Gloucester

County Arms (P)

Millbrook Street (off Barton Street at Vauxhall Inn)
Taunton (PC)
Large single-bar pub with robust atmosphere, adjoining the New Country Hotel not far south of the Cross. Good food.

Gloucestershire

Peter Dominic (OL)
72 Northgate Street
☎ (0452) 25686
Dymock Farmhouse (B)
Near Gloucester BR station.

Gotherington

TILLYS CIDER ▲
Moat Farm, Malleson Road
☎ (024267) 6807

Great Barrington

Weekdays: 11–2.30; 6.30–11

Fox Inn (P)
Off A40
☎ (04514) 385
Coates (PC)
A stone built pub by the River Windrush. Meals and snacks lunchtime and evenings; garden; accommodation; skittle alley.

Greet

Weekdays: 11–3; 6–11

Harvest Home (P)
Near Winchcombe
☎ (0242) 602430
Weston (PC)
Lively village pub with garden and function room. Meals and snacks.

Guiting Power

Farmers Arms (P)
Off A436 in village centre
☎ (04515) 358
Weston (H)
Ivy clad pub in typical Cotswold village. Meals; garden.

Halmore

SUMMERS' CIDER

Slimbridge Lane
☎ (0453) 811218

Hillersland

Weekdays: 12–3; 7–11, Sunday: 12–3; 7–10.30

Rock Inn (P)
On B4432, near Coleford
☎ (0594) 32367
Bulmer (H)
17th century country inn near Symonds Yat, with superb views of the Wye Valley, on the edge of the Forest of Dean. Snacks at most times; family room; garden.

Kineton

Weekdays: 11–2.30; 6–11

Halfway House (P)
2 miles south of Ford on B4077
☎ (04515) 344
Bulmer (PC)
Country pub near Cotswold Farm Park. Meals and snacks; garden; accommodation.

Leighterton

Weekdays: 11–2.30; 7–11

Royal Oak (P)
4 miles south of A46/A4135 junction
☎ (066689) 250
Bulmer (PC)
Bright but tastefully modernised pub with friendly atmosphere. Meals and snacks lunchtime and evenings; children's room (summer only); access for disabled.

Leonard Stanley

Monday–Friday: 11–2.30; 6–11, Saturday: 11–3; 6–11, Sunday: 12–3; 7–10.30

White Hart (P)
The Street
☎ (045382) 2702
Bulmer (H)
Meals and snacks; garden.

Littledean

Monday–Saturday: 12–3; 7–11, Sunday: 12–3; 7–10.30

Kings Head (P)
Broad Street
☎ (0594) 24474
Bulmer (H)
Locals' corner pub with piano. Bar snacks.

Little Washbourne

Weekdays: 11–2.30; 6–11

Hobnails Inn (P)
On A438
☎ (0242) 620237
Bulmer (PC)
Long, low 15th century building in the same family for 240 years. Two thoroughly traditional bars, restaurant, children's room, garden and skittles alley.

Lower Swell

Weekdays: 11–2.30; 6–11, Sunday: 12–2; 7–10.30

Golden Ball (P)
On B4068
☎ (0451) 30247
Weston (PC)
Cotswold pub in pretty village, with stream running close by. Meals and snacks lunchtime and evenings; garden; accommodation.

Lydney

Cross Keys (P)
Church Road
☎ (0594) 41619
Bulmer (H)
Meals and snacks; garden.

Greyhound (P)
☎ (0594) 42670
Bulmer (PC)
Meals and snacks; garden.

Weekdays: 11–11, Sunday: 12–3; 7–10.30

Swan Hotel (P)
Hill Street
☎ (0594) 842834
Bulmer (H)
Victorian pub with two bars. Meals and snacks 12–2.15; 7–10; restaurant; outdoor drinking area; accommodation; function room.

Micheldean

Old Smithy Off Licence (OL)
Weston (PC)

Mickleton

Weekdays: 11–2.30; 6.30–11

Kings Arms (P)
High Street (B4632)
☎ (0386) 438257
Bulmer (PC)
Pleasant stone built pub. Meals and snacks; garden.

Moreton in Marsh

Swan (P)
At junction of A429 and A44
Bulmer (PC)
Meals and snacks. Near Moreton in Marsh BR station.

Wellington (P)
London Road (A44)
☎ (0608) 50396
Bulmer (H)
Imposing stone pub on edge of town. Snacks; children's room; garden. Near Moreton in Marsh BR station.

Weekdays: 10.30–2.30; 6–11.

White Horse (P)
On A429
☏ (0608) 50120
Bulmer (PC)
Small and simple. Meals and snacks; garden.

Nailsworth

COTSWOLD CIDER ▲
Bottle Green Drinks Company, Spring Mills Estate, Avening Road
☏ (045383) 4050

Flynns Restaurant (P)
3 Fountain Street
☏ (045383) 5567
Cotswold Cider (B)
Restaurant with finest English ingredients prepared in the French manner with a touch of Australia!

Williams Kitchen Delicatessen (OL)
3 Fountain Street
☏ (045383) 2240
Cotswold Cider (B)

Nether Westcote

Weekdays: 11–2.30; 6.30–11 (open all day on Bank Holidays)

New Inn (P)
Off A424
☏ (0993) 830827
Bulmer (H)
Small and hidden away on north side of village. Meals and snacks lunchtime and evenings (including vegetarian dishes); garden with Aunt Sally; camping on adjoining site.

Newent

DYMOCK FARMHOUSE CIDER ▲
Three Choirs Vineyards Ltd., Rhyle House, Welsh House Lane
☏ (0531) 85555

North Cerney

Bathurst Arms (P)
On A435
☏ (028583) 281
Dunkerton (B)
Unspoilt pub on Cheltenham to Cirencester road. Extensive bar menu and a la carte menu; riverside garden; letting rooms.

North Nibley

Monday–Friday: 12–2.30; 7–11, Saturday 12–3; 7–11, Sunday 12–3; 7–10.30.

New Inn (P)
Waterley Bottom
☏ (0453) 3659
Inch (PC)
Hard to find pub in delightful countryside. Meals and snacks lunchtime and evenings; children's play area; large garden; accommodation.

Oddington

Weekdays: 11–2.30; 6–11.

Horse & Groom (P)
Upper Oddington (off A436 2½ miles from Stow on the Wold)
☏ (0451) 30684
Taunton (H)
16th century Cotswold stone inn in delightful village; inglenook fireplace. Meals and snacks lunchtime and evenings; restaurant; children's room; garden; accommodation.

Pillowell

Weekdays: 11–3; 7–11, Sunday: 12–2.30; 7–10.30.

Swan Inn (P)
☏ (0594) 562477
Bulmer (E)
Forest of Dean local near disused railway line. Snacks; patio.

Quenington

Weekdays: 11–3; 6–11.

Keepers Arms (P)
☏ (028575) 249
Westons Old Rosie (H)
Former gamekeepers' cottages. Meals and snacks; restaurant; garden; accommodation.

Ruspidge

Monday–Friday: 7–11, Saturday: 12–11, Sunday: 12–3; 7–10.30.

New Inn (P)
2 miles south west of Cinderford on B4227
☏ (0594) 24508
Bulmer (H)
Bland (H)
Local village pub with piano. Garden.

Weekdays: 11–11 most days.

Rising Sun Inn (P)
Ruspidge Road
☏ (0594) 22783
Bulmer (E)
Snacks.

Shuthonger

Weekdays: 11–2.30; 6–11.

Crown (P)
On A38 north of Tewkesbury
☏ (0684) 293714
Weston's Old Rosie (H)
Specialises in food. Meals lunchtime all week; evening meals except Sunday and Monday; separate restaurant; camping facilities nearby.

Sling

Weekdays: 11–11.

Okepool Inn (P)
On B4228 two miles outside Coleford
☏ (0594) 33277
Bulmer
Dean Forest village pub with meals lunchtime and evening; children's room; garden; access for disabled; separate games room.

Stanton

Summer weekdays: 11–11, Winter weekdays: 11–2.30; 6–11.

Mount (P)
Old Snowshill Road (at top of hill leading from village)
☏ (038673) 316
Weston (H)
Popular pub. Meals lunchtime and evening; large garden; access for disabled; woodlice racing and boules!

Staverton

Weekdays: 11–2.30; 5.30–11.

House in the Tree (P)
Haydens Elm (on B4063)
☏ (0242) 680241
Bulmer (E)
Snacks; garden.

Stonehouse

Monday–Friday: 11–3; 6–11, Saturday: 10–3; 6–11, Sunday: 12–3; 7–10.30.

Brewers Arms (P)
Gloucester Road (B4008 at edge of town)

☎ (045382) 2621
Bulmer (H)
Popular basic town local half a mile from railway station. Snacks; children's room; garden.

Weekdays: 11–11, Sunday: 12–3; 7–10.30.

Royal Arms (P)
Bath Road (B4008)
☎ (045382) 2718
Bulmer (H)
Friendly local with plenty of banter. Snacks lunchtime. 300 yards from Stonehouse BR station.

Monday–Friday: 11–3; 6–11, Saturday: 11–2.30; 6.30–11.

Spa (P)
Oldends Lane (opposite factory estate)
☎ (045382) 2327
Bulmer
Popular, cosy little pub on industrial estate near the station. Meals lunchtime, evenings Friday and Saturday only; outdoor drinking area.

Stow on the Wold

Bell (P)
Park Street
☎ (0451) 30663
Bulmer (PC)
Overlooking small green. Snacks; garden.

Queens Head (P)
Market Square
☎ (0451) 30563
Weston (H)
Fine old Cotswold town centre pub. Meals and snacks; outdoor drinking area.

Stratton

Weekdays: 10.30–2.30; 6–11, Sunday: 12–2; 7–10.30.

Plough Inn (P)
Gloucester Road, Cirencester (on A417 1 mile from town centre)
☎ (0285) 653422
Weston (PC) (H) (J)
Pleasant and friendly pub. Bar snacks 12–2; 7.30–9; garden.

Stroud

Monday–Thursday: 10–2.30; 5–11, Friday–Saturday: 10–11, Sunday: 12–2; 7–10.30.

Greyhound Inn (P)
Gloucester Street (junction with King Street)
Bulmer (H)
Basic two bar town centre pub. Snacks; pool table.

Mother Nature (OL)
2 Bedford Street
☎ (04536) 78202
Cotswold Cider (B)

Tewkesbury

Anchor (P)
High Street
☎ (0684) 296614
Weston (PC)
Plain, town centre local. snacks lunchtime and evenings; full meals lunchtime; coffee room; accommodation.

Weekdays: 11–2.30; 6.30–11.

Berkeley Arms (P)
Church Street (near the cross)
☎ (0684) 293034
Bulmer (PC)
17th century town centre inn, with access through alley way. Snacks lunchtime.

Kings Head (P)
Barton Street
☎ (0684) 293267
Bulmer (H)
Robust town centre local.

Tirley

Haw Bridge Inn (P)
On B4213
☎ (045278) 316
Weston (H)
On bank of River Severn. Snacks; garden.

Twyning

Weekdays: 11–3; 6–11 (Bank Holidays 11–11)

Village Inn (P)
On village green
☎ (0684) 293500
Bulmer (PC)
Pleasant pub with good atmosphere. Meals and snacks; garden; skittle alley, barbecues.

Upper Lydbrook

Weekdays: 11–11.

Masons Arms (P)
Hawsley
☎ (0594) 61210
Bulmer (H)
One of the most isolated, and perhaps the most attractive, pub in the Forest of Dean. Children's play area; garden; function room.

Wainlodes

Weekdays: 11–3; 6–11.

Red Lion (P)
Wainlodes Hill, Norton
☎ (0452) 730251
Weston (H) (PP)
On the bank of the River Severn, with caravan and camping park, and excellent fishing. Snacks lunchtime and 7–10; garden; holiday cottage and chalet to let; children's room.

Wanswell

Weekdays: 11–3; 6.30–11.

Salmon Inn (P)
On B4068 between Berkeley and Sharpness
☎ (0453) 811306
Bulmer (PC)
Convenient for Berkeley Castle, Slimbridge Wildfowl Trust, and Sharpness Marina. Meals and snacks lunchtime and 7.30–10; children's room and large children's lawn.

Whitecroft

Miners Arms (P)
Bulmer (H)
Two bar village local. Snacks; skittle alley.

Royal Oak (P)
Bulmer (H)
Typical Forest of Dean local. Snacks; garden.

Winchcombe

Weekdays: 11.30–2.30; 5.30–11.

Corner Cupboard (P)
☎ (0242) 602303
Bulmer (H)
Westons Old Rosie (H)
Old stone built inn in Cotswold town. Snacks lunchtime; restaurant Tuesday–Saturday 7.15–8.30; outdoor drinking area; self catering accommodation.

Withington

Weekdays: 11–2.30; 6–11.

Kings Head (P)
☎ (024289) 216
Weston (PC)
Unspoilt pub hidden away. Snacks; garden.

Woodcroft

Weekdays: 11–3; 6–11, Sunday: 12–3; 7–10.30.

Rising Sun (P)
On B4228
☎ (0291) 622470
Taunton (H)
Friendly one-bar pub with garden. Meals and snacks.

Wotton under Edge

Royal Oak (P)
Haw Street
☎ (0453) 842316
Bulmer (H)
Pleasantly modernised inn with garden. Meals and snacks. Accommodation.

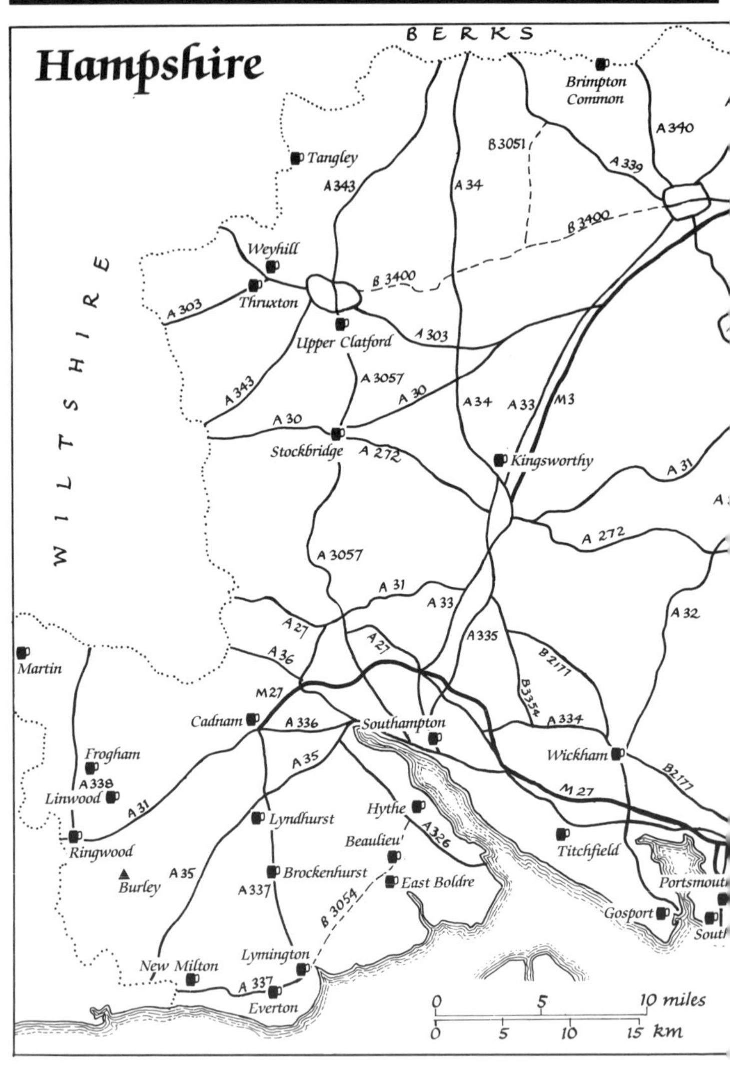

Beaulieu

Weekdays: 9–6 all week.

Abbey Stores (OL)
High Street
☎ (0590) 612240
New Forest (J) (PL)
Supermarket and post office also.

Brimpton Common

Weekdays: 11.30–3; 5.30–11, Sunday: 12–3; 7–10.30

Pineapple (P)
On B3051 between Tadley and Kingsclere
☎ (07356) 4376
Bulmer (H)
16th century thatched pub on Berkshire border: distinctive hewn tables of British elm. Meals and snacks all times except Sunday evenings; separate restaurant early evening; garden.

Brockenhurst

Purkess Supermarket (OL)
31 Brookley Road
☎ (0590) 22322
New Forest (PL)

Burley

NEW FOREST CIDER ▲
Littlemead, Pound Lane
☎ (04253) 3589

Cadnam

White Hart (P)
☎ (0703) 812277
Bulmer (H)
Pleasant New Forest pub.

East Boldre

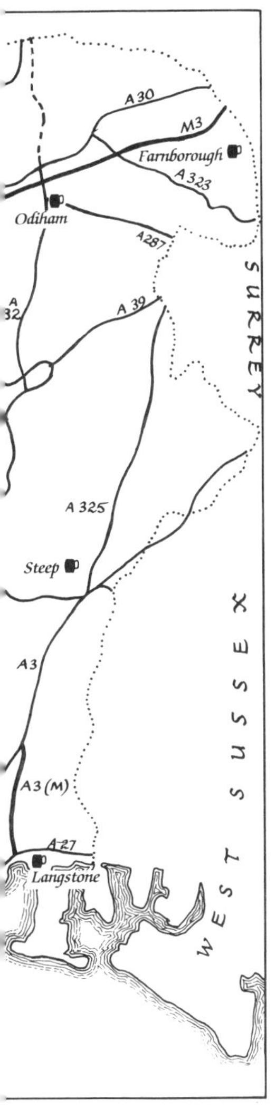

Monday–Friday: 11–2.30; 6–11, Saturday: 11–11, Sunday: 12–3; 7–10.30

Turfcutters Arms (P)
Main Road (south of B3054 at Hatchet Pond)
☏ (0590) 612331
Bulmer (H)
Snacks 12–2; 7.30–10: garden.

Everton

Monday–Friday: 10.30–2.30; 6–11, Saturday: 10.30–3; 6–11, Sunday: 12–3; 7–10.30

Crown Inn (P)
Old Christchurch Road (just off A337, 2 miles east of Lymington)
☏ (0590) 42655
Bulmer (H)
The pub has been a drinking house for well over 500 years! Interesting smoke screen windows; log fire in winter. Meals and snacks 12–1.45; 7–9.45; garden; camping facilities nearby; live music on Thursday and Saturday nights; pool table.

Farnborough

Weekdays: 9–10.30, Sunday: 12–3; 7–10.30

Carty's (OL)
56 Queens Road
☏ (0252) 545417
Weston (PC) (J) (PL) (BB) (DJ)
Convenience store, specialising in ales, ciders and strong lagers. Near Ash BR station.

Fordingbridge

Mace Shop (OL)
Sandy Balls Holiday Park, Godshill
☏ (0425) 56065
New Forest (PL)

Frogham

Weekdays: 11–3; 6–11, Sunday: 12–3; 7–10.30

Foresters Arms (P)
Abbots Well Road (2 miles east of Fordingbridge)
☏ (0425) 52294
New Forest (PC)
Perrys Cider (H)
On edge of New Forest; start of many walks and pony treks. Meals weekdays 12–2; 7–10, Sunday: 12–2; 7–9.30; children's room; large garden.

Gosport

Weekdays: 11–3; 6–11, Sunday: 12–3; 7–10.30

Park Hotel (P)
Park Road, Alverstoke
☏ (0705) 583074
Bulmer (H)
Large Victorian building overlooking Gosport Park and Hasler Lake in quiet residential part of town. Meals all opening hours; outdoor drinking area; accommodation; resident talking parrot.

Weekdays: 11–11, Sunday: 12–3; 7–10.30

Royal Arms (P)
37 Stoke Road
☏ (0705) 581740
Bulmer (H)
Traditional pub with listed iron canopy over pavement. Snacks all times; outdoor drinking area.

Hythe

Weekdays: 11–3; 6–11

Lord Nelson (P)
High Street (near ferry)
☏ (0703) 842169
Bulmer (PC)
Waterfront pub, originally a customs house. Lunchtime bar snacks; garden overlooking Southampton Water; access for disabled.

Weekdays: Monday–Friday: 11–2.30; 6–11, Saturday: 11–3; 6–11

Travellers Rest (P)
Hart Hill, Frost Lane (off Frost Lane on Solent Way)
☏ (0703) 842356
Bulmer (PC)
Off the beaten track, an old Pilgrims Way between Hythe and Bucklers Hard. Meals and snacks lunchtime; garden.

Kingsworthy

Weekdays: 11–3; 5.30–11 (all day on Bank Holidays)

Cart & Horses (P)
London Road (A33/A333 junction, near M3 junction 9)
☏ (0962) 882360
Bulmer (PC)
Large rambling roadhouse, catering for all needs. Good selection of food at all times; restaurant; children's room; children's playground and large garden; access for disabled; bar billiards; skittle alley.

Langstone

Weekdays: 11–11, Sunday: 12–3; 7–10.30

Royal Oak (P)
19 High Street (turn left on approach to the causeway to Hayling Island)
☏ (0705) 481325
Bulmer (H)
Splendid historic pub in picturesque setting – at high water you can sail right up to the front door!

Inside there are large log fires and a stone flagged floor. Meals 12–3; 6–10; restaurant; outdoor drinking area; camping facilities nearby.

Linwood

High Corner Inn (P)
☎ (0425) 473973
New Forest (PC)
Multi-roomed pub with large garden and children's play area. Bar snacks and meals are in demand but the pub also has a public bar with traditional games. Popular in summer.

Red Short Inn (P)
☎ (0425) 475792
New Forest (PC)

Lymington

Spar Stores (OL)
Pennington
New Forest (PL)

Victoria Wine (OL)
116 High Street
☎ (0590) 72700
New Forest (PL)

Lyndhurst

Country Store (OL)
43-47 High Street
☎ (042128) 2654
New Forest (PL)

Martin

Weekdays: 11–3; 6–11

Coote Arms (P)
Martin Drove End (on A354)
☎ (072589) 220
Bulmer (H)
Roadside inn. Full bar menu, hot and cold meals; Sunday lunches; garden; caravans welcome; pool table; clay pigeon shoot every other week.

New Milton

Victoria Wine (OL)
3 Milton Grand Parade, Christchurch Road
☎ (0425) 614423
New Forest (PL)

Victorian Wine (OL)
73 Station Road
☎ (0425) 610028
New Forest (PL)
Near New Milton BR station.

Odiham

Weekdays: 11–3; 5.30–11

Waterwitch (P)
Colt Hill (off Main Street in dead end road leading to canal)
☎ (025671) 2778
Bulmer (H)
Old waterways pub with garden leading down to the Basingstoke Canal, where boats can be hired. Meals and snacks all times; restaurant; garden.

Portsmouth

Weekdays: 11–11, Sunday: 12–3; 7–10.30

Bottoms Up (OL)
7 Kingston Road, Buckland
☎ (0705) 830760
Rich (PC)
Fratton BR station nearby.

Weekdays: 10.30–11

Brewery Tap (P)
17 London Road, North End (southern end of North End shopping area)
☎ (0705) 699943
Langdon (PP)
One room pub which sprang out of the doomed Southsea Brewery: geared to the drinker's needs. Meals and snacks 12–11; outdoor drinking area.

Weekdays: 12–3; 5–10.30, Sunday: 7–10.30

Wishing Well (OL)
18 Copnor Road, Copnor
☎ (0703) 669451
Zum (PC)

Ringwood

Contented Toad Delicatessen (OL)
Unit 2, The Granaries, Pedlars Walk
☎ (0425) 471340
New Forest (PL)

Victoria Wine (OL)
33 Southampton Road
☎ (0425) 472080
New Forest (PL)

Southampton

Weekdays: 10–3.30; 6.30–11

North Star (P)
91 St. Marys Street
☎ (0703) 229789
Bulmer (H)
Meals.

Monday–Friday: 10–3; 5–11, Saturday: 10–11, Sunday 12–3; 7–10.30

Rover Inn (P)
266 Shirley Road, Shirley
☎ (0703) 772882
Bulmer (H)

Weekdays: 10–11

Sun Hotel (P)
Weston Lane, Woolston
☎ (0703) 448339
Bulmer (H)

Southsea

Weekdays: 11–11, Sunday: 12–3; 7–10.30

Bold Forester (P)
177 Albert Road
☎ (0705) 823609
Bulmer (H)
Large former Longs pub with well preserved exterior and refurbished single split level bar; plenty of dark wood and subdued lighting: popular with gregarious students; circular pool. Meals 12–2; outdoor drinking area.

Weekdays: 8.30–10, Sunday: 8.30–1; 7–10.30

Britannia Wine (OL)
54 Victoria Road North
☎ (0705) 829309
Thatcher (F)
Near Fratton BR station.

Weekdays: 11–11

Eastney Cellars (P)
56 Cromwell Road
☎ (0705) 826249
Bulmer (H)

Weekdays: 9–11 all week.

Pompey Beer Shop (OL)
62 Elm Grove
☎ (0705) 756118
Rich (PC)

Monday–Friday: 10.30–2.30; 6–11, Saturday: 11–11

Royal Marine Artillery Tavern (P)
58 Cromwell Road, Eastney
☎ (0705) 820896
Bulmer (PC)
Surprisingly large street corner pub opposite the Royal Marine barracks, with friendly but vociferous landlord. Meals 12–2; 8–11 on Friday and Saturday; children's room; outdoor drinking area.

Steep

Monday–Friday: 10.30–2.30; 6–11, Saturday: 10.30–3; 6–11, Sunday: 12–3; 7–10.30

Harrow (P)

Turn off A325 at Sheet
☏ (0730) 62685
Bulmer (PC)
Small unspoilt country pub in peaceful setting, a short walk from Petersfield. Meals and snacks lunchtime and evenings; garden; access for disabled.

Stockbridge

Weekdays: 11–2.30; 6–11, Sunday: 12–3; 7–10.30

White Hart Inn (P)

High Street
☏ (0264) 810475
Taunton (H)
Meals and snacks; accommodation.

Tangley

Weekdays: 11–2.30; 6–11 (supper licence to midnight): Sunday: 12–3; 7–10.30

Fox (P)

Between Tangley and Hatherden
☏ (026470) 276
Wilkins (PC)
300 year old wayside pub in area of special scenic beauty: specialises in food. Meals and snacks 12–2; 6.30–10; separate restaurant; garden; access for disabled; camping facilities nearby.

Thruxton

Weekdays: 11–2.30; 6–11, Sunday 12–3; 7–10.30

White Horse (P)

Below A303 Thruxton bypass
☏ (026477) 2401
Bulmer (H) – summer only
Part thatched grade 2 listed building; near Thruxton race track and hawk conservancy. Meals evenings 7–9.15 except Sunday and Monday; snacks 12–2.15; and 7–9.15 except Sunday and Monday; children's room; garden.

Titchfield

Weekdays: 11–2.30; 6–11, Sunday: 12–3; 7–10.30

Wheatsheaf Inn (P)

East Street
☏ (0329) 42965
Bulmer (H)
Mentioned in Doomsday Book. Meals and snacks lunchtime and evenings; restaurant; garden.

Upper Clatford

Monday–Thursday: 11–2.30; 6–11, Friday–Saturday: 11–3; 6–11, Sunday 12–3; 7–10.30

Crook & Shears (P)

Main Street (east of A343 at Abbots Ann)
☏ (0264) 61543
Bulmer (PC)
365 year old thatched village local near River Avon. Meals and snacks all sessions except Mondays; children's room, garden; excellent facilities for disabled (local disabled group meet here).

Wickham

Weekdays: 10–3; 4.45–11, Sunday: 12–2.30; 7–10.30

Kings Head (P)

The Square
☏ (0329) 832123
Bulmer (H)
Old coaching inn. Bar snacks all times, full meals until 45 minutes before closing; children's room; outdoor drinking area/garden; camping facilities nearby; skittle alley for private hire.

Weyhill

Weekdays: 11.30–2.30; 6–11, Sunday: 12–2.30; 7–10.30

Weyhill Fair (P)

On A342 just north of A303 ring road
☏ (026477) 3631
Regular guest ciders (PC) (H)
Meals and snacks lunchtime and evenings; children's room; garden.

METHODS OF DISPENSE
(B) Bottle (BB) Bag in box (CK) Carry keg (DJ) glass demijohn (E) Cask and electric pump (F) Flagon (H) Cask and hand pump (J) glass jar (PC) polycask (PL) plastic container (PP) polypin (W) wooden cask

KEY TO MAPS
⊕ town or village with one or more real cider or perry outlets
▲ location of cider or perry maker selling direct to public from premises

Hereford & Worcester

Herefordshire

Allensmore

Locks Garage (OL)
☏ (098121) 206 and 439
Dunkerton (J)

Bishopswood

Weekdays: 11–4; 6–11 (summer holiday season): 12–3; 7–11 other times.

Kerne Bridge Inn (P)
On B4228
☏ (0600) 890495
Bulmer (PC)
Views over River Wye to Goodrich Castle; Meals and snacks all sessions; children's room; garden.

Bridge Sollars

Nelson (P)
On A438
☏ (098122) 208
Weston (PC)
In pretty Wye Valley village. Meals and snacks; children's room; garden and patio.

Nelson Service Station (OL)
☏ (098122) 239 or 656
Dunkerton (B)
A fill up for you and your car?

Brimfield

Roebuck (P)
Off A49
☏ (058472) 230
Dunkerton (B)
Meals lunchtime and evenings; restaurant.

Bromyard

Monday–Wednesday: 11–3; 7–11, Thursday–Saturday: 11–11

Bay Horse (P)
21 High Street
☏ (0885) 482635
Westons Old Rosie (PC)
Black and white pub built in 1557. Meals and snacks all opening hours; restaurant; outdoor drinking area/garden; camping facilities nearby.

Weekdays: 10–10, Sunday: 12–2; 7–9.30

Port of Call (OL)
58 High Street
☏ (0885) 482367
Dunkerton (J)

White Horse (P)
Old Road
☏ (0885) 82279
Weston (PC)
Old two bar town pub. Snacks.

Canon Pyon

Weekdays: 11–2.30; 6–11

Plough (P)
On A4110
☏ (043271) 577
Bulmer (PC)

Originally a pub cum blacksmiths shop. Meals and snacks all sessions; restaurant; garden; skittle alley, pool table.

Carey

Weekdays: 11–2.30; 6–11 (summer): 12–2.30; 7–11 (winter)

Cottage of Content (P)
1½ miles north east of Hoarwithy
☎ (043270) 242
Weston (H) – summer
Built 500 years ago as farm cottages, a condition of the tenancy being that one should be maintained as an ale and cider house! Meals and snacks lunchtime and evenings; children's room; garden; accommodation; access for disabled.

Craswell

Bulls Head (P)
Weston (PC)
Old pub with beams and stone floor; in hilly country at end of Monnow valley.

Dinmore

Weekdays: 9–5 all days except Christmas

Dinmore Fruit Farm (OL)
On A49 Hereford to Leominster road below Dinmore Hill
☎ (056884) 261
Dunkerton (PC) (PL)
Dymock Farmhouse (B)
Weston (PC) (PL)
PYO apples, pears, plums soft fruit and veg in season: farm also sells local specialities. Camping facilities nearby.

Eardisley

GREAT OAK CIDER & HONEY CO. ▲
Roughmoor
☎ (05446) 400

Felton

Crozens Arms (P)
☎ (043278) 213
Weston (H)
Georgian pub with accent on food and sport. Meals and snacks lunchtime and evenings; children's room.

Fownhope

Forge & Ferry (P)
Ferry Lane (off B4224)
☎ (043277) 391
Weston (PC)
Small pub with much character situated down lane leading to the river. Meals and snacks lunchtime and evenings; children's room; garden.

Weekdays: 11–2.30; 6–11, Sunday: 12–2.30; 7–10.30

Green Man Inn (P)
On B4224 six miles south east of Hereford)
☎ (043277) 243
Weston (PC)
Timber framed inn dating from 1485; in 18th and 19th centuries the petty sessional court was held here: the pub's name is after a previous owner. Meals and snacks lunchtime, and evenings till 10; garden; accommodation; camping facilities one mile away. Hotel residents enjoy fishing rights on River Wye.

Goodrich

Weekdays: 11–3; 6.30–11

Cross Keys (P)
just off A40
☎ (0660) 890203
Bulmer (H)
Friendly two bar village inn near Goodrich Castle. Meals and snacks; garden.

Weekdays: 9–5.30 (closed for lunch 12.30–1.30)

Jolly's (OL)
☎ (0660) 890352
Weston (J)

Halmonds Frome

Weekdays: 12–2.30; 5–11, Sunday: 12–3; 7–10.30

Majors Arms (P)
Off A4103 at top of Fromes Hill, Bishops Frome
☎ (053186) 371
Westons Farm Brand (PC)
16th century free house, with dramatic views of five counties. Snacks and meals 12–2.30 and 7.30–10 except Sunday and Monday evening; garden; camping in grounds by arrangement.

Hardwicke

Weekdays: 11–2.30; 6–11

Royal Oak (P)
Near Hay on Wye, on B4348 at junction with B4352
☎ (04973) 248
Westons Old Rosie (PC)
16th century timber framed pub in beautiful countryside high above the Wye. Meals lunchtime and evening till 10; vegetarian dishes always available; garden; accommodation.

Hereford

Monday–Tuesday: 11–2.30; 5–11, Wednesday–Thursday: 11–4; 5–11, Friday–Saturday: 11–11, Sunday: 12–3; 7–10.30

Barrels (P)
69 St. Owen Street (400 yards east of town hall)
☎ (0432) 274968
Bulmer (H)
Westons Vintage (PC)
Formerly a coaching inn, the Lamb Hotel; now a students' and locals' pub near city centre. Snacks lunchtime; live music Saturday nights. Hereford BR station half a mile.

Weekdays: 11–2.30; 6–11

Brewers Arms (P)
Eign Road (on B4224)
☎ (0432) 273746
Bulmer West Country (H)
Locals' pub on outskirts of city. Bar snacks; morning coffee; garden.

Weekdays: 11–3; 7–11, Sunday: 12–3; 7–10.30

Bricklayers Arms (P)
St. Owen Street (opposite fire station)
☎ (0432) 274998
Bulmer (H)
Westons Old Rosie (PC)
City centre pub. Snacks. Half a mile from Hereford BR station.

Weekdays: 11–2.30; 6–11

Buckingham Hotel (P)
Whitecross Road
☎ (0432) 276087
Bulmer (H)
Roadside locals' pub. Outdoor drinking area.

Hereford & Worcester

BULMER'S TRADITIONAL DRAUGHT CIDERS
H.P. Bulmer Ltd., UK Drinks Division, The Cider Mills, Plough Lane
☎ (0432) 270622

Castle Pool Hotel (P)
Castle Street
☎ (0432) 56321
Weston (PC)
Built in 1850 as a residence for the Bishop of Hereford, beside the remains of the castle moat: a haunt of wild fowl. Bar and restaurant meals; garden; accommodation.

Weekdays: 9–5 (closed in January)

Cider Museum (OL)
Pomona Place (off Whitecross Road)
☎ (0432) 270662
King Offa (F)
An essential port of call for all cider enthusiasts, showing the history of cider making from earliest times to modern mechanical methods. The cider is the Museum's own brand.

Weekdays: 11–2.30; 6–11

Crown Inn (P)
St. Martins (by Greyfriars Bridge roundabout)
☎ (0432) 351227
Bulmer (H)
Basic boozer on edge of city centre. Snacks; outdoor drinking area; children's room.

Dickinsons (OL)
14 Bridge Street
☎ (0432) 353720
Dunkerton (B)
Bulmer (DJ)
Symonds (DJ)
Westons (J)
Westons Perry (DJ)
Half a mile from Hereford BR station.

Tuesday–Saturday: 7–9.30 (last orders)

Effy's Restaurant (P)
96 East Street
☎ (0432) 59754
Dunkerton (B)
Within half a mile of Hereford BR station.

Golden Lion (P)
Grand Stand Road
☎ (0432) 272383
Weston (H)
Locals' pub near the racecourse, once two cottages; interesting Victorian windows. Snacks; garden.

Green Dragon Hotel (P)
Broad Street
☎ (0432) 272506
Dunkerton (B)
Hereford's premier hotel, a fine Georgian building with 19th century facade and cast iron balcony. Meals and snacks lunchtime and evenings; accommodation.

Monday–Friday: 11–3, Saturday: 12–11, Sunday: 12–3

Heart of Oak (P)
Edgar Street
☎ (0432) 276056
Bulmer (E)
Part of pub was once a bakery. Meals lunchtime; children welcome; garden.

Monday–Tuesday: 10–2.30; 6–11, Wednesday–Saturday: 10–11, Sunday: 12–3; 7–10.30

Horse & Groom (P)
Eign Street (opposite eye hospital)
☎ (0432) 355026
Bulmers West Country (E)
Basic city pub: cider only available in public bar. Rolls, sandwiches, lunchtime bar snacks; outdoor drinking area.

Peter Dominic (OL)
56 Broad Street
☎ (0432) 269150
Dunkerton range (F)
Half a mile from Hereford BR station.

Weekdays: 11–11 (summer); 11–3; 5–11 (winter)

Saracens Head (P)
1–5 St. Martins Street (on old bridge over River Wye)
☎ (0432) 275480
Bulmer (H)
Westons Old Rosie (PC) – summer
One of Hereford's oldest buildings. Lunchtime meals; separate restaurant; patio. Half a mile from Hereford BR station.

Weekdays: 9–5.30

Shop Under the Clock (OL)
11 Commercial Road
☎ (0432) 268279
Dunkerton range (F)
Knight (PC) (PL)
Weston range (F)
Near Hereford BR station and bus station.

Weekdays: 11–2.30; 6–11

Sun Inn (P)
St. Owen Street
☎ (0432) 266403
Bulmer (W)
Old city centre pub with a cider following; only cider from the wood to be found in the county. Cider served only in public bar. Snacks lunchtime; outdoor drinking area. Half a mile from Hereford BR station.

Hoarwithy

Weekdays: 11–2.30; 6–11

New Harp Inn (P)
5 miles northwest of Ross on Wye
☎ (043270) 213
Bulmer (H)
Pleasant pub in middle of riverside village, partly hidden behind trees. Meals and snacks. Garden.

How Caple

How Caple Grange Hotel (P)
☎ (098986) 208
Dunkerton (B)
Hotel with restaurant and bar; function facilities; garden.

Kingsland

Corners Inn (P)
On B4360 off A4110
☎ (056881) 385
Weston (PC)
17th century pub, which used to have its own cider press. Snacks; children's room.

Monument Inn (P)
Junction of A4110 and B4360
☎ (056881) 311
Weston (PC)
Built in 1799, and named after the monument outside, which commemorates the battle at nearby Mortimers Cross: a one time cider house.

Kingstone

Masons Arms (P)
On B4349
☎ (0981) 250223
Weston (H)
17th century village inn.

Kington

Weekdays: 9–5.30

Gourmets Corner (OL)
High Street
Great Oak (F)

Weekdays: 9–5.30

Husseys Off Licence (OL)
High Street
Dunkerton full range (B)

Monday–Thursday: 10–1; 4–10, Friday–Saturday: 10–10, Sunday: 12–2; 7–9

Kington Off Licence (OL)
15 High Street
☏ (0544) 230987
Dunkerton (B)
Symonds (PC)

Kinnersley

Weekdays: 11–2.30; 6–11

Kinnersley Arms (P)
On Letton road out of Kinnersley, adjacent to bridge over old railway
☏ (05446) 240
Bulmer (H)
Taunton (H)
Unspoilt country inn, formerly the station hotel. Meals and snacks all sessions; restaurant; garden; accommodation.

Ledbury

Weekdays: 11–2.30; 6–11

Brewery Inn (P)
Bye Street (opposite cattle market)
☏ (0531) 4272
Weston (H)
Unspoilt pub with two rooms served from unique small corner bar – more like being in someone's living room! Dates from 15th century. Children's room; outdoor drinking area. Half a mile from Ledbury BR station.

Monday–Friday: 12–3; 6–11, Saturday: 12–11, Sunday: 12–3; 7–10.30

Full Pitcher (P)
The Wharf (on new Ledbury bypass)
☏ (0531) 2688
Westons Old Rosie (H)
Large pub overlooking cricket pitch. Meals and snacks 12–9; children's room; garden; camping facilities nearby.

Weekdays: 11–2.30; 6–11

Plough Hotel (P)
The Homend
☏ (0531) 2911
Bulmer (H)
Old coaching inn, and still residential. Meals and snacks all sessions; restaurant; accommodation; skittle alley. Half a mile from Bedbury BR station.

Weekdays: 11–11, Sunday: 12–3; 7–10.30

Seven Stars (P)
The Homend
☏ (0531) 2824
Weston (PC)
16th century inn. Morning coffee; lunchtime and evening meals; full bar menu – home cooking; garden; accommodation.

Weekdays: 9–8, Sunday: 12–2

Vine Stores (OL)
11 High Street
☏ (0531) 2665
Dymock Farmhouse (B)
Weston – all range.

Weekdays: 11–2; 6.30–11

White Hart (P)
Church Street
☏ (0531) 2620
Weston (PC)
Good value local.

Leominster

Bodega Wines (OL)
28 High Street
☏ (0568) 2003
Weston (PC)

Hop Pole (P)
Bridge Street
☏ (0568) 4194
Bulmer (E)
Busy cider house at north end of town.

Whitbread Flowers (OL)
26 Broad Street
☏ (0568) 2002
Weston (PC) (J)

Lingen

Weekdays: 12–3; 7–11, Sunday: 12–3; 7–10.30

Royal George (P)
☏ (0544) 267322
Weston (PC)
Remote 17th century pub, which serves as post office and shop – one of only three in the country. Snacks; meals by arrangement; children's room; garden.

Little Hereford

FRANKLINS CIDER 
The Cliffs (2 miles west of Tenbury Wells on A456)
☏ (0584) 810488

Longhope

Valley Off Licence (OL)
Weston (PC)

Luston

Weekdays: 11–2.30; 6–11

Balance (P)
On B4361 3 miles north of Leominster
☏ (0568) 5757
Bulmer (H)
400 year old pub, originally a wool weighing station, hence the name. Beware of Bessie the ghost, who hid some money there after the War, and still guards it! Meals and snacks; restaurant; garden.

Lyonshall

Penros Court Restaurant (P)
☏ (0544) 239720
Dunkerton (B)
Restaurant in a superbly restored group of medieval timber-framed buildings.

Weekdays: 11–2.30; 7–11

Royal George Inn (P)
On A480
☏ (05448) 210
Bulmer (E)
16th century timber framed inn which was once a cidermill with its own orchard. Meals and snacks; restaurant; garden; accommodation; games room.

Much Marcle

LYNE DOWN CIDER ▲
Lyne Down Farm (off A449 Ross road $1\frac{1}{2}$ miles south of village)
☏ (053184) 691

WESTON'S CIDER

Bounds
☎ (053184) 233

Orleton

Weekdays: 11–2.30; 6–11

Boot Inn (P)
On old road through village centre, just off B4361 midway between Leominster and Ludlow
☎ (056885) 228
Westons Old Rosie (PC)
Old rambling half timbered village inn: once a butcher's shop with a slaughter house at the back, then became a pub cum small holding selling rough cider. Meals and snacks all sessions; garden.

Pembridge

DUNKERTON'S CIDER ▲
Hays Head, Luntley
☎ (05447) 653

Weekdays: 11–3; 6–11

New Inn (P)
Market Square
☎ (04547) 427
Bulmer (H)
Dates from 1311, and dominates this picture book village. Meals and snacks; restaurant; garden; accommodation.

Weekdays: 12–3; 7–11

Red Lion (P)
☎ (04557) 473
Westons Old Rosie (PC) (J)
Traditional country pub with beams and log fires. Bar snacks and meals all opening hours; accommodation.

Monday–Tuesday, Thursday–Saturday: 6.30–5.30, Wednesday and Sunday: 6.30–1

Ye Olde Steppes Stores (OL)
High Street
☎ (05447) 310
Dunkerton (B)

Peterchurch

Boughton Arms Hotel (P)
On B4348
☎ (09816) 208
Weston (PC)
Nearby is a fine Norman church, restored with a fibre glass spire! Snacks lunchtime and evenings; meals evenings; restaurant, garden; accommodation; a clean air pub.

Nags Head (P)
☎ (09816) 271
Weston (PC)

Peterstow

BROOME FARM CIDER ▲
Broome Farm
☎ (0989) 62824

Red Lion Inn (P)
On A49 at Winters Cross
☎ (098987) 202
Broome Farm (PC)
A nice change – a closed pub which has been reopened! Meals and snacks; garden.

Pixley

Weekdays: 11–2.30; 6.30–11, Sunday: 12–2.30; 7–10.30

Trumpet Inn (P)
At junction of A438 and A417
☎ (053183) 277
Weston (PC)
400 year old timber framed pub. Snacks all times; garden.

Ridgeway Cross

PULLEN FARM CIDER ▲
The Country Produce Store, Pullens Farm (on B4220 half a mile off A449)
☎ (088684) 599

Ross on Wye

7.30–10 All Week

Gwalia (OL)
27–29 Broad Street
☎ (0989) 63282
Dunkerton (PC) (B)
Farmers Tipple (J) (PL)
Weston (PC) (DJ) (J)
Old fashioned shop with original signs inside and out.

Monday–Friday: 10–3, Saturday: 10–11

Horse & Jockey Inn (P)
New Street
☎ (0989) 768180
Westons Old Rosie (PC)
Weston (J)
Bulmer (PC)
Quiet back street local. Snacks lunchtime; skittle alley.

Man of Ross (P)
Wye Street
☎ (0989) 64597
Weston (PC)
Jacobean pub in town centre. Snacks lunchtime and evenings.

Monday: 10–2.30, Tuesday–Saturday: 10.30–2.30; 7–9.30

Meaders Hungarian Restaurant (P)
1 Copse Cross Street
☎ (0989) 62803
Dunkerton (B)

Weekdays: 9.30–5.30, Sunday (in summer): 11–6

Patio Cafe (P)
45 High Street
☎ (0989) 62217
Dunkerton (B)

Pencraig Hotel (P)
☎ (098984) 306
Dunkerton (B)
Country hotel.

Weekdays: 11–11

Rosswyn Hotel (P)
17 High Street
☎ (0989) 62733
Broome Farm (PP)
15th century freehouse with notable wall carvings, beams, and four poster beds. Snacks 12–10; meals 7.30–9.30; restaurant; outdoor drinking area/garden.

Ryefield House Hotel
Gloucester Road
☎ (0989) 63030
Dunkerton (B)
Accommodation.

Weekdays: 10–11

Stag (P)
5 Henry Street
☎ (0989) 62893
Bulmer (W)
Enthusiastic cider pub near bus stop: use it while you wait!

St. Owens Cross

Weekdays: 11.30–2.30; 6.30–11

New Inn (P)
at junction of A4137 and B4251, 4 miles west of Ross on Wye
☎ (098987) 274
Weston (H) – summer only
The inn was actually "new" in 1540: a posting inn, with

the great half timbered barn used for stabling and changing the horses: fine settles and carved bar in lounge. Meals and snacks lunchtime and evenings (last orders 9.30); garden; accommodation; caravan site nearby.

Stoke Lacy

SYMONDS' CIDER ▲
Symonds Cider & English Wine Company, Cider Mills & Winery
☏ (08853) 411

Storridge

KNIGHT'S CIDER ▲
Crumpton Oaks Fruit Farm
☏ (0684) 574594

Symonds Yat

Saracens Head (P)
☏ (0600) 890435
Weston (PC) (J)
On bank of River Wye, with a passenger ferry; ideal area for canoeing, camping, walking and fishing. Meals and snacks lunchtime and evenings; restaurant; children's room; garden; accommodation.

Symonds Yat West

Weekdays: 11–11 (summer): 11–2.30; 6–11 (winter)

Ye Olde Ferrie Inne (P)
just off B4164
☏ (0600) 890232
Bulmer (PC)
Riverside setting; ferry crossing. Meals and snacks 11–2; 7–10; restaurant; riverside patio and picnic area; accommodation; cream teas; gift shop; boat hire.

Tarrington

Foley Arms (P)
On A438
☏ (043279) 217
Weston (H)
Georgian red brick hotel in village surrounded by hop fields; fine Norman church nearby. Snacks lunchtime and Monday–Thursday evenings; large garden; accommodation.

Weobley

Weekdays: 10–11

Jules Cafe (P)
Broad Street
☏ (0544) 318206
Dunkerton (B)

Weekdays: 8–5.30

R. E. Williams & Sons (OL)
8 Broad Street
☏ (0544) 318205
Dunkerton (B)

Whitney on Wye

Weekdays: 11–2.30; 7.30–11

Rhydspence Inn (P)
In lay-by off A483 on Welsh border
☏ (04973) 262
Dunkerton (H)
Timber framed 14th century inn in Kilvert country near Hay on Wye. Meals and snacks, lunchtime and evenings; restaurant; large garden with superb views; accommodation; access for disabled to bar, but not to toilets.

Wigmore

Weekdays: 11–11, Sunday: 12–3; 7–10.30

Ye Olde Oak Inn (P)
☏ (056886) 247
Weston (PC)
Old world inn with inglenook fireplace. Meals all times; restaurant; garden; accommodation; camping facilities nearby.

Woolhope

Weekdays: 11–2.30; 6–11

Crown Inn (P)
In village centre near church
☏ (043277) 468
Bulmer (H)
300 year old village local. Meals and snacks all sessions; garden.

Yarpole

Weekdays: 11.30–3; 6.30–11

Bell Inn (P)
Green Lane (off B4361, near church)
☏ (056885) 359
Bulmer (H)
17th century black and white village pub in beautiful surroundings: adjacent cider mill has been converted into lounge bar. Meals and snacks lunchtime and evenings till 10.30; children's room; garden.

Worcestershire

Arley

New Inn (P)
Pound Green
☏ (0299) 401271
Weston (H)
Near Severn Valley Railway station.

Astley Burf

Weekdays: 11.30–2.30; 6–11

Hampstall Inn (P)
On B4196
☏ (02993) 2600
Bulmer (H)
Used to be a cider house: on the bank of the River Severn. Meals lunchtime and evenings; private fishing; moorings for patrons.

Berrow

Duke of York (P)
Rye Cross
Weston (PC)
Friendly pub with two bar areas. Good value food Wednesday to Sunday. Large garden.

Berrow Green

Weekdays: 12–3; 6.30–11

Admiral Rodney (P)
1 mile south of Martley on B4197
☏ (0886) 21375
Westons Old Rosie (PC)
Ancient pub with superb views, on Worcester Way long distance footpath. Meals and snacks 12–3; 6.30–10; restaurant; children's room; outdoor drinking area/garden; accommodation; access for disabled; camping facilities in grounds.

Bewdley

Weekdays: 10–10, Sunday: 12–2; 7–10

Tipplers (OL)
70 Load Street

☎ (0299) 403354
Dunkerton (B)
Knights Crumpton Oaks (W)
Weston (PC) (B) (J)

Bredon

Weekdays: 12–2.30; 7–11

Royal Oak Inn (P)

☎ (0684) 72393
Bulmer (H)
Old coaching inn with traditional interior. Bar food lunchtime and evenings; garden.

Bretforton

Weekdays: 10–3; 6–11

Fleece (P)

The Cross (50 yards off B4035)
☎ (0386) 831173
Westons Farm Brand (PC)
Westons Old Rosie (PC)
14th century farmhouse, converted into a pub in 1848, and now owned by the National Trust: interior unchanged for many years. Meals and snacks lunchtime and evenings; children's room; garden; access for disabled; camping facilities nearby.

Royal British Legion Club (P)

Black Bull (PC)

Broadway

Arnolds (OL)

99 High Street
☎ (0386) 852427
Black Bull (PC)

9–5 Every day from August–Christmas

Cotswold Orchards (OL)

☎ (0386) 45241
Weston (PC)

Crown & Trumpet Inn (P)

Church Street
☎ (0386) 853202
Bulmer (H)
Cotswold stone pub in tourist centre. The locals have their own cider mugs and cider horns which they all use! Meals and snacks all sessions; garden; accommodation.

Caunsall

Weekdays: 11–3.30; 7–11, Sunday: 12–3; 7–10.30

Anchor Inn (P)

High Street
☎ (0562) 850254
Bulmer (PC)
Country pub near Staffordshire and Worcestershire Canal. Snacks lunchtime and evenings; outdoor drinking area; camping facilities nearby.

Claines

Weekdays: 11–11, Sunday: 12–3; 7–10.30

Mug House (P)

Claines Lane
☎ (0905) 56649
Weston (PC)
Over 600 years old, believed to be the only pub in England in a churchyard. Bar snacks all day; outdoor drinking area/garden; camping facilities nearby (*not* in the churchyard!)

Conderton

Weekdays: 11–3; 6–11, Sunday: 12–3; 7–10.30

Yew Tree (P)

☎ (038689) 364
Westons Old Rosie (H)
16th century village pub under Bredon Hill. Bar snacks every lunchtime, 12–2; evenings 7–10 except Tuesday.

Cookley

Weekdays: 11–3; 6–11

Bulls Head (P)

Bridge Road
☎ (0384) 850242
Weston (PC)
Village pub near Staffordshire and Worcestershire Canal – an ideal overnight mooring venue. Snacks and meals all opening hours; children's room; outdoor drinking area/garden camping facilities nearby.

Defford

Monkey House (P)

☎ (0386) 750234
Bulmer Special Dry (W)
Unmarked and unspoilt, a genuine cider house: a rare chance to experience the past!

Droitwich

Gardeners Arms (P)

Vines Lane
☎ (0905) 772936
Weston (PC)
Pleasant, friendly pub opposite the park. Lunchtime snacks.

Eckington

Bell (P)

☎ (0386) 750205
Bulmer (PC)
Friendly pub near bridge over the Avon. Snacks lunchtime; children welcome inside when wet (the weather, not the children!); garden.

Weekdays: 11–3; 6–11

Crown Inn (P)

Church Street
☎ (0386) 750472
Bulmer (PC)
Cosy atmosphere, inglenook fireplace, in village pub. Meals and snacks 11–2; 6.30–10; children's room; garden; pool room.

Elmley Castle

Monday–Friday: 11–2.30; 6–10.30, Sunday: 12–2; 7–10.30 (closed Saturday)

Plough (P)

☎ (0386) 74269
Home Made (H)
A pub which makes its own cider – beer hardly gets a look in! Bredon Hill is conveniently nearby for you to walk off the after affects, should you need to. Meals lunchtime.

Evesham

Weekdays: 11–11, Sunday: 12–3; 7–10.30

Angel Vaults (P)

Port Street
☎ (0386) 47188
Bulmer (H)

Beewell (OL)

Vine Street
☎ (0386) 443757
Dunkerton (B)
Health food and delicatessen.

Boaters Wine Bar (P)

58 Bridge Street
☎ (0386) 2349
Dunkerton (B)
Wine bar and brasserie near

River Avon, good overnight moorings nearby.

Evesham Working Mens Club (P)
8 Merstow Green
☏ (0386) 2069
Black Bull (PC)

Fairfield Inn (P)
Battleton Road
☏ (0386) 41292
Bulmer (H)

Robbins (OL)
33–35 Port Street
☏ (0386) 6161
Black Bull (PC)
Licensed tea room adjacent: coffee; light lunches; high teas – Monday to Saturday 9–5.

Royal Oak (P)
Vine Street
☏ (0386) 2465
Bulmer (H)

Feckenham

Lygon Arms (P)
☏ (052789) 3495
Bulmer (H)

Fladbury

Craycombe Farm Shop (OL)
☏ (0386) 860732
Black Bull (PC)
Dunkerton (B)

Grimley

Weekdays: 11–3; 6–11, Sunday: 12–3; 7–10.30

Camp House Inn (P)
Camp Lane (Off A443)
☏ (0905) 640288
Bulmer (E)
Unspoilt pub on banks of River Severn. Snacks 12–2; 6–8; children's room; garden.

Hallow

Thursday, Saturday, Sunday: 12–2.30, Monday–Wednesday, Friday: 7–11

Fox Inn (P)
Monkwood Green
☏ (08866) 326
Weston (PC)
Common land and woods; nature conservation area. Garden.

Hampton

Working Mens Club (P)
Workman Road
☏ (0386) 2719
Black Bull (PC)

Harvington

Weekdays: 12–3; 5.30–11

Dog Inn (P)
Worcester Road (north of Evesham)
☏ (056283) 253
Westons Old Rosie (H)
Old coaching inn. Bar snacks 12–2; 5.30–9.30; meals 12–2; 7–10; restaurant; outdoor drinking area/garden; children's play area; camping facilities nearby; barbecues.

Headless Cross

Weekdays: 12–11, Sunday: 12–3; 7–10.30

Seven Stars (P)
75 Birchfield Road
☏ (0527) 402138
Bulmer (H)
Three roomed locals' pub: public bar, lounge and games room. Superb value lunchtime meals.

Himbleton

Galton Arms (P)
Near Droitwich
☏ (090569) 672
Weston (PC)
Village local in beautiful setting. Meals and snacks except Monday lunchtime; restaurant; garden.

Kempsey

Weekdays: 12–3; 6–11

Queens Head (P)
Main Road
☏ (0905) 820572
Bulmer (PC)
Oak beamed bars. Snacks lunchtime; garden with play area and patio.

Kidderminster

Boars Head (P)
Worcester Street
☏ (0562) 740004
Weston (PC)
Town centre pub near main shopping centre. Lunchtime meals.

Chester Tavern (P)
Chester Road North
☏ (0562) 740184
Bulmer (H)
Lively local with a warm welcome. Snacks.

Monday–Friday: 11–2.30; 6–11, Saturday: 11–11

Coopers Arms (P)
Canterbury Road
☏ (0562) 745413
Weston (PC)

Horn & Trumpet (P)
Park Lane
☏ (0562) 69512
Weston (PC)

Weekdays: 10–11, Sunday: 12–3; 7–10.30

Prince Albert (P)
Bewdley Road
☏ (0562) 753705
Bulmer (PC)
Good cider plus warm and friendly service! Bar snacks all times; children's room; outdoor drinking area/garden. Near Kidderminster BR station.

Weekdays: 11.30–3; 6.30–11

Woodfield Tavern (P)
Woodfield Street
☏ (0562) 740173
Bulmer (PC)
A back street local.

Leigh Sinton

BLACK BULL CIDER ▲
Norbury's Cider Company, Crowcroft
☏ (0886) 23306

Littleton

Littleton & Cleeve Prior Royal British Legion Club (P)
School Lane, Middle Littleton
☏ (0386) 830439
Black Bull (PC)

Lower Broadheath

Monday–Friday: 12–3; 6–11, Saturday: 11–11, Sunday: 12–3; 7–10.30

Dew Drop Inn (P)
Bell Lane
☏ (0905) 641774
Westons Old Rosie (PC)
Country pub in small village on Elgar route. Bar snacks 12–2; 7–9 except Sundays; children's room; award

winning garden; lots of children's play equipment.

Malvern

Mill Farm Shop (OL)
Mill Farm, Guarlford Road
☏ (06845) 69861
Dunkerton (B)

Oak Inn (P)
Worcester Road, Malvern Link
☏ (06845) 4756
Weston (H)

Phillips Off Licence (OL)
Court Road
Weston (J)

Red Lion (P)
St. Annes Road
☏ (06845) 3563
Weston (PC)
Town centre pub. Snacks lunchtime; restaurant.

Warwick House (OL)
Wells Road
☏ (06845) 61721
Dunkerton (B)

Offenham

Weekdays: 7–11

Offenham Royal British Legion Club (P)
Main Street
Black Bull (PC)

Overbury

Weekdays: 11–3; 6–11

Star Inn (P)
Crashmore Lane
☏ (038689) 316
Bulmer (H)
Meals available until 9 weekdays, 9.30 weekends; children's menu; room where children can eat with parents; garden; accommodation.

Peopleton

Crown Inn (P)
☏ (0905) 840222
Bulmer (H)
Welcoming pub with strikingly attractive exterior. Bar food.

Pershore

Monday–Friday: 11.30–3; 6.30–11, Saturday: 11.30–4; 6.30–11

Talbot Inn (P)
52 Newland
☏ (0386) 553575
Bulmer (H)
In back street near Abbey. Meals all sessions; garden.

Monday–Thursday: 11–3.30; 6–11, Friday: 11–4.30; 6–11, Saturday: 11–11

Victoria Hotel (P)
60 Newland
☏ (0386) 553662
Bulmer (E)
Near Pershore Abbey. Meals all sessions; garden.

Redditch

Waggon & Horses (P)
Beoley Road
☏ (0527) 62183
Bulmer (H)

Wine Rack (OL)
Mason Road
Weston (J)

Monday–Friday: 12–2.30; 6–11, Saturday: 12–4; 6–11

Woodland Cottage (P)
Mount Pleasant
☏ (0527) 402299
Weston (PC) (H)
Attractive small town pub. Bar snacks 12–2; outdoor drinking area/garden; access for disabled. Near Redditch BR station.

Shenstone

Weekdays: 11–3; 6.30–11

Plough (P)
Just off A450 3 miles south east of Kidderminster
☏ (056283) 340
Weston (PC)
Despite its proximity to the urban Midlands, everything a good rural local pub should be. Snacks; families welcome; garden.

Stourport

Clifford (P)
Lower Lickhill Road
☏ (02993) 3899
Weston (PC)

Tenbury Wells

Clockhouse Grocers (OL)
14 Market Street
☏ (0584) 810596
Weston (J)

Weekdays: 11–2.30; 6–11

Crow Hotel & Spa Room (P)
Teme Street
☏ (0584) 810503
Weston (PC)
Pleasant hotel near River Teme. Bar lunches; restaurant.

Tenbury Butchers (OL)
23 Teme Street
☏ (0584) 810266
Weston (J)

Wickhamford

Weekdays: 10–2.30; 7–11

Sandys Arms (P)
☏ (0386) 830535
Bulmer (H)

Wolverley

Weekdays: 11.30–2.30; 6–11

Lock Inn (P)
Wolverley Road
☏ (0562) 850581
Bulmer (PC) (H)
On Staffordshire and Worcestershire Canal, with lock in grounds. Open fires, no juke box. Meals and snacks 11.30–2.15; 6.30–9; outdoor drinking area; camping facilities nearby; Lock Stock and Barrel Folk Club on Friday evenings.

Worcester

Berwick Arms (P)
250 Bath Road
☏ (0905) 351335
Weston (H)

Monday–Friday: 11.30–2.30; 5–11, Saturday: 11.30–11, Sunday 12–3; 7–10.30

Brewery Tap (P)
50 Lowesmoor
☏ (0905) 21540
Severn Cyder (H)
Pleasant pub full of atmosphere – no mod cons to spoil the style of this traditional English drinking house – good cider and good food.

Weekdays: 11.30–2.30; 5.30–11

Crown & Anchor (P)
233 Hylton Road
☏ (0905) 421481
Bulmer (PC)
Pub by River Severn. Snacks lunchtime all week; garden; skittle alley.

Food for Thought (OL)
20 Mealcheapen Street
☏ (0905) 29537
Dunkerton (B)
Delicatessen and restaurant.

Gun Tavern (P)
Newtown Road
☏ (0905) 352335
Weston (H)

Melbourne Street Stores (OL)
36 Melbourne Street
☏ (0905) 25720
Black Bull

Weekdays: 11.30–2.30; 5.30–11, Sunday: 12–3; 7–10.30

Mount Pleasant Inn (P)
London Road
☏ (0905) 351282
Westons Old Rosie (PC) (H)
Looks very small from outside, but is deceptively spacious. Meals and snacks 12–2; 7–9; garden. Near Worcester Shrub Hill BR station.

Northwick Arms (P)
Vine Street
☏ (0905) 51379
Weston (H)
Pleasant side street pub wth garden. Snacks.

Pause for Thought (OL)
159 London Road
☏ (0905) 360458
Weston (J)

Wheatsheaf (P)
192 Henwick Road
☏ (0905) 423077
Weston (PC)
Pleasant pub overlooking racecourse and the River Severn. Garden. Snacks.

Weekdays: 9.15–6

Worcester Wine Cellars (OL)
Cornmarket
☏ (0905) 26228
Weston (PC)

Wythall

Weekdays: 11–2; 6–10

Hollywood Wines (OL)
Hollywood Lane
☏ (021) 430 7692
Bulmer (PC) (W)
Langdon (PP) (J) (PL)
Weston (PC) (J)
Near Crimes Hill BR station.

The Cider Museum, Hereford.

Hertfordshire

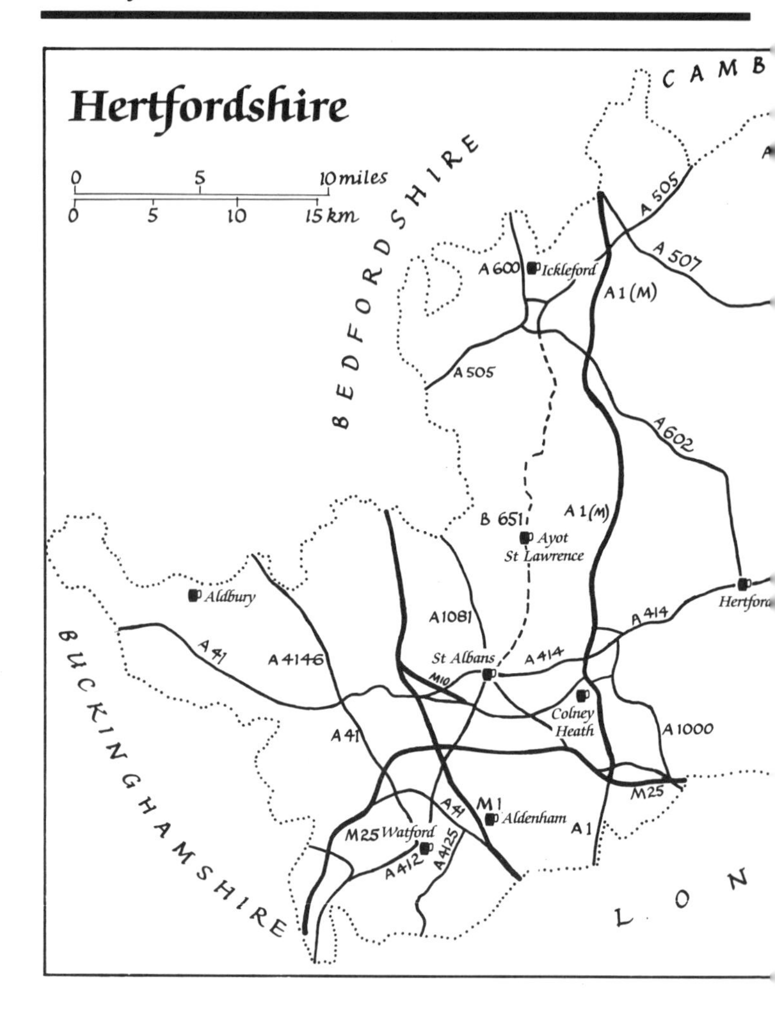

Aldbury

Monday–Friday: 12–3; 6–11, Saturday: 12–11, Sunday: 12–3; 7–10.30

Valiant Trooper (P)

Trooper Road
☏ (044385) 203
Weston (H)
Popular and pretty village local with tiled public bar with wood burning stove. Two quieter rooms lie beyond and there is a garden out the back. Meals.

Aldenham

All day all week

Church Farm Shop (OL)

Old Radlett Road
☏ (0923) 857443
Westons Old Rosie (PC)
Westons Vintage (PC)
Westons Perry (PC)
Also sell real ale, bread, cheese and homemade pies, plus full range of farm produce. Snacks and tea room in summer; children's room; accommodation.

Ayot St. Lawrence

Weekdays: 11.30–2.30, Sunday: 12–2; 7–10.30

Brocket Arms (P)

Shaws Corner
☏ (0438) 820250
Lane (PC)
15th century inn near George Bernard Shaw's home, now owned by National Trust. A la carte meals; garden.

Barley

Weekdays: 12–2.30; 6–11

Fox & Hounds (P)

High Street (on B1368)
☏ (076384) 459
Bulmer (H)
The inn dates from the 15th century, and the timber framed building was converted from a farmhouse in 1797: in centre of a conservation area. Meals and snacks all sessions; restaurant; garden.

Colney Heath

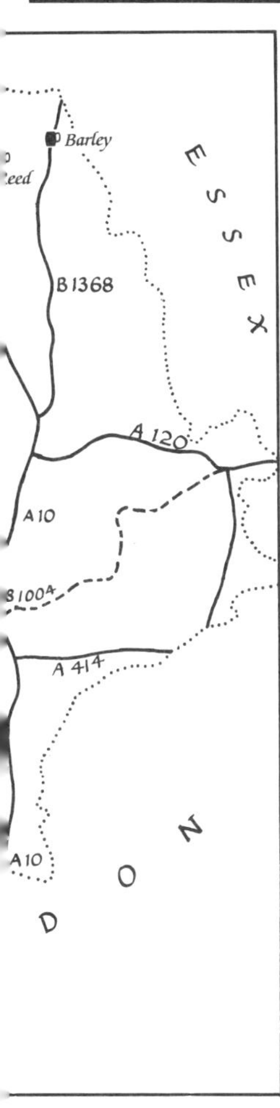

Weekdays: 11–11

Crooked Billet (P)
88 High Street
☎ (0272) 22128
Guest ciders (PC)
Unspoilt cottage style village pub. Meals and snacks lunchtime and evening; garden with mini zoo; access for disabled; camping facilities nearby; folk singing Thursday evenings.

Hertford

Monday–Friday: 12–2.30; 5.30–11, Saturday: 12–3; 7–11, Sunday: 12–3; 7–10.30

White Horse (P)
33 Castle Street
☎ (0992) 550127
Zum (PC)
Guest ciders (PC)
Tiny town centre free house. Lunchtime food weekdays; no music or fruit machines.

Ickleford

Monday–Wednesday: 11–3, Thursday–Friday: 11–4, Saturday: 11–11

Cricketers (P)
107 Arlesley Road (off A600)
☎ (0462) 32629
Westons Scrumpy (PC)
Westons Old Rosie (H)
Lively village alehouse, warm, friendly and comfortable. Good value food (not Sunday) includes vegetarian option. Carpet bowls and shut-the-box played. Garden and overnight accommodation.

Reed

Weekdays: 10.30–2.30; 5.30–11

Cabinet (P)
High Street (turn off A10 opposite transport cafe, then first right and first left)
☎ (076384) 366
Westons Old Rosie (H)
Comfortable weather boarded building with large garden. Difficult to find but worth trying. Meals.

St. Albans

Weekdays: 11.15–2.30 (3 on Saturday); 5.30–11.

Rose & Crown (P)
St. Michaels Street (400 yards off A4147
☎ (0727) 51903
Various guest ciders (PC)
About a mile from city centre, but well worth the walk: a Georgian pub behind a brick facade. The nearby Kingsbury Water Mill Museum should also be visited. The ciders usually include some rare varieties. Snacks lunchtime; patio garden at rear; folk music on Thursday nights.

Watford

Blakes (P)
96 Queens Road
☎ (0923) 247697
Weston (H)
Meals and snacks all sessions; outdoor drinking area. Near Watford Junction BR station.

West Herts Sports Club (P)
Park Avenue
☎ (0923) 229239
Symonds (PC)
Bar snacks and meals; children's room; outdoor drinking area. Near Watford Junction BR station.

Isle of Wight

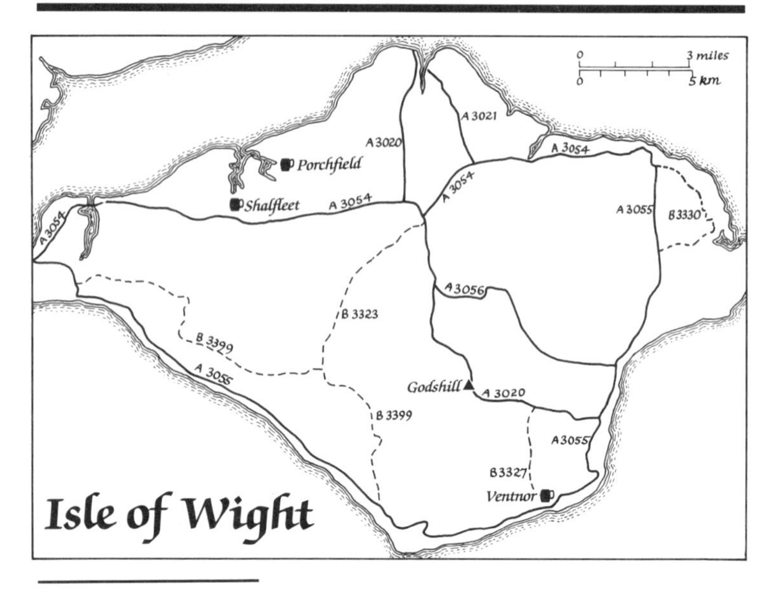

Godshill

GODSHILL FARMHOUSE CIDER ▲
The Cider Barn
☎ (0983) 840680

Porchfield

Porchfield Stores (OL)
North of A3054 west of Parkhurst Forest
Inch (J) (PL)
Village stores supplying all grocery and household needs.

Shalfleet

Weekdays: 11–11 (summer)

New Inn (P)
Yarmouth Road (A3054)
☎ (098378) 314
Bulmer (H)
A popular venue for yachtsmen. Specialises in fresh fish: meals and snacks all sessions; terrace.

Ventnor

Weekdays: 10.30–11.30, Sunday: 12–3; 7–10.30

Blenheim (P)
9 High Street
☎ (0983) 853633
Bulmer (H)
Pleasant little town pub of character. Snacks.

Vinetum Britannicum:
OR A
TREATISE
OF
CIDER,
And other Wines and Drinks extracted from Fruits Growing in this Kingdom.
With the Method of Propagating all ſorts of Vinous FRUIT-TREES.
And a DESCRIPTION of the New-Invented INGENIO or MILL,
For the more expeditious making of *CIDER*.
And alſo the right way of making METHEGLIN and BIRCH-WINE.

The Second Impreſſion; much Enlarged.

To which is added, A Diſcourſe teaching the beſt way of Improving BEES.

With Copper Plates.

By *J. Worlidge*. Gent.

LONDON,
Printed for *Thomas Dring*, over againſt the Inner-Temple-gate; and *Thomas Burrel*, at the Golden-ball under St *Dunſtan's* Church in *Fleet-ſtreet*. 1678.

Kent

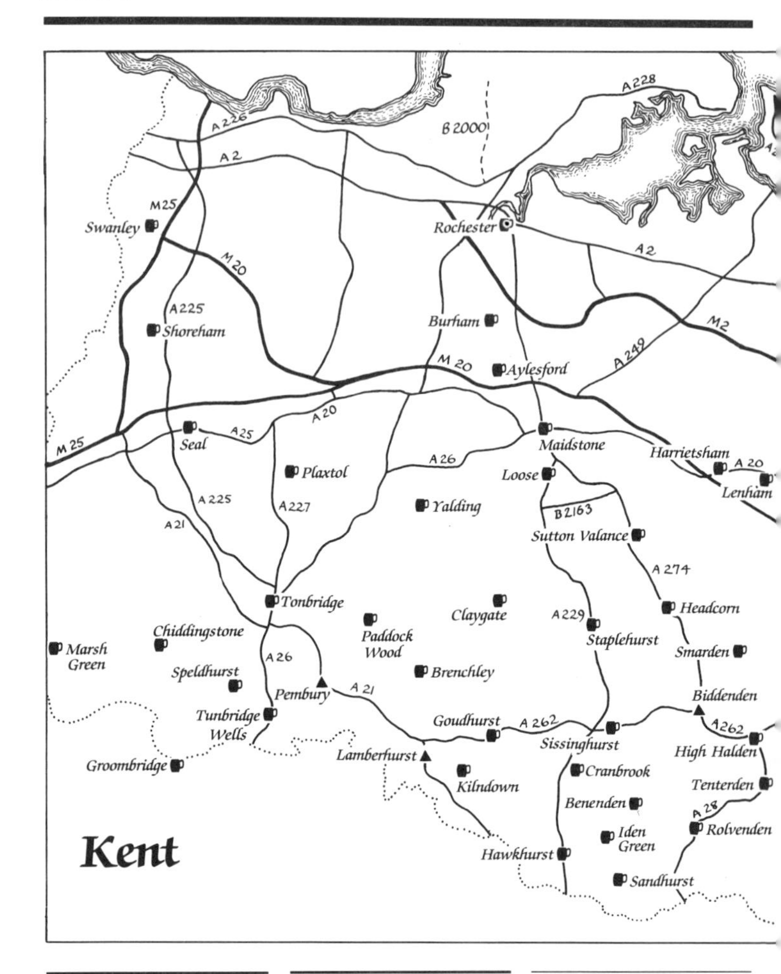

Aldington

Post Office Stores (OL)
☏ (023372) 246
Biddenden (B)

Appledore Heath

Victoria Arms (P)
1 mile north of Appledore
☏ (023383) 359
Biddenden (PC)
Snacks; garden.

Ash

Weekdays: 8–10, Sunday: 10–10

Poparound (OL)
31 The Street
☏ (0304) 812251
Theobolds (J)

Ashford

Weekdays: 11–10

Beaver Road Off Licence (OL)
36 Beaver Road
☏ (0233) 622904
Biddenden (PC) (BB) (PL)
Thatcher (PC) (BB) (PL)
Near Ashford BR station.

Bottles (OL)
31 Court Wurtin,
Beaver Lane
☏ (0233) 28660
Biddenden (PC)

Bungalow Stores (OL)
212 Kingsnorth Road
Biddenden (B)

Wheatsheaf (P)
66 Lower Denmark Road
☏ (0233) 621807
Biddenden (PC)

Aylesford

Weekdays: 11–2.30; 6–11

Little Gem (P)
19 High Street
☏ (0622) 717510
Biddenden (PC)
Kent's smallest pub, dating from 12th century. Bar snacks 12–2. Near Aylesford BR station.

Barfreston

Yew Tree (P)
☏ (0304) 830288
Theobold (PL)
Meals and snacks.

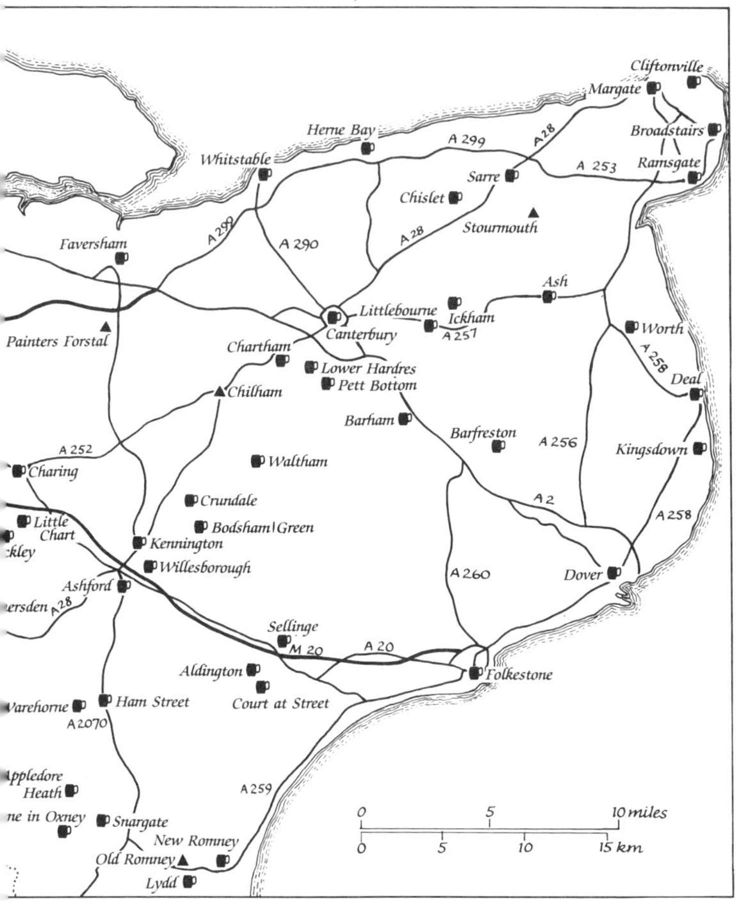

Barham

Weekdays: 11–3; 6–11, Sunday: 12–3; 7–10.30

Duke of Cumberland (P)

The Street
☏ (0227) 831396
Bulmer (H)
Friendly village local. Bar snacks 12–2; 6–9; meals 6–9; children's room and play area; garden; pets corner; accommodation; access for disabled; caravan park.

Benenden

Weekdays: 8.30–1; 2.15–5 (half day Wednesday)

Benenden Stores and Post Office (OL)

The Street
☏ (0580) 240508
Biddenden (B)

Bethersden

Weekdays: 11–2.30; 6–11

Royal Standard (P)

Ashford Road (A28)
☏ (023382) 280
Biddenden (J)
Well restored country pub with good views over the Weald. Meals and snacks 12–2; 7–9.30; garden.

Biddenden

BIDDENDEN CIDER ▲

Biddenden Vineyards Ltd., 'Little Whatmans'
☏ (0580) 291726

Monday–Tuesday, Thursday–Saturday: 8–1; 2–5.30, Wednesday 8–1

Post Office (OL)

24 High Street
☏ (0580) 291201
Biddenden (B)

Weekdays: 11–2.30; 6–11

Red Lion (P)

High Street
☏ (0580) 291347
Biddenden (B)
15th century inn at heart of medieval village. The sign on the green opposite commemorates the famous Siamese twins who lived in the village in the 16th century. Meals and snacks 11.30–1.30; 7–9.30; restaurant; garden; accommodation.

Weekdays: 11–2.30; 6–11, Sunday 12–2.30; 7–10.30

Three Chimneys (P)

On A262 west of village

☏ (0580) 291472
Biddenden (PC)
The pub is said to have been given its name by French prisoners of war from the nearby Sissinghurst Castle during the Seven Years War, a corruption of "Trois chemins" – or "three ways", after the adjacent road junction. Meals and snacks 11.30–2; 6.30–10; restaurant; children's room; garden.

Turners Stores (OL)
2 High Street
☏ (0580) 291205
Biddenden (B)

Woodlands Filling Station (OL)
Tenterden Road (B2082)
☏ (0580) 291473
Biddenden (B)

Bodsham Green

Weekdays: 11.30–2.30; 6.30–11, Sunday: 2–3; 7–10.30

Timber Batts Inn (P)
2½ miles off Stone Street (B2068)
☏ (023375) 237
Biddenden (PC)
Extensive range of home made hot and cold bar snacks and lunches; restaurant open by reservation Monday–Saturday; spacious gardens with play facilities for children.

Brenchley

Monday–Tuesday, Thursday–Friday: 8.30–1; 2.15–5.30, Wednesday, Saturday: 8.30–1

Bournes Stores (OL)
High Street
☏ (089272) 2066
Biddenden (B)

Brenchley Wine Co (OL)
The Bournes, High Street
☏ (089272) 3094
Biddenden (B)

Broadstairs

Continental Corner (OL)
13 Charlotte Street
☏ (0843) 61766
Biddenden (B)

Burham

Weekdays: 12–3.30; 6–11, Sunday: 12–3; 7–10.30

Toastmaster Inn (P)
65 Church Street
☏ (0634) 61299
Weston (PC)
Zum (PC)
Popular free house with a collection of pewter tankards. Good quality home cooked bar meals 12–2; 7–10 every day; restaurant open on Friday and Saturday.

Canterbury

Weekdays: 11–10

The Beer Shop (OL)
83 Northgate
☏ (0227) 457839
Biddenden (PC)
Theobold (PC)

Weekdays: 11–3; 6–11

Cherry Tree (P)
Whitehorse Lane
☏ (0227) 451266
Biddenden (H)
Snacks lunchtime and evenings. Town pub just off main street.

Monday–Friday: 11–2.30; 7–11, Saturday: 11–11, Sunday: 12–2.30; 7–10.30

Falstaff Tap (P)
St. Dunstans Street (near Westgate)
☏ (0227) 462138
Bulmer (H)
Pleasant old pub refurbished with stripped wood decor. Snacks.

Weekdays: 11–11

Rose & Crown (P)
76 St. Dunstans Street
☏ (0227) 463583
Bulmer (H)
Pub with garden and offering overnight accommodation. Occasional discos.

Simple Simons (P)
3 Church Lane, St. Radigunds
☏ (0227) 762355
Theobold (E)
Near Canterbury West BR station.

Charing

Weekdays: 9–1; 2.15–5.15, Sunday: 10–1

The Charing Stores (OL)
4 High Street
☏ (023371) 2325
Biddenden (B)

Wady & Brett (OL)
High Street
☏ (023371) 2318
Biddenden (B)
Near Charing BR station.

Chartham

George Inn (P)
Shalmsford Street
☏ (0227) 738253
Theobold (PC)
Noted for its outstanding real food. Restaurant attached.

Chatham

Monday–Thursday: 10–10, Friday–Saturday: 9 am–10.30 pm, Sunday 12–3; 7–10.30.

Wine Trader (OL)
3–5 Watling Street
☏ (0634) 578267
Biddenden (B)
Also an excellent range of scrumpy ciders.

Chiddingstone

Weekdays: 11–3; 6–11, Sunday: 12–3; 7–10.30

Castle Inn (P)
☏ (0892) 870247
Biddenden (PC)
Ancient pub in preserved village, an ideal place to wait for the *other* castle to open. Bar food 11–2.45; 6–10.45 during week; 12–2.45; 7–10.15 on Sunday; restaurant open 12–2; 7.30–9.30; children welcome in all eating areas; garden.

Chilham

Browns Kitchen Shop (OL)
High Street
☏ (0227) 730597
Theobold (PC)

PIPPIN CIDER ▲
Badgers Hill Fruit Farm (on Chilham bypass–A252)
☏ (0227) 730537

Chislet

Weekdays: 12–11, Sunday: 12–3; 7–10.30

Six Bells Inn (P)
☏ (022786) 373
Biddenden (PC)
Fully restored Georgian pub with wealth of panelling;

open log fires, and a regency cooking range. Snacks all opening hours; meals 12–3; 7–10; children's room; outdoor drinking area and garden; accommodation; access for disabled; camping facilities nearby.

Claygate

Weekdays: 11–3; 6–11, Sunday: 12–3; 7–10.30

White Hart (P)
On B2162 south of Collier Street
☏ (089273) 313
Biddenden (H)
Comfortable country inn with log fires. Meals and snacks 12–2.30; 7–10 (morning coffee from 10.30); restaurant; large garden with table service; camping facilities nearby. Booking is advised for meals at weekends: essential on Sunday.

Cliftonville

Dane Wine Merchants (OL)
57 Upper Dane Road
☏ (0843) 290085
Theobold (B)

Court at Street

Welcome Stranger (P)
On B2067
☏ (023372) 400
Biddenden (PC)
Small, quiet one-bar pub ideal for a chat and a pint or two. On the hills above Romney Marsh, near Port Lymne Zoo Park and Gardens. Snacks.

Cranbrook

Monday–Tuesday; Thursday–Saturday: 9–1; 2–5.30, Wednesday: 9–1

Perfect Partners (OL)
7 Stone Street
☏ (0580) 712633
Biddenden (B)

Crundale

Weekdays: 11.30–2.30; 6.30–11 (closed Mondays except Bank Holidays)

Compasses (P)
Sole Street
☏ (022770) 300
Biddenden (PC)
A 16th century show place on the North Downs above Wye. Meals all sessions except Sunday evening; children's room; garden.

Deal

Grocery Basket (OL)
56 Church Lane
Theobold (B)

Dover

Tuesday–Friday: 12–2; 6.30–10, Saturday: 6.30–10

Cabin Restaurant (P)
91 High Street
☏ (0304) 206118
Biddenden (PC)
Traditional English cooking. Biddenden Special Reserve and Perry also available in bottles.

Park Inn (P)
1–2 Park Place, Ladywell
☏ (0304) 206471
Bulmer (H)
Rambling and spacious free house close to historic Maison Dieu and convenient for Priory Station, Children's room.

Triangle Newsmart (OL)
1 Bewsbury Cross Lane, Whitfield
☏ (0304) 821488
Biddenden (B)

Weekdays: 9–10

Unwins (OL)
13 Worthington Street
☏ (0304) 201406
Biddenden (W) (DJ)

Weekdays: 11–11

White Horse (P)
St. James Street
☏ (0304) 202911
Bulmer (H)
A rare survival of old Dover, with long established rowing club connections. Meals lunch-time; children's room; outdoor drinking area.

Faversham

Shipwrights Arms (P)
Hollowshore (access along unmade road across marshes from Oare Road)
☏ (0795) 533163
Biddenden (PC)
At confluence of two creeks north of the town, fine river panorama and yachting centre. Snacks lunchtime and evenings; children's room; garden.

Folkestone

Weekdays: 10–2; 6–10

Alexandra Wine (OL)
37–39 Canterbury Road
☏ (0303) 57573
Biddenden (B)
Inch (B)

Weekdays: 8–6

Coolinge Stores (OL)
Alton House, Shorncliffe Road
☏ (0303) 54977
Biddenden (B)

Dover Road Off Licence (OL)
40 Dover Road
☏ (0303) 52405
Biddenden (B)

Weekdays: 10–10, Sunday: 12–3; 7–10

Grapevine (OL)
34 The Old High Street
☏ (0303) 44497
Biddenden (B)
Theobolds (B) (PC)

Wine Centre (OL)
182 Dover Road
☏ (0303) 50592
Biddenden (B)

Goudhurst

Burgess Stores (OL)
High Street
☏ (0580) 211206
Biddenden (B)

Weekdays: 11–2.30; 6,30–11, Sunday: 12–2.30; 7–10.30

Green Cross (P)
Station Road (A262)
☏ (0580) 211200
Biddenden (PC)
Small, friendly family run inn near "Finchcocks". Do not be misled by the address – you can no longer get there by train! Meals and snacks 12–2; 7–9.30; restaurant; garden; accommodation.

Groombridge

Weekdays: 11–2.30; 6–11, Sunday: 12–3; 7–10.30

Crown Inn (P)
Groombridge Hill
☏ (0892) 864742
Biddenden (PC)
16th century brick and tile hung inn overlooking the green. Bar snacks to a la

carte menu; restaurant; garden; accommodation.

Ham Street

VG Stores (OL)
Falstead House
☏ (023373) 2206
Biddenden (B)

Harrietsham

Weekdays: 11–3; 7–11

Ringlestone Inn (P)
Ringlestone Road (between Harrietsham and Wormshill)
☏ (0622) 859207
Biddenden (PC)
Pippins (PC)
Guest ciders (PC)
High on the North Downs north of the village, an unspoilt medieval lamplit tavern, with oak beams, log fires, and 17th century furniture Famous for its traditional English pies: comprehensive menu lunchtime and evenings; restaurant; patio; 2 acre garden. Guest ciders include Burrow Hill from Somerset, and Really Fowl from Cornwall.

Hawkhurst

Weekdays: 9–1; 2.15–7.30 (Wednesday: 9–1 only), Sunday: 12–2

The Wine Cask (OL)
Highgate Hill
☏ (0580) 753080
Biddenden (B)

Headcorn

Weekdays: 9–1; 5–10, Sunday: 12–2; 7–9

The Chalet (OL)
North Street
☏ (0622) 890288
Biddenden (PP) (J)
Weston (PP)
Near Headcorn BR station.

Weekdays: 8–7 all week

The Village Shop (OL)
7 High Street
☏ (0622) 890339
Biddenden (B)

Herne Bay

Lee Aperitif (OL)
2 Poplar Drive, Greenhill
☏ (0227) 369446
Theobold (B)

Shutters Wine Bar (P)
85 Mortimer Street
☏ (0227) 368388
Biddenden (PC)
Within half a mile of Herne Bay BR station.

High Halden

R & P Dawes (OL)
General Stores, White House Stores
☏ (023385) 304
Biddenden (B)

Ickham

Weekdays: 11–2.30; 6–11, Sunday: 12–3; 7–10.30

Duke William (P)
The Street
☏ (0227) 721308
Biddenden (PC)
In centre of village: near Howletts Zoo Park. Meals and snacks all sessions; restaurant; children's room; garden.

Iden Green

Weekdays: 8–5.30

Iden Green Stores (OL)
☏ (0580) 240668
Biddenden (B)

Woodcock (P)
☏ (0580) 240529
Biddenden (PC)
Isolated pub, well worth finding. Bar meals (not Sunday).

Kennington

Knotts Off Licence (OL)
Faversham Road
Biddenden (B)

Kilndown

Globe & Rainbow (P)
Rogers Rough Road
☏ (0892) 890283
Biddenden (PC)
A rambling, renovated Victorian building. Bar meals, restaurant in evenings, family room and garden.

Kingsdown

Rising Sun (P)
Cliff Road
☏ (0304) 373983
Theobold (PC) – summer
Picturesque weatherboarded pub. Still has the old "Cash Register" style handpumps for serving beer. Meals.

Lamberhurst

OWLET CIDER ▲
Owl House Fruit Farm
☏ (0892) 890553

Victoria House Stores (OL)
Biddenden (B)

Lenham

Lurcocks Off Licence (OL)
The Square
Biddenden (B)

Littlebourne

Weekdays: 8.30–6, Sunday: 12–1

Farm Shop (OL)
28 High Street
☏ (0227) 721495
Theobolds (J)
Old fashioned village shop that sells everything.

Little Chart

Post Office (OL)
☏ (023384) 262
Biddenden (B)

Loose

Linton Road Stores (OL)
48 Salts Avenue
☏ (0622) 43481
Biddenden (B)

Lower Hardres

Tuesday–Friday: 11.30–2.30; 6.30–11, Saturday: 11.30–3; 6.30–11, Sunday: 12–3; 7–10.30 (closed on Mondays)

Three Horseshoes (P)
Catts Wood Road
☏ (022770) 333
Lane (PC)
Zum (PC)
Country pub with old fashioned furnishings and vintage buses. Snacks lunchtime; dinner/lunch parties by arrangement; garden; occasional jazz festivals. If lost ask for "Lower *Hards*". Ciders on offer may vary.

Lydd

Monday–Wednesday: 8–5.30, Thursday–Friday: 8–8, Saturday: 8.30–6.30, Sunday: 9–6

Corner Store (OL)
1 Dengemarsh Road
☎ (0679) 20005
Biddenden (B)

West End Stores (OL)
84 High Street
☎ (0679) 20493
Biddenden (B)

Maidstone

Maidstone Wine Making Centre (OL)
53 Hardy Street
☎ (0622) 677619
Weston (PC) (J)
Westons Perry (PC)

Minstrel Wine Bar
4a Knightrider Street
☎ (0622) 55655
Biddenden (PC)
Old building with character. Meals and snacks lunchtime and evenings. Within half a mile of Maidstone East and West BR stations.

Barnacles Crab & Oyster House (P)
1 King Street
☎ (0843) 223207
Theobold (E)

Benjamin Beale (P)
10 Buck Hill
☎ (0843) 223997
Theobold (PC)
Half a mile from Margate BR station, on the sea front. Family room and arcade amusements. Excellent value meals.

Weekdays: 10.30–1.30; 2.30–9

Country Wines (OL)
1 High Street
☎ (0843) 299564
Theobold (B)
Near Margate BR station.

Liquor Locker (OL)
55 Canterbury Road
☎ (0843) 294202
Biddenden (B)

Weekdays: 10.30–11; Sunday: 7–10.30

Watsons' Cottage (P)
19 High Street
☎ (0843) 224466
Biddenden
Weston (PC)
Town centre free house. Meals and snacks all day; separate family room and dining room.

Marsh Green

Weekdays: 11.45–3; 7–11, Sunday: 12–3; 7–10.30

Wheatsheaf Inn (P)
Marsh Green Road (between Edenbridge and Lingfield)
☎ (0732) 864380
Biddenden (PL)
Delightfully refurbished country pub. Bar snacks 12–2.30; 7–10; restaurant 7.30–10; garden.

New Romney

Davisons (OL)
24 High Street
☎ (0678) 62994
Biddenden (B)

Monday–Thursday: 11–3; 6–11, Friday–Saturday: 11–11

Prince of Wales (P)
Fairfield Road (turn up George Lane from High Street)
☎ (0679) 62012
Biddenden (PC)
Homely locals' pub. Patio drinking area. Good value bar snacks at lunchtimes.

Old Romney

JESSAMINE FARM CIDER ▲
Jessamine Farm (on A259)
☎ (0679) 62850

Paddock Wood

Davisons (OL)
Commercial Road
Pippin (B)
Near Paddock Wood BR station.

Painters Forstal

PAWLEY FARM CIDER ▲
Kimberlea (near village centre)
☎ (0795) 532043

Pembury

PIPPINS CIDER ▲
Pippins Cider Company, Pippins Farm, Stonecourt Lane
☎ (089282) 4624

Pett Bottom

Weekdays: 11.30–3.30; 6.30–11

Duck Inn (P)
Near Bridge. Take Bridge turn off from A2
☎ (0227) 830354
Pippin (PL)
Pretty country pub set in picturesque Kentish valley. Meals 11.30–2; 6.30–11; snacks 11.30–2; 6.30–10; separate restaurant; garden.

Plaxtol

Monday–Friday: 11–2.30; 6–11, Saturday: 11–3; 6–11

Golding Hop (P)
Sheet Hill (turn east off A227 and follow signs)
☎ (0732) 882150
Weston (PC)
In a hard to find valley just north of the village. Meals and snacks lunchtime and evenings on weekdays; large garden opposite.

Papermakers Arms (P)
The Street
☎ (0732) 810407
Weston (H)
Just a local village pub. Bar snacks Saturday and Sunday lunchtimes; Friday, Saturday and Sunday evenings; children's room; outdoor drinking area/garden; access for disabled.

Rorty Crankle Inn (P)
School Lane
☎ (0732) 810254
Biddenden (B)
In case you are wondering, the name is Anglo Saxon for "Happy Corner"! Meals and snacks lunchtime and evenings.

Pluckley

Weekdays: 11.30–2.30; 6–11, Sunday: 12–3; 7–10.30

Dering Arms (P)
Station Road (south of village, adjoining BR station)
☎ (023384) 371
Biddenden (F)
Former hunting lodge of the Dering Estate. Bar food. Garden.

Heasmans Store (OL)
☎ (023384) 371
Biddenden (B)

Ramsgate

Cliffs End Post Office (OL)
54 Foads Lane, Cliffsend

☎ (0843) 593225
Theobold (B)

Weekdays: 10–10, Sunday: 12–2; 7–10

North Star (OL)
162 Margate Road
☎ (0843) 587705
Inch range (J)
Theobold range (J)

Square Dozen (OL)
144 Grange Road
☎ (0843) 592419
Theobold (B)
Near Ramsgate BR station

Rochester

Weekdays: 10–2; 4.30–9.30

Rochester Wines & Beers (OL)
5 Victoria Street
☎ (0634) 827518
Owlet (B)

Rolvenden

HOOK'S CIDER PRESS
Oak Cottage, 15 Hastings Road

Sandhurst

Johnsons (OL)
☎ (058085) 227
Biddenden (B)

Sarre

Kings Head (P)
☎ (0843) 47247
Theobold (W)

Seal

Five Bells (P)
Church Road
☎ (0732) 61503
Biddenden (PC)
Small low-ceilinged well-kept free house in back street. Parking not easy. Meals.

Sellinge

Sellinge Stores (OL)
☎ (030381) 2102
Biddenden (B)

Shoreham

Weekdays: 10.30–2.30 (3 Saturday); 6–11, Sunday: 12–3; 7–10.30

Royal Oak (P)
2 High Street (in centre of village, off A225)
☎ (09592) 2319
Weston (DJ)
The heart of the village community. Meals and snacks lunchtime; outdoor drinking area. Half a mile from Shoreham BR station.

Monday–Friday: 8.30–6, Saturday: 8.30–1, Sunday: 10–1

Village Stores (OL)
High Street
☎ (09592) 2018
Weston (DJ) (J)
Half a mile from Shoreham BR station.

Sissinghurst

D. C. Hemsted (OL)
Biddenden (B)

Smarden

Weekdays: 11.30–2.30; 6–11.

Bell (P)
Bell Lane
☎ (023377) 283
Biddenden (PC)
Ancient inn with oak beams and inglenook fireplaces, between Smarden and Headcorn in typical orchard and oast country. Good choice of meals and snacks 12–2; 6.30–10.30 all sessions; children's room; garden; accommodation. Headcorn BR station approx. 2 miles.

Snargate

Weekdays: 11–3; 7–11.

Red Lion (P)
On A2080 Brenzett to Appledore Road
☎ (06794) 648
Biddenden (PC)
A tiny isolated free house on the Romney Marsh, unaffected by "progress": marble bar top, real fires. The pub holds the key to the village church opposite, which you should also visit. Garden.

Speldhurst

Weekdays: 11–2.30; 6–11, Sunday: 12–3; 7–10.30.

George & Dragon (P)
opposite village church
☎ (0892) 863125
Bulmer (H)
Medieval timber framed inn, dating back to 1212, with stone flagged floors. Good range of meals lunchtime and evenings; restaurant; garden.

Staplehurst

Staplehurst Village Stores (OL)
Station Road
☎ (0580) 891319
Biddenden (B)
Near Staplehurst BR station.

Stone in Oxney

Crown Inn (P)
The Street
☎ (023383) 267
Biddenden (PC)
Delightfully remote, on the edge of Romney Marsh; the Military Canal and RHDR Railway are within easy reach. Meals and snacks lunchtime and evenings except Sunday evening.

Stourmouth

Weekdays: 11–3; 6.30–11.

Rising Sun Inn (P)
The Street (B2046)
☎ (0227) 722220
Theobold (PC)
Good fishing nearby in River Stour. Meals and snacks 12–2; 7–10 weekdays; 12–1.30; 7–10 Sundays; children welcome if taking meals; garden.

Stourmouth

THEOBOLDS CIDER ▲
Heronsgate Farm
☎ (0227) 722275

Sutton Valance

The Village Shop (OL)
Broad Street
☎ (0622) 843313
Biddenden (B)

Swanley

Weekdays: 11–1; 5–10, Sunday 12–2; 7–10.

Real Ale Shop (OL)
31 Azalea Drive
☎ (0322) 63221
Zum (PC)
Adjacent to Swanley BR station.

Tenterden

Davisons (OL)
106 High Street
☎ (05806) 2939
Biddenden (B)

Wilkes Freezer Shop (OL)
Ashford Road, St. Michaels (A28)
☎ (05806) 3277
Bidenden (B)

Tonbridge

Monday: 9–5,
Tuesday–Thursday: 11–2; 4–9,
Friday–Saturday: 10–2; 4–9.30,
Sunday: 12–2; 7–9.

Priory Wine Cellars (OL)
64 Priory Street
☎ (0732) 359784
Pippins (B)

Tunbridge Wells

Dowlings Stores (OL)
81 Forest Road
☎ (0892) 34975
Biddenden (B)

Waltham

Monday, Wednesday-Saturday: 11.30–2.30; 7–11 (closed all day Tuesday).

Lord Nelson (P)
Church Lane
☎ (022770) 628
Biddenden (PC)
High in the Kentish hills, in good walking country. Meals and snacks all sessions; large garden with glorious views; access for disabled.

Warehorne

Worlds Wonder (P)
☎ (023373) 2431
Biddenden (PC)

Warren Street

Harrow Inn (P)
☎ (0622) 858727
Biddenden (PC)
On the North Downs, once the forge and rest house for travellers on the nearby Pilgrims Way. Snacks lunchtime and evenings; meals evenings; restaurant; garden.

Whitstable

Harbour Lights (P)
Beach Walk
☎ (0227) 264767
Theobold (E)
Large sea front bar within half a mile of Whitstable BR station. Occasional live music. Snacks (not Sunday evening)

Willesborough

Willesborough Wines (OL)
139 Church Road
☎ (0233) 24128
Biddenden (B)

Worth

Weekdays: 11–2.30; 6.30–11.

St. Crispin (P)
The Street (off A258)
☎ (0304) 612081
Theobold (PC)
Meals and snacks lunchtime and evening; garden; accommodation; facilities for camping nearby; local game of Bat and Trap played.

Yalding

Beauchamps (OL)
The Swan Fruit Shop, High Street
☎ (0622) 814486
Biddenden (B)

White Hart, Claygate

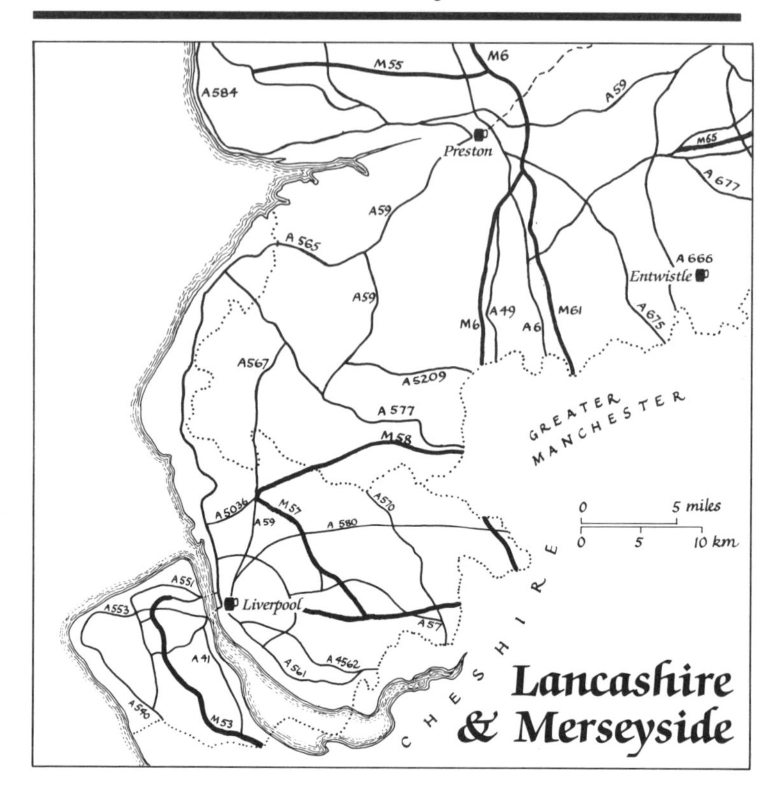

Lancashire

Entwistle

Monday: 6–11 (closed lunchtime except Bank Holidays): Tuesday–Friday: 12–11 (July–September): 12–2.30; 6–11 (October–June): Saturday: 12–11, Sunday: 12–10.30.

Strawberry Duck (P)
Overshires Road
☎ (0204) 852013
Bulmer (H)
Remote pub next to station, near Wayoh reservoir: popular with walkers. Meals lunchtime and evenings; all day Sunday to 9.30; garden; accommodation; live music.

Preston

Monday–Thursday: 11–3; 6–11, Friday and Saturday: 11–4; 6–11, closed Sunday lunch.

New Britannia (P)
6 Heatley Street
☎ (0772) 534224
Bulmer (PC)
Small, popular side street pub near the Polytechnic and convenient for the railway station. Often crowded. Meals lunchtime.

Monday–Friday: 5–10, Saturday: 11–2; 5–10, Sunday: 12–2; 7–10.

Real Ale Shop (OL)
47 Lovat Road
☎ (0772) 201591
Countryman
Cornish Scrumpy
Thatcher
Near Preston BR station.

Merseyside

Liverpool

Weekdays: 12–12, Sunday evening entrance fee – band night.

Everyman Bistro (P)
9 Hope Street (below Everyman Theatre, over road from RC Cathedral)
☎ (051) 708 9545
Bulmer (H)
Large basement eating house with plenty of atmosphere. Food all day, including vegetarian dishes; children's room. Near Liverpool Lime Street BR station, and Central Metro station.

Weekdays: 11–11, Sunday: 12–3; 7–10.30

Swan (P)
86 Wood Street
☎ (051) 709 5281
Thatcher (PC)
One roomed pub in side street, near city centre. Meals and snacks lunchtime and evenings. Near Liverpool Lime Street BR station, Central Metro station.

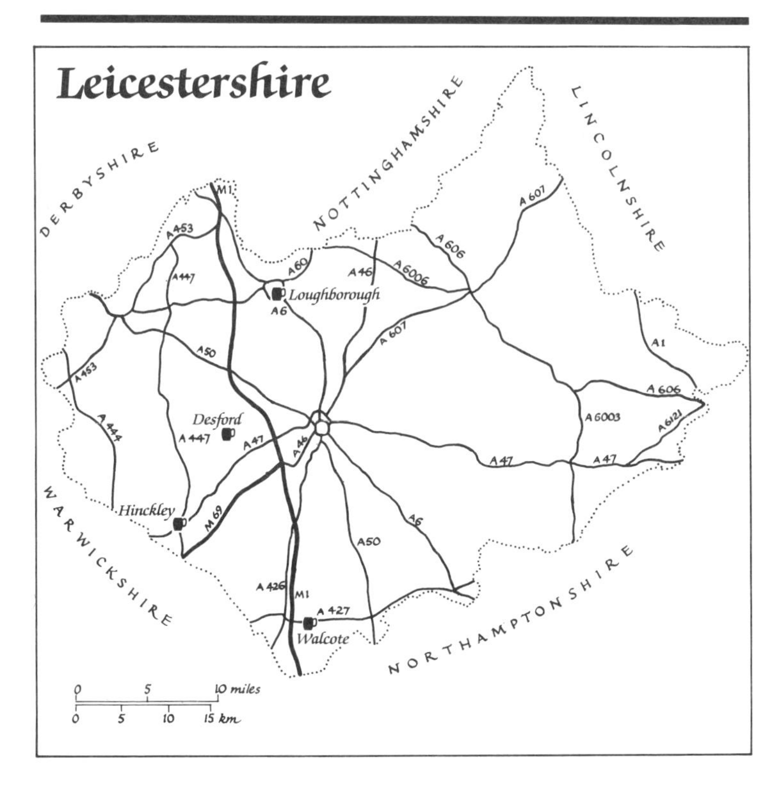

Desford

Weekdays: 11.30–2.30; 5.30–11, Sunday: 12–2.30; 7–10.30.

Olde Lancaster Inn (P)

Station Road
☎ (04557) 2589
Bulmer (H)
Four roomed, oak beamed, country inn. Meals lunchtime and evenings; garden.

Hinckley

Rugby Road Wine Cellars (OL)

83 Rugby Road
☎ (0455) 631403
Weston (J)

Kegworth

Cap & Stocking (P)

20 Borough Street
☎ (0509) 674814
Thatcher (PP)
Small pub hidden down back streets. Stuffed animals in the bar. Petanque played. Cider and real ales served from jugs filled in the cellar. Garden. Meals lunchtimes and evenings (7–7.45 only).

Loughborough

Monday–Tuesday: 7–10, Wednesday–Thursday: 12–2; 5.30–10, Friday: 11–2; 5.30–10.30, Saturday: 11–1; 5.30–10.30, Sunday 12–2; 7–10.

Jug & Bottle (OL)

16 Albert Promenade
☎ (0509) 261174
Weston (PC)
Wide range of ciders in bottles and jars.

Walcote

Weekdays: 11–3; 6–11, Sunday: 12–2.30; 7–10.30.

Black Horse (P)

Lutterworth Road (A427 near M1 junction 20)
☎ (04555) 2634
Weston (DJ)
Outwardly a typical English country pub near Foxton Locks and Stanton Hall. The landlady is Thai however and apart from the English cider and real ales Thai food is served along with Singha beer. Garden.

Lincolnshire

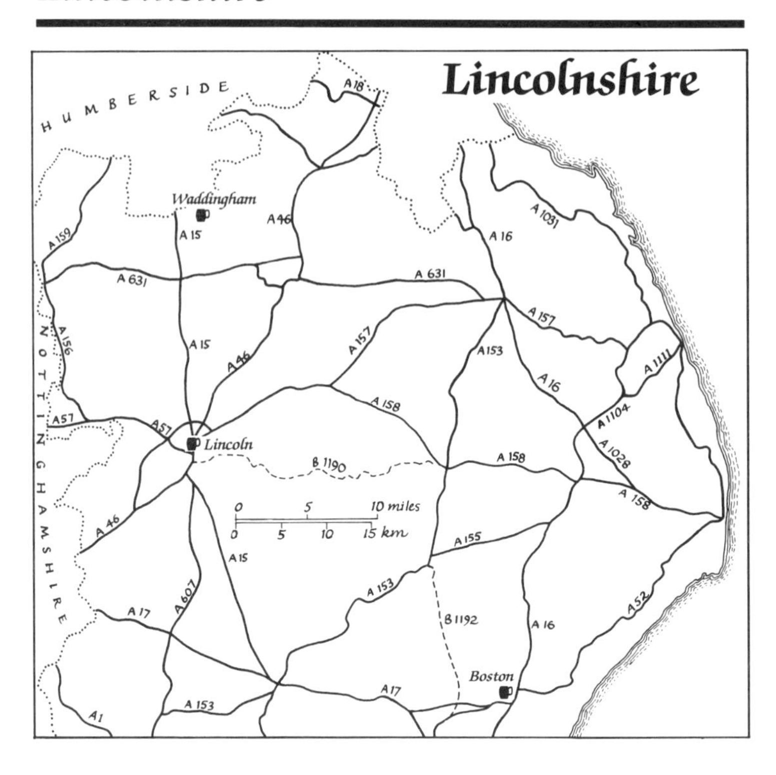

Boston

Monday–Friday: 10.30–3; 6–11, Saturday: 11–11.

Eagle (P)

144 West Street
☎ (0205) 61116
Symonds (H)
Popular and busy bar with comfortable lounge, not far from Station. a meeting place for various organisations including a folk club. Good value lunchtime bar menu; restaurant open on Sundays. Outdoor drinking area. The cider is *not* on fake handpumps!

Lincoln

Jolly Brewer (P)

Broadgate
☎ (0522) 528583
Bulmer (H)
1930s Art Deco style pub in easy reach of city centre. Meals lunchtime; garden.

Weekdays: 10.30–10.30.

Small Beer (OL)

91 Newland Street West
(off A57)
☎ (0522) 28628
Symonds (PC)
Other draught ciders available to order.

Weekdays: 11–11.

Victoria (P)

Union Road (behind Castle)
☎ (0522) 536048
Bulmer (H)
Busy pub behind the castle with amazingly varied clientele. Excellent lunches but food only occasionally available in evenings.

Waddingham

Lunchtimes: March–November: 12–3, November–March: 12–2.30 (not Mondays): Evenings: 7–11, Sunday: 7–10.30. Closed Christmas and New Year.

Cider Centre (P)

Brandy Wharf, River Ancholme (on B1205 Gainsborough to Grimsby Road)
☎ (06527) 364
Haymaker (BB)
James White (F)
Inch (BB)
Weston (J) (PC)
Westons Perry (PC)
A complete cider centre with tavern, orchard, and museum: a popular location on the River Ancholme; good fishing and towpath walks. Possibly the largest selection of ciders in Europe – over 60! Bar meals daily from extensive menu.

THE CIDER IN SPAIN FALLS MAINLY ON THE FLOOR

The Asturias Way of Dispense

Tony Flatman

So often we think of cider as an English drink, without considering equally strong traditions of cider-making in parts of Western Europe, and to some extent worldwide. In this, and future editions of the Guide, we hope to present a little of the flavour of ciders from outside the UK.

We start with Asturias, a coastal province in the north of Spain, and centred on the major cities of Oviedo and Gijon. This is traditionally a very prosperous part of Spain, with industries ranging from coal mining and steel to agriculture and forestry, the latter helped by the climate, which is that of Green Spain – similar to Northern rather than Southern Europe. Tourism is low key: being cut off from the rest of the country by high mountain ranges, the province has tended to go its own way. This separation is not just from the south, but also from the east, where the Basque provinces have very different traditions.

Cider is the traditional drink of Asturias rather than wine, and the cider (sidra) is drunk in true cider houses (sidrerias) which are found in every town or village. They usually serve one house cider, plus the usual range of spirits and soft drinks, and often a draught beer. The cider is stored in corked green bottles. It is a deep orange in colour, completely still in the bottle, and slightly cloudy, being made entirely by natural processes. It is about the strength of a normal English farm cider.

The unique feature of drinking cider here is its manner of serving. The bottle is held above the barman's head with arm outstretched, and the glass in his other hand close to knee height, so the lip is directly below the neck of the bottle. Some barmen will rotate the glass slightly at this point. The cider is poured by gradually tilting the bottle to the horizontal, where it drops some five feet, strikes the side of the glass, and falls to the bottom, where in its now aerated state the flavour is considered to be much improved: it is drunk immediately.

The bottle contains just over a pint, enough for five or six "shots". Usually each customer has his own glass, but sometimes a glass is shared, with a shot of cider supplied to each customer in turn. The cider is brought by the bottle, not by the glass. While serving the barman will fix his eye on a spot in the middle distance, and move the glass by instinct if it is not lined up correctly. Some look at the glass – it could be dangerous to look at the bottle. The glass is a standard shape – straight sides widening towards the rim – and is made of very thin glass, which helps in the pouring.

It must be asked whether this process actually does improve the taste of the cider, as it obviously increases the work the barman has to do. The freshly-poured cider certainly has different and more lively taste to that which it has only a few moments later. However, even in its flat state it is perfectly acceptable to an English palate – though apparently not to a Spanish one.

As you might expect, a lot of cider gets spilt: often the glass and bottle are not lined up correctly at the start – the fall of the cider has to be on the edge of the glass for maximum impact, so some rebounds out of the glass. The dregs are not drunk, as it is considered the cider has by then become flat again, added to which the sediment in the bottle renders the last part

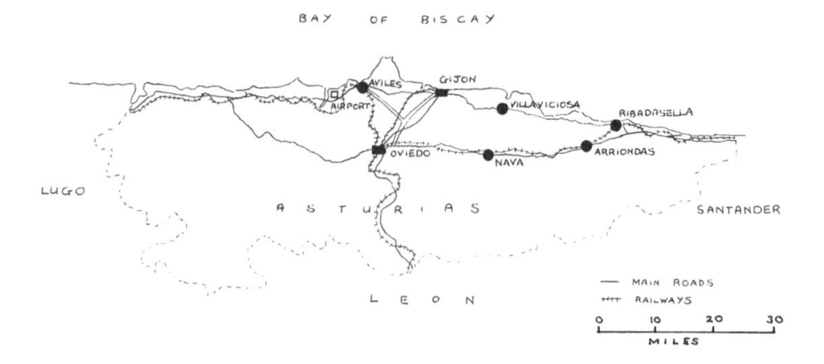

undrinkable. Up to about a fifth of the bottle is thus wasted, but at around 75p per bottle this is not too critical.

The waste cider either goes into wooden buckets placed round the bar, or sometimes into a natural channel at the base of the bar where pouring takes place. Sawdust is also often sprinkled around the bar area – a sidreria is hardly the place for carpets.

Though there is a first impression of messiness on the floor, sidrerias can range from stand-up drinking establishments up to excellent restaurants.

It is interesting to compare the attitudes towards drinking traditional cider between our West Country and Asturias. In both cases there are clearly bars which choose to serve cider, and others that do not. In both cases, too, the bars are not usually "upmarket". However, despite this, the sidrerias tend to attract a much wider spectrum of drinkers than would a cider bar in the UK. Business men, families, and, groups of women are equally likely to be seen; though it is apparently not done for a woman to indulge in the pouring routine.

The bottles are unlabelled. Only the imprint on the cork identifies the cider maker, though you may also find occasional clues on the crates. The different ciders vary little in taste, and many are sold under a common name, eg. "El Gaitero" from Villaviciosa. It is described as "natural cider". However there does seem to be some competition – for example, Sidra Fanjul won the first price at the Nava Festival of Cider in 1989. It is possible after a while to distinguish between ciders, some being particularly dry, and others having a fuller taste. Somehow, though, the cider always seems to taste better if you drink it near where it is made.

Come with me now on a trip round Asturias: we shall use only public transport, for obvious reasons. We shall start in the main cities of Oviedo and Gijon, then pass through the apple growing country around Villaviciosa and Nava, and continue east to the seaside towns of Ribadasella and Arriondas, which is the departure point for the mountains. These sidrerias are my favourites, there are many more. You will not find much English spoken, so I hope you have brushed up on your Spanish.

Our first port of call in Oviedo is the Sidreria El Piguena, at 2 Calle Gascona, which serves Cortina Coro cider from Villaviciosa. It has a typical format of a bar fronting a restaurant, which also extends upstairs. What is special here is the good mix of customers, being near the central area, and the excellent range of snacks (tapas) some of which are free, while others, like the fine seafood, have to be paid for. It is a good place to acclimatise to the sidreria scene.

Just up the road is the Sidreria A Munieira (7 Calle Gascona). This is notable not only for the Roza cider from Nava, but also for the fresh crab, which they are just bringing in, and are stacking round the bar as we sit here.

It is unusual in having a draught cider: chilled and filtered, but only slightly carbonated. Although it is somewhat sweeter than its natural counterpart it makes an interesting comparison.

On our way to the station we'll call in at the Sidreria Venecia (14 Calle Doctor Casal): it serves Corsino cider from Nava, and besides the lively bar there is an excellent restaurant.

Gijon is an impressive town: it is a commercial port, and also has a yacht marina and a tourist beach, but combines all of them so well you are hardly aware of the others. The sidrerias are less impressive here – perhaps we are unlucky: the Sidreria el Llagarin at 1 Calle Mieres is the pick of the bunch. It is unusual in having a central pool of water where the bottles are cooled before serving. The cider is again Corsino from Nava.

We must stop at Villaviciosa. We are right in the heart of the cider making country, with the scent of apples hanging in the air: it is the Asturias equivalent of Taunton and is clearly prosperous from its cider. There are some fine bars here: the Sidreria El Congreso (by the town hall) serves an excellent El Fugitivo local cider, and has a very friendly atmosphere and good seafood tapa. They've just bought us another bottle, after I made a technically inept attempt at a pour!

To the back of the town now, and the rather obscurely situated Sidreria la Ballera, and another fine cider, this time Angelon from Nava. The bar is notable for its house mirror and posters, featuring the various types of Spanish cheese and a collection of drip mats – including a Boddington's beer mat!

Just beyond the town hall, and serving the local Cortina Coro cider, is the Sidreria El Roxu, with a good atmosphere and a helpful landlord. Two things are constant in every sidreria – the hams hanging behind the door and the television set in front of it. This is the first bar which hasn't had a television.

In Ribadasella we've come to the Meson Tinin Cornidas, on the east bank facing the river. It is a lively bar, with friendly staff, and an English-speaking customer tells us that they have a refinement to the Asturias style of pouring cider – doing it behind one's back, though they don't seem to be doing it today. Again the cider is Cortina Coro. Our last stop is Arriondas, where we have two bars to visit. The first, the Sidreria la Bolera, is set back in a shaded garden off the main street, and serves El Pilonu cider from Nava. An area has been set aside to play an outdoor game of bowls or skittles, and in a hollowed out tree trunk some guinea pigs have set up home.

Also in the main street is the Sidreria Mirador. They have served us Cortina Coro, but the crates indicate other ciders are for sale. The landlord is clearly a cider enthusiast, and pictures and posters adorn his walls. One notice from the Regional (government) office is of particular interest, as it seems to indicate a threat to cider trees, which would be clearly recognised in the UK. A translation reads: "Cider cannot survive on its own. Campaign for the Replanting and Improvement of Orchards. The disease arfueyu [a technical word which does not seem to have any equivalent in English] is common among very old apple trees. Replanting of these apple trees is the only way to get an adequate crop. You will receive: for every apple tree free of disease five new apple trees, for every diseased or unproductive tree pulled up ten new trees"

(*Any further information about either ciders from Asturias, or any other area, will be gratefully received for inclusion in future editions of the Guide. ED*)

Greater London

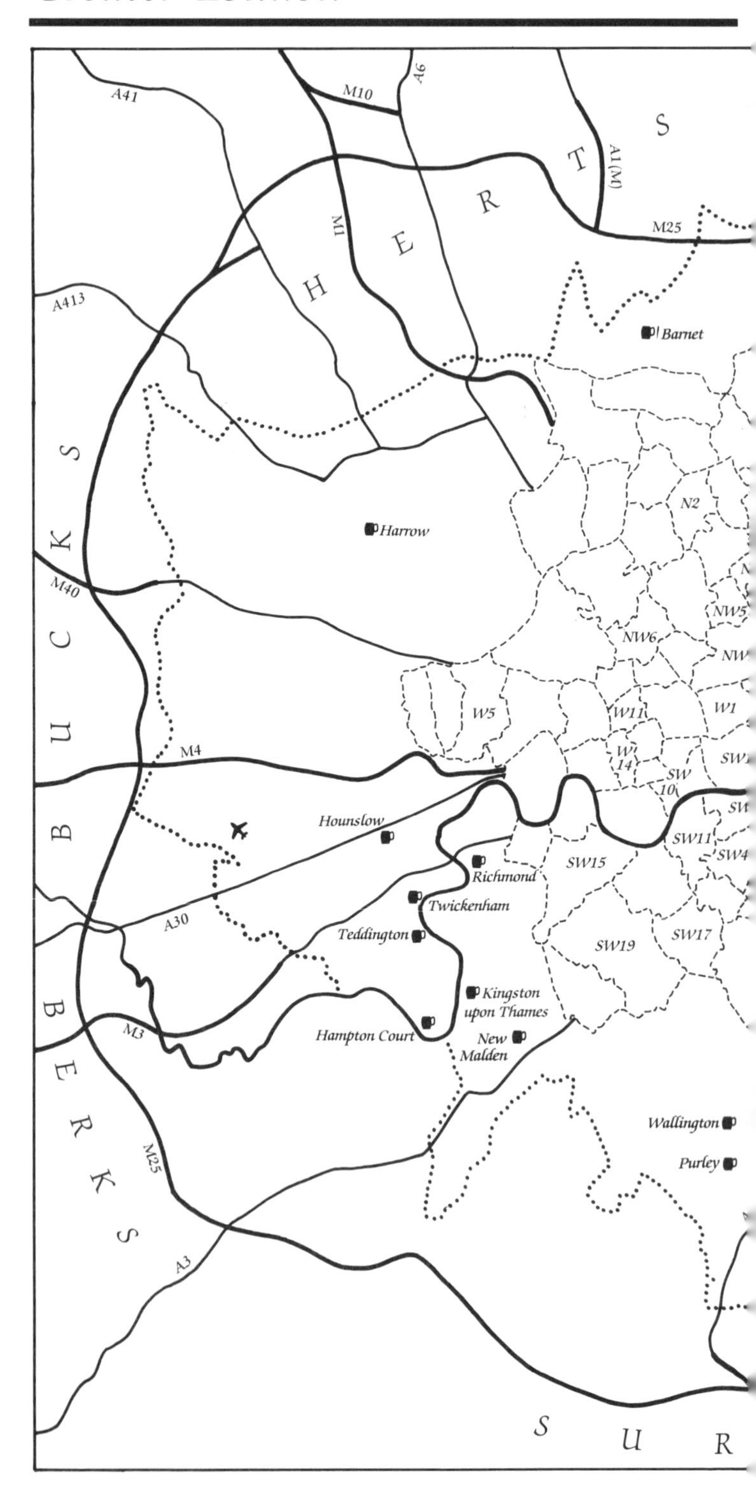

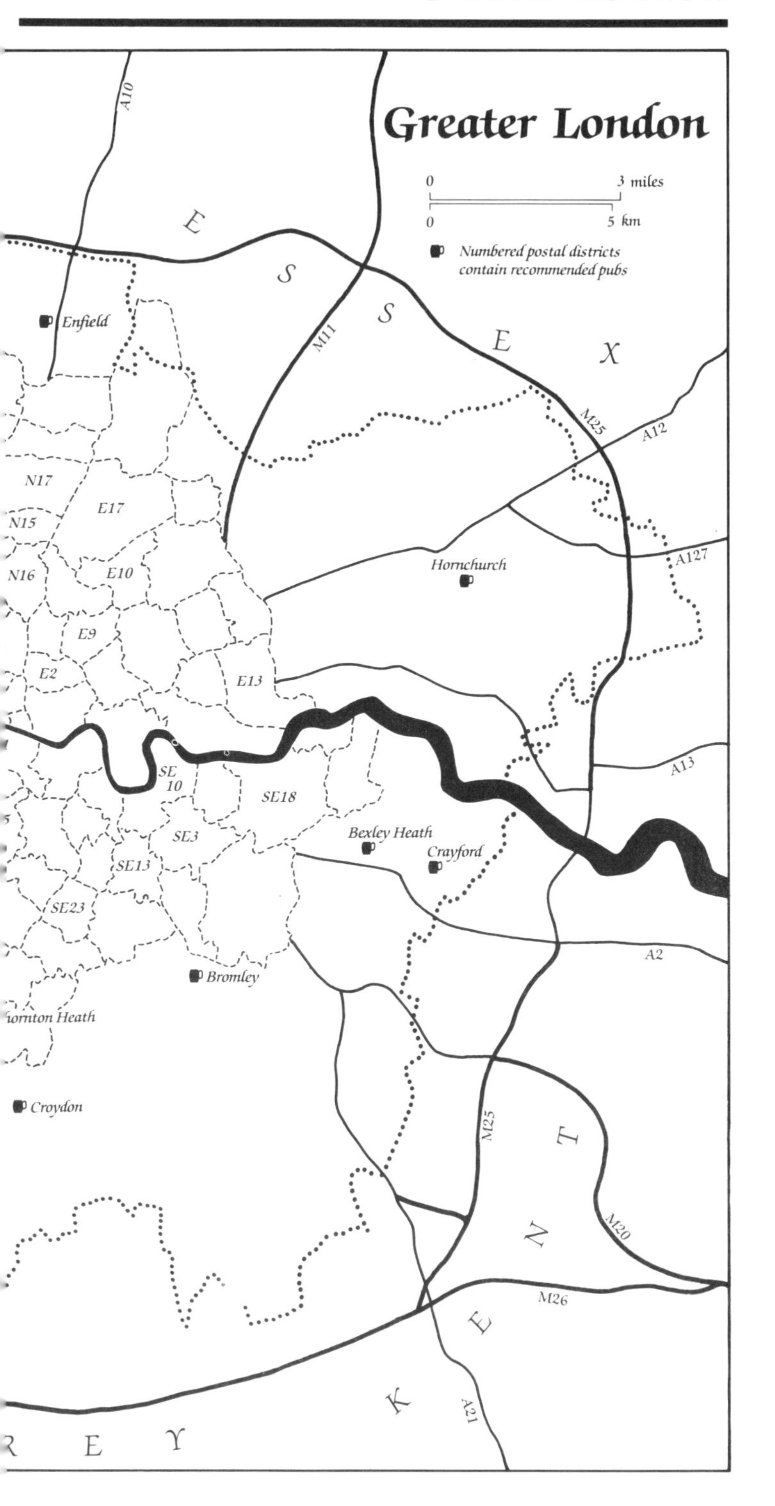
Greater London
0
3 miles
0
5 km
Numbered postal districts contain recommended pubs
E
S
S
E
X
A10
M11
M25
A12
A127
A13
A2
M25
M20
M26
A21
Enfield
N17
E17
N15
N16
E10
E9
E2
E13
SE 10
SE18
SE3
SE13
SE23
Hornchurch
Bexley Heath
Crayford
Bromley
Croydon
T
N
E
K
E
Y

Greater London

W1 – West End

Monday–Friday: 8.30–6, Saturday 9.30–5.30.

Cranks (OL)
8 Marshall Street
☏ (071) 437 2915
Aspall (B)

Glassblower (P)
42 Glasshouse Street
Bulmer (H)
Sawdust on the floor and gas lit. Landlord has an extensive collection of breweriana on display. Outdoor drinking area. Bar food. Near Piccadilly tube station.

Wholefood (OL)
24 Paddington Street
☏ (071) 935 3924
Aspall (B)
Retail shop selling organically grown produce, including wine.

WC1

Weekdays: 11–11, Sunday: 12–3; 7–10.30.

Sun (P)
63 Lambs Conduit Street
☏ (071) 405 8278
Jumpy Scrap (H)
Zum (H)
Popular venue for London University students: vast beer selection; cellar tours most nights – a notorious den of iniquity! Snacks and meals all times; outdoor drinking area.

EC1

Pheasant & Firkin (P)
166 Goswell Road
☏ (071) 253 7429
Weston (H)
Basic and straightforward drinking house, and very popular, particularly with University students. Brewery on premises but cider is from Herefordshire. Lunches.

EC1 – Clerkenwell

Weekdays: 11–11.

Thomas Wethered (P)
Rosaman Street
☏ (071) 278 9983
Bulmer (H)
Hot and cold food always available; carvery roast, Sunday lunch. near Farringdon BR and Underground station.

EC1

Monday–Friday: 11–11, Saturday: 11–3; 5.30–11, Sunday: 12–3; 7–10.30.

Three Compasses (P)
66 Cowcross Street, Smithfield
☏ (071) 253 3368
Bulmer (H)
Bar food all hours; restaurant Monday–Friday lunchtimes; jazz piano Tuesday evening and Sunday lunchtime.

E2 – Bethnal Green

Marksman (P)
254 Hackney Road
☏ (071) 739 7393
Burrow Hill (PC)
Refurbished freehouse with young clientele.

E9

Summer: weekdays: 11–11, Sunday: 12–3; 7–10.30.

Falcon & Firkin (P)
360 Victoria Park Road, Hackney
☏ (081) 985 0693
Westons Old Rosie (H)
Ex David Bruce home brew pub.

E10 – Leyton

Weekdays: 11–11, Sunday:12–3; 7–10.30.

Drum (P)
567 Lea Bridge Road
☏ (081) 539 6577
Westons Farmhouse (DJ) (J)
Westons Special (DJ) (J)
Westons Vintage (DJ) (J)
A freehouse with *no music*, leaving customers to enjoy conversation quietly and easily, amid a decor of drums and other instruments. Meals and snacks 12–3.30. Near Walthamstow Central BR and Underground stations.

E10 – Leyton

Hare Wines (OL)
24 Rigg Approach
☏ (071) 588 6986
Cornish Scrumpy (PL)

E13 – Plaistow

Phantom & Firkin (P)
140 Balaam Street
☏ (081) 472 2024
Westons Old Rosie (H)
Another former David Bruce brewpub. Meals and snacks lunchtime and evenings.

E17 – Walthamstow

Weekdays: 11–11.

College Arms (P)
807 Forest Road
☏ (081) 531 8001
Weston (H)
Former shop, converted into a pub – rather a reverse from the normal trend! Meals lunchtime and evening.

Elphinstones (OL)
485 Forest Road
☏ (081) 527 2080
Cornish Scrumpy – range.

Hornchurch

Monday–Friday: 12–2.30; 6–11, Saturday 11–2.30; 6–11, Sunday: 12–2; 7–10.30 (unless no show on)

Queens Theatre, Pit Bar (P)
Billet Lane
☏ (04024) 43333
Coates (PC)
Large modern theatre with wide range of entertainment. The cider is not advertised, so please ask for it. Bar snacks 10 am – evening interval (times vary); meals 12–2; children roam freely; access for disabled; trad jazz Sunday lunchtime – 5p surcharge per drink to cover expenses. Near Emerson Park BR station (Romford–Upminster branch).

N1 – Hackney

Monday–Friday: 11–7.30, Saturday: 10–4 (closed Sunday)

The Beer Shop (OL)
8 Pitfield Street
☏ (071) 739 3701
Biddenden (B)
Dunkerton (B)
Inch (B)
Westons Farm Brand (PC)
Westons Old Rosie (PC)
Also Cidre Breton from France. Near Old Street Underground station.

N1 – Kings Cross

Monday–Friday: 11–11, Saturday: 12–1.

Malt & Hops (P)
33 Caledonian Road

☎ (071) 837 9558
Bulmer (H)
Expensive but welcome freehouse in central London's cider desert. Meals and snacks lunchtime and evenings. Only 200 yards from Kings Cross and St. Pancras BR and Underground stations.

N2 – East Finchley

Grogblossom (OL)
160 High Road
☎ (081) 883 3588
James White (H)

Monday–Friday: 11–3; 5.30–11, Saturday: 11–11, Sunday: 12-3; 7–10.30.

Welch's (P)
130 High Road
☎ (081) 444 7444
Guest Ciders (PC)
The cider brand varies, but is most often Wilkins or Coombes: it is always dry. Snacks all sessions; meals 12–2.30.

N4 – Finsbury Park

Old Suffolk Punch (P)
10–12 Grand Parade, Green Lanes
Westons Farm Brand (DJ)
Meals lunchtime. *No* music. Cider is kept in a chilled cabinet – please ask for it. Near Harringay Stadium BR station.

White Lion of Mortimer (P)
125/127 Stroud Green Road
Weston Farm Brand (DJ)
Ornate glazed tile and timber interior, conservatory at rear: no music. Cider stored in chilled cabinet – please ask. Meals lunchtime; outside drinking area in front of pub. Half a mile from Finsbury Park BR and Underground stations.

N7 – Highbury

Weekdays: 12–11.

Flounder & Firkin (P)
54 Holloway Road
☎ (071) 609 9574
Weston (H)
Another basic and popular Firkin pub bringing good cider into a real cider desert. Meals. Also guest ciders including Inch, James White, and Zum.

N15 – South Tottenham

Goat (P)
414/416 West Green Road
Weston (DJ)
Victorian decor. Meals and snacks lunchtime.

N16 – Stoke Newington

Tanners Hall (P)
145 High Street
☎ (071) 249 6016
Westons (J)
Ornate Victorian decor with glazed conservatory at rear; no music. Meals and snacks lunchtime.

N17 – Tottenham

Weekdays: 11–11, Sunday: 12–3; 7–10.30.

Boar (P)
413 Lordship Lane
☎ (081) 801 6179
Westons Old Rosie (H)
No music of any kind (so don't whistle?) Library. Bar snacks 12–7; full meals 12–2.30; garden. Near Wood Green BR station.

Elbow Room (P)
503–505 High Road
Weston (PP)
Meals and snacks lunchtime. A no music zone, welcome for conversationalists.

Weekdays: 11–11, Sunday: 12–3; 7–10.30.

Moon Under Water (P)
423 Lordship Lane (corner of Downhills Way)
☎ (081) 889 7397
Weston (PP)
Corner pub with one spacious bar; no music. Meals and snacks lunchtime; outdoor drinking area; access for disabled. Near Turnpike Lane Underground station.

N19 – Upper Holloway

Weekdays: 11–11, Sunday: 12–3; 7–10.30.

Dog (P)
17–19 Archway Road (A1)
☎ (071) 263 0429
Westons Farm Brand (H)
No music or pool tables, ideal for a quiet drink and chat. Bar snacks 12–2.30; outdoor drinking area. Near Upper Holloway BR station.

Hornsey Tap (OL)
498 Hornsey Road
☎ (071) 263 1650
Cornish Scrumpy – range
Near Crouch Hill BR station.

J. J. Moons (P)
37 Landseer Road (between Hornsey Road and Holloway Road)
☎ (071) 263 4658
Westons Old Rosie (H)
Large single bar back street local: no music, just good conversation! Hot and cold food lunchtime; outdoor drinking area in front of pub. Near Upper Holloway BR station, and Archway Underground station.

Barnet

Moon Under Water (P)
148 High Street (A1000)
Weston (DJ)
A fascinating long dark drinking arcade, culminating in a splendid glass vaulted conservatory. No music. Hot and cold meals and snacks lunchtime – 12–2.30 weekdays; 12.30–2 Sunday; includes vegetarian dish; outdoor drinking area at rear. Half a mile from High Barnet Underground station.

Enfield

Moon Under Water (P)
115/7 Chase Side
Weston (PP)
Traditional pub atmosphere with no music. Meals and snacks at lunchtimes.

NW1 – Camden Town

Weekdays: 12–4; 5.30–11, Sunday: 12–3; 7–10.30.

Victoria (P)
2 Mornington Terrace
☎ (071) 387 3804
Wilkins (PC)
A rare central London outlet for this prize winning cider, though it is not openly displayed, and you may

need to ask for it by name. Snacks, including vegetarian dishes, lunchtime and evenings.

NW1 – Camden Town

Fuzzock & Firkin (P)
77 Castle Road
☎ (071) 267 4855
Westons Old Rosie (H)
Another former David Bruce "Firkin" good, basic and popular brewpubs.

NW6 – West Hampstead

Grogblossom (OL)
253 West End Lane
☎ (071) 794 7808
James White (PC)
Weston (H)

Harrow on the Hill

Weekdays: 11–11, Sunday: 12–3; 7–10.30.

Kings Head Hotel (P)
88 High Street
☎ (081) 422 5541
Weston (PC) (PL)
Meals and snacks 11–2.30; restaurant; children's room; garden; accommodation.

SE1 – Southwark

Monday–Friday: 11–11, Saturday: 12–3; 6–11, Sunday: 12–3; 7–10.30.

George Inn (P)
77 Borough High Street (in George Inn Yard, 100 yards south of St. Thomas Street)
☎ (071) 407 2056
Bulmers West Country (H)
The only galleried inn left in London, rebuilt in 1676: frequented by Charles Dickens, and mentioned by him in his book "Little Dorrit": now a National Trust property. Snacks and meals in downstairs bars and restaurant; outdoor drinking area in George Inn Yard. Near London Bridge BR and Underground stations.

Weekdays: 11.30–3; 5–11.

Goose & Firkin (P)
47–48 Borough Road
☎ (071) 403 3590
James White (H)
Westons Old Rosie (H)
London's first "Firkin" pub providing a very successful blend of basicness and trendiness. Bar snacks all sessions; live music every night, usually piano. Near Elephant and Castle BR and Underground stations, and Borough Underground station.

SE3

Monday–Friday: 11–9.30, Saturday: 10–2; 3–9.30, Sunday and Bank Holidays: 12–2; 7–9.

Bitter Experience (OL)
129 Lee Road, Lee Green
☎ (081) 852 8819
Haymaker (PC) Zum (PC)
Near Lee BR station.

SE5 – Camberwell

Phoenix & Firkin (P)
Windsor Walk (in Denmark Hill railway station buildings)
☎ (071) 701 8282
Westons Old Rosie (H)
Built in the burnt out remains of the old station booking hall – hence the name: virtually a railway museum of memorabilia. Snacks all sessions; no children permitted.

SE10 – Greenwich

Weekdays: 11–3; 6–11, Sunday: 12–2; 7–10.30.

Richard I (P)
52 Royal Hill
☎ (081) 692 2996
Bulmer (PC)
Popular traditional pub. Snacks 11–2; meals 12–2.15. Near Greenwich BR station.

SE13 – Lewisham

Fox & Firkin (P)
316 Lewisham High Street
☎ (081) 690 8925
Westons Old Rosie (H)
Spit and sawdust style brewpub. Snacks all sessions; Sunday lunch; live music most nights, singalong at weekends. Near Ladywell BR station.

SE23 – Forest Hill

Two Brewers (OL)
97 Dartmouth Road
☎ (081) 699 1326
Weston (PC)

Bexleyheath

Monday–Friday: 12–2; 4–9.30, Saturday: 10–2; 3–9.30, Sunday and Bank Holidays: 12–2; 7–9.

Bitter Experience (OL)
216 Broadway
☎ (081) 304 2839
Haymaker (PC)
Zum (PC)

Bromley

Monday: 5–9, Tuesday–Friday: 12–3; 5–10, Saturday: 11–11, Sunday: 12–2; 7–9.

Bitter End (OL)
139 Masons Hill
☎ (081) 466 6083
Westons Old Rosie (PC)
Westons Vintage (PC)
Zum (PC)
Quarter of a mile from Bromley South BR station.

Oddbins (OL)
26 High Street
☎ (081) 290 1382
Weston (J)
Opposite Bromley South BR station.

Crayford

Monday–Thursday: 11–2.30; 6–11, Friday–Saturday: 11–4; 6–11.

White Swan (P)
143 Crayford Road (on A207)
☎ (0322) 521115
Weston (H)
Near to greyhound stadium, popular with younger drinkers. Lunchtime meals except Sunday; outdoor drinking area. Near Crayford BR station.

Croydon

Weekdays: 11–3; 5–11.

The Old Windsor Stores (OL)
3 Lower Coombe Street
☎ (081) 688 2945
Bulmer (H)
Haymaker (PC)

Purley

Bin 449 (OL)
449 Purley Way
☎ (081) 680 0477
Weston (J)

Thornton Heath

Chateau Colleen (OL)

71 Beulah Road
☏ (081) 653 0963
Weston (J)

Wallington

Sante Distributors (OL)
19 Church Lane
☏ (081) 647 8827
James White (J)

W5 – Ealing

Weekdays: 9–5.30.

Cornucopia (OL)
64 St. Marys Road
☏ (081) 579 9431
Dunkerton (J)

W11 – Notting Hill

Frog & Firkin (P)
41 Tavistock Crescent
☏ (071) 727 9250
Weston (H)
Meals and snacks lunchtime and evenings; live music. Typically popular, "Firkin" basic pub.

W14 – West Kensington

Weekdays: 11–11, Sunday: 12–3; 7–10.30.

Frigate & Firkin (P)
24 Blythe Road
☏ (071) 602 1412
Westons Old Rosie (H)
Yes folks, yet another "Firkin" pub bringing real cider to the throats of thirsty Londoners! Meals and snacks all day.

Hounslow

Weekdays: 11–11, Sunday: 12–3; 7–10.30.

Royal Albion (P)
58 Hibernia Road
☏ (081) 572 8461
Taunton (H)
Friendly side street local. Meals all sessions; garden; lending library; pool table; quiz night Thursday. Near Hounslow BR station.

SW1 – Victoria

Chimes (P)
26 Churton Street, Pimlico
☏ (071) 821 7456
Biddenden (F)
Weston (H) cider and perry
English restaurant and cider/wine bar, the nearest thing to a cider house in central London. Restaurant downstairs, snacks and cider on ground floor. The standard measure is $\frac{1}{2}$ pint, but there is the alternative of a 2 pint pottery jug. Snacks 12–2.30; meals 6–10; no snacks Sunday, but meals 7–10; outdoor drinking area.

SW2 – Brixton

Liquor Supply (OL)
94 Acre Lane
☏ (071) 737 1205
Weston (J)

SW4 – Clapham

Jacks Off Licence (OL)
2c Binfield Road
☏ (071) 622 7065
Weston (J)

SW8 – South Lambeth

Lavigna Off Licence (OL)
43 Dorset Road
☏ (071) 735 8656
Weston (J)

SW10 – Chelsea

Weekdays: 11–11, Sunday: 12–3; 7–10.30.

Ferret & Firkin in the Balloon up the Creek (P)
114 Lots Road
☏ (071) 352 6645
Westons Old Rosie (H)
The "Firkin" pub with the longest name. Near Chelsea Creek. Cold food all day to 10.30; hot food 12–3; live music every night.

SW11 – Battersea

Nature Garden (OL)
62 Lavender Hill
James White (J)

SW15 – Putney

Weekdays: 11–11.

White Lion (P)
14 Putney High Street
☏ (081) 785 3081
Westons Old Rosie (H)
Well restored Victorian pub. Lunchtime meals. Near Putney BR station, and Putney Bridge Underground station.

SW17 – Tooting

KWT Foodshow (OL)
Bellvue Parade, Wiseton Road
☏ (081) 767 5390
Dunkerton (B)

SW19 – Merton

Texemp Ltd (OL)
190 Merton High Street
☏ (081) 543 3339
Weston (J)
Near South Wimbledon Underground station.

Kingston Upon Thames

Bentalls (OL)
Wood Street
☏ (081) 546 1001
Dunkerton (B)
Near Kingston BR station.

Weekdays: 11–11, Sunday: 12–3; 7–10.30

Flamingo Brewery (P)
88 London Road
☏ (081) 541 3717
Bulmer (H)
Large Edwardian street corner pub with a recently added brewery. Meals and snacks all opening hours; children's room; outdoor drinking area/garden; live jazz; games available. Near Kingston BR station.

McCluskeys Free Off Licence (OL)
22 Bloomfield Road
☏ (081) 546 8655
Cornish Scrumpy (J) (PL)
Weston (J)
Near Kingston and Surbiton BR stations.

New Malden

Weekdays: 11–1; 5.30–10

The Wine Cask & Delicatessen Bar (OL)
161 South Lane
☏ (081) 949 8185
Zum (PC)

Richmond

Weekdays: 11–11, Sunday: 12–10.30

Pig & Parrot (P)
Kew Gardens Station
☏ (071) 332 1162
Weston (H)
On station platform; half a mile from Kew Gardens themselves. Bar snacks till 9; full meals till 7; outdoor drinking area.

Teddington

Weekdays: Tuesday–Friday: 9–7, Saturday: 9–4

Bay Tree (OL)
190 Stanley Road
☏ (081) 977 3727
Dunkerton (J) range
Delicatessen specialising in traditional British food and drink. Near Fulwell BR station.

Twickenham

Weekdays: 12–3; 6–10.30

Chimes (P)
19–21 York Street
☏ (081) 892 4794
Biddenden (F)
Weston (H) cider and perry
English restaurant/cider and wine bar. Meals lunchtime and evenings all sessions.

ZUM ZIDER (D)
West Country Products,
Lyon House, 51 Lion Road
☏ (081) 892 4114

WASSAIL TO THEE OLD APPLE TREE!

Now that even Royalty are known to talk to the plants, the time has surely come to look seriously at the age old custom of wassailing. The word comes from the Anglo Saxon "Waes Hal", which means "be of good health". It was originally used as a greeting, but over the years it developed into a mid-winter festival, in which people wished good health and prosperity to each other, their orchards, and animals. In a very dilute form, the greeting and good wishes on a Christmas card for a "happy new year" carry on the tradition, but *real* wassailing is still alive and well, and takes place in several places across the country.

The date for the ceremony varied, but it mostly occurred on either Old Christmas Eve (January 5) or Old Twelfth Night (January 17). The farmer, his family and friends, and often the entire village, would gather in the orchard, armed to the teeth with sticks and shot guns, and carrying with them a bowl of the best cider, with a piece of toast floating in it. The cider would be poured over the roots of the best tree, which would then be addressed in song:

"Old apple tree we wassail thee
And hope that thou wilt bear
For the Lord doth know where we shall be
Till apples come another year.

For to bear well and to bloom well
So merry let us be
Let every man take off his hat
And shout to the old apple tree.

Old apple tree we wassail thee,
And hope that thou wilt bear
Hats full, caps full,
Buckets full and bags full,
And a little heap under the stair."

Further to make their point, the company would then proceed to thrash the unfortunate tree with their sticks, shoot at it, and bang kettles and trays to create an almighty din. At the same time the piece of toast, now well soaked in cider, would be placed in the branches of the tree, usually by a small boy, as an offering to the robins, who were the messengers of the goddess of the apple trees, Pomona. It was presumably hoped that the robins would return to court sufficiently sober to convey an accurate report of the proceedings to their mistress.

There was, as with many old customs, some rudimentary logic – those present would doubtless have told you they were driving out the evil spirits from the tree, but firing at the tree, and bashing its trunk, would probably have dislodged the insects, which would then have been eaten by the birds.

During the last hundred years the practice has largely died out, most modern apple growers resorting to chemical sprays to ward off the evil spirits. But wassailing now shows signs of making a comeback: the Taunton Cider Company, no less, reintroduced it in the 1970s: the first year they recorded a bumper crop, and they have wisely kept it up ever since. A splendid young lady, known as the "Wassail Queen", graces the proceedings, though whether she gets hoisted up into the branches with a piece of toast to commune with the robins is not clear.

Not far away, at Carhampton, wassailing takes place every January 17 in the orchard behind the Butchers Arms; in Devon, a similar event occurs at Dunkeswell, on the Somerset border, and further into Devon, as you will read elsewhere in the Guide, the villagers of Combeinteignhead have lately revived the custom. In Herefordshire Weston's Cider Company have found a spot of wassailing does their trees a power of good, and at the other side of the country, in deepest Lincolnshire, the Cider Centre at Waddingham holds a Lincolnshire Wassailing Sunday, on the nearest Sunday lunch to the thirteenth day after the twelfth Day of Christmas.

Next January, why not go and sing to a tree? If you get caught, you can always blame us!

Greater Manchester

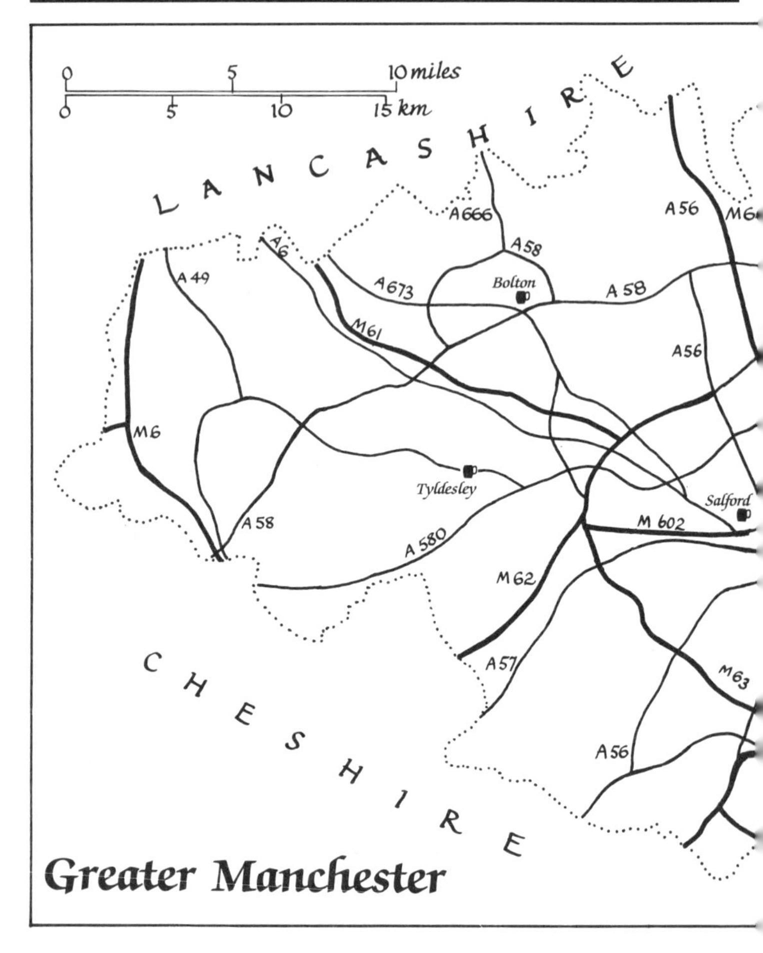

Ashton Under Lyne

Weekdays: 12–2.30; 6–11, Sunday: 12–3; 7–10.30

Witchwood (P)

152 Old Street
☏ (061) 344 0321
Thatcher (PC)
Recently renovated but retains a vibrant, spit and sawdust, heavy metal atmosphere. Lunchtime snacks. Rock bands Tuesday, Thursday, Saturday and Sunday nights.

Bolton

Weekdays: 11–11

Olde Man & Scythe Inn (P)

6–8 Churchgate
Bulmer (H)
Bolton's oldest pub. The present building dates from 1636 and was recently refurbished with plush blue seats and stools replacing ancient leather. Two side rooms and long bar. Lunches.

Denshaw

Golden Fleece (P)

41 Oldham Road
☏ (04577) 876877
Bulmer (H)

Delph

Cottage Hotel (P)

Huddersfield Road (A62)
☏ (04577) 871885
Bulmer (H)
Accommodation.

Gorton

Monday–Saturday: 10 am–10.30 pm, Sunday: 11–10

Doreen & Alan Wharf (OL)

Reddish Lane (B6167)
Harvester (PC)
Grocers and off Licence, opposite the Pomona pub, which despite the name has no cider! Near Reddish North BR station.

Weekdays: 11–11, Sunday: 12–3; 7–10.30

Railway (P)

Pottery Lane (on Manchester Ring Road – A6010, just south of junction with Ashton Old Road – A635)
Frampton (PC)

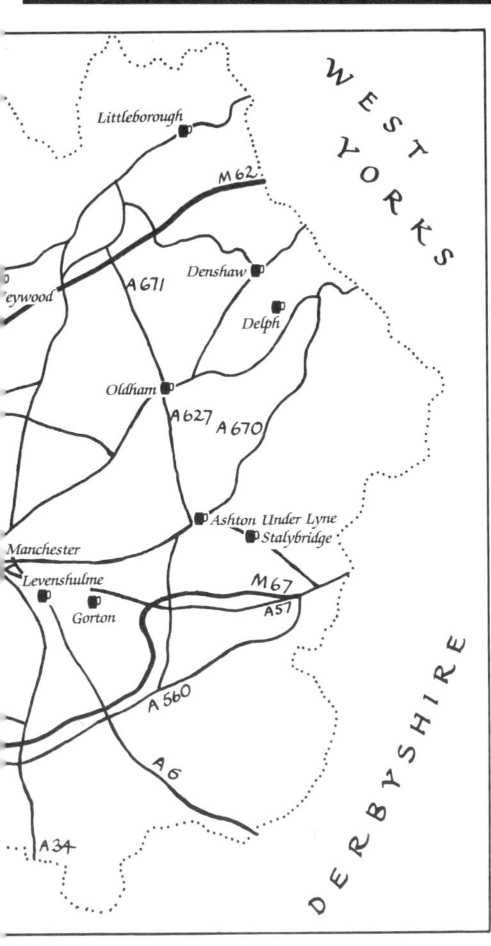

Westons Special Vintage (PC)
Reopened brewery tap, with railway photographs of local interest. Meals Monday–Friday lunchtime; snacks all reasonable times. Near Ashburys BR station.

Heywood

Monday–Friday: 12–3; 5–11, Saturday: 12–4; 7–11, Sunday: 7–10.30

Browns No. 1 Bar (P)

41 Bridge Street (on A58 just west of town centre)
☏ (0706) 625240
Frampton (PP)
Compact, bustling one-roomed bar converted from a hairdresser's into an Amsterdam style "Brown" bar.

Levenshulme

Weekdays: 8.30–1.30; 3.30–9

Bottle Corner (OL)

40 Forest Range (turn left off Albert Road from station)
☏ (061) 224 1600
Westons Old Rosie and Scrumpy (PL)
Near Levenshulme BR station.

Littleborough

Monday–Thursday: 11.30–2; 4.30–11, Friday: 11–11, Saturday: 11.30–3.30; 6–11

Red Lion (P)

6 Halifax Road (under the arches)
☏ (0706) 78195
Bulmer (H) (PC)
Follow footpath to canal and Red Lion is next to railway station. Ciders are Traditional, West Country Dry and Extra Dry: 3 handpumps. Snacks 12–2; 5–7; garden; live music Wednesday, Friday, Saturday, Sunday.

Manchester City Centre

Weekdays: 11–11, Sunday: 12–3; 7–10.30

Beer House (P)

Angel Street (off Rochdale Road – A664)
☏ (061) 832 1452
Hartland (PC)
James White (PC)
Thatcher (H)
Westons Special Vintage (PC)
Basic boozer for devotees of good cider. Simple but filling lunchtime snacks; cider range subject to change. Near Manchester Victoria BR station.

Monday–Friday: 11.30–10, Saturday: 11.30–3; 6–10, Sunday: 12–3; 7–10.30

Lass O'Gowrie (P)

36 Charles Street
☏ (061) 273 6932
Bulmer (H)
Popular city centre pub, often frequented by students: brewhouse on view from bar; naked gas flame lights. Meals lunchtime.

Weekdays: 11–11, Sunday: 12–2; 7–10.30

Salisbury (P)

2 Wakefield Street (off Oxford Road)
☏ (061) 236 4347
Bulmer (H)
Popular city centre pub, much frequented by students from nearby Polytechnic. Snacks lunchtime and evenings; meals 12–2. Adjoins Oxford Road BR station.

Oldham

Weekdays: 11.30–11, Sunday: 12–3; 7–10.30

Auld Lang Syne (P)

14 Manchester Road, Werneth
☏ (061) 626 6336
Various (PC)
Owned by Oldham Council (due for demolition – so hurry!). Sunday lunch;

excellent juke box; heavy duty football table. Near Werneth BR station.

Salford

Monday–Thursday: 12–2.30; 4.30–11, Friday: 12–11, Saturday: 12–2.30; 7.30–11, Sunday: 12–2.30; 7.30–10.30

Crescent (P)

20 The Crescent (on A6 near Salford Royal Hospital)
☎ (061) 736 5600
Various (H)
Relaxing freehouse near nature trail and Lowry Collection. Lunchtime snacks; access for disabled; bar billiards. Cider range varies: Biddenden, Frampton, Inch, Dunkerton, Thatcher and Weston. Near Salford Crescent BR station.

Stalybridge

Monday–Tuesday: 5–11, Wednesday–Friday: 12–3; 5–11, Saturday: 12–3; 7–11, Sunday: 7–10.30

Buffet Bar (P)

Stalybridge Railway Station (Platform 1)
☎ (061) 338 2020
Various (PP)
Original Victorian railway buffet, with marble top bar; privately owned. Snacks all opening hours; children welcome; outdoor drinking area; folk singers Saturday evenings.

White House (P)

Water Street (near bus station)
Frampton (PC)
Lively, no-frills former Cunningham's of Warrington brewery pub.

Tyldesley

Half Moon Inn (P)

115–117 Elliott Street
☎ (0942) 873206
West Country Scrumpy (PC)
Hectic town centre pub, very popular especially with young people and at weekends. Separate games room. Lunchtime snacks.

Traditional cider making: preparing the "cheese".

Norfolk

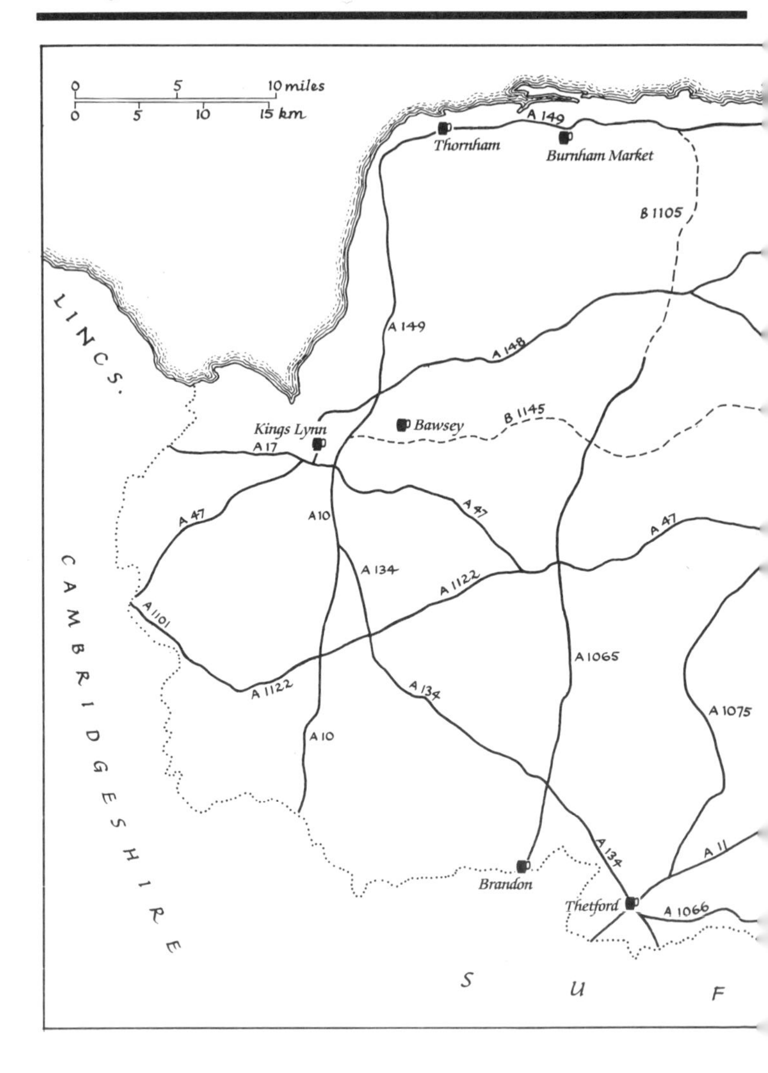

Attleborough

Monday–Wednesday: 10.30–2.30; 5.30–11, Thursday–Saturday: 10.30–11, Sunday: 12–3; 7–10.30

Griffin Hotel (P)

Church Street (next to church)
☏ (0953) 452149
Potmere Farm (H) – summer only
16th century town centre hotel with beamed walls and ceilings. Meals and snacks lunchtime and evenings; restaurant; outdoor drinking areas; accommodation; access for disabled; camping facilities nearby. Near Attleborough BR station.

POTMERE FARM CIDER ▲

Norfolk Cider Company, Potmere Farm, Hargham Road
☏ (0953) 456168

White Lodge (P)

London Road
☏ (0953) 452474
Potmere Farm (PC)
Comfortable pub with atmosphere. Meals and snacks; restaurant.

Banham

Olde Garden House (Banham Cider House) (P)

Greyhound Lane
☏ (0953) 860437
Norfolk Scrumpy (PL)
Potmere (H)
A wellknown local institution, about a mile west of the village. Meals lunchtime all days; garden; camping facilities in grounds.

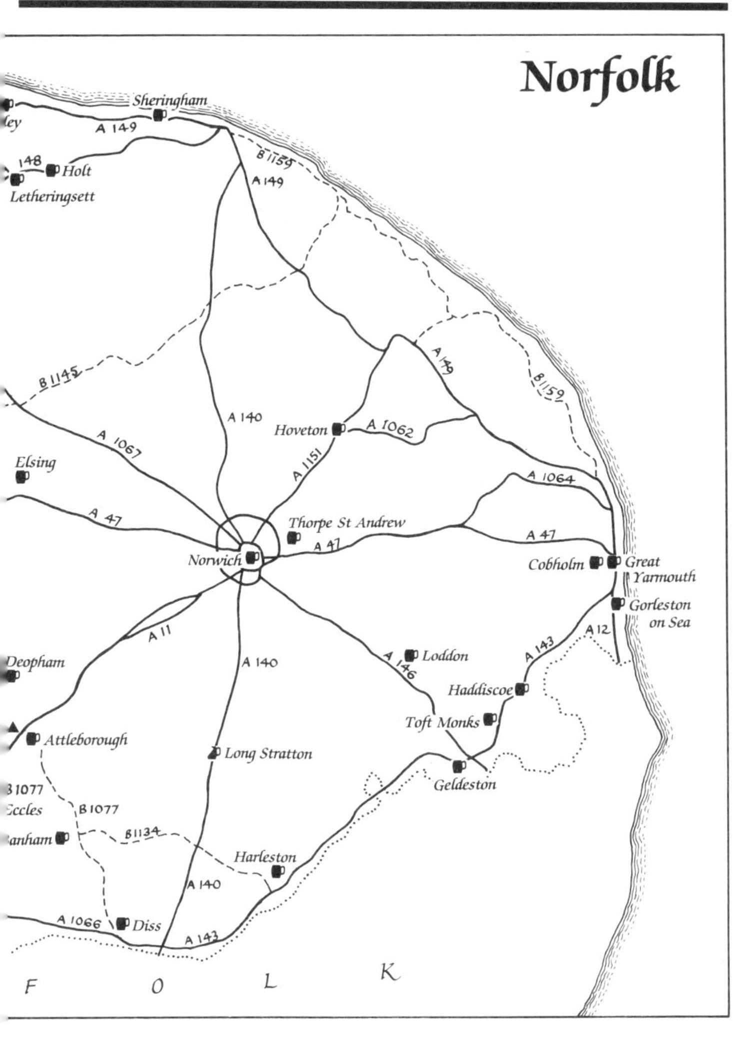

Bawsey

Weekdays: 11–2.30; 7–11

Sandboy (P)

Gayton Road
☎ (055383) 557
Bulmer (H)
Popular pub set in woodland area suitable for picnics and walks, just outside Kings Lynn. Family room and garden. Meals. Facilities for disabled people.

Brandon

Peter Dominic (OL)

3–5 High Street
☎ (0842) 810241
James White (J)

Burnham Market

Satchells (OL)

North Street
☎ (0328) 738272
James White (J)

Cley

Monday–Saturday: 9–5

Picnic Fare (OL)

Cley Forge
☎ (0263) 740037
James White Cider (B)
James White Apple Wine (B)
Norfolk Apple Wine (B)

Cobholm

Salisbury Arms (P)

Lucas Road (near Great Yarmouth)
☎ (0493) 655242
James White (PP)

Deopham

Victoria Inn (P)

Church Road
☎ (0953) 850783
James White (PP)
Village local for one of the most dispersed villages in Norfolk. Meals and snacks; garden.

Norfolk

Diss

Peter Dominic (OL)
Cuthberts Stores, 36 Mere Street
☎ (0379) 642084
James White (J)

Eccles

Old Railway Tavern (P)
Eccles Station (near A11)
☎ (095387) 788
Potmere Farm (PC)
Excellent sociable pub with teams for darts, crib and petanque. Good value food to suit local tastes (not Sunday lunch). Garden, family room and facilities for disabled people.

Elsing

Weekdays: 12–2.30 (except Monday); 7–11, Sunday: 12–3; 7–10.30

Mermaid Inn (P)
Church Street (2 miles north of A47)
☎ (036283) 640
James White (PP) (PL)
17th century country freehouse with real fire. Bar snacks to 2 and 10.30; meals evenings 7–10; Sunday lunchtime; restaurant; children's room; garden.

Geldeston

Weekdays: 11–11

Locks Inn (P)
Station Road (on Suffolk border)
☎ (050845) 414
James White (PC)
At the upper limit of navigation on the River Waveney: a beamed riverside building dating from 1680. Meals lunchtime and evenings; children's room; garden; accommodation; camping facilities.

Gorleston on Sea

8 am–9 pm All week

Beccles Road Supermarket (OL)
59 Beccles Road
☎ (0493) 602071
Inch (J)

Weekdays: 9 am–10.30 pm, Sunday: 12–2; 7–10.30

The Odd Bottle (OL)
49–50 Bells Road
☎ (0493) 663140
James White (J)
Off licence with home brew section. Camping facilities nearby.

Great Yarmouth

Weekdays: 12–3; 7–11

Flints (P)
46 St. Georges Road
☎ (0493) 842196
James White (PC)
Pool table, padded bar and fairy lights.

Red Herring (P)
24–25 Havelock Road
☎ (0493) 853384
Bulmer (H)
James White (PP)

Weekdays: 11–11

Talbot (P)
Howard Street North (behind west side of market place)
☎ (0493) 843175
Guest ciders (PC)
Occasional guest perry (PC)
Small one roomed bar with good social mix. Lunchtime meals. Near Vauxhall BR station.

Terrys (OL)
7 St. Peters Road
James White (J)

Haddiscoe

Pampas Lodge Caravan Site (P)
Beccles Road
☎ (050277) 265
James White

Harleston

Duke William (P)
28 Redenhall Road
☎ (0379) 853183
James White (PP)
Comfortable two bar local with low beamed ceiling, built in 1650. Meals and snacks; garden.

Holt

Weekdays: 8.30–5

Larners of Holt (OL)
10 Market Place
☎ (0263) 712323
James White (B)

Hoveton

Norfolk Fayre (OL)
Wroxham Barns, Tunstead Road
☎ (06053) 3762
James White (J)

Kings Lynn

Peter Dominic (OL)
☎ (0553) 763879
James White (J)
Within half a mile of Kings Lynn BR station.

Letheringsett

Kings Head (P)
On A148
☎ (0263) 712691
James White (J)
Two bar inn close to the River Glaven, popular with tourists and locals. Meals and snacks; garden.

Loddon

A. A. Cook (OL)
13 Church Plain
☎ (0508) 20631
James White (J)

Long Stratton

Wine Box (OL)
The Street
☎ (0508) 30283
James White (J)

Norwich

Barwell & Jones (OL)
118 Sprowston Road
☎ (0603) 484966
James White (J)

Weekdays: 8–5

Clipper Wholesale (OL)
Unit 4 Caley Close
James White (PP)
Cash & carry.

Der Weinkeller (P)
5 St. Johns Close, Hall Road
James White (J)

Horse & Dray (P)
137 Ber Street
☎ (0603) 624741
Bulmer (H)
Snacks and meals lunchtime; evening meals by arrangement; restaurant; children's room; outdoor drinking area.

Hotel Norwich (P)
Boundary Road
☎ (0603) 787260
James White (J)
Friendly hotel bar with local trade. Lunchtime and evening meals.

Weekdays: 11–11
Jubilee (P)
26 St. Leonards Road
☎ (0603) 618734
Various (PC)
Victorian corner pub with two bars. Meals and snacks lunchtime and evenings; outdoor drinking area; access for disabled; pool room. Near Norwich Thorpe BR station.

Weekdays: 11–11, Sunday: 12–3; 7–10.30
Pottergate Tavern (P)
23 Pottergate
☎ (0603) 614589
Wilkins (H)
Meals 12–3; 5–10: snacks 12–10. Access for disabled. Boring 1920s facade hides a well-run, popular city centre pub. Open all day for good food, beers and ciders.

Weekdays: 11–11
Reindeer (P)
10 Dereham Road (just outside city walls)
☎ (0603) 666821
Coombes (PC)
Plain, comfortable, split-level pub with its own brewery. Good lunchtime food. Notable netball team, phat played.

Weekdays: 10.30–11, Sunday: 12–3; 7–10.30
Ribs of Beef (P)
24 Wensum Street
☎ (0603) 619517
James White (PC)
Guest Ciders (PC)
Riverside position with mooring. Home cooked food lunchtime; children's room. The guest ciders include Coombes, Inch, and Thatcher.

Thorpe Wine Stores (OL)
186 Yarmouth Road
☎ (0603) 33532
James White (J)

Monday–Saturday: 10–10, Sunday: 12–2; 7–9
Vintages Off Licence (OL)
98 Thorpe Road
☎ (0603) 624840
James White (B)

Weekdays: 11–11
White Lion (P)
73 Oak Street
☎ (0603) 620630
Guest ciders (H)
Excellent, basic, town centre freehouse. Meals lunchtime and evenings; access for disabled.

Wine Warehouse (OL)
59 Dereham Road
☎ (0603) 612839
James White (B)

Sheringham

Peter Dominic (OL)
37 High Street
☎ (0263) 822508
James White (J)

Thetford

Peter Dominic (OL)
44 King Street
☎ (0842) 752274
James White (J)

Thornham

Weekdays: 11–3; 6–11, Sunday: 12–3; 7–10.30
Lifeboat Inn (P)
Sea Lane
☎ (04826) 236
Bulmer (H)
Ex-smugglers inn overlooking marshes. Meals lunchtime and evenings; children's room; garden.

Thorpe St. Andrew

Monday–Friday: 11–2.30; 7–11, Saturday: 11–10, Sunday: 12–3; 7–10.30
Gordon (P)
88 Gordon Avenue (600 yards off Harvey Lane)
☎ (0603) 34658
Bulmer (H)
Popular local on Norwich outskirts. Lunchtime meals; garden; access for disabled.

Toft Monks

Weekdays: 11.30–2.30; 6.30–11
Toft Lion (P)
Yarmouth Road (near Beccles)
☎ (050277) 702
James White (PC)
Friendly local pub, modernised but comfortable. Meals at lunchtimes and all evenings except Tuesdays. Garden, family room and overnight accommodation.

Northamptonshire

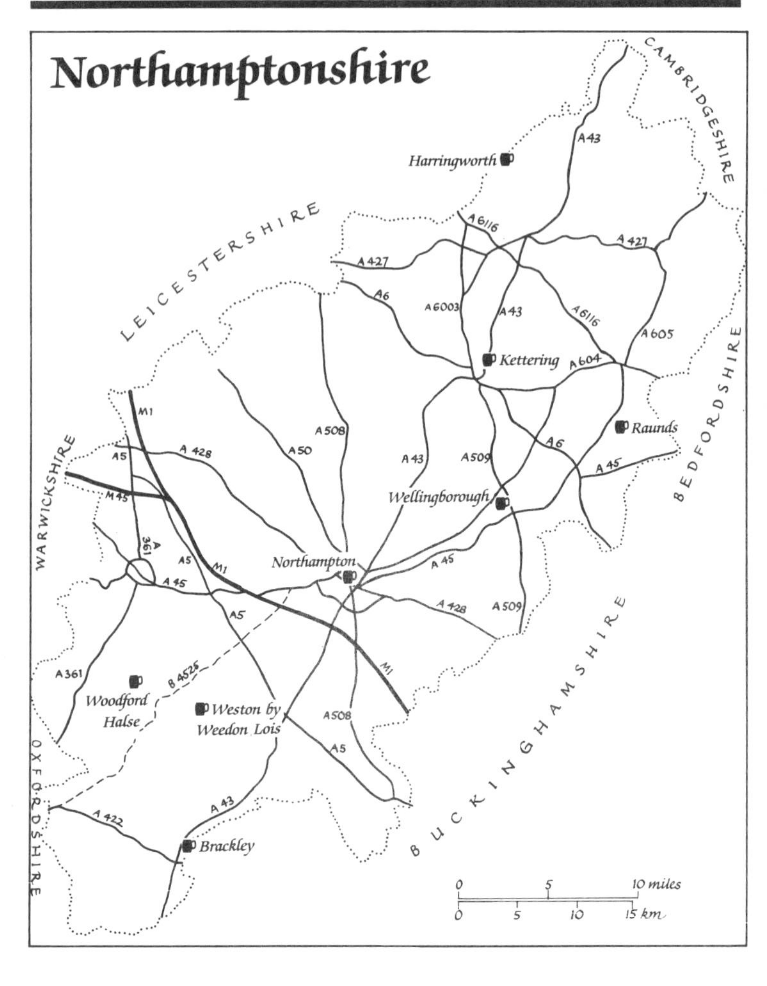

Brackley

Weekdays: 12–2.30; 7–11

Greyhound (P)

101 High Street (on old A43)
☎ (0280) 70331
Bulmer (H)
Attractive low ceilinged lounge bar. Meals and snacks; separate restaurant; outdoor drinking area; access for disabled.

Harringworth

Weekdays: 11–2.30; 6.30–11

White Swan (P)

Seaton Road
☎ (057287) 543
Bulmer (PC) – summer
A Grade 2 listed building with a fine 16th century staircase. A small bar and a larger lounge used mainly by diners. Six letting bedrooms, all ensuite.

Kettering

Monday–Thursday: 11–3; 5.30–11, Friday and Saturday: 11–11

Melton Arms (P)

33 Melton Street
☎ (0536) 518818
Bulmer (H)
Locals' pub five minutes walk from town centre. Snacks.

11.30–2.30; 5.30–11, Sunday: 12–3; 7–10.30

Robin Hood (P)

Northall Street (just off town centre)
☎ (0536) 514395
Bulmer (H)
Locals' pub with a sporty feel. Snacks lunchtime; garden. Near Kettering BR station.

Monday–Friday: 11–2.30; 6–11, Saturday: 11–11

Shire Horse (P)

18 Newland Street
☎ (0536) 519078
Bulmer (PC)
Bar snacks lunchtime; garden.

Northampton

Monday–Friday: 12–2; 6–10, Saturday: 10–10, Sunday: 7–9.30

Beer Agency (OL)

34 Derby Road (off Kettering Road, near

Racecourse)
☏ (0604) 37670
Weston (PC)
Specialises in real ale and cider.

Weekdays: 11–11

King Billy (P)
Commercial Street
☏ (0604) 21307
Bland (PC)
Near town centre, close to Carlsberg Lager factory. Bar snacks; live music Tuesday and Thursday.

Raunds

Monday–Friday: 11–3; 6–11, Saturday and Bank Holidays: 11–11

World Upside Down (P)
8 Marshalls Road (off A605)
☏ (0933) 623328
Bulmer (H)
Named after the reputed lifestyle of an early landlord. Lunchtime meals except Sundays; garden; bar billiards; live music on alternate Friday evenings.

Wellingborough

Monday–Thursday: 10–2; 4–9.30, Friday: 10–2; 4–10, Saturday: 10–10, Sunday: 12–2; 7–9.30

Jug & Bottle (OL)
54 Midland Road
☏ (0933) 71134
Guest Ciders (PC)

Weston by Weedon Lois

Weekdays: 12–2.30; 6.30–11

Crown Inn (P)
6 miles north of Brackley, on the Helmdon road
☏ (029576) 328
Weston (PP)
Large 16th century farmhouse, with stone flagged floors. Separate restaurant; meals and snacks all opening hours; garden; children's room; Northants Skittles; bar billiards.

Woodford Halse

Monday–Thursday: 11.30–3; 6–11, Friday and Saturday: 11–11

Fleur de Lys (P)
South Street (south end of village, on Eydon road)
☏ (0327) 61526
Wilkins (PP)
Brick and stone built village local, with long single room divided up into three separate areas. Snacks lunchtime; garden.

Vinetum Britannicum:
OR A
TREATISE
OF
CIDER;
And other Wines and Drinks extracted from Fruits Growing in this Kingdom.
With the Method of Propagating all ſorts of Vinous FRUIT-TREES.
And a DESCRIPTION of the New-Invented INGENIO or MILL, For the more expeditious making of *CIDER*.
And alſo the right way of making METHEGLIN and BIRCH-WINE.

The Second Impreſſion, much Enlarged.

To which is added, A Diſcourſe teaching the beſt way of Improving BEES.

With Copper Plates.

By *J. Worlidge*. Gent.

LONDON,
Printed for *Thomas Dring*, over againſt the Inner-Temple-gate; and *Thomas Burrel*, at the Golden-ball under St *Dunſtan's* Church in *Fleet-ſtreet*. 1678.

Northumberland, Tyne and Wear

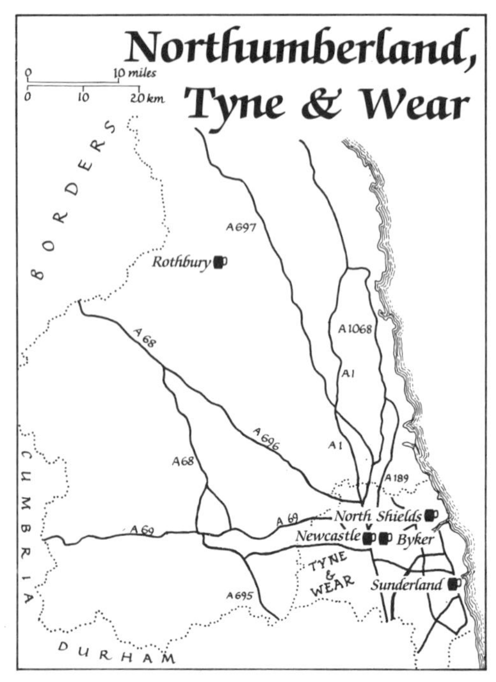

Byker

Weekdays: 11–11

Cumberland Arms (P)

Byker Buildings, Byker (below Byker Bridge, on hill opposite Newcastle)
☎ (091) 265 6151
Bland (H)
Unspoilt basic boozer with bare boards and display of bottles of commemorative ales. Outdoor drinking area. Between Byker and Manors stations.

Newcastle

Weekdays: 11–11, Sunday: 12–3; 7–10.30

Blackie Boy (P)

11 Groat Market
☎ (091) 232 0730
Bulmer (H)

Weekdays: 11–11

Broken Doll (P)

85 Blenheim Street
☎ (091) 232 1047
Bulmer (H)
Centre of the city's modern music scene, popular with young people. Bar snacks lunchtime; live entertainment. Near Newcastle BR and Metro stations.

Weekdays: 11–11

Cooperage (P)

32 The Close, Quayside
☎ (091) 232 8286
Coates (H)
14th century building, once a cooperage. Bar snacks lunchtime, meals all day; restaurant. Near Newcastle Central BR and Metro stations.

North Shields

Weekdays: 11–11, Sunday: 12–3; 7–10.30

Tynemouth Lodge Hotel (P)

Tynemouth Road (A193)
☎ (091) 257765
Thatcher (H)
Very popular free house on main road and not far from Tynemouth Metro Station. Lunches.

Weekdays: 11–11, Sunday: 12–3; 7–10.30

Wolsington House (P)

Burdon Main Row
☎ (091) 257 8487 and 258 5758
Thatcher (PC)
Unspoilt dockland pub in entrance to Appledore ship Repair Yard. Family room.

Rothbury

Newcastle Hotel (P)

Front Street
☎ (0669) 20334
Bulmer (H)

Sunderland

Weekdays: 11–11 (closed Sunday and Bank Holiday lunchtimes)

Borough (P)

Vine Place (in town centre opposite cinema)
☎ (091) 567 7909
Bulmer (H)
Popular with shoppers and students. Meals lunchtime. Near Sunderland BR station.

Monday–Thursday: 12–3; 7–11, Friday–Saturday: 11–11

Pilot Cutter (P)

Harbour View, Roker (on A183 coast road)
☎ (091) 567 1402
Bulmer (PC)
Nautical theme and harbour view, near Roker Park. Outdoor drinking area. Bulmer and guest ciders only available seasonally – please check first.

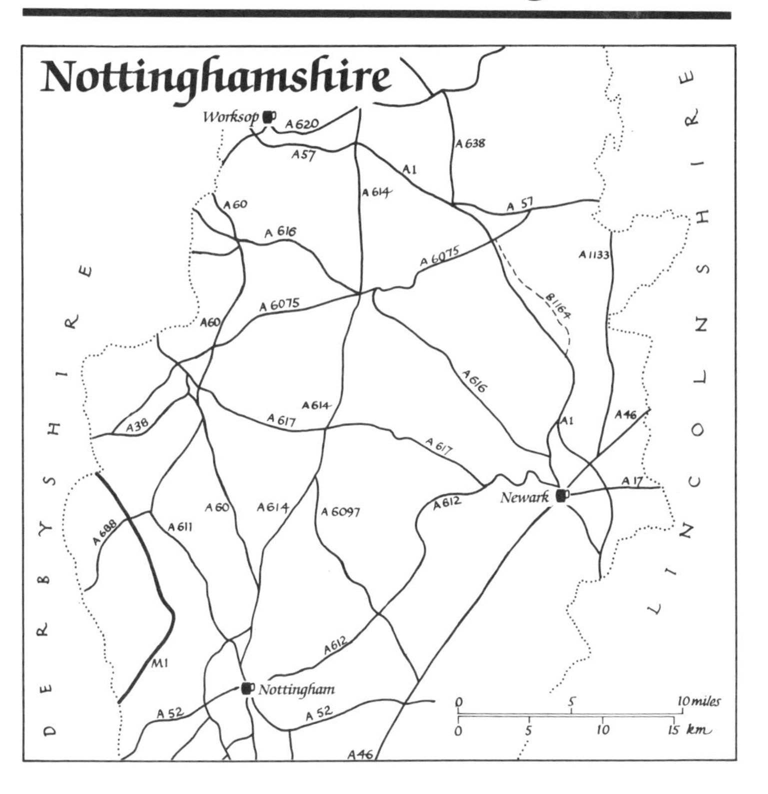

Newark

Weekdays: 11.30–3;
7 (Friday: 5)–11

Malt Shovel (P)

25 North Gate
☎ (0636) 702036
Bulmer (H)
Popular town freehouse. Lunchtime meals; outdoor drinking area; access for disabled. Near Newark Castle and Northgate BR stations.

Nottingham

Weekdays: 10.30–3; 5.30–11

FMC Brewhouse (P)

54 Canal Street
☎ (0602) 506795
Bulmer (H)
Unusually, a Whitbread pub which brews its own beer, known as Fellows, Morton and Clayton.

Weekdays: 11–11

Turf Tavern (P)

Upper Parliament Street
☎ (0602) 474817
Bulmer (H)
Excellent one-roomed local, unusual in a street mainly taken over by café bars. Meals and snacks (not Sunday evening.)

Worksop

Weekdays: 9 am–10 pm

Royson Vintners (OL)

81 Worksop Road, Woodsetts
☎ (0909) 569117
James White (J)
Near Worksop BR station.

Oxfordshire

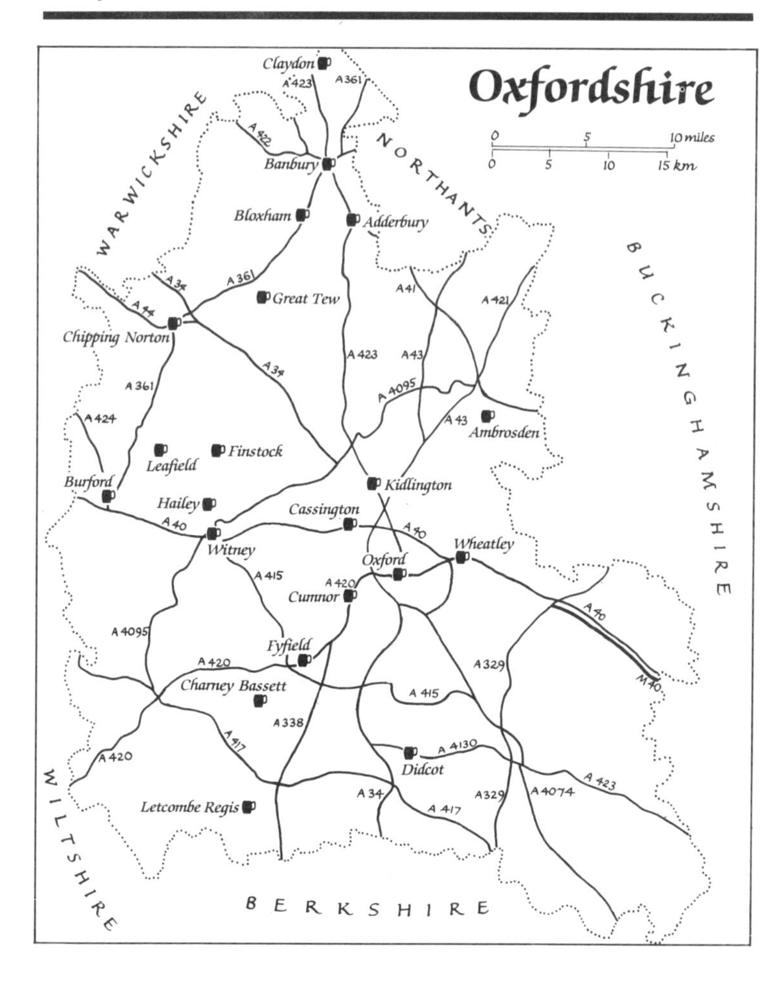

Adderbury

Weekdays: 11–3; 5.30–11, Sunday: 12–3; 7–10.30

Bell Inn (P)
High Street (A423)
☎ (0295) 810338
Westons Old Rosie (H)
Westons Farm Brand (H)
Westons Vintage (PP)
Meals and snacks 12–2; snacks evenings 6–8; meals 6–12; restaurant; garden.

Ambrosden

Turner Arms (P)
Merton Road
☎ (0869) 2468
Weston (PC) (J)
Modernised local in ancient village in the Ray valley.

Banbury

The Bacon Slice (OL)
White Lion Walk
James White (PP) (J) (B)
Off licence outlet for Vitis Wines

evenings only

Vitis Wines (Wholesaler)
29 Kingsway
☎ (0295) 251786
James White (PP) (J) (B)
Off licence at the Bacon Slice qv.

Bloxham

Weekdays: 10.30–2.30; 6–11

Elephant & Castle (P)
Humber Street (off A361)
☎ (0295) 720383
Bulmer (PC)
Fine four storey mid 17th century building in picturesque north Oxfordshire village. Lunches except Sunday; children's room; garden.

Burford

Weekdays: 11–2.30; 6–11, Sunday: 12–2.30; 7–10.30

Lamb (P)
Sheep Street (off High Street)
☎ (099382) 3155
Bulmer (PC)
15th century Cotswold stone hotel with antique furniture and flag stone floors. Meals lunchtime and

evenings; children's room; accommodation.

Cassington

Chequers Inn (P)
Off A40
☎ (0865) 881390
Weston (J)
Recently refurbished pub with good choice of food, including carvery. Good, friendly service. Family room and garden.

Charney Bassett

Chequers (P)
Off A420
☎ (023587) 642
Weston (H) (J)
In Vale of White Horse, near Pusey House and Gardens. Meals and snacks lunchtime and evenings; garden.

Chipping Norton

Weekdays: 10.30–11

Red Lion (P)
Albion Street
☎ (0608) 44641
Bulmer (PC)
Backstreet pub up hill off market place. Meals lunchtime and evenings; outdoor drinking area.

Claydon

Weekdays: 12–2.30; 7–11

Sun Rising (P)
Off A423 in village centre
☎ (029589) 393
Bulmer (H) – summer
Convenient overnight stop on the nearby Oxford Canal. Meals and snacks lunchtime and evenings; garden.

Cumnor

Weekdays: 11–3; 5.30–11

Bear & Ragged Staff (P)
Appleton Road (off A420, between Appleton and Cumnor village)
☎ (0865) 862329
Weston (H)
Comfortable 17th century inn full of charm and character; roaring log fires in winter. Hot and cold bar snacks all sessions; restaurant with English and French cuisine: 12–2; 7–10; special Sunday lunches and vegetarian menus; garden.

Didcot

Weekdays: 11–3; 5.30–11, Sunday: 12–3; 7–10.30

Prince of Wales (P)
Station Road
☎ (0235) 813207
Weston (PC)
Near Didcot Stream Railway Centre, and Didcot Parkway BR station. Meals lunchtime and evenings; garden; accommodation.

Finstock

Crown Inn (P)
School Road
☎ (099386) 431
Weston (H)
Traditional local in pleasant stone village.

Fyfield

Weekdays: 11–2.30; 6.30–11, Sunday 12–3; 7–10.30

White Hart (P)
Off A420
☎ (0865) 390585
Weston (H)
15th century half timbered and tiled building, originally a hospital or chantry for the poor, leased as a tavern by St. Johns College – though they still reserve the right to reside there "in time of pestilence". Antiquarian bookshop in nearby Manor House. Home made food, lunchtime and 7–10; restaurant; children's room; garden.

Great Tew

Weekdays: 11.30–2.30; 6–11 (closed Monday lunchtime), Sunday: 7–10.30

Falkland Arms (P)
☎ (060883) 653
Guest ciders (PC)
18th century thatched pub in centre of Cotswold conservation village, with flagstone floor. Lunchtime snacks in summer; folk music. The ciders will surprise you with their variety.

Hailey

Weekdays: 11–2.30; 6–11

King William IV (P)
Off A4074 towards Ipsden, at White Horse PH
☎ (0491) 680675
Coates (PL)
Superb country pub, popular with walkers due to proximity of Ridegeway Path. Bar snacks all opening hours; outdoor drinking area.

Kidlington

Weekdays: 10.30–4; 6.30–11

Britannia (P)
Church Street
☎ (08675) 2038
Westons Farm Brand (J)
Westons Old Rosie (J)
Lunchtime snacks; garden with climbing frame, seesaw, and swings; camping facilities nearby.

Leafield

Fox Inn (P)
The Greens
☎ (099387) 647
Weston (PC)

Letcombe Regis

Sparrow (P)
South Street
☎ (02357) 3228
Weston (H) (J)
At foot of Lambourn Downs; take narrow winding lane south of church. Meals and snacks lunchtime; large garden with children's facilities.

Oxford

Coach & Horses (P)
62 St. Clements
☎ (0865) 243170
Weston (H)
Late 18th century pub, over Cherwell Bridge from city.

Gardeners Arms (P)
39 Plantation Road
☎ (0865) 59814
Weston (H)
Traditional North Oxford local, popular with town and gown. Meals and snacks; garden.

Weekdays: 10.30–2.30; 6.30–11

Globe (P)

Cranham Street, Jericho (off Walton Street)
☏ (0865) 57759
Westons Old Rosie (H)
Peaceful side street pub. Lunchtime meals; outdoor drinking area; accommodation. Near Oxford BR station.

Weekdays: 11–11, Sunday: 12–3; 7–10.30

Horse & Jockey (P)
69 Woodstock Road
☏ (0865) 52719
Weston (H)
Close to Radcliffe Hospital. Food bar with extensive range of hot and cold meals and snacks all sessions; garden.

Monday–Friday: 11–2.30; 6–11, Saturday: 11–3; 6–11, Sunday: 12–3; 7–10.30

Isis Tavern (P)
Near Iffley Lock
☏ (0865) 247006
Westons Old Rosie (H)
Isolated Thames side pub with no road access, formerly a farmhouse. Lunchtime meals; riverside garden; skittle alley.

Kings Arms (P)
40 Holywell Street
☏ (0865) 242369
Weston (H) (J)
Popular 17th century pub in heart of University area, opposite Bodlieian New Library and Sheldonian Theatre. Hot and cold snacks lunchtime and evenings.

Weekdays: 10–8

Oddbins (OL)
Unit 10, 263 Banbury Road, Summertown
☏ (0865) 52407
Weston (J)

Weekdays: 11–11

Turf Tavern (P)
4 Bath Place (off Holywell Street)
☏ (0865) 243235
Westons Old Rosie (H)
Famous 13th century tavern in peaceful oasis in the middle of the city, approached only by two narrow passageways from Holywell Street. Hot and cold food lunchtime and evenings; outdoor drinking in courtyard; access for disabled.

Wheatsheaf (P)
Wheatsheaf Yard (off High Street)
☏ (0865) 242276
Weston (H)
Crowded pub in heart of the city. Meals and snacks all sessions.

Wheatley

Weekdays: 11–3.30; 6–11

King & Queen (P)
High Street
☏ (08677) 3443
Weston (H)
15th century pub, with beamed ceilings, open fires, and garden.

Witney

Weekdays: 10–11

Red Lion Hotel (P)
Corn Street
☏ (0993) 703149
Westons Old Rosie (H)
Small friendly town centre hotel with good tap room. Bar snacks 10–10; outdoor drinking area; accommodation; round pool table.

Witney

Monday–Wednesday: 10–2.30; 5–11, Thursday–Friday: 10–4; 5–11, Saturday: 10–4; 6.30–11, Sunday: 12–3; 7–10.30

Royal Oak (P)
17 High Street
☏ (0993) 702576
Weston (PL)
In main shopping area. Meals except Sundays; garden.

METHODS OF DISPENSE
(B) Bottle (BB) Bag in box (CK) Carry keg (DJ) glass demijohn (E) Cask and electric pump (F) Flagon (H) Cask and hand pump (J) glass jar (PC) polycask (PL) plastic container (PP) polypin (W) wooden cask

KEY TO MAPS
🍺 town or village with one or more real cider or perry outlets
▲ location of cider or perry maker selling direct to public from premises

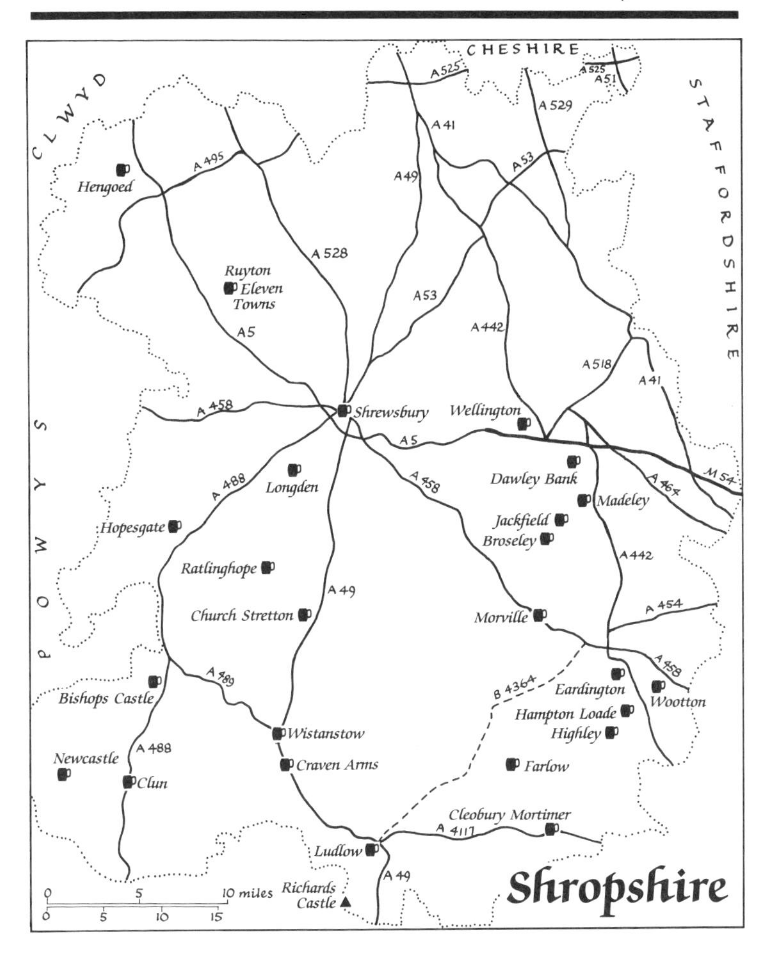

Bishops Castle

Philips Wine Shop (OL)
Spar Stores
Weston – full range

Weekdays: 11.30–2.30; 6.30–11

Three Tuns (P)
Salop Street
☎ (0588) 638797
Weston (H)
Medieval coaching inn at centre of town: one of the original home brew pubs – tours are available. Snacks lunchtime; full meals lunchtime and evenings; outdoor drinking area.

Broseley

Pheasant Inn (P)
Church Street
☎ (0952) 882943
Weston (PC)

Church Stretton

Weekdays: 9 am–9.30 pm, Sunday: 12–3; 7–9.30

Bikold (OL)
6 Sandford Avenue
☎ (0694) 722081
Dunkerton – full range
Weston – full range

Bucks Head Hotel (P)
42 High Street
☎ (0694) 722898
Weston (H)

Cleobury Mortimer

Weekdays: 11–3; 6–11

Bell Inn (P)
Lower Street
☎ (0299) 270305
Bulmer (H)
Unspoilt inn of character.

Clun

White Horse Inn (P)
The Square
☎ (05884) 305
Weston (PC)

Craven Arms

Aston Munslow Garage and Off Licence (OL)
☎ (058476) 280
Weston (J)

Dawley Bank

Weekdays: 12–3; 6.30–11

Bulls Head (P)
☎ (0952) 503378
Weston (PC)

Shropshire

Eardington

Springfield Stores (OL)
Near Bridgnorth
Weston (J)

Farlow

Gate Hangs Well (P)
Near Cleobury Mortimer
☎ (0584) 890273
Weston (PC)
Snacks lunchtime; meals evenings; restaurant; garden; touring caravan site.

Hampton Loade

Weekdays: 11–11

Unicorn (P)
Chelmarsh
☎ (0746) 861515
Weston (J) (PC)
Near Hampton Loade station on privately run Severn Valley Railway: down the road at the River Severn is a current powered ferry. Out of season 3 pint jars of draught cider are sold. Meals and snacks all sessions; terrace within sight and sound of the railway.

Hengoed

Weekdays: 7–11, Sunday: 12–2; 7–10.30

Last Inn (P)
On back road from Oswestry to Weston Rhyn
☎ (0691) 659747
Weston (H)
Surprisingly large country inn, which would be the envy of many a town community centre! Home cooking all sessions; separate restaurant, games, and children's rooms; large function room; access for disabled; live entertainment at weekends.

Highley

Monday–Thursday: 11–3; 6–11, Friday–Saturday: 11–11

Bache Arms (P)
High Street
☎ (0746) 861266
Bulmer (PC)
In village served by Severn Valley Railway steam trains, from Kidderminster to Bridgnorth. Bar snacks 12–2; 7–10; outdoor drinking area/garden; camping facilities nearby; function room; bowling green.

Hopesgate

Weekdays: 11–3; 7–11. Closed Mondays except Bank Holidays

Stables Inn (P)
Near Minsterley – turn right at Hope (off A488), and right at crossroad
☎ (074383) 344
Westons Old Rosie and Special Vintage (F) (PL). Occasional guest ciders
Small pub overlooking Hope Valley, free of juke box and fruit machines. Meals lunchtime and Thursday–Saturday evenings. Garden; camping facilities.

Jackfield

Weekdays: 12–3; 6–11, Sunday: 12–3; 7–10.30

Boat Inn (P)
Ferry Road (access by footbridge from Coalport side of river)
☎ (0952) 882178
Westons Vintage (PC)
Riverside pub in Ironbridge heritage site; near Coalport china museum. Lunchtime meals; garden; access for disabled; camping facilities nearby.

Longden

Tankerville Arms (P)
☎ (0743) 860395
Weston (PC)

Ludlow

Country & Gardens (OL)
22 Corve Street
☎ (0584) 2010
Dunkerton (B)
Near Ludlow BR station.

Feathers (P)
Bull Ring
☎ (0584) 5262
Dunkerton (B)
Set right in the heart of this attractive, historical town.

Weekdays: 11–11 (May–September): 11–2.30; 6–11 (winter)

Bull Hotel (P)
The Bull Ring
☎ (0584) 3611
Weston (PC)
14th century timber framed building. Bar food lunchtime 12–2.15 Monday–Saturday; outdoor drinking area.

Madeley

Park Inn (P)
Park Street
☎ (0952) 583086
Weston (PC)
Comfortable, refurbished pub on edge of former village park. Garden. Families welcome.

Weekdays: 12–11, Sunday: 12–3; 7–10.30

Pheasant (P)
Coalport Road
☎ (0952) 684454
Weston (PC)
Hidden among the trees of the Ironbridge Gorge, overlooking Blists Hill Museum. Meals at lunchtimes, family room and garden.

Red Lion (P)
Park Street
☎ (0952) 592294
Weston (PC)
Excellent example of a mining town pub, retaining its character amongst the New Town development.

Morville

Acton Arms (P)
☎ (074631) 209
Weston (PC)
Pleasant roadside inn reputedly the most haunted in Britain. Renowned for good food; fresh fish a speciality (no meals Sunday evening). Enclosed children's play area plus garden. Disabled access.

Newcastle on Clun

Crown Inn (P)
☎ (05884) 271
Weston (H)
Pub in quiet border village.

Ratlinghope

Monday: 6–11, Tuesday–Saturday: 12–2.30; 6–11, Sunday: 12–3; 7–10.30

Horseshoe Inn (P)
Bridges
☎ (058561) 260
Weston Special Vintage (PC) (J)
Westons Old Rosie (PC) (J)
Unspoilt 16th century inn in a secluded valley between the Long Mynd and the Stiperstones. Bar snacks

12–2; outdoor drinking area; camping facilities nearby.

Richards Castle

FORGE FARM FAMOUS CIDERS ▲
The Forge (on A4361)
☎ (058474) 672

Ruyton Eleven Towns

Monday–Friday: 12–3; 7–11, Saturday: 12–5; 7–11, Sunday: 12–3; 7–10.30

Bridge Inn (P)
☎ (0939) 260651
Weston (PC)
The Manor once contained eleven townships.

Shrewsbury

Coracle Inn (P)
Sundorne Road
☎ (0743) 52818
Weston (J)
Basic bar and trendy lounge. Garden at rear.

Globe Inn (P)
Coleham Head, Longden Coleham
☎ (0743) 54059
Weston (PC)
Until recently known as the Black Horse.

Weekdays: 10.30–3; 6–11

Old Bell (P)
115 Abbey Foregate
☎ (0743) 56041
Weston Old Rosie (DJ)
18th century pub near Lord Hills column (highest Doric column in Britain). Access for disabled from rear entrance; separate bar billiards, pool and juke box room.

Proud Salopian (P)
Smithfield Road
Weston (PC)
Named after Thomas Southam. Five minutes from Station.

Seven Stars (P)
Coleham Head, Longden Coleham
☎ (0743) 52108
Weston (PC)
Home of local folk music club. Impromptu singalongs.

Wellington

Mondays–Tuesday, Thursday–Saturday: 9.30–6, Wednesday: 10–2

Tudor Wines (OL)
15 Market Square
☎ (0752) 255297
Weston Scrumpy
Weston Vintage

Wistanstow

Weekdays: 11.30–2.30; 7–11, Sunday: 12–2; 7–10.30

Plough Inn (P)
Near Craven Arms
☎ (0588) 673251
Weston (PC)
Village local and the Wood Brewery tap. Excellent home-cooked food using local produce. Large lounge and public bar. Garden. Disabled access.

Wootton

Cider House (P)
Near Bridgnorth (off A442 at Quatt or A458 at Broad Oak)
☎ (0746) 780285
Bulmer (E) (H) (PC)
Once a Bulmer's cider house, now independent; in delightful countryside. A day out combining the Severn Valley Railway is highly recommended – Hampton Loade station is about 2 miles to the west. Hot and cold food; large garden.

Somerset

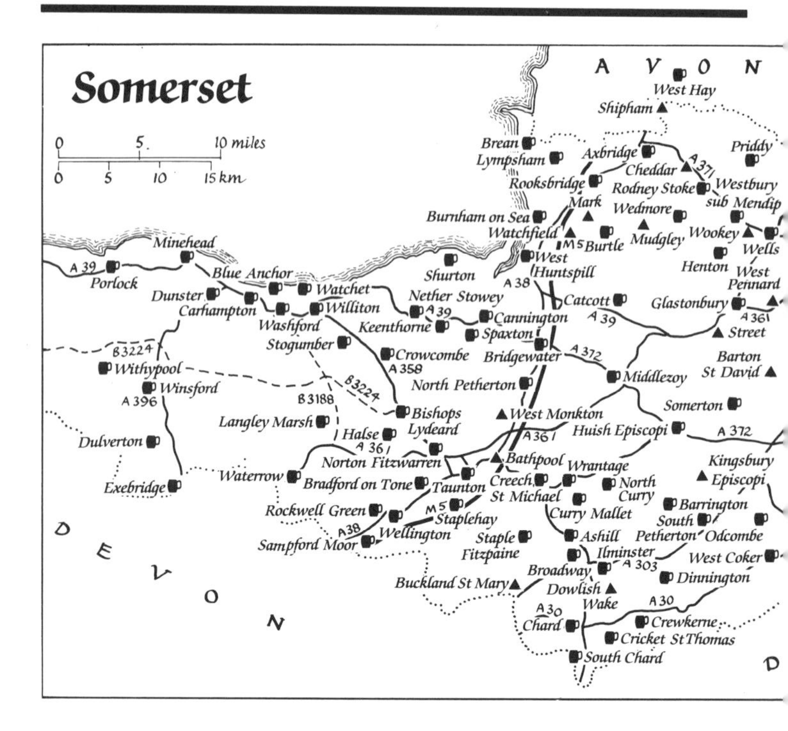

Ashill

ASHILL CIDER ▲
Ashill Farm
☏ (0823) 480513

Axbridge

Broadway House Caravan and Camping Park (OL)
Axbridge Road
☏ (0934) 742610
Country Fayre

Monday–Friday: 11–2.30; 6.30–11, Saturday: 11–3; 6.30–11, Sunday: 12–2.30; 7–10.30

Lamb Inn (P)
The Square
☏ (0934) 732253
Thatcher (H)
Rambling pub in square opposite King John's hunting lodge. Large terraced beer garden. Unusual bar made out of bottles. Accommodation available. Family room and garden. Lunchtime and evening meals (except Sunday evening).

Barrington

Royal Oak (P)
☏ (0460) 53455
Burrow Hill (PC)
Taunton (PC)
Freehouse in a picturesque village. Meals. Outdoor drinking area.

Barton St. David

WHITEHEAD'S CIDER ▲
Tootle Bridge Farm
☏ (0458) 50220

Bathpool

HENRY'S CIDER ▲
Tanpits Cider Farm, Dyers Lane
☏ (0823) 270663

Beckington

Weekdays except Tuesday: 11–2.30; 6–11 (11.30 Friday and Saturday): Sunday: 12–3; 7–10.30

Foresters Arms (P)
Goose Street (off A361)
☏ (0373) 830864
Cheddar Valley (PC)

Snacks; meals lunchtime and evenings.

Binegar

Weekdays: 11–2.30; 7–11, Sunday: 12–3; 7–10.30

Horse & Jockey Inn (P)
Off A37
☏ (0749) 840537
Thatcher (PC)
Meals and snacks lunchtime and evenings – deep pan pizza speciality (not Tuesday or Sunday); garden with children's pets corner.

Bishops Lydeard

Weekdays: 10.30–2.30; 6–11, Sunday: 12–3; 7–10.30

Bell Inn (P)
☏ (0823) 432968
Taunton (H)
Large village pub with oak beams and inglenook fireplaces. Renowned locally for its good food at good prices; family room; garden; patio; games room; two skittle alleys.

Blue Anchor

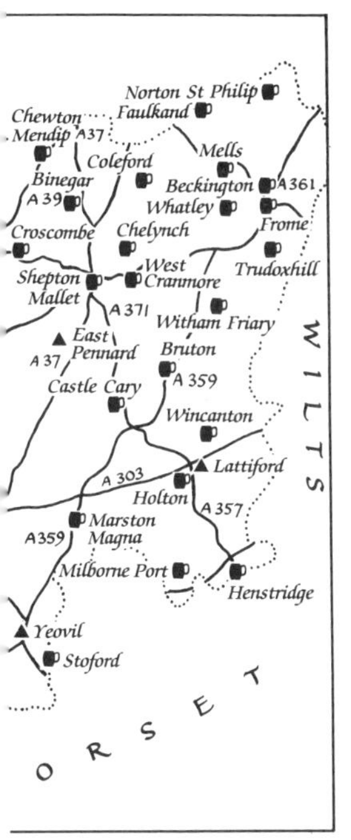

Weekdays: 11–2.30; 6.30–11, Sunday: 12–3; 7–10.30

Blue Anchor (P)
☏ (0934) 40239
Rich (PC)
Good views of bay from garden; bar meals; children's room; accommodation.

Weekdays: 8–8

Blue Anchor Camp Shop (OL)
☏ (064382) 1336
Sheppy

Bradford on Tone

SHEPPY'S CIDER ▲
Three Bridges (on A38)
☏ (082346) 233

Brean

Weekdays: 10–10, Sunday: 12–3; 7–10 (summer): 12–2; 6–8, Sunday: 12–2 (winter)

Allens (OL)
South Road
☏ (027875) 247
Langdon (PC)
Rich (PP)
Sheppy (PL)

Bridgwater

Bath Road News (OL)
167 Bath Road
☏ (0278) 424307
Lane (PL)

Bristol & Exeter (P)
135 St. John Street
☏ (0278) 423722
Lane (H)
Taunton (H)
Near Bridgwater BR station: the pub's name derives from the original title of the line. A good basic cider pub.

Dawes Farm Shop (OL)
Huntworth (on A38)
Lane (PC)
Sheppy (PC)
Exceptionally convenient for M5 Motorway users being located alongside the junction to the south of Bridgwater.

K & C Stores (OL)
15 North Street
☏ (0278) 423124
Lane (PL)
Rich (BB)
Ciders are sold in ½ and 1 gallon containers: Lanes – medium and dry; Rich – medium.

7–7 All week

Minimarket (OL)
133 Taunton Road
☏ (0278) 422961
Rich (PC)

Moorland Stores (OL)
Moorland Road
Lane (PC)

North Pole (P)
North Street
☏ (0278) 51930
Taunton (H)
Small, homely town local.

Oakhill Stores (OL)
58 Wellington Road
☏ (0278) 423801
Lane (PL)

Broadway

Weekdays: 11–2.30; 7–11

Bell Inn (P)
Off A303 in centre of village
☏ (0460) 52343
Taunton (H)
Friendly village local which incorporates a restaurant (meals lunchtimes and evenings). Garden.

Bruton

Castle Inn (P)
High Street
☏ (074981) 812211
Churchill (PC)
Origin of the cider unclear – is this what won the War? Meals and snacks lunchtime include Indian food; garden; skittle alley. Half a mile from Bruton BR station.

Royal Oak (P)
Coombé Street
Taunton (PC)
Bar snacks; pool room; skittle alley. The cider is kept in the back room, so please ask for it by name. Near Bruton BR station.

Weekdays: 11–3; 5.30–11

Sun Inn (P)
High Street
☏ (0749) 813493
Taunton (PC)
Bar snacks 12–2; meals 5.30–10; separate dining area; children's room; camping facilities nearby. Near Bruton BR station.

Buckland St. Mary

VICKERY'S CIDER ▲
Hisbeers Farm, Hare Lane
☏ (046034) 378

Burnham on Sea

Beeline Wines (OL)
12 Regent Street
☏ (0278) 786531
Sheppy

Burtle

Weekdays: 11.30–3.30; 6.30–11

Olde Burtle Inn (P)
☏ (0278) 722269
Wilkins (PC)
16th century moorland inn with games room. Bar meals, children's room and garden.

Cannington

Monday–Friday: 11.30–2.30; 6.30–11, Saturday: 11.30–3.30; 6.30–11, Sunday: 12–3; 7–10.30

Malt Shovel Inn (P)
Blackmore Lane (off A39)
☏ (0278) 653432
Rich (PC)

Somerset

Many roomed country inn in quiet lane, with pleasant views of Quantock Hills. Meals and snacks all sessions; restaurant; children's room; garden; accommodation; area for limited number of caravans; skittle alley.

Carhampton

Butchers Arms (P)
On A39
☏ (064382) 333
Taunton (PC)
Wassailing still takes place in January in the adjoining orchard. Meals and snacks lunchtime and evenings; children's room; garden; accommodation.

Castle Cary

Weekdays: 10–5.30 (closed Sunday)

Castle Cary Vineyard (OL)
Honeywick House
☏ (0963) 50323
Rosies (J) (PL)
Half a mile from Castle Cary BR station.

Sherston Wine Company (OL)
The Pitchings, Market Square
☏ (0963) 50124
Rosies (BB)

Waggon & Horses (P)
Ansford (on A371)
☏ (0963) 50495
Thatcher (H)
Meals and snacks lunchtime and evenings; restaurant; garden; skittle alley. Half a mile from Castle Cary BR station (via footpath to A371).

Monday–Friday: 10.30–2.30; 5.30–11, Saturday: 10.30–11, Sunday: 12–2.30; 7–10.30

White Hart (P)
Fore Street
☏ (0963) 50255
Taunton (H)
Popular town centre pub. Meals and snacks lunchtime and evenings; accommodation; skittles; bar billiards.

Catcott

Weekdays: 11.30–2.30; 6–11, Sunday: 12–3; 7–10.30

King William Inn (P)
Off A39
☏ (0278) 722374
Wilkins (PC)
Popular out of town pub on edge of moor, north of village. Meals; garden; new extension with discovered well; skittle alley.

Chard

8–6 All week

Carpenters Stores (OL)
Furnham Road (A358)
☏ (04606) 3202
Perrys Cider (PL)
Vickery (PL)
General store. Take away snacks all day.

Wey & Co (OL)
19a High Street
☏ (04606) 2546
Sheppy

Working Mens Club & Institute (P)
Fore Street
☏ (04606) 3112
Vickery (PC)

Cheddar

ASHWOOD CIDER
▲
'Ashwood', Shipham Hill
☏ (0934) 742393

Weekdays: 10–6

The Cider Shop (OL)
Cheddar Valley Cheese Depot, The Gorge
☏ (0934) 743113
Derrick (B)
Rich (PC)

DERRICK'S CIDER
▲
Cheddar Valley Cheese Depot, The Gorge
☏ (0934) 743113

Weekdays: 11–2.30; 6–11

Kings Head Inn (P)
Silver Street
☏ (0934) 742153
Taunton (H)
15th century inn. Bar snacks; a la carte menu; children's room; function room; internal courtyard.

WEST COUNTRY CIDER SUPPLIES (D)
67 Redcliffe Street
☏ (0934) 744121

Weekdays: 11–3; 5.30–11

White Hart (P)
The Bays
Taunton (PC)
Cosy pub just off the Gorge road. Garden. Meals lunchtimes and evenings. Also operates an off licence for Taunton Traditional Cider in the adjoining outhouse.

Chelynch

Weekdays: 11.30–2.30; 6.15–11 (closed Monday lunchtime)

Poachers Pocket (P)
☏ (0749) 88220
Wilkins (PC)
Bar meals 11.30–2.30; full meals 6.15–9.45; restaurant; children's room; garden.

Chewton Mendip

Shop: Monday–Saturday: 9–5: Restaurant: daily 10.30–4.30 (closed mid January–mid February): Cheese and cider on sale in restaurant on Sundays.

Chewton Cheese Dairy (OL)
Cheddar Road (off A39 in Chewton Mendip)
☏ (076121) 666
Burrow Hill (PL)
Perrys Cider (PL)
Sheppy (B)
A working cheese maker with a produce shop and restaurant. You can watch the cheese being made while you eat.

Coleford

Weekdays: 12–2.30; 7–11

Eagle (P)
Highbury (at top of village)
☏ (0373) 812440
Taunton (E)
Hot and cold menu; skittle alley; function room.

Weekdays: 12–2.30; 6–11.

Kings Head (P)
☏ (0373) 812346
Bulmer (PC) (H)
Rural country pub in village on edge of Mendip hills; traditional atmosphere.

Creech St. Michael

Weekdays: 11–2.30; 6.30–11.

Riverside Tavern (P)
Bull Street (near church)
☏ (0823) 442257
Bulmer (E)
In village 3 miles from Taunton on canal to Bridgwater.

Crewkerne

Monday–Wednesday: 11–2.30; 6–11, Thursday–Saturday: 11–11.

Castle Inn (P)
West Street
☏ (0460) 72791
Bulmer (H)
Taunton (H)
Terraced pub with comfortable interior and extraordinary fireplace. Skittle alley.

Railway Tavern (P)
South Street
Taunton (H)
Half a mile from Crewkerne BR station.

Weekdays: Monday–Friday: 5–9.30, Saturday: 12–9.30, Sunday: 12–1.30; 7–9.30.

Spencers (OL)
3 North Street
☏ (0460) 75006
Sheppy

Cricket St. Thomas

Cricket St. Thomas Estate (OL)
☏ (046030) 755
Country Fayre
Sheppy

Croscombe

Weekdays: 12–2.30; 7–11. (closed Monday lunch November–March)

Bull Terrier (P)
On A371 in centre of village
☏ (0749) 343658
Wilkins (PC)
15th century building in pattern of a medieval house: fine beams, fireplace and ceiling. The unique name has attracted bull terrier owners worldwide! Comprehensive menu including vegetarian dishes: 12–2; 7–9.30 (to 1.45 Sunday lunch; to 10 Saturday evening); no food Sunday evening or Mondays November–March; family room; accommodation.

Crowcombe

Weekdays: 10–3; 5.30–11.

Carew Arms (P)
☏ (09848) 631
Taunton (PC)
Old local in idyllic location in foothills of the Quantocks. Snacks; children's room; garden; accommodation.

Curry Mallet

Bell Inn (P)
☏ (0823) 480310
Lane (PC)
Small, friendly village local.

Dinnington

Weekdays: 11–3; 6–11.

Rose & Crown Inn (P)
Near Hinton St. George
☏ (0460) 52397
Burrow Hill (PC)
Taunton (H)
Vickery (PC)
Home of Dinnington Docks and Railway Preservation Society, and the famous Green Arrows Formation Lawnmower Team! Snacks 11–2.15; 7–10; full meals 12 noon–2.30; 7–10.30; children's room; probably the largest play area in west for small pub; mobile home for letting; skittle alley.

Dowlish Wake

PERRY'S FARMHOUSE CIDER ▲
Perry's Cider Mills
☏ (04505) 2681

Weekdays: 11–2.30; 6–11.

New Inn (P)
In village centre, 1 mile south of A303
☏ (0460) 52413
Perrys Cider (PC)
Stone built 300 year old pub, just down the street, from Perry's Cider Mill. Meals and snacks all sessions; children's room, garden; access for disabled; skittles; table skittles.

Dulverton

Weekdays: 11–11 (summer): restricted hours in winter.

Rock House Inn (P)
1 Jury Road
☏ (0398) 23558
Taunton (H)
Quiet town local serving meals lunchtimes and evenings. Outdoor drinking area; accommodation; shooting and fishing by arrangement.

Weekdays: 8–1; 2–5.30: Sunday: 9.30–1; 2.30–5.30.

The Tantivy (OL)
Fore Street
☏ (0398) 23465
Countryman (J) (PL)
Inch (PC) (J) (PL)
Palmerhayes (PC) (PL)
Sheppy (J) (PL)
Off licence with confectionery, tobacco, and quality gifts.

Dunster

Weekdays: 11.30–2.30; 7–11.

Castle Hotel (P)
5 High Street
☏ (0643) 821445
Taunton (PC)
Busy hotel with ballroom; interesting ceiling in public bar. Lunch dinner and snacks in restaurant; children welcome; garden; accommodation; pool table.

Weekdays: 11–3; 6.30–11.

Foresters Arms (P)
West Street
☏ (0643) 821313
Bulmer (H)
Interior features a thatched bar. Bar meals; outdoor drinking area; accommodation.

Weekdays: 8–6 (shop): 6.30–10 (takeaway)

Tamarack Stores (OL)
13 Marsh Street
☏ (0643) 821324
Sheppy

East Pennard

AVALON CIDER ▲
Avalon Vineyard, The Drove (off Wraxall to West Pennard Road)
☏ (074986) 393

Exebridge

11–2.30; 6–11: Sunday: 12–2.30; 7–10.30.

Anchor Inn (P)
☏ (0398) 23433
Palmerhayes (DJ)
Sheppy (J)
On the bank of the River Exe, with fishing from the lawns. Meals and snacks 12–2; restaurant; children's room; garden; accommodation; access for disabled; camping facilities nearby.

Faulkland

Weekdays: 12 noon–11 as required.

Faulkland Inn (P)

On A366
☏ (037387) 312
Taunton (H)
Spacious, comfortably furnished country inn. Meals lunchtime and evenings; snacks; garden; skittles; pool table.

Tuckers Grave Inn (P)
On A366
☏ (037387) 230
Cheddar Valley (PC)
Traditional cider and ale house, a small farm cottage which has doubled as an inn for over 200 years. Snacks; garden.

Frome

Monday–Friday: 11–11: Saturday: 10–11.

Angel (P)
King Street
☏ (0373) 62369
Taunton (H)
Meals and snacks 11–2.30; 6–8.30; restaurant; children's room; outdoor drinking area; accommodation; pool room.

Weekdays: 11–2.30; 6–11.

First & Last (P)
Wallbridge
☏ (0373) 62642
Bulmer (PC)
Lunches; garden; accommodation. Near Frome BR station.

Weekdays: 11–3; 6–11; Saturday: 11–11.

Lamb & Fountain (P)
57 Castle Street
☏ (0373) 63414
Taunton (PC)
The cider centre of the town: little else is drunk, and you probably will be too! Snacks lunchtime.

Weekdays: Monday-Friday: 11–3; 6–11: Saturday: 11–11.

Sun Inn (P)
6 Catherine Street
☏ (0373) 73123
Thatcher (H)
Popular former coaching inn in old part of town. Lunchtime meals except Sundays; accommodation, half a mile from Frome BR station.

Trinity (P)
31 Vallis Ways (A362)
☏ (0373) 63603
Taunton (H)
Previously called the Globe; games oriented local. Bar food; pool table; skittles.

Weekdays: 11–2.30; 6.30–11.

Weaver (P)
6 The Butts
☏ (0373) 63733
Bulmer (PC)
Meals and snacks lunchtime and evenings.

Glastonbury

Weekdays: 11–11: Sunday: 12–3.

Fairfield (P)
31 Benedict Street
☏ (0458) 31442
Wilkins (PC)

King William (P)
Market Place
☏ (0458) 31473
Taunton (PC)
Pleasant place to wait for or chat with friends. Live music most weekends. Family room.

Weekdays: 11–4; 5–11 (summer): 11–2.30; 5–11 (winter)

Riflemans Arms (P)
Chilkwell Street
☏ (0458) 31023
Wilkins (PC)
Several roomed pub, dating from 13th century, strategically placed for the ascent of Glastonbury Tor – and to retire to afterwards! Meals lunchtime except Sunday; children's room; garden; pool room.

Stevens Stores (OL)
Northload Street
Avalon (B)
Country Fayre (B) (S)
Inch (BB) (PL)
Wilkins (PL)

The Truckle of Cheese (OL)
33 High Street
☏ (0458) 32116
Country Fayre (B)
Inch (B)

Halse

Weekdays: 11–3; 6–11.

New Inn (P)
☏ (0823) 432352
Taunton (H)
Compact old inn in friendly village. Meals and snacks; restaurant; garden; accommodation

Henstridge

Weekdays: 11–2.30; 5.30–11: Sunday: 12–2; 7–10.30

Bird in Hand (P)
Ash Walk (off A30, ½ mile along A357 towards Blandford)
☏ (0963) 62255
Taunton (PC)
Classic village pub with beams and low roof. Meals and snacks lunchtime and evenings; skittle alley, function room.

Henton

Weekdays: 11.30–3; 7–11.

Olde Punch Bowl Tavern (P)
On Wells to Wedmore road
☏ (0749) 72212
Wilkins (PC)
Lively roadside pub with bar food and meals available all week; restaurant and grill room.

Holton

Monday–Friday: 11–2.30; 5.30–11: Saturday 11–11: Sunday: 12–3; 7–10.30.

Old Inn (P)
Just south of A303, near Wincanton
☏ (0963) 32002
Rosies (BB)
Taunton (PC)
Village inn. Originally a smithy. Meals and snacks lunchtime and evenings; garden.

Huish Episcopi

Rose & Crown (P)
On A372
☏ (0458) 250494
Burrow Hill (W)
Known locally as 'Eli's', a pub with no bar, just a tap room and various rooms to retreat to with your drink. Family room; garden; access for disabled; skittles; pool table.

Ilminster

Lord Nelson Inn (P)
☏ (0406) 52532
West Country Scrumpy (PC)

Weekdays: Monday–Thursday: 11.30–2.30; 7–11: Friday: 11.30–4; 7–11: Saturday: 11–11.

White Horse (P)
Bay Hill
☏ (0460) 54616
Taunton (PC)
Vickery (PC)

Friendly family local. Snacks 12–2; children's room; outdoor drinking area/garden: children's play area.

Keenthorne

Weekdays: 11–11: Sunday: 12–3; 7–10.30.

Cottage Inn (P)
On A39 near Nether Stowey
☎ (0278) 732355
Coombes (PC)
Lane (PC)
Very popular roadhouse with large family/pool room. Meals and bar snacks. Garden and camping facilities on site.

Kingsbury Episcopi

BURROW HILL SOMERSET CIDER ▲
Pass Vale Farm, Burrow Hill
☎ (0460) 40782

Rusty Axe (P)
Stembridge (between village and Burrow Hill)
Burrow Hill (PC)

Wyndham Arms (P)
☎ (0935) 823239
Burrow Hill (PC)
Meals and snacks lunchtime and evenings; garden; skittle alley.

Langley Marsh

Weekdays: 12–2.30; 7–11: Sunday: 12–2; 7–10.30.

Three Horseshoes (P)
☎ (0984) 23763
Perrys Cider (PC) (W)
Small, friendly pub with real fire and vast collection of photos of old cars. Interesting traditional and vegetarian menu – puddings especially recommended. Garden. Table skittles.

Lattiford

ROSIES CIDER ▲
Rose Farm on A357
☎ (0963) 33680

Lympsham

Sanders Super Fruit (OL)
West Home Nurseries
☎ (0934) 812652
Sheppy

Mark

COOMBES TRADITIONAL FARMHOUSE CIDER ▲
Japonica Farm
☎ (027864) 265

Weekdays: 11–2.30; 6–11: Sunday: 12–2.30; 7–10.30.

Pack Horse (P)
On B3139 adjoining church
☎ (027864) 209
Wilkins (PC)
Impressive village pub sympathetically refurbished in traditional style. Lunchtime meals, also evening meals for hotel guests. Garden. Accommodation.

Marston Magna

Marston Magna Stores (OL)
☎ (0935) 850215
Rosies (BB)

Mells

Monday–Friday: 11–3; 6–11: Saturday: 11–3.30; 4.30–11.

Talbot Inn (P)
☎ (0373) 812254
Wilkins (PP)
15th century coaching inn with central cobbled courtyard. Meals and snacks lunchtime and evenings.

Middlezoy

Monday: 7–11: Tuesday–Saturday 12–2.30; 7–11.

George Inn (P)
42 Main Road
☎ (082369) 215
Oak Farm Cider (PC)
17th century free house near site of Battle of Sedgemoor. Lunchtime meals except Monday; evening meals except Sunday and Monday; accommodation; access for disabled; camping facilities nearby; skittle alley, pool room.

Milborne Port

Weekdays: 10.30–2.30; 5.30–11.

Queens Head (P)
High Street (A30)
☎ (0963) 250314
Rosies (PC)
Taunton (H)
Basic village pub with separate restaurant and skittle alley. Excellent food lunchtimes in bar and evenings in restaurant. Piano. Garden. Bed and Breakfast.

Minehead

9–5.30 all week.

Minimarket (OL)
45 The Avenue
☎ (0643) 3979
Perrys Cider (PC) (BB) (J) (PL)
Sheppy (PC) (BB) (J) (PL)

Peter Dominic (OL)
12 The Parade
☎ (0643) 2072
Country Fayre (B)

Mudgley

WILKINS' FARMHOUSE CIDER ▲
Lands End Farm
☎ (0934) 712385

Nether Stowey

Monday–Wednesday; Friday–Saturday: 8–5.30: Thursday: 8–8: Sunday and Bank Holidays: 10–5.30 (summer): weekdays: 8–5 (winter).

Stowey Court Farm
☎ (0278) 732207
Rich (PC)
Sheppy

North Curry

White Hart (P)
☎ (0823) 490439
Lane (PC)

North Petherton

Monday–Friday: 11–3; 6–11: Saturday: 11–11: Sunday: 12–3; 7–10.30.

Globe Inn (P)
High Street
☎ (0278) 662999
Bulmer (H)
Taunton (H)
Snacks; garden. skittle alley.

Norton Fitzwarren

Weekdays: 11–3; 6–11: Sunday: 12–3; 7–10.30.

Ring of Bells (P)
On A361
☎ (0823) 275995
Taunton (H)
Lively pub with two carpeted bars and spacious skittle alley cum family room, the local for the

Somerset

Taunton Cider Company. Bar meals, garden and disabled access. Camping facilities nearby.

Norton Fitzwarren

TAUNTON TRADITIONAL CIDER
The Taunton Cider Company
☎ (0823) 83141

Norton St. Philip

Weekdays: 10.30–2.30; 6–11.

Fleur de Lys (P)
The Plain (On A366)
☎ (037387) 333
Bulmer (PC)
Snacks.

Odcombe

Weekdays: 12–3; 7–11.

Masons Arms (P)
☎ (093586) 2591
Taunton (H)
14th century longhouse; sit in fireplace; beamed ceiling. Bar snacks 12–2.30; garden.

Porlock

Porlock Fare (OL)
High Street
☎ (0643) 862515
Country Fayre (B)

Weekdays: 10.30–2.30; 5.30–11.

Ship Inn (P)
High Street
☎ (0643) 862507
Perrys Cider (PC)
13th century inn at foot of Porlock Hill. Meals and snacks all sessions; children's room; garden; accommodation; camping facilities nearby.

Priddy

Weekdays: 11.30–2.30; 6.30–11: Sunday: 12–2.30; 7–10.30.

Hunters Lodge (P)
1½ miles northwest of Mendip TV mast off A39
☎ (0749) 72275
Stott (PC)
High in the Mendips, popular with walkers and cavers. Meals and snacks lunchtime, snacks only in evenings; garden; accommodation; camping facilities nearby.

Weekdays: 12–2.30; 7–11: Sunday: 12–2.30; 7–10.30.

New Inn (P)
Signposted off B3135
☎ (0749) 76465
Perry's Cider (PC)
15th century farmhouse on village green, with stone flagged floors. Lunchtime and evening meals, including vegetarian dishes; children's room; garden; accommodation; access for disabled; camping facilities nearby; skittles.

Rockwell Green

Weekdays: 11–3; 6–11.

Weavers Arms (P)
102 Rockwell Green
☎ (082347) 2466
Bulmers West Country (PC)
Local village pub. Bar snacks lunchtimes 12–2 except Sundays; access for disabled; skittle alley.

Rodney Stoke

Bucklegrove Caravan Park (OL)
☎ (0749) 870261
Derrick (PC)

Rooksbridge

Weekdays: 12–2.30; 7–11: Sunday: 7–10.30.

Wellington Arms (P)
Bristol Road (A38)
☎ (0934) 750106
Wilkins (PC)
Small free house. Garden.

Samford Moor

Weekdays: 12–2.30; 6–11.

Blue Ball (P)
Off A38
☎ (082347) 3112
Bulmer (H)
Taunton (H)
Weston (H)
Rural local with good range of cider. Good pub food; garden with outstanding views.

Shepton Mallet

Weekdays: 11–2.30; 7–11; Sundays: 12–3, 7–10.30.

Bell Hotel (P)
2 High Street
☎ (0749) 5393
Taunton (PC)
Meals and snacks lunchtime; accommodation.

COATES FARMHOUSE CIDER
Showerings Ltd., Kilver Street
☎ (0749) 3333

Monday–Tuesday; Thursday–Saturday: 8.30–5.30: Wednesday: 8.30–2.

The Delicatessen (OL)
36 High Street
☎ (0749) 4523
Sheppy (J)
Large range of traditional English and international cheeses.

Monday–Friday: 12–2; 7–11: Saturday: 11–2.30; 7–11: Sunday: 12–2; 7–10.30.

Showerings Sports & Social Club (P)
Town Lane
☎ (0749) 2461
Wilkins (PC)
Snacks 12–2; 7–10; full meals by arrangement; skittle alley.

Shepton Montague

Weekdays: 12–2; 6.30–11 (summer); 6–11 (winter)

Montague Inn (P)
400 yards off A359, one mile east of A359/A371 crossroads
☎ (0749) 813213
Sandford (PC)
Remote but convivial country pub. Lunchtime meals (Saturday and Sunday only in winter); garden; accommodation.

Shipham

ART'S SOMERSET SCRUMPY ▲
Lilypool Farm
☎ (0934) 743994

Miners Arms (P)
The Square
☎ (093484) 2146
Thatcher (H)
Welcoming, traditional village local. Meals and snacks lunchtime and evenings; restaurant; games room.

Shurton

Weekdays: 11–2.30; 6–11.

Shurton Inn (P)
☎ (0278) 732695
Lane (H)

Cottage style country inn close to Quantock Hills. Meals and snacks 12–2; 7–10; restaurant; children's room; outdoor drinking area; accommodation; camping facilities nearby.

Somerton

Monday–Tuesday; Thursday–Saturday: 9–1; 2–7: Wednesday: 9–1. (closed all day Sunday).

Longmires (OL)
West Street
☏ (0458) 72326
Country Fayre (PL)
Taunton (PC)

Weekdays: 11–3; 6–11: Sunday: 12–3; 7–10.30.

Royal Oak (P)
☏ (0458) 72758
Vickery (PC)
Pub with strong sporting connections – two football teams! Access for disabled.

South Chard

Weekdays: 11.30–2.30; 6.30–11.

Perry Street Club (P)
☏ (0460) 20239
Taunton (H)
Vickery (PC) (PL)
C.I.U. Club. Meals and snacks 12–2; 7–10; outdoor drinking area/garden; camping facilities nearby; snooker, pool, skittles.

South Petherton

Weekdays: 11–3; 7–11.

Wheatsheaf (P)
39 Silver Street (off A303)
☏ (0460) 40382
Burrow Hill (W)
Taunton (PC)
Town local

Spaxton

Weekdays: 11–2.30; 7–11: Sunday: 12–3; 7–10.30.

Lamb Inn (P)
Barford Road
☏ (027867) 350
Bulmer (H)
Village local adjacent to Agapemone (Victorian commune). Snacks; meals; particularly fine garden.

Staple Fitzpaine

Weekdays: 11–3; 5.30–11

Greyhound Inn (P)
☏ (0823) 480227
Taunton (H)
Much extended old pub serving meals and snacks. Restaurant – including candle lit dinners, Friday Fish Day, and Sunday Special. Garden. Accommodation. Function facilities available.

Staplehay

Weekdays: 11.30–2.30; 6.30–11

Crown Inn (P)
Honiton Road
☏ (0823) 272560
Taunton (PC)
Friendly, comfortable local serving both restaurant meals and bar snacks. Skittle alley and pool table.

Stoford

Weekdays: 11–2.30; 6–11, Sunday: 12–3; 7–10.30

Royal Oak (P)
The Green
☏ (0935) 75071
Taunton (PC)
Snacks. Half a mile from Yeovil Junction BR station.

Stogumber

Weekdays: 11–2.30; 6–11, Sunday: 12–3; 7–10.30

White Horse Inn (P)
In village centre, opposite church
☏ (0984) 56277
Sheppy (H) – summer only
Near Quantocks and Brendon Hills. Home made and extensive meal and snack menu all sessions; restaurant; garden; accommodation; access for disabled.

Street

HECKS' FARMHOUSE CIDER ▲
9 and 11 Middle Leigh
☏ (0458) 42367

Weekdays: 10.30–2; 6.30–11

Royal British Legion Club (P)
3–5 Farm Road
☏ (0458) 42873
Wilkins (PC) (PP)

West Country Garden Supplies (Supplier)
39 Brooks Road
☏ (0458) 45505 and (0483) 37848
Rich (PC)
An agency which delivers Rich's Cider direct from Somerset to anywhere in Surrey, on a once a month basis as required.

Taunton

Cheddon Road Stores (OL)
97 Cheddon Road
☏ (0823) 278960
Lane (PC)

County Stores (OL)
52 North Street
☏ (0823) 72235
Sheppy

Weekdays: 8.30–6

Essjays (OL)
14 Priorswood Place
☏ (0823) 252304
Lane (PL)

Weekdays: Monday–Friday: 7 am–8 pm, Saturday: 7–6

King Stores (OL)
88 Eastleigh Road
☏ (0823) 275354
Henrys

Manor Fare (OL)
93 Galmington Road
☏ (0823) 336351
Sheppy

Threshers Wine Merchants (OL)
29 East Reach
☏ (0823) 335927
Sheppy

Weekdays: 8.30 am–9 pm

Victoria Wine (OL)
40 East Street
☏ (0823) 272128
Sheppy (PL)

Wheeltappers (P)
Station Road
☏ (0823) 88557
Taunton (H)
Adjoins south side of Taunton BR station – ideal as a waiting room!

Trudoxhill

Monday–Friday: 12–2.30; 7–11, Saturday: 11.30–2.30; 7–11

White Hart (P)
½ mile south of A361 at Nunney Catch
☏ (0373) 84324
Old Barnie (PC)
Comfortable atmosphere in this village pub with new brewery at rear. Menu caters for vegetarians. Garden.

Washford

Weekdays: 11–3; 5.30–11

Washford Inn (P)
☏ (0984) 40256
Taunton (H)
Next to Washford station on the privately operated West Somerset Railway. The public bar being appropriately decorated. Meals and snacks 12–2; 7–10.30; restaurant; children's room; garden; accommodation.

Watchet

Weekdays: 11–11

Anchor (P)
Anchor Street
☏ (0984) 31387
Taunton (H)
Extended back street local with outdoor drinking area. Snacks.

Weekdays: 10.30–4 (summer), 3 (winter); 6–11, Sunday: 12–3; 7–10.30

Bell Inn (P)
Market Street (opposite museum, near harbour)
☏ (0984) 31379
Sheppy (PC)
Old multi-roomed pub, popular with local boatmen. Meals lunchtime and evenings; children's room; access for disabled; camping facilities nearby.

Country Kitchens (OL)
Henry (PL)

Harbour Stores (OL)
Sheppy

Weekdays: 8–8

Sunnybank Caravan Park (OL)
Doniford
☏ (0984) 32237
Sheppy
A happy small caravan park, where you can come for a holiday, and be made happier drinking Sheppy's Farm Cider!

Watchfield

RICH'S SOMERSET FARMHOUSE CIDER ▲
Mill Farm
☏ (0278) 783651

Waterrow

Weekdays: 11–2.30; 6–11

Rock Inn (P)
☏ (0984) 23293
Sheppy (PC)
One bar hotel built against a rock face. Meals lunchtime and evenings; separate restaurant; garden across the road; accommodation, camping facilities up the road.

Wedmore

COUNTRY FAYRE CIDER
Knee Cracker Cider Ltd.
☏ (0934) 712801

Weekdays: 11–2.30; 7–11

New Inn (P)
Coombe Batch
☏ (0934) 712099
Wilkins (PC)
Simple village pub with a variety of meals and snacks lunchtimes and evenings (not Sunday evening). Garden.

Wellington

Weekdays: 9–5.30

The Cheese & Wine Shop (OL)
11 South Street
☏ (082347) 2899
Sheppy

Concorde Wines (OL)
The Wine Cellar, 12 Cornhill Arcade
☏ (082347) 7565
Sheppy

Weekdays: 9–9

The Wine Cellar (OL)
22 High Street
☏ (0823) 667565
Sheppy (PP) (DJ) (J) (PL)
Haymaker (DJ) (J) (PL)

Wells

Monday–Friday: 11–2.30; 5–11, Saturday: 11–11, Sunday: 12–3; 7–10.30

Cheddar Valley Inn (P)
22 Tucker Street
☏ (0749) 72807
Taunton (H)
Named after the one time nearby railway: old fashioned traditional public bar. Snacks all sessions; outdoor drinking area.

Peter Dominic (OL)
28 High Street
☏ (0749) 72005
Country Fayre (B)

Westbury Sub Mendip

Weekdays: 11–3; 7–11

Westbury Inn (P)
On A371 Wells to Cheddar road
☏ (0749) 870223
Wilkins (PP)
Attractive country inn. Good and reasonable food from sandwiches to steaks 12–2.30; 7–9.30; restaurant; outdoor drinking area; camping facilities nearby.

West Cranmore

Weekdays: 11.30–2.30; 6.30–11

Strode Arms (P)
Off A361, near headquarters of East Somerset Railway
☏ (074988) 450
Wilkins (PC)
Country pub by village duck-pond. Meals and snacks lunchtime and evenings; garden; pool table.

West Coker

Royal George (P)
11 High Street
☏ (093586) 2334
Taunton (PC)
Busy main road pub. Lots of brass, but a bit modern and characterless. Meals and snacks lunchtime and evenings. Garden.

West Hay

Weekdays: 11–2.30; 6–11, Sunday: 12–3; 7–10.30

Bird in Hand (P)
Main Road
☏ (04586) 229
Wilkins (PC)
Friendly village pub with garden and children's room. Bar meals served.

West Huntspill

Weekdays: 12–11

Crossways Inn (P)
On A38
☏ (0278) 783756
Rich (PC)
17th century inn. Excellent

meals and snacks; restaurant. Garden. Accommodation.

West Monkton

LANE'S CIDER ▲
Overton
☏ (0823) 412345

Monday–Tuesday, Thursday–Friday: 9–5.30 (closed 1–2): Wednesday, Saturday: 9–1, closed Sunday.

Post Office Stores (OL)
☏ (0823) 412201
Lane (BB)
300 year old post office stores in home village of Lane's Cider. Danish spoken! (the proprietor is Bjarne Nielsen).

West Pennard

NAISH'S CIDER ▲
Piltown Farm
☏ (07489) 260

Whatley

Weekdays: 11–3; 6–11, Sunday: 12–3; 7–10.30

Sun Inn (P)
Near Frome
☏ (0373) 84219
Bulmer (PP)
Good bar snacks and meals all times; restaurant; outdoor drinking area/garden.

Williton

Monday–Friday: 11–2.30; 5.30–11, Saturday: 11–11

Wyndham Arms (P)
High Street
☏ (0984) 32381
Taunton (H)
Popular town local with good beer (or cider) garden. Bar meals.

Wincanton

Weekdays: 11–2.30; 6–11

Dolphin Hotel (P)
High Street
☏ (0463) 32215
Bulmer (H)
Rosies (PC)
Meals and snacks lunchtime and evenings; garden; accommodation.

Railway Inn (P)
Station Road
☏ (0963) 32252
Taunton (H)
You have missed the last train – it ran in March 1966! Games oriented pub; snacks; skittles, table skittles, pool table, shove ha'penny; darts.

Winsford

Weekdays: 9–1; 2–5.30

Winsford Stores (OL)
☏ (064385) 201
Hancock (B)

Witham Friary

Weekdays: 11–3; 6–11

Seymour Arms (P)
3 miles south of A361 from Nunney Catch
Bulmer (PC)
Taunton (PC)
Old local, with central serving hatch. Garden; children's room; bar billiards.

Withypool

Weekdays: 11–2.30; 6–11, Sunday: 12–2; 7–10.30

Royal Oak Inn (P)
Off B3223
☏ (064383) 506
Hancock (PC)
2 bars with oak beams. Meals and snacks; restaurant; garden; accommodation.

Wookey

STOTT'S SUPERB CIDER ▲
Shotts Farm
☏ (0749) 74731 or 73323

Wrantage

Weekdays: 12–2.30; 7–11

Canal Inn (P)
☏ (0823) 480210
Lane (PC)
18th century inn. Meals and snacks 12–2; 7–9.30; restaurant; large garden with tree house.

Yeovil

Weekdays: 11–11, Sunday: 12–3; 7–10.30

Alexandra (P)
South Western Terrace (next to old station car park)
☏ (0935) 23723
Taunton (H)
Traditional town centre pub. Meals lunchtime.

Monday–Thursday: 11–2.30; 6–11, Friday–Saturday: 11–3.30; 6–11, Sunday: 12–3; 7–10.30

Black Horse (P)
The Avenue, Recklesford (next to District Hospital)
☏ (0935) 23878
Taunton (H)
Small edge of town local. Bar snacks 12–2; meals 6–10; outdoor drinking area.

BRYMPTON D'EVERCY CIDER ▲
Brympton d'Evercy House
☏ (093586) 2528

Monday–Thursday: 10.30–2; 5.30–11, Friday–Saturday: 10.30–3.30; 5.30–11

Globe & Crown (P)
South Street
☏ (0935) 23328
Taunton (H)
Lively town centre local with strong cider following. Snacks all sessions.

Monday–Friday: 11–11, Saturday: 10.30–11, Sunday: 12–3; 7–10.30

Royal Marine (P)
Great Western Terrace (just off A30 near Pen Mill BR station)
☏ (0935) 74350
Taunton (H)
Meals lunchtime and evenings; pool table.

Weekdays: 8.30 am–10 pm all week.

Suzy Fruits (OL)
257 Stiby Road
☏ (0935) 32204
Perrys Cider (PC)
Sheppy (PC)
Here the customer is never right, is abused and trained to serve him or herself, but always leaves with a smile!

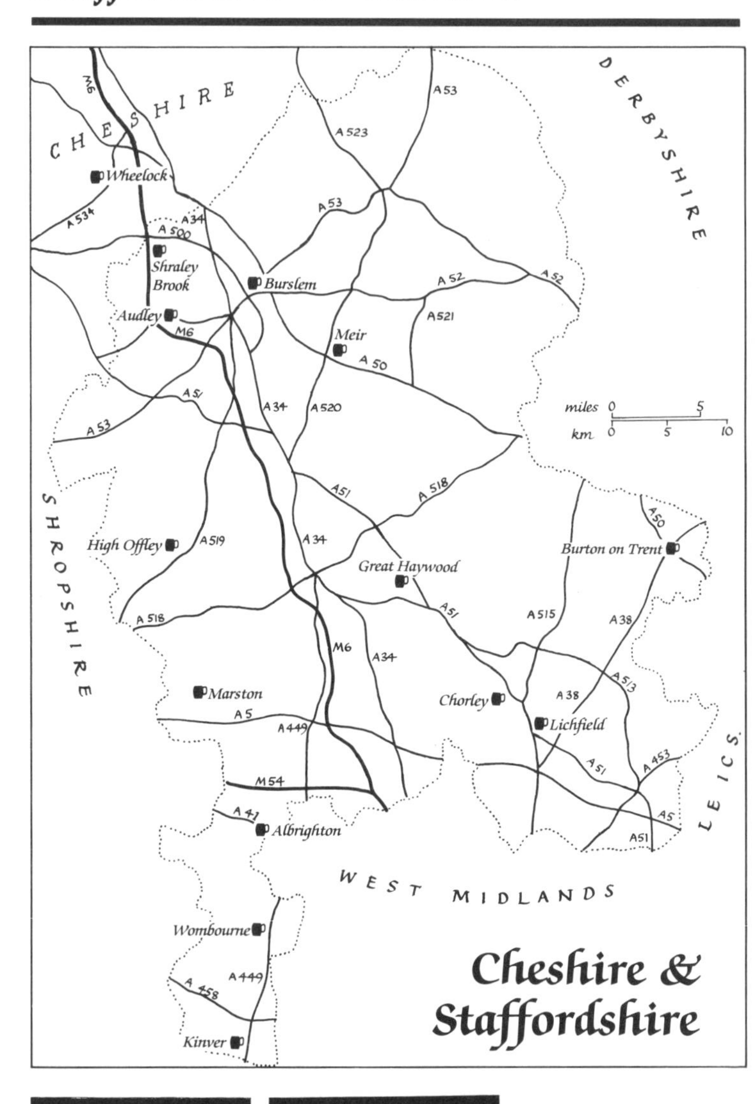

Cheshire

Wheelock

Weekdays: evenings only: 8–11, and Sunday: 12–2

Commercial (P)
Crewe Road (just west of A534 near canal bridge no. 154)
☎ (0270) 760122
Bulmer (PC)
Georgian house turned into a pub; old fashioned atmosphere, wicker seats. Sunday lunchtime cheeseboard.

Staffordshire

Albrighton

Albrighton Wines (OL)
16 High Street
☎ (090722) 3619
Weston (J)

Audley

Weekdays: 9 am–10.30 pm

Audley Off Licence (OL)
2 Mellard Street
☎ (0782) 720320
Inch
Thatcher
Guest Ciders
Range of ciders is from Somerset, Devon, Dorset, Cornwall, Herefordshire, Gloucestershire and Kent.

Burslem

Weekdays: 12–2.30; 5.30–11, Sunday: 12–3; 7–10.30

Travellers Rest (P)
239 Newcastle Street; Middleport

☎ (0782) 810418
Westrays (H)
Traditional real ale freehouse. Home made meals and snacks every lunchtime and all evenings except Sunday; garden; live music almost every night and some Sunday lunchtimes. Cider only available intermittently.

Burton on Trent

Weekdays: 11.30–3; 5.30–11

Burton Bridge (P)
24 Bridge Street
(A50 – western end of Trent Bridge)
☎ (0283) 36596
Black Bull (PC)
Thatcher (PC)
Brewery tap for Burton Bridge Brewery. Very friendly and well worth a visit. Skittle alley. Jazz club, meets Thursday. Bar snacks 12–2 except Sunday.

Monday–Saturday: 7.30 am–10 pm, Sunday: 10–1; 7–10

J & J Off Licence & Stores (OL)
167 Waterloo Street
☎ (0283) 64516
Broadoak (PL)
Near Burton BR station.

Weekdays: 12–3; 6–11, Sunday: 12–3; 7–10.30

Studbakers (P)
91–93 Moor Street
(opposite fire station)
☎ (0283) 510435
Westons Old Rosie (PC)
American style diner with separate bar area (Jaspers Bar): American and Mexican food predominates. Meals and snacks all opening hours; restaurant; outdoor drinking area; access for disabled. Near Heritage Brewery Museum. Near Burton on Trent BR station.

Chorley

Nelson (P)
Padbury Lane (near Lichfield)
☎ (05436) 5084
Westons Special Vintage (H)

Endon

Westrays Cider & Traditional Beer Supplies (D)
220 Leek Road
☎ (0782) 504441

Great Hayward

Weekdays: 11.30–2.30; 6–11

Coach & Horses (P)
☎ (0889) 270324
Weston (F)
Near Trent & Mersey Canal.

High Offley

Weekdays: 11–3; 6–11, Sunday: 12–2; 7–10.30

Anchor Inn (P)
On bank of Shropshire Union Canal 2 miles north west of Norbury Junction
☎ (078574) 569
Westons Farm Brand (PC) (J)
Westons Vintage (PC) (J)
Delightful oasis for the landlubber, and excuse to stop for the navigator! Sandwiches; garden overlooking canal; fishing and camping facilities.

Kinver

Weekdays: 11–4; 7–11

Cross (P)
Dark Lane (just off High Street)
☎ (0384) 872435
Weston (PC)
Pub with character in centre of West Midlands commuter village. Convenient for travellers on the Staffordshire and Worcestershire Canal.

Lichfield

Weekdays: 11–3; 5.30–11

Duke of York (P)
Church Street
☎ (0543) 255171
Westons Special Vintage (PC)
Westons Old Rosie (H)
Victorian lounge; beamed bar; good views over city and Cathedral. Meals lunchtime and evenings; children's room; garden; accommodation. Near Lichfield BR station.

Marston

Weekdays: 12–4; 6–11 (winter 7–11)

Fox (P)
Church Eaton
☎ (0785) 840729
Weston (PC)
Country freehouse, popular with cyclists. Meals and snacks lunchtime and evenings; garden; access for disabled; camping facilities nearby.

Meir

Weekdays: 12–2; 6–10.30, Sunday: 12–2; 7–10.30

Good Cheer Cellars (OL)
34 Stansmore Road
☎ (0782) 322745
Westrays (F)

Shraley Brook

Monday–Friday: 12–3; 6.30–11, Saturday: 11–11

Rising Sun Inn (P)
Knowle Bank Road
(off A52)
☎ (0782) 720600
Westons Old Rosie (PC)
Westons Vintage (PC)
Cosy and intimate free house with plain bar and larger L-shaped lounge. Pleasant outdoor drinking area. Lunchtime and evening meals. "Smart casual wear" required.

Wombourne

Monday–Friday: 11–3; 6–11, Saturday: 11–11, Sunday: 12–3; 7–10.30

Mount Pleasant (P)
Ounsdale Road
☎ (0902) 3240
Westons Old Rosie (PC)
Up hill from Staffordshire and Worcestershire Canal.

Weekdays: 11–11, Sunday: 12–3; 7–10.30

Red Lion (P)
Old Stourbridge Road
☎ (0902) 892270
Westons Old Rosie (PC)
Farmers Tipple (PC)
Old coaching inn. Meals lunchtime; camping facilities nearby.

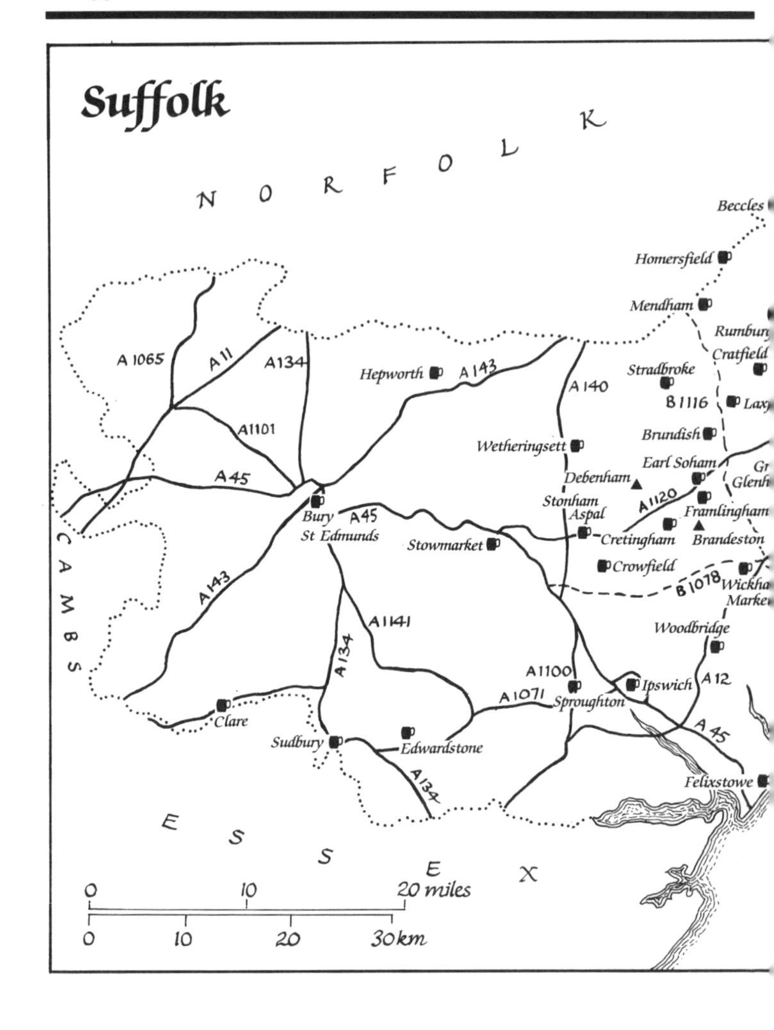

Aldeburgh

Cross Keys (P)
Crabbe Street
☏ (072885) 452637
James White (H)
Low-ceilinged, plainly furnished 16th century pub with huge chimney and wood-burning stoves. Bar meals.

Beccles

St. Peters House Hotel (P)
Old Market
☏ (0502) 713203
James White (B)

Blundeston

Country Cookin (OL)
27 The Street
James White (J)

Blythburgh

Monday–Friday: 11–2.30; 6–11, Saturday: 11–3; 6–11, Sunday: 12–3; 7–10.30

Queens Head (P)
Southwold Road
☏ (050270) 404
James White (PP)
500 year old thatched smugglers' inn, with ghost. Snacks 12–2; 7–10; meals 12–2 (Sunday: 7–9); children's room; garden.

Brandeston

JAMES WHITE SUFFOLK CIDER ▲
The Suffolk Cider Company Ltd., The Cider House, Friday Street
☏ (072882) 537

Weekdays: 11–2.30, 5.30–11.

Queens Head (P)
☏ (072882) 307
James White (H)
Old style pub in wonderful countryside. Meals and snacks 12–2; 6–9.30; children's room; outdoor drinking area/garden; accommodation; camping facilities in grounds.

Brundish

Crown (P)
Framlingham Road
☏ (072876) 277
James White (PP)

Bungay

Weekdays: 9–6.

Peter Dominic (OL)
18 Broad Street
☏ (0986) 2803
James White (J)

Bury St. Edmunds

Abbey Wines (OL)
28 Angel Hill
☏ (0284) 704995
James White (B)

Edmunds (OL)
33 Brentgovel Street
☏ (0284) 705604
James White (B)

Weekdays: 8.30–6.

Peter Dominic (OL)
22 Abbeygate Street
☏ (0284) 753041
Bulmers West Country (PC)

Clare

Weekdays: 10.30–1; 2–6.30; early closing Wednesday at 1, Sunday: 12–2.

The Clare Jug & Bottle (OL)
High Street (near Sudbury)
☏ (0787) 278433
Symonds

Weekdays: 12–2.30; 7–11.

Seafarer Hotel (P)
Nethergate Street
☏ (0787) 277449
Various (PC)
Specialises in fresh home cooked foods; log fire for chilly nights; beautiful traditional landscaped garden; hotel has en-suite rooms and full hotel facilities.

Cratfield

Cratfield Poacher (P)
Bell Green
☏ (098683) 206
James White (B)
Meals and snacks lunchtime and evenings; garden; pool room; eagle owl resident on premises.

Cretingham

New Bell Inn (P)
☏ (072872) 419
James White (PC)
16th century beamed inn in attractive village. Meals and snacks lunchtime and evenings; children's room; garden.

Crowfield

Rose Inn (P)
Debenham Road
☏ (047339) 368
James White (PP)

Debenham

ASPALL CYDER ▲
Cyder House, Aspall Hall
☏ (0728) 860510

Dunwich

Weekdays: 11–3; 6–11.

Ship Inn (P)
☏ (072873) 219
James White (B)
Period pub on coast. Lunchtime and evening meals; children's room; garden; accommodation.

Earl Soham

Victoria (P)
On A1120
☏ (072882) 758
James White (B)
Local country pub with friendly atmosphere and a brewery in the back yard. Home made bar food lunchtimes and evenings. Garden. Local musicians often spontaneously entertain.

Edwardstone

Weekdays: 11.30–2.30; 6.30–11.

White Horse (P)
Mill Green, 1 mile north of Boxford off A1071
☏ (0787) 211211
Castlings Heath Cottage Cider (W)
Traditional Suffolk pub with a good selection of games including steel quoits. Excellent value bar food all week, full meals Thursday to Sunday inclusive (book for Sunday lunch). Garden.

Felixstowe

Weekdays: 10.30–5 (6 Sundays) – May 1st – September 30th.

Q Tower (P)
South Hill
☏ (0394) 285735
James White (J)
Restaurant and tea room situated in a dry moat of a Martello tower: features exhibitions on Martello towers; also art exhibitions. Full meals 11.45–2.45, also evening bookings by groups up to 9 pm. Near Felixstowe BR station.

Framlingham

Weekdays: 8.30–5.30.

Carvey & Webb (OL)
29 Market Hill
☏ (0228) 724106

Suffolk

Aspall (B)
James White (B)

Great Glenham

Crown (P)
☏ (072878) 693
James White (PP)
Open-plan lounge bar with a side eating room and wood burning stove. Good value food. Accommodation.

Halesworth

Market Place Wine Shop (OL)
Market Place
☏ (08867) 2563
James White (J)

Warners Wine Bar (P)
The Thoroughfare
☏ (09867) 282110
James White (B)

Hepworth

Duke of Marlborough (P)
☏ (0359) 50272
James White (PP)

Homersfield

Weekdays: 11–2.30; 6–11, Sunday: 12–3; 7–10.30.

Black Swan (P)
On Norfolk border, near Harleston
☏ (098686) 204
James White (PC)

Ilketshall St. Lawrence

PARADISE CIDER ▲
Cherry Tree Farm (on A144 Bungay to Halesworth Road)
☏ (098681) 353

Ipswich

Monday–Friday: 9–1; 2.30–6, Saturday: 9–1.

Barwell & Jones (OL)
94 Rushmere Road
☏ (0473) 727426
James White (B)

Cosssticks (OL)
20 Tackett Street
☏ (0473) 221210
James White (B)

Monday–Friday: 11–2.30; 5–11, Saturday: 11–11.

Greyhound (P)
9 Henley Road
☏ (0473) 252862
James White (PP)
Town pub refurbished in Victorian style. Bar snacks 12–2; 6–9; outdoor drinking area. Near Ipswich BR station.

Lord Nelson (P)
81 Fore Street
☏ (0473) 54072
James White (PP)
Dates from 1663. Children's room; accommodation; access for disabled. Near swimming pool.

Peter Dominic (OL)
22 Carr Street
☏ (0473) 252600
James White (J)

Peter Dominic (OL)
46 Queensway
☏ (0473) 726284
James White (J)

Wolsey Theatre Bar (P)
Civic Drive
☏ (0473) 218911
James White (J)

Laxfield

Weekdays: 11–3; 6–11, Sunday: 12–3; 7–10.30.

Kings Head (P)
Goramsmill Lane
☏ (098683) 395
James White (PC)
600 year old unspoilt ale house, known locally as "The Low House": no bar, order your drink at the cellar door! Meals and snacks all sessions; restaurant.

Leiston

White Horse Hotel (P)
Station Road
☏ (0728) 830694
James White (H)
18th century hotel, once deeply involved in smuggling. Meals and snacks lunchtime and evening; garden; children's room; accommodation.

Lowestoft

Carlton Road General Stores (OL)
28 Carlton Road
☏ (0502) 516285
James White (B)

Jonathan Whites Off Licence (OL)
62–64 Stanley Street
James White (J)

Jug & Bottle (OL)
161 St. Margarets Road
☏ (0502) 664423
James White (B)

Lawson Road Off Licence (OL)
65–67 Lawson Road
☏ (0502) 516263
James White (J) (PP)

Weekdays: 8.30–5.30.

Peter Dominic (OL)
57 London Road North
☏ (0502) 572719
James White (J)

Triangle Tavern (P)
St. Peters Street (A12)
☏ (0502) 82711
James White (PC)
Town centre local. Meals and snacks lunchtime and evening; outdoor drinking area. Near Lowestoft BR station.

Mendham

Sir Alfred Munnings Country Hotel (P)
Studio Corner (on Norfolk border)
☏ (0379) 852358
Potmere Farm (PC)
Cheerful, large, open-plan hotel bar and restaurant. Family room.

Oulton Broad

Cheese Shop (OL)
74 Beccles Road
James White (B)

Tooles Off Licence (OL)
159 Victoria Road
James White (J)

Rumburgh

Rumburgh Buck (P)
☏ (098685) 257
James White (PC)
Very traditional – once the Priory guest house. Garden; children's room.

Saxmundham

Weekdays: 9–4.30.

Hayloft (P)
26a High Street
☏ (0728) 2895
James White (B)
17th century tea room and restaurant; outdoor drinking and eating area; camping facilities nearby. Near Saxmundham BR station.

Peter Dominic (OL)
6 South Entrance, Main Road
☏ (0728) 2053
James White (J)

Snape

Crown Inn (P)
Bridge Road
☏ (072888) 324
James White (PP)

Golden Key (P)
Priory Road
☏ (072888) 510
James White (J)
Contemporary styled yet traditional pub with attractive garden. Meals.

Weekdays: 11–3; 5.30–11, Sunday: 12–3; 7–10.30.

Plough & Sail (P)
Snape Maltings
☏ (072888) 302 or 413
Aspall (B)
The Maltings' own pub, part of a remarkable collection of 19th century buildings on the bank of the River Alde, including the world famous concert hall, restaurants, shops, galleries, and a centre for activity holidays and river trips. Fresh, home-cooked snacks and lunches.

Somerleyton

Weekdays: 11–3; 6–11.

Dukes Head (P)
Slugs Lane (off B1074)
☏ (0502) 730281
James White (PC)
Family pub on the Broads, with good views. Meals lunchtime and evenings; children's room; garden.

Southwold

Weekdays: 10.30–3; 6–11.

Crown (P)
91 High Street
☏ (0502) 722275
James White (J)
Georgian coaching inn. Meals and snacks 12.30–2; 7.30–9.45; restaurant; outdoor drinking area; accommodation; regular winebreaks; music evenings.

Sproughton

Beagle (P)
Old Hadleigh Road
☏ (047386) 455
James White (J)
Large free house converted from a row of whitewashed cottages. Comfortable lounge and friendly bar, beamed throughout. Healthy home-cooked food (not Sunday or Bank Holidays). Family room, garden and disabled access.

Stonham Aspal

Tuesday–Sunday: 10–5.30.

Stonham Barns (OL)
Pettaugh Road (A1120)
☏ (0449) 711755
James White (B)
A farm shop with much more! Restaurant 12–2; garden centre; large all glass country produce shopping centre; pick your own from July onwards.

Stowmarket

Peter Dominic (OL)
11 Ipswich Street
☏ (0449) 612026
James White (J)

Stradbroke

Weekdays: 11–2.30; 6.30–11, Sunday: 12–3; 7–11.

Queens Head (P)
Queens Street (B1118)
☏ (037984) 384
James White (PC)
Timbered 15th century inn. Meals and snacks lunchtime and evenings; garden; accommodation.

Sudbury

Peter Dominic (OL)
8 Old Market Place
☏ (0787) 72144
James White (J)

Thorpeness

Dolphin Inn (P)
☏ (0728) 852681
James White (PP)
Bar snacks and a la carte restaurant – specialises in grills and seafood; barbecue in summer; children welcome; garden; accommodation.

Westleton

Crown Inn (P)
The Street
☏ (072873) 273 or 239
James White (H)
Well kept village inn with bric-a-brac furnished bar and a conservatory. Accommodation and good bar food. Garden.

Weekdays: 11.30–2.30; 6–11, Sunday 12–2.30; 7–10.30.

White Horse (P)
Darsham Road
☏ (072873) 222
James White (B)
Next to village pond. Meals and snacks 12–2; 6.30–9; garden; accommodation; camping facilities nearby.

Wetheringsett

Weekdays: 11–3; 5–11.

Cat & Mouse (P)
Pages Green
☏ (0728) 860765
James White (PC)
Wilkins (PC)
Guest cider (PC)
Heavily beamed pub in rural surroundings. Meals lunchtime, and evenings by reservation; children's room and play area; garden; accommodation; caravan.

Wickham Market

Taylors Superfare (OL)
66 High Street
☏ (0728) 746275
James White (B)

Woodbridge

Weekdays: 9–5; 6.30–10.

Barwells & The Cross Inn (OL)
2 Church Street
☏ (03943) 3288
Aspall (B)
James White (B)
An off licence with a small bar – but the bar sells only Dry Blackthorn.

Riverside Restaurant (P)
Quayside

☏ (03943) 2587
James White (J)
Renowned for quality and service. Children welcome; outdoor seating available; access for disabled; no smoking area.

Weekdays: 11–11.
Seckford Arms (P)
Seckford Street (300 yards along Seckford Street from Market Square)
☏ (03943) 444
James White (PP)
Bar food 12–2.15; 6.30–9: a la carte dining room evenings from 7 on Thursday to Sunday (please book); family room; accommodation; shove ha'penny.

Yoxford

Eliza Acton Restaurant (P)
Tunshaven, Old High Road
☏ (072877) 637
James White (J)

COMMON GROUND IN FIGHT TO SAVE OUR ORCHARDS

As you can see from Anthony Gibson's "State of the Apple", orchards in Britain could soon be in terminal decline. They are disappearing at an alarming rate: not just due to farmers giving up cider making, but for housing, new roads, and "cost effective" crops. 100 years ago there were some 23,000 acres of orchards in Devon alone, more than any other county. Now the figure for Devon and Cornwall combined is barely 1,500 acres. The situation in other counties is probably even worse.

Even where cider makers are replacing old trees, and planting new orchards, these are almost all bush varieties. They also contain far fewer varieties of fruit than did the old standard orchards: over 6,000 different varieties of apple have been recorded, and at one time as many as 200 different types might be found in just one orchard. Although you will through the pages of this Guide come across a number of evocative old names, these are regrettably the exceptions – nowadays only nine varieties dominate in commercial orchards.

Though wassailing, and a quiet winter prayer to the Goddess Pomona, may help this year's fruiting, it does little to halt the long-term slide. Recently however, the conservation group Common Ground has launched a campaign to preserve old orchards and plant new ones. Common Ground believes that with the disappearance of the traditional orchards with their tall standard trees we are losing a vital part of the British landscape and a wealth of cultural association – besides, of course, the essential ingredient of real cider and perry, the vintage fruit varieties!

The group stresses the value of old orchards for many purposes: they can be rich habitats for wild life – birds, plants and animals; they have a long tradition of multiple use – as places to graze sheep, pigs and geese, for the production of honey, and as places of enjoyment; they are a rich source of poetic symbolism and ideas. Old varieties of fruit are also irreplaceable sources of genetic diversity and disease-resistant strains for the future. Above all, says the group, orchards are important places imbued with local cultural significance.

Common Ground's campaign runs parallel with that of APPLE – aiming to halt the increasing standardisation and blandness of mass produced cider and perry, mainly concocted from imported apple concentrate and a cocktail of additives. This Save Our Orchards campaign is part of Common Ground's

Tree's, Woods and the Green Man project, which aims to heighten people's awareness of the cultural, aesthetic and spiritual value of trees and woods, as well as their ecological importance. It has produced a campaign leaflet outlining what is happening to orchards, why they are important, and what can be done to save them. It has also published a book, "Orchards – a guide to local conservation", which describes how to find and conserve local varieties of fruit, with examples of local initiatives; and there is a touring exhibition "Orchards – photographs from the West Country".

By these, and other means, Common Ground hopes to create a secure future for orchards, old and new, in the local landscape.

Further information about Common Ground's Campaign to Save Old Orchards and Plant New Ones can be obtained by sending an SAE to "Save Our Orchards", Common Ground, 45 Shelton Street, London WC2H 9HJ. Copies of the Campaign leaflet are also available from the same address; single copies free with an SAE, £1 for 10.

The book "Orchards, a guide to local conservation", edited by Common Ground, 80pp, £4.95, ISBN 1 870364 08 2, (£6.00 including postage and packing), also from Common Ground.

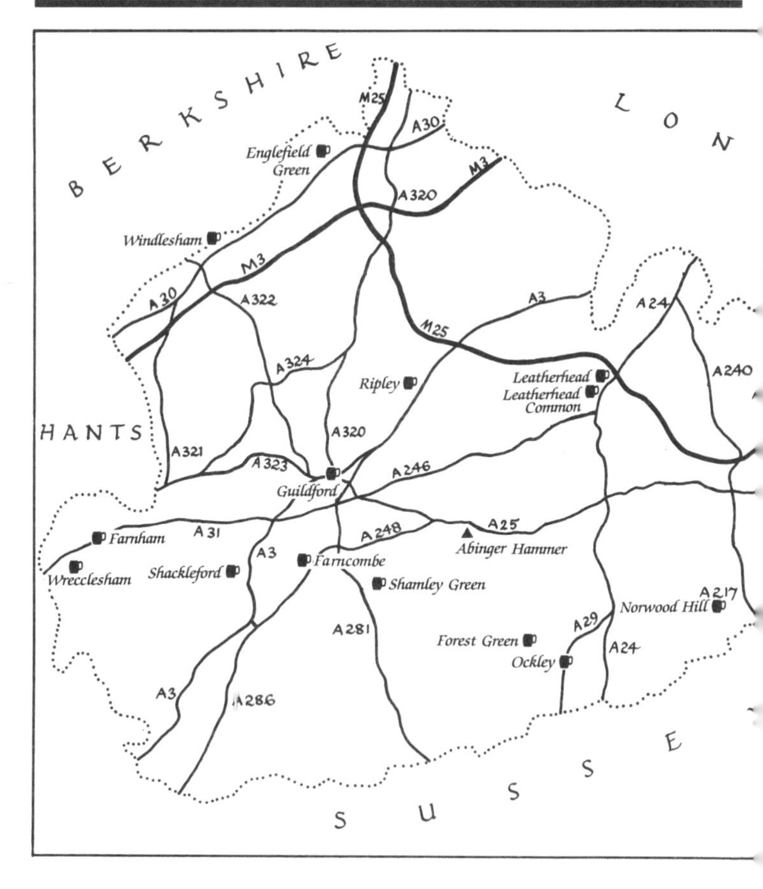

Abinger Hammer

BARNARD CIDER

▲

'Grassmere' (on A25 next to Post Office)
☎ (0306) 730941

Englefield Green

Weekdays: 11–3; 5.30–11.

Beehive (P)

Middle Hill (off A30)
☎ (0784) 31621
Bulmer (H)
Small busy pub near Windsor Great Park and Runnymede. Meals and snacks lunchtime and evenings; garden; access for disabled.

Farncombe

Weekdays: 11–2.30; 6–10.30 (11 F & S); Sunday: 12–2; 7–10.30

Ram Cider House (P)

Catteshall Lane (off Catteshall Road)
☎ (04868) 21093
Bulmer (E)
A must for the cider enthusiast! Just south of Catteshall Lock on the River Wey, but could be in the deep west! Large 16th century wattle and daub building, with 3 bars. Good value food; large attractive garden.

Farnham

Monday–Tuesday, Thursday–Saturday: 9–9, Wednesday: 9–1; 5–9, Sunday: 12–2; 7–9

Lion Brewery (OL)

West Street
☎ (0252) 715749
Dunkerton (B)
Free off licence on site of old Farnham United Brewery. Near Farnham BR station.

Fickleshole

Monday–Friday: 11–2.30; 6–11, Saturday: 11–11

White Bear (P)

Fairchildes Road
☎ (0959) 73166
Westons Vintage (H)
Rambling rural pub, originally farm cottages, dating from 15th century, and dominated by a large white bear in the forecourt, brought here in 1877 when the building became a pub. Surprisingly remote, considering the proximity of the New Addington Estate! Meals and snacks all sessions; children's room, garden.

Forest Green

Weekdays: 11–11

Parrot (P)

Horsham Road (off A29)

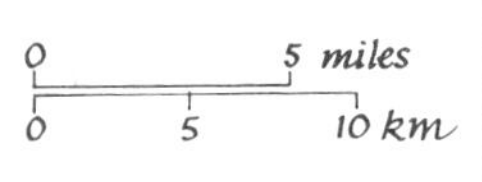

☏ (030670) 339
Bulmer (H)
Country inn overlooking village green and cricket ground. Meals and snacks all opening hours, breakfasts from 9; separate restaurant; large garden with play equipment for children; live music on Sunday evenings.

Guildford

Weekdays: 11–2.30; 5.30–11

Clavadel Hotel (P)
Epsom Road (A246) at junction with Pit Farm Road
☏ (0483) 572064
Westons Old Rosie (H)
Guildford's only free house. Meals and snacks lunchtime and evenings; restaurant; garden; accommodation. Near London Road BR station.

Leatherhead

Thorncroft Vineyard (OL)
Highlands Farm, Headley Road
☏ (0372) 372558
Cotswold Cider (B)

Leatherhead Common

Weekdays: 10–3; 5.30–11

Star (P)
243 Kingston Road
☏ (037284) 2416
Bulmer (H)
Straddles the London/Surrey border between Chessington and Leatherhead, within easy reach of Chessington Zoo: interesting collection of guns. Good range of hot and cold food all sessions; garden; access for disabled.

Merstham

Monday–Friday: 11–2.30; 5.30–11, Saturday: 11–3; 5.30–11

Inn on the Pond (P)
Nutfield Marsh Road, Nutfield Marsh
☏ (0737) 43000
Bulmer (H)
Although dating from 1603, the building only became a pub in 1988: it is next to the pond and cricket pitch: inside are many original beams and two real fires. Meals and snacks all sessions; garden; children's room; two squash courts available for hire.

Norwood Hill

Tuesday–Friday: 10–2.30, Saturday–Sunday: 10–4 (closed Monday)

Orchard Shop (OL)
Rickettswood Road (250 yards west of "Fox Revived" pub on Leigh to Charlewood road)
☏ (0293) 862186 and 862766
Gray (PC)
Weston (PC)
Various (PC)
A cider oasis; taste before you buy; containers provided, or bring your own. Also mulling spices; local apple juice, organic fruit and vegetables.

Ockley

Weekdays: 10.30–2.30; 5.30–11

Red Lion (P)
Stane Street (on A29)
☏ (0306) 211032
Bulmer (H)
Beefeater Steak House. Meals and snacks all sessions; separate restaurant; garden.

Ripley

Stansfield Bros (OL)
37–43 Newark Road
☏ (0483) 225261
James White (J)

Shackleford

Weekdays: 11–2.30; 5.30–11

Cyder House (P)
Peperharrow Road (off A3)
☏ (0483) 810360
Taunton (H)
A private house converted into a cider house, but now an ordinary pub, which happily still sells cider. (*Not however to be confused with the nearby Ram Cider House at Farncombe*). Meals and snacks lunchtime and evenings; children's room; garden.

Shamley Green

Farmers Fare (OL)
☏ (0483) 892411
Weston (J)

Windlesham

Monday–Thursday: 11–2.30; 5.30–11, Friday–Saturday: 11–3; 5.30–11

Half Moon (P)
Church Road (off A386, near church)
☏ (0276) 73329
Weston (H)
Pleasant, characterful pub with welcoming log fire. Large garden with children's play area. Lunchtime meals Monday to Saturday.

Wrecclesham

Monday–Friday: 11–2.30; 5–11, Saturday: 11–11

Sandrock (P)
Sandrock Hill Road, Upper Bourne (off B3384 at Shortheath crossroads)
☏ (0252) 715865
Wilkins (PC)
Recently extended, family-owned and run free house specialising in real ales and ciders and home cooking. Garden. Lunchtime meals. Bar billiards.

East Sussex

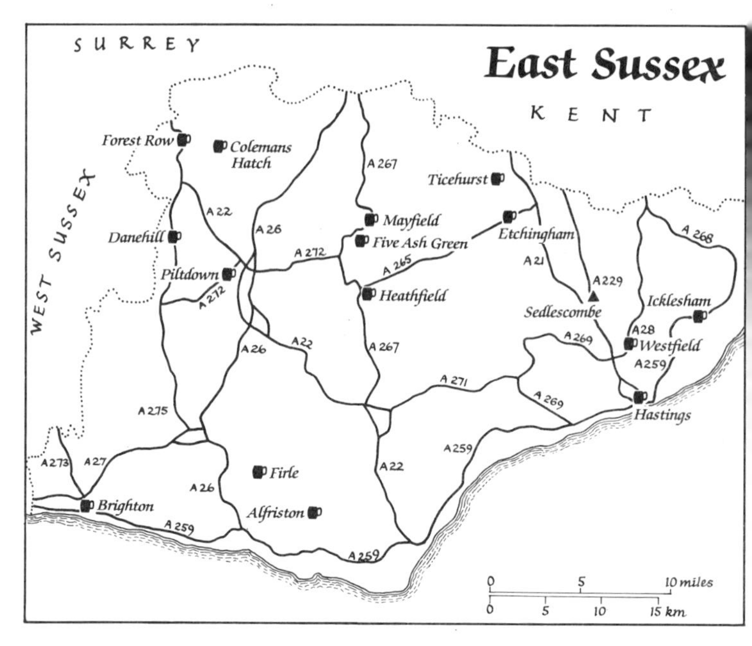

Alfriston

English Wine Centre (OL)
Drusillas
☎ (0323) 870532
Biddenden (B)

Brighton

Weekdays: 10.30–11
Albion (P)
28 Albion Hill (behind old Tamplins brewery)
☎ (0273) 604439
Bulmer (H)
Side street local with one bar on two levels. Outdoor drinking area; two bar billiard tables.

Weekdays: 11–11
Edinburgh Hotel (P)
67a Upper Gloucester Road
☎ (0273) 27075
Long Ashton (B)
Meals and snacks all sessions.

Weekdays: 11–11
Nobles Bar (P)
New Road
☎ (0273) 68240
Thatcher (PC)
Friendly free house close to Theatre Royal and Dome Theatre. Tiny bar with extra seating upstairs.

Weekdays: 11–3; 5.30–11
Quadrant (P)
12–13 North Street
☎ (0273) 26432
Guest Ciders (H)
Town centre pub. Meals. Ciders range from Bulmers West Country, Symonds, Rich, and Zum.

Weekdays: 11–3; 6–11
Sir Charles Napier (P)
50 Southover Street
☎ (0273) 601413
Bulmer (H)
Busy but deceptively spacious corner local. Lunchtimes snacks served as well as full range of Gales country wines. Children's room and outdoor drinking area.

Weekdays: 11–2; 5–11, Sunday: 12–3; 7–10.30
Southover Wines (OL)
80–81 Southover Street
☎ (0273) 600402
Inch (PC)
Long Ashton (B)
Perrys Cider (PC)
Thatcher (PC)
Also a range of barrels and polypins for order on 24 hours notice. Guest ciders from West Country and France always available. Near Brighton BR station.

Weekdays: 12–2.30; 5.30–11
Sussex Yeoman (P)
7 Guildford Road
☎ (0273) 27985
Long Ashton (B)
Turn sharp right out of Brighton BR station, and the pub is 100 yards up Guildford Road. Snacks lunchtime.

Windsor Tavern
46 Windsor Street
☎ (0273) 23490
Burrow Hill (PC)
Recently converted freehouse. Snacks lunchtime.

Colemans Hatch

Hatch Inn (P)
Near B2110
☎ (034282) 2363
Weston (H)
Secluded one-bar pub in the Ashdown Forest, near Hartfield. Snacks. Family room.

Danehill

Weekdays: 11–2.30; 6–11 (longer hours in summer)
Coach & Horses (P)
School Lane ($\frac{3}{4}$ mile north east of village off A22)

☎ (082574) 369
Rich (PC)
Unspoilt rural pub. Meals lunchtime and evenings; restaurant; garden; bar billiards.

Monday–Tuesday, Thursday–Saturday: 8–6, Wednesday: 8–1, Sunday: 10–1

The Etchingham Stores (OL)
On A265
☎ (058081) 289
Biddenden (B)
Near Etchingham BR station.

Firle

English Farm Cider Centre (OL)
Middle Farm on A27 between Firle and Selmeston
☎ (032183) 303 or 411
Various (PC) (B) (J) (BB)
A permanent cider exhibition, awaiting your inspection! Sample many ciders from all over the country, from Sussex, Kent, Herefordshire, Worcestershire, Norfolk, Suffolk, Devon, and Somerset. Also a selection of quality farm produce.

Five Ash Down

Weekdays: 11–3; 6–11, Sunday: 12–3; 7–10.30

Fireman's Arms (P)
☎ (082581) 2191
Various (PC) (PP)
Many railway pictures and relics. Bar snacks 12–2; 6.30–9; children's room; garden; bar billiards; pool table; shove ha'penny. A mile and a half from Buxted BR station.

Forest Row

Davies Stores (OL)
The Square
☎ (034282) 3955
Weston (J)

Hastings

The Cheese Board (OL)
High Street, Old Town
Biddenden (B)
A comprehensive selection of cheeses also on sale, to complement the cider.

Hercules Enterprises (OL)
45 Springfield Road, St. Leonards
☎ (0424) 712272
Biddenden (B)

Hollington Wine Stores (OL)
55 Blackman Avenue, Hollington (1 miles north of town)
☎ (0424) 420494
Biddenden (B)

Weekdays: 6.30 am–9 pm, Sunday: 8–12.30

Post Office Stores (OL)
Milward Road
☎ (0424) 425417
Biddenden (J)

Heathfield

Heathfield Wine Stores (OL)
Commerce House
☎ (04352) 2109
Biddenden (B)

Icklesham

Monday–Friday: 11–3; 6–11, Saturday: 11–11

Queens Head (P)
Parsonage Lane (turn off A259 at east end of village)
☎ (0424) 814552
Thatcher (PC) – May – October
Tile hung country inn peacefully situated with splendid views from garden. Meals and snacks lunchtime and evenings; access for disabled.

Mayfield

Carpenters Arms (P)
Fletching Street (near A267)
☎ (0435) 873294
Biddenden (BB)
Friendly, half-timbered pub dating back to 17th century with a separate restaurant offering home-cooked food. Garden.

Piltdown

Old Spot Farm Shop (OL)
On A272 near Piltdown
☎ (082572) 3929
Aspall (B)
Inch (DJ) (PL)
Small farm shop with rare English cheeses: also a chance to visit the pigs after which the farm is named, for a small charge.

Sedlescombe

BATTLE VINTAGE CYDER ▲
Garnett Bros., Oaklands Farm, Moat Lane
☎ (0424) 42587

Ticehurst

Duke of York (P)
High Street, The Square
☎ (0580) 200229
Biddenden (B)
Lively village local. Lunchtime meals; garden.

Westfield

10–5 every day from Easter to Christmas; winter weekdays only

Carr Taylor Vineyards (OL)
(off A28)
☎ (0424) 752501
Battle Vintage (B)

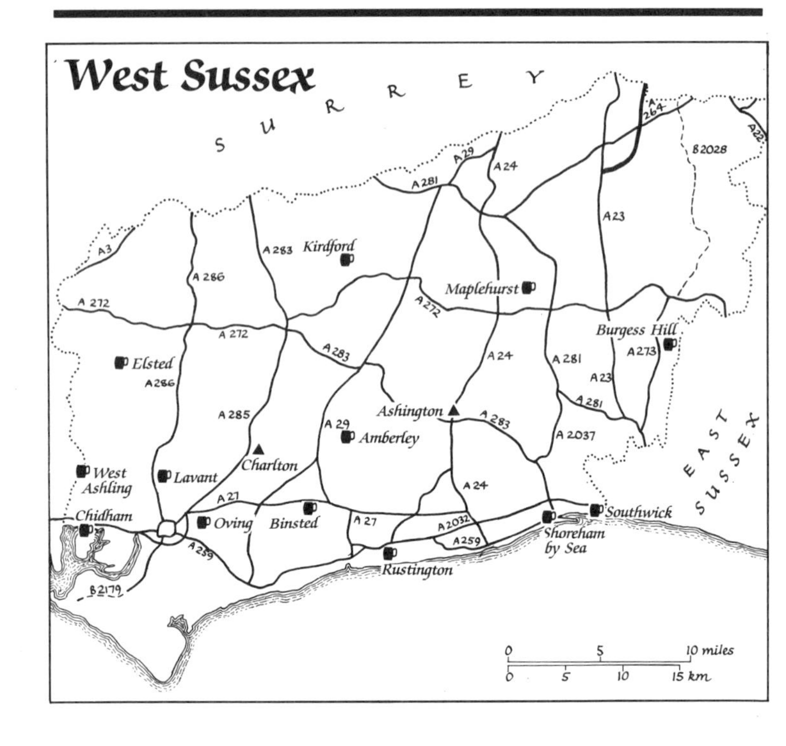

Amberley

Sportsman (P)
Rackham Road (east end of village)
Churchward (PC)
Despite a modern exterior the pub has an older, comfortable interior, with three bars and a terrace giving superb views over the Wild Brooks. Meals lunchtime and evenings; games room.

Ashington

FRIAR'S CIDER ▲
Woolvens Farm,
Billingshurst Lane
☎ (0903) 892273

Binsted

Black Horse (P)
Binsted Lane (off A27/B2132)
☎ (0243) 551213
Bulmer (PC)
Beautiful garden and views. Meals and snacks all sessions; restaurant; accommodation. Designated Tourist Information Centre.

Burgess Hill

Weekdays: 11–11

Watermill (P)
Worlds End, Leyland Road
☎ (04446) 5517
Bulmer (H)
Single-bar locals' pub in the "World's End" part of town 300 yards from Wivelsfield Station. Home-made food a speciality.

Charlton

SUSSEX BARN CYDER ▲
Charlton Barns
☎ (024363) 762

Chidham

Old House at Home (P)
Cot Lane
Churchward (PC)
Remote pub near Chichester Harbour. Food lunchtime and evenings. Children's room, garden and overnight accommodation.

Elsted

Weekdays: 11–3; 6–11, Sunday: 12–3; 7–10.30

Three Horseshoes (P)
Near Midhurst
☎ (0730) 825746
Churchward (PC)
Country pub with children's room and garden. Meals, including vegetarian lunchtimes and evenings (except Sunday evening).

Kirdford

10–5 all week

Kirdford Growers Country Shop (OL)
Pound Lane
☎ (040377) 274
Rich (W)

Lavant

Earl of March (P)
Lavant Road (A286)
Churchward (PC) – summer only
Deceptively large roadside pub specialising in home-made food (particularly game in season). Open-plan arrangement allows for quiet

dining area and space for families. Dogs welcome. Garden. Disabled person's access. Availability of cider intermittent; check first.

Maplehurst

Weekdays: 12–2.30; 6–11; Sunday: 12–3; 7–10.30

White Horse (P)

Park Lane (between A281 Monks Gate and A272)
☎ (0403) 871208
Burrow Hill (PC) – summer only
Deep in Sussex Weald, with excellent views: widest bar in Sussex. Snacks lunchtime and early evening; children's room; large garden; access for disabled.

Oving

Weekdays: 11–2.30; 6–11, Sunday: 12–2.30; 7–10.30

Gribble Inn (P)

Off A259
☎ (0243) 786893
Inch (PC)
16th century thatched house. Meals and snacks lunchtime and 6.30–9.30; children's room; large garden.

Rustington

Weekdays: 11–3; 5–11

Smugglers Roost (P)

125 Sea Lane
☎ (0903) 785714
Churchward (PC)
Various (PC)
Welcome oasis in Littlehampton area! Meals and snacks lunchtime and 7–9.30; restaurant; children's room; garden; 100 yards from beach.

Shoreham by Sea

Weekdays: 10.30–2.30; 7–12

Bridge Inn (P)

87 High Street
☎ (0273) 452477
Bulmer (H)
Meals and snacks; restaurant; children's room; patio; garden; facilities for disabled.

Crab Tree (P)

6 Buckingham Road
☎ (07917) 3083
Bulmer (H)
Cider only found in public bar. Large garden; pool room. Adjacent to Shoreham by Sea BR station.

Weekdays: 11–3; 6–11

Schooner (P)

64 High Street
☎ (0273) 452527
Bulmer (H)
Quiet, two bar pub with original etched windows. Good bar snacks.

Southwick

Threshers (OL)

45 Southwick Square
☎ (0273) 592790
Inch (PL) (B)
Near Southwick BR station.

West Ashling

Weekdays: 10.30–3; 5.30–11, Sunday: 12–3; 7–10.30

Richmond Arms (P)

Mill Road ($\frac{1}{4}$ mile west of B2146)
☎ (0243) 575730
Thatcher (PC)
Adjoins duck pond. Meals and snacks lunchtimes Monday–Saturday; children's room; garden.

Old cider mill in action.

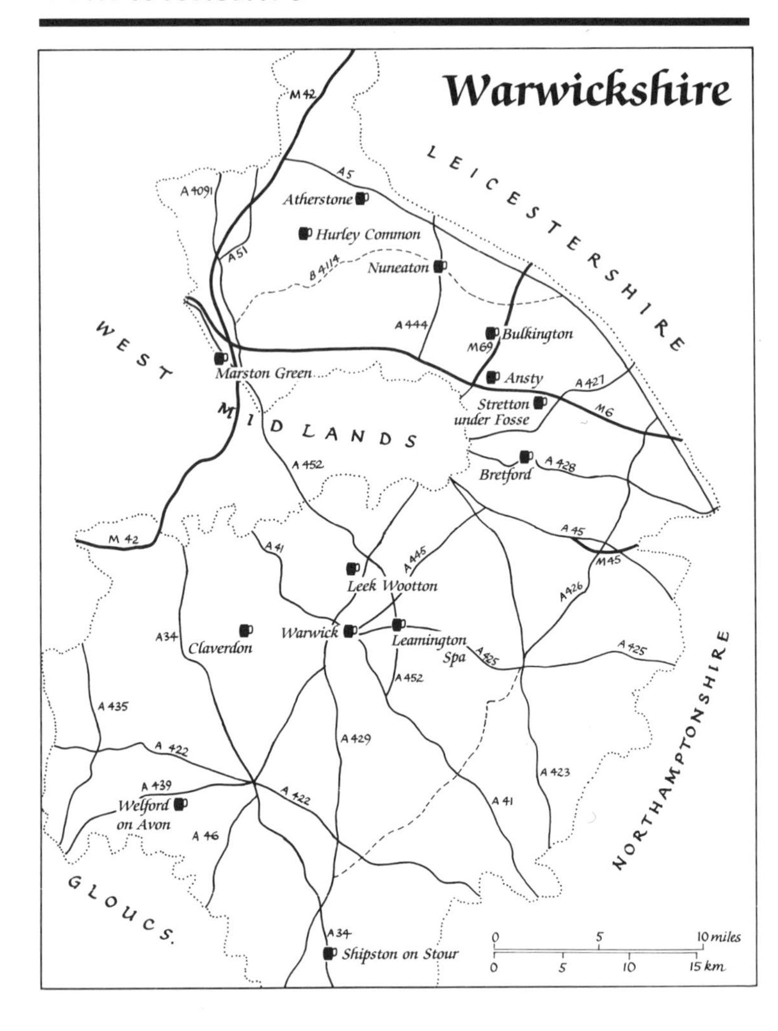

Ansty

Crown (P)

☎ (0203) 612822

Westons Special Vintage (PC)

Very busy local with garden, near Oxford Canal between Stretton Shop and Hawkesbury Junction. Meals.

Atherstone

Cloisters Wine Bar (P)

66 Long Street

☎ (0827) 717293

Weston (PC)

Bretford

Weekdays: 11–3; 6.30–11, Sunday: 12–3; 7–10.30

Queens Head (P)

Fosse Way (B4029)

☎ (0203) 542671

Bulmer (H)

Meals weekday evenings and Sunday lunch; snacks all sessions; separate restaurant; large garden with swings, slides and climbing frames; access for disabled.

Bulkington

Chequers Street Off Licence (OL)

Chequers Street

Westons Old Rosie (PC)

Westons Special Vintage (PC)

Claverdon

Weekdays: 11–2.30; 5.30–11

Red Lion (P)

Station Road

☎ (0926) 842291

Westons Old Rosie (PC) (W)

Attractive position with lovely views. Meals 12–2; 7–10; bar snacks all hours; outdoor drinking area/garden; access for disabled. Near Claverdon BR station.

Hurley Common

White Hart (P)
216 Hurley Common
☏ (0827) 872315
Westons Old Rosie (PC)

Leamington Spa

Beer Engine (P)
39 Clements Street
☏ (0926) 335758
Weston (J) (PC)

Black Horse (P)
Princes Street
☏ (0926) 425169
Bulmer (H)
Popular local serving snacks lunchtimes and evenings.

Leek Wootton

Weekdays: 11–3; 6–11, Sunday: 12–2.30; 7–10.30

Anchor (P)
Warwick Road (on main road in centre of village)
☏ (0926) 53355
Weston (PC)
Popular locals' bar complemented by a plush lounge. Food bar serving excellent meals (not Sunday). Garden. Access for disabled.

Marston Green

Monday: 12–1; 6–10.30, Thursday–Friday: 11.30–1; 6–10.30, Saturday: 11.30–2; 6–10.30, Sunday: 7–10.30.

Ye Old Village Wine Lodge (OL)
6 Elmdon Road
☏ (021) 779 3089
Weston (PC)

Nuneaton

Hop Pole (P)
16 Arbury Road
☏ (0203) 343346
Weston (H)

Shipston on Stour

Weekdays: 12–2.30; 7–11, Sunday: 12–3; 7–10.30

Black Horse Inn (P)
Station Road
☏ (0608) 61617
Bulmer (E)
16th century thatched inn. Meals and snacks 12–2; 7–10; restaurant; garden.

Stretton Under Fosse

Weekdays: 11–2.30; 7–11, Sunday: 12–2.30; 7–10.30

Union Jack (P)
On A427
☏ (0788) 832517
Weston (PC)
Village local. Meals and snacks all sessions except Monday; dining room; garden; access for disabled; skittles.

Warwick

Weekdays: 11–2.30; 6–11

Cape of Good Hope (P)
66 Lower Cape
☏ (0926) 498138
Bulmer (H)

Welford on Avon

Weekdays: 11–3; 6–11

Bell Inn (P)
Binton Road
☏ (0789) 750353
Bulmer (H)
Well kept 17th century pub in riverside village, with low-beamed ceilings and a flagstoned floor in the public bar. Meals and snacks, family room and garden.

METHODS OF DISPENSE
(B) Bottle (BB) Bag in box (CK) Carry keg (DJ) glass demijohn (E) Cask and electric pump (F) Flagon (H) Cask and hand pump (J) glass jar (PC) polycask (PL) plastic container (PP) polypin (W) wooden cask

KEY TO MAPS
- town or village with one or more real cider or perry outlets
- ▲ location of cider or perry maker selling direct to public from premises

West Midlands

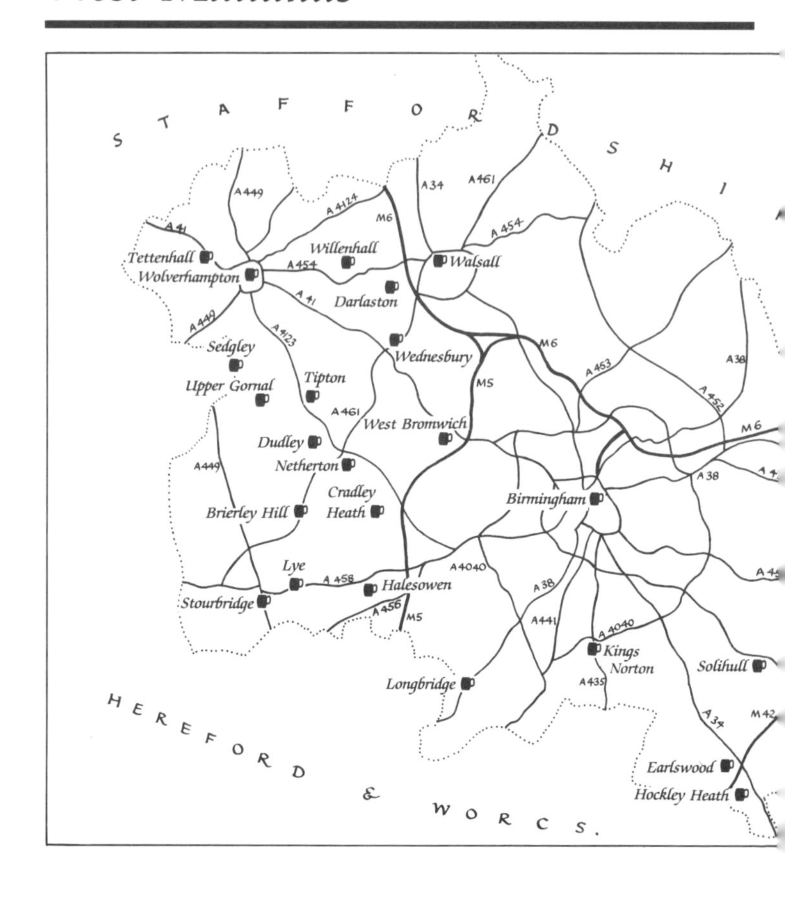

Birmingham – City Centre

White Swan (P)

116 Sherlock Street
(A441 – junction of Hurst Street and Sherlock Street)
☎ (021) 622 6717
Coates (PC)
A glance round the bar will make you think you are in the West Country, rather than the middle of Birmingham! Near New Street BR station.

Brierley Hill

Crystal Tavern (P)

19 Dudley Road
☎ (0384) 265773
Weston (PC)

New Inn (P)

Dudley Road (A461)
☎ (0384) 73792
Weston (PC)
Near town centre. Small and friendly with open fires.

Weekdays: 12–2.30; 7–11

Robin Hood (P)

Merry Hill, Quarry Park
☎ (0384) 77756
Weston (PC)

Royal Oak (P)

258 Stourbridge Road, Holly Hill
☎ (0384) 75950
Westons Old Rosie (PC)

Waterloo Inn (P)

Mill Street
☎ (0384) 79281
Westons Special Vintage (PC)
Pleasant bar, comfortable lounge in mock Tudor style.

Coventry

Broomfield Tavern (P)

14–16 Broomfield Place, Spon End
☎ (0203) 228506
Bulmer (H)
Meals lunchtime and evenings; outdoor drinking area; regular folk sessions.

Cradley Heath

Marina Mini Market (OL)

25 Park Road, Quarry Bank
☎ (0384) 69108
Weston (J)

Wharf (P)

Station Road
Westons Old Rosie (PC)
Near Cradley Heath BR station.

Darlaston

Monday–Friday: 12–2.30; 7–11, Saturday: 12–11, Sunday: 12–3; 7–10.30

Prince of Wales (P)

Walsall Road
☎ (021) 526 2010

West Midlands

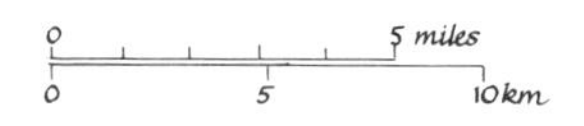

Bulmer (H)
Lively bar and small lounge, with occasional live entertainment. Hot and cold food Monday–Saturday lunchtimes; children welcome; large garden.

Weekdays: 10–10.30 all week.

Rose Park Off Licence (OL)

144 Wolverhampton Street (opposite George Rose Park)
☎ (021) 526 2571
Langdon (PC)

Dudley

Weekdays: 11.30–3.15; 6.30–11

British Oak (P)

Salop Street, Eve Hill
☎ (0384) 236297
Bulmer (H)
Skittain Home made (H)
Old local on main Sedgley road in the shadow of the Eve Hill flats (the three hilltop blocks – highest point West of the Urals). The traditional pub has been opened out and a brew-house and cider works added. Bar snacks. Evening meals. Near Dudley Port and Coseley BR stations.

Monday–Thursday: 10.30–3.30; 5–11, Friday–Saturday: 10.30–11, Sunday: 12–3; 7–10.30

Empire Tavern (P)

Trindle Road
☎ (0384) 54337
Bulmer (H)
Just off town centre. Meals lunchtime.

King & Queen (P)

Stafford Street
Weston (PC)
Conveniently located near town centre.

Weekdays: 11–2.30; 6–11

Lamp Tavern (P)

High Street (on A459 just down the hill from Hansons brewery)
☎ (0384) 54129
Westons Old Rosie (H)
Busy pub at west end of town centre. Extensive range of malt whiskies. Lunchtime meals; outdoor drinking area; large children's play area with climbing structures.

Earlswood

Monday–Friday: 12–2.30; 6–11, Saturday: 12–11

Bulls Head (P)

Limekiln Lane, Salter Street (off B4102)
☎ (021) 728 2335
Coates (PC)
Two room country pub, popular with Sunday cyclists. Separate dart throw, tiled floor in bar. Two outdoor drinking areas including lawn with swing and slides. Meals. Ask for "the scrumpy".

Halesowen

Monday–Thursday: 12–2.30; 7–11; Friday and Saturday: 11–11

Waggon & Horses (P)

21 Stourbridge Road (A458)
☎ (021) 550 4989
Weston Old Rosie (H)
A superb "beer festival" pub with ten handpumps. Occasional live music and quizzes; pool table and cosy snug.

Hockley Heath

Blue Bell Cider House (P)

Warings Green Road
☎ (05646) 3607
Bulmer (E)
A cider house on the Stratford Canal, with moorings for visitors. Meals and snacks lunchtime Monday–Saturday.

Kings Norton

Monday–Friday: 11.30–2.30; 5.30–11, Saturday: 11–3; 5.30–11, Sunday 12–3; 7–10.30

Navigation Inn (P)

1 Wharf Road
☎ (021) 459 1652
Bulmer (E)
Old world outside, modern inside. Bar snacks – hot and cold servery – 12–2; 6–8.45; children's play area with equipment; outdoor

drinking area/garden; access for disabled.

Longbridge

Weekdays: 11.30–10, Sunday: 12–3; 7–10.30

Patrick's Trad Ales (OL)

129 Longbridge Lane
☎ (021) 477 8650
Westons Vintage (PC)

Lye

Monday–Thursday: 10.30–3; 5–11, Friday–Saturday: 10–11, Sunday: 12–3; 7–10.30

Windmill Inn (P)

90 Dudley Road
☎ (0384) 423313
Weston (PC)
Small local near the railway station.

Netherton

Weekdays: 12–3; 7–11

Blue Pig (P)

St. Andrews Street
☎ (0384) 239595
Weston (PC)
Thriving corner pub on the church hill. Bright and friendly. Garden.

Sedgley

Weekdays: 11.30–3; 7.30–11

Grand Junction (P)

High Holborn
☎ (09073) 2980
Weston (PC)
Gornal Stone corner pub with a lounge decorated like a railway carriage.

Solihull

Monday–Friday: 12–2; 5.30–10, Saturday: 11–3; 5–10, Sunday: 12–2; 7–9.45

Bernies Real Ale Off Licence (OL)

266 Cranmore Boulevard, Shirley
☎ (021) 744 2827
Somerset Scrumpy (E) (H)

Stourbridge

Moorings (P)

78 Lower High Street, Amblecote
☎ (0384) 374124
Westons Old Rosie (H)

Tettenhall

Monday–Friday: 12–3; 6–11, Saturday: 12–3; 7–11, Sunday: 12–3; 7–10.30

Mitre (P)

Lower Green (near Wolverhampton)
☎ (0902) 753487
Weston (PC)
Pleasant old pub by village green. Varied rooms, deservedly popular with wide range of people. Garden. Meals lunchtimes (except Sunday)

Tipton

Weekdays: 12–3.30; 6–11, Sunday: 12–3; 7–10.30

Melting Pot (P)

Dudley Port (on A461 close to canal aqueduct and railway bridge)
☎ (021) 557 8886
Bulmer (PC)
Bright and bustling local with a warm welcome, near Dudley Port Station. Family room and outdoor drinking area.

Monday–Thursday: 11.30–2.30; 6–11, Friday–Saturday: 11.30–3; 6–11, Sunday: 12–3; 7–10.30

Old Court House (P)

Lower Church Lane, Dudley Port (on B4163 400 yards off A461 at Dudley Port, opposite police station)
☎ (021) 520 2865
Westons Farm Brand (PC)
One roomed pub with wide variety of clientele. Meals lunchtime and evening except Sunday; outdoor drinking area. Near Dudley Port BR station.

Upper Gornal

Monday–Friday: 12–3.30; 7–11, Saturday: 12–3; 6.30–11, Sunday: 12–3; 7–10.30

Crown (P)

Holloway Street, Ruiton (400 yards off A459)
☎ (09073) 4035
Bulmer (H)
An old home brew house. Children's room; outdoor drinking area.

Walsall

Weekdays: 10–10

Khalsa Wines (OL)

5 West Bromwich Street, Caldmore
☎ (0922) 29875
Langdon (F)
Near Walsall BR station.

Monday–Tuesday: 7–11, Wednesday–Friday: 12–3; 7–11, Saturday: 11–11, Sunday: 12–3; 7–10.30

Manor House (P)

Mill Street, Ryecroft
☎ (0922) 20104
Westons Old Rosie (H)
Meals and snacks 12–3 (Wednesday–Sunday); 7–10.30; restaurant; private suite; facilities for conferences and meetings; paved outdoor eating and drinking area.

Wednesbury

Weekdays: 10–11

Turks Head (P)

Lower High Street
☎ (021) 556 9370
Westons Traditional (H)
Westons Old Rosie (H)
Recently modernised local. Snacks.

West Bromwich

Monday–Friday: 12–2.30; 6–11, Saturday: 12–3; 6–11, Sunday: 12–3; 7–10.30

Sow & Pigs (P)

Hill Top (on A41, 1 mile from Carters Green, opposite Trotters Lane)
☎ (021) 553 3127
Bulmer (J)
Two roomed local, little altered over the years. Outdoor drinking area.

Willenhall

Monday–Thursday: 12–3; 6–11, Friday–Saturday: 11–11, Sunday: 12–3; 7–10.30

Brewers Droop (P)

Wolverhampton Street
☎ (0902) 607827
Bulmer (H)
Meals and snacks 12–3; 6–9.30; outdoor drinking area.

Monday–Friday: 11–11, Saturday: 11.30–11, Sunday: 12–3; 7–10.30

Falcon (P)

Gomer Street West
☎ (0902) 633378
Westons Old Rosie (H)

Snacks 12–2. Comfortable two-room free house with a loyal local following. Stocks wide ranges of ales and whiskies as well as cider so mind the slope in the lounge! Garden.

Wolverhampton

Monday–Friday: 11.30–2.30; 6–11, Saturday: 11.30–3.30; 6–11, Sunday: 12–2.30; 7–10.30

Alexandra (P)
Clifton Street, Chapel Ash
☏ (0902) 25317
Bulmer (PC)
Pleasant one-room pub on western edge of town centre. Meals.

Monday–Thursday: 11–2.30; 6–11, Friday: 11–3; 6–11, Saturday: 11–3.30; 6–11, Sunday: 12–2.30; 7–10.30

Combermere Arms (P)
90 Chapel Ash (A41)
☏ (0902) 21880
Bulmer (PC)
A pub which could easily be mistaken for an ordinary terraced house! Tree growing in gents (could it be a lava tree?); outdoor drinking area; access for disabled at rear; pool table.

Weekdays: 11–2; 5–10.30

Farmers Off Licence (OL)
81 Aldersley Road
☏ (0902) 755666
Westons Farm Brand (PC)
Corner shop within easy reach of navigable canal.

Monday–Thursday: 11–3; Friday–Saturday: 11–11, Sunday: 12–3; 7–10.30

Feathers (P)
102 North Street
☏ (0902) 26924
Weston (PC)
Small local behind football ground. Meals and snacks lunchtime; garden.

Weekdays: 11–11

Great Western (P)
Sun Street (down steps under Wolverhampton BR station, turn right across front of old low level station)
☏ (0902) 351090
Bulmer (H)
A railway buff's paradise; railway memorabilia, photos and prints; necktie collection above central bar; no juke box. Meals and snacks 11.45–2.15 weekdays; outdoor drinking area. Near Wolverhampton BR station.

Paget Arms (P)
Park Lane
☏ (0902) 731136
Weston (PC)
Huge housing estate local recently splendidly refurbished. A choice of bars including a most attractive terrace around the back. Meals.

Wiltshire

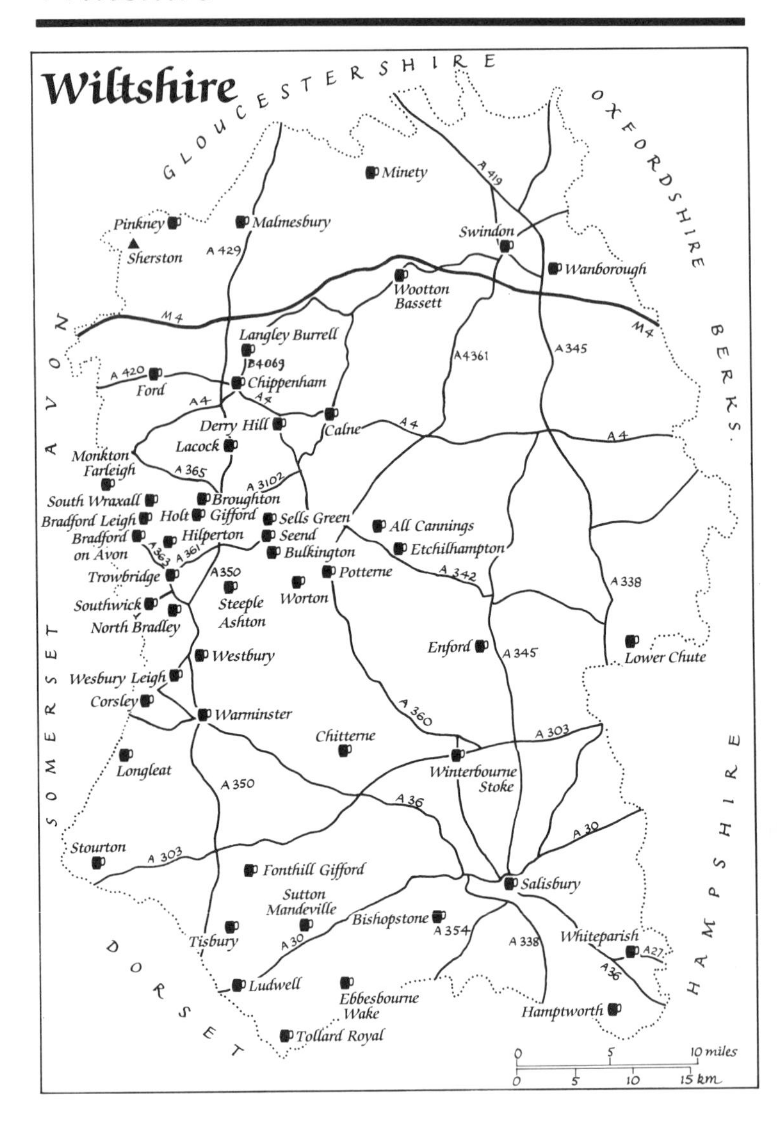

All Cannings

Weekdays: 11–2.30; 7–11, Sunday: 12–3; 7–10.30

Kings Arms (P)

☎ (038086) 328

Bulmer (PC)

Hard to find local in village on Kennett and Avon Canal. Bar snacks all opening times; garden; camping facilities nearby; small bore rifle range

Bishopstone

Weekdays: 10.30–2.30; 6–11, Sunday: 12–3; 7–10.30

Three Horse Shoes (P)

☎ (0722) 780491

Bulmer (H)

Taunton (PC)

Unaltered village watering hole. Garden; facilities for camping nearby.

Bradford on Avon

Dog & Fox (P)

Ashley Road (to north of town, about ½ mile west of A363 Bath road)

☎ (02216) 3257

Bulmer (PC)

Totally unspoilt country pub. Snug public and "front parlour" style lounge and large garden. Meals and snacks available.

George (P)
67 Woolley Street
☏ (02216) 5650
Bulmer (H)
Spacious pub with imposing frontage, formerly a farmhouse. Snacks; garden.

Kings Arms (P)
Coppice Hill
☏ (02216) 5005 or 4441
Bulmer (H)
Popular town centre pub. Lunchtime food.

Weekdays: 11–11

Rising Sun (P)
Winsley Road
☏ (02216) 2354
Bulmer (H)
Friendly locals' pub. Bar snacks all times; outdoor drinking area/garden; camping facilities nearby; frequent live music. Near Bradford on Avon BR station.

Bradford Leigh

Weekdays: 11–2.30; 6.30–11, Sunday: 12–3; 7–10.30

Plough Inn (P)
On B3109
☏ (02216) 2037
Bulmer (PC)
Large unspoilt roadside pub. Extensive menu; large garden.

Broughton Gillford

Monday–Friday: 11–2.30; 6.30–11, Saturday: 11–11.

Bell on the Green (P)
Off B3107
☏ (0225) 782309
Bulmer (H)
Village pub on edge of common. Meals and snacks lunchtime and evenings; garden; camping facilities nearby.

Bulkington

Bell (P)
☏ (030882) 741
Bulmer (PC)
One-bar local with nice garden. Collection of keys and traps. Snacks.

Calne

Buckeridge Wine Merchants (OL)
6 High Street
☏ (0249) 812381
Dunkerton (B)

Chitterne

Weekdays: 11–11

Kings Head (P)
☏ (0985) 50269
Bulmer (H)
Small village pub. Bar snacks and full meals 12–2; 6–9; garden with children's slide; one letting bedroom – sleeps 3 people.

Chippenham

Borough Arms (P)
34 Gladstone Road
☏ (0249) 652342
Bulmer (H)
Basic two-bar pub with pool room. Lunchtime meals; garden. Near bus station.

Weekdays: 11–11

Three Crowns (P)
London Road Causeway (A4)
☏ (0249) 652388
Bulmer (PC)
Bar snacks 11–2.30.

Corsley

Wednesday–Friday: 11.30–2.30, Saturday: 12–3: all weekday evenings: 6.30–11.

Cross Keys (P)
Lyes Green (½ mile off A362)
☏ (037388) 406
Bulmer (H)
Free house near Cley Hill. Meals lunchtime and evenings; children's room; garden; camping facilities nearby; skittle alley and bar skittles.

Derry Hill

Weekdays: 11–2.30; 6–11, Sunday: 12–2.30; 7–10.30

Lansdowne Arms (P)
On A342
☏ (0249) 812422
Bulmer (PC)
Victorian gothic pub opposite entrance to Bowood House and gardens. Meals and snacks 11–2; 6.30–10; restaurant; garden.

Ebbesbourne Wake

Weekdays: 11–2.30; 6–11.

Horseshoe (P)
2 miles south of A30 – turn off at Fovant
☏ (0722) 780474
Lazy Daisy (PC)
West Country Scrumpy (PC)
18th century inn at foot of old ox drove. Meals and snacks lunchtime and evenings; children's room; garden; accommodation; access for disabled.

Enford

Monday–Friday: 11.30–3; 7–11, Saturday: 11.30–11, Sunday: 12–3; 7–10.30.

Swan (P)
☏ (0980) 70338
Various (PP)
17th century thatched freehouse; cosy beamed bar with open fire, friendly local with atmosphere. Meals and snacks 12–2; 7–9.30; outdoor drinking area/garden.

Etchilhampton

Wayside Shop (OL)
☏ (038086) 470
Dunkerton (B)
Whole food and organic produce shop.

Fonthill Gifford

Weekdays: 11–2.30; 7–11

Beckford Arms (P)
Off B3089 on road from Hindon to Tisbury
☏ (0747) 870385
Bulmer (PC)
Stone built 17th century inn; log fires: good lakeside and woodland walks. Meals and snacks lunchtime and evenings; garden; accommodation; camping nearby.

Ford

Monday–Friday: 11–3; 6–11, Saturday: 11–11, Sunday: 12–3; 7–10.30

White Hart (P)
Off A420 – Colerne signpost
☏ (0249) 782213
Thatcher (PC)
West Country Scrumpy (PC)
Old inn in picturesque setting by trout stream. Meals and snacks lunchtime and evening; restaurant; children's room; garden; accommodation; access for disabled.

Hamptworth

Monday–Friday: 11.30–2.30; 6–11, Saturday and Bank

Wiltshire

Holidays: 11.30–11, Sunday: 12–3; 7–10.30

Cuckoo Inn (P)
Off B3079
☏ (0794) 390302
Wilkins (PC)
Popular, basic pub in quiet rural setting on edge of New Forest. Good garden for children. Snacks.

Hilperton

Lion & Fiddle (P)
Trowbridge Road (A361)
☏ (02214) 2824
Bulmer (PC)
Lounge overlooks sheltered garden. Public bar and children's room also available. Meals lunchtimes and evenings. Accommodation.

Holt

Tollgate (P)
Ham Green
☏ (0225) 782326
Bulmer (H)
Large, single bar pub specialising in food. Garden.

Lacock

George Inn (P)
4 West Street
☏ (0249) 73263
Bulmer (PC)
Taunton (PC)
Picturesque old pub. Snacks 12–2; garden with swings and aviary.

Langley Burrell

Weekdays: 11.30–2.30; 6–11

Brewery Arms (P)
The Common
☏ (0249) 652707
Bulmer (PC) (H)
Village pub, situated on "Maud Heath's Causeway". Meals and snacks 12–2; 7–10; children's room; outdoor drinking area/garden.

Longleat

Weekdays: 11–3; 6–11, Sunday: 12–2.30; 7–10.30

Bath Arms (P)
Horningshan, off B3092
☏ (098533) 308
Wilkins (PC)
Elegant pub in Longleat estate village. Meals and snacks lunchtime and evenings; children's room if eating; garden; accommodation.

Lower Chute

Weekdays: 11–3; 6–11

Hatchet Inn (P)
Near Andover
☏ (0264) 70229
Bulmer (PL)
300 year old thatched pub. Meals and snacks – fresh food menu – 12–2.30; 7–10; restaurant; outdoor drinking area/garden; accommodation.

Ludwell

Grove House Hotel (P)
☏ (074788) 365
Lazy Daisy (PC)
Accommodation.

Malmesbury

Borough Arms (P)
Oxford Street
☏ (0666) 822551
Bulmer (H)
Basic, noisy pub with a pool table.

Minety

Weekdays: 12–3; 6.30–11

White Horse (P)
☏ (0666) 860284
Bulmer (H)
Meals and snacks 12–2; 7–11; restaurant, children's room; garden; sun terrace overlooking lakeside setting; function suite.

Monkton Farleigh

Weekdays: 12–3; 6–11

Kings Arms (P)
☏ (0225) 858705
Taunton (H)
Old stone built pub with monastic connections. Meals and snacks lunchtime and evenings; restaurant; graden.

North Bradley

Rising Sun (P)
61 Woodmarsh (on A363)
☏ (02214) 2453
Bulmer (PC)
Busy village pub. Snacks; garden; pool table.

Pinkney

Weekdays: 11–2.30; 6–11

Eagle Inn (P)
☏ (0666) 840528
Weston (PC)
Basic village pub – a vanishing species.

Potterne

Bell (P)
On A360
☏ (0380) 3067
Bulmer (H)
One-bar local festooned with pewter and horse brasses. Meals.

Salisbury

Weekdays: 11–11

Anchor & Hope (P)
59 Winchester Street
☏ (0722) 27890
Taunton (H)
City centre pub with good cider following. Snacks lunchtime and evenings; families welcome; secluded garden.

Bird in Hand (P)
North Street
☏ (0722) 27238
Taunton (H)
Back street local. Near Salisbury BR station.

Weekdays: 12–2.30; 5.30–11.15

Mo's Restaurant (P)
62 Milford Street
☏ (0722) 331377
Bulmer (PC)
Popular town centre bistro with home cooking. Half a mile from Salisbury BR station.

Seend

Weekdays: 12–3; 6.30–11, Sunday: 12–3; 7–10.30

Brewery Inn (P)
The Cleeve
☏ (030882) 463
Taunton (PC)
Locals' pub with downstairs games room and good atmosphere, near Kennet and Avon Canal. Lunchtime snacks. Children's room. Garden.

Sells Green

Weekdays: 11–2.30; 6–11

Three Magpies (P)
On A365
☏ (0380) 828389
Taunton (PC)
Hospitable roadside inn offering snacks lunchtime and evenings; evening

meals; Sunday roast; children welcome; large children's garden; camping and caravanning facilities; pool table.

Semington

Weekdays: 11–3; 6–11

Somerset Arms (P)

High Street (A350)
☏ (0380) 870067
Bulmer (H)
400 year old roadside pub, once the property of the Duke of Somerset. Meals and snacks lunchtime and evenings; garden; accommodation en suite – 11 rooms.

Sherston

Weekdays: 10–2.30; 6.30–11, Sunday: 12–3; 7–10.30

Carpenters Arms (P)

☏ (0666) 840665
Westons Old Rosie (PC)
Westons Perry (PC)
Unspoilt and natural, even to scrubbed tops to bar tables. Meals and snacks all sessions; garden.

SELLERS' CIDER ▲

The Vineyard
☏ (0666) 840716

Steeple Ashton

Weekdays: 11–2.30; 6.30–11

Longs Arms (P)

One mile south east of A350
☏ (0380) 870245
Taunton (H)
Old coaching inn in a pretty village: bar was once used as a magistrate's court. Meals and snacks lunchtime and evenings; garden.

Southwick

Farmhouse Inn (P)

Frome Road
☏ (0225) 764366
Bulmer (H)
Converted farmhouse with exposed stone and white plastered walls. Restaurant. Garden.

South Wraxall

Monday–Friday: 11.30–2.30; 5.30–11, Saturday: 11–3; 5.30–11

Longs Arms (P)

Upper South Wraxall (½ mile west of B3109)
☏ (02216) 4450
Bulmer (PC)
Two bar village local. Meals lunchtime, and Wednesday to Saturday evenings; garden; access for disabled.

Stourton

Weekdays: 11–2.30; 7–11, Sunday: 12–3; 7–10.30

Spread Eagle Inn (P)

At entrance to Stourhead Gardens
☏ (0747) 840587
Rosies (BB)
Hot and cold buffet lunch every day; bar meals every evening; dinner a la carte in restaurant; morning coffee and afternoon teas November–Easter; accommodation.

Sutton Mandeville

Lances (P)

North of A30
☏ (072270) 220
Lazy Daisy (PC)
Good local pub with jovial atmosphere. Children's room and swings in garden. Accommodation. Meals.

Swindon

Weekdays: 10–10, Sunday: 12–3; 7–10

Sansons (OL)

91 Farringdon Road (opposite Railway Village)
☏ (0793) 538756
Thatcher (PC)
Fill up your own containers, or buy ½ gallon containers from the shop. Thought to be the only real cider outlet in the town – don't miss it!

Tisbury

Weekdays: 11–11

Cross (P)

Hindon Lane
☏ (0747) 871130
Taunton (H)
An old cider house, once the haunt of highwaymen. Snacks 11–2.30; meals 7–10; restaurant; garden. Half a mile from Tisbury BR station.

Tollard Royal

King John Hotel (P)

☏ (07256) 207
Lazy Daisy (PC)
Friendly one-bar local. In the heart of Cranborne Chase. Meals.

Trowbridge

Weekdays: 12–2.30; 6.30–11

Anchor & Hope (P)

64 Frome Road (A361)
☏ (0225) 752794
Bulmer (H)
Lively local with two-board darts room. Lunches.

Black Swan (P)

1 Adcroft Street
☏ (02214) 2600
Bulmer (H)
Detached pub with pleasant decor. Meals and snacks lunchtime and evenings; large garden and play area.

Greyhound (P)

61 Mortimer Street
☏ (02214) 62135
Bulmer (H)
Friendly popular local with large single bar. Meals and snacks lunchtime; garden; pool table. Near Trowbridge BR station.

John Bull (P)

Westfield Road
Bulmer (H)
A modern estate pub.

Rose & Crown (P)

Stallard Street
☏ (0225) 752862
Bulmer (H)
Comfortable pub near Trowbridge BR station. Meals.

Monday–Friday: 11–2.30; 6–11, Saturday: 11–3.30; 7–11, Sunday: 12–3; 7–10.30

Twelve Bells (P)

2 Seymour Road
☏ (0225) 752905
Bulmer (PC)
Comfortable locals' pub dominated by pool tables. Meals and snacks lunchtime and evenings.

Wanborough

Monday–Thursday: 11–2.30, Friday–Saturday: 11–11

Harrow Inn (P)

☏ (0793) 790622
Weston (H)
Lovingly restored 17th century thatched inn; beamed bars replete with stuffed fauna on three levels. One of the three cavernous fireplaces houses a fan-operated spit. Meals. Garden.

Wiltshire

Warminster

Bell & Crown (P)
66 Deverill Road (on A350 1 mile out of town)
☎ (0985) 212774
Taunton (H)
Multi-level bar with comfortable seating. Meals and snacks lunchtime and evenings; children's room; garden.

Masons Arms (P)
East Street
Taunton (H)
Busy town centre pub. Near Warminster BR station. Lunchtime food.

Westbury

Weekdays: 10.30–11

Castle Inn (P)
Bratton Road
☎ (0373) 822615
Taunton (PC)
Modern, mock-Spanish decor in this friendly local.

Monday–Friday: 11–2.30; 5.30–11, Saturday: 11–11, Sunday: 12–3; 7–10.30

Crown Inn (P)
Market Place
☎ (0373) 822828
Taunton (PC) (H)
Small town centre hotel. Meals and snacks Monday–Saturday, 12–2; 7.30–10; accommodation; pool table.

Monday–Friday: 11.30–3; 6.30–11, Saturday: 11.30–4; 6.30–11, Sunday: 12–3; 7–10.30

Horse & Groom (P)
Alfred Street
☎ (0373) 822854
Taunton (H)
Popular two-bar local with large food trade. Large garden with stream.

Weekdays: 11–11, Sunday: 12–3; 7–10.30

White Lion (P)
Market Place
☎ (0373) 822700
Taunton (H)
Homely two-bar pub with pool room catering mainly for younger people. Lunchtime meals. Accommodation.

Westbury Leigh

Weekdays: 12–2.30; 6–11

Phipps Arms (P)
On A3098
☎ (0373) 822809
Bulmer (H)
Pleasant village pub. Extensive menu; garden; accommodation.

Whiteparish

Monday–Friday: 11–2.30; 6–11, Saturday: 11–3; 6–11, Sunday: 12–3; 7–10.30

Kings Head (P)
The Street (on A27 – near Salisbury)
☎ (0794) 884287
Bulmer (H)
Traditional, unspoilt village local offering a welcoming and friendly atmosphere. Meals lunchtime and evening; garden; camping facilities nearby.

Winterbourne Stoke

Bell (P)
High Street
☎ (0980) 620445
Bulmer (H)
Busy roadside pub. Snacks lunchtime and evenings; garden.

Wootton Bassett

Longleaze Stores (OL)
Longleaze
Weston (PC)

Worton

Rose & Crown (P)
High Street
☎ (0380) 4202
Bulmer (H)
Beamed bar in 300 year old former forge. Meals and snacks lunchtime and evenings; children's room; garden; bar billiards.

Blands... a sad loss to cider making.

Yorkshire & Humberside

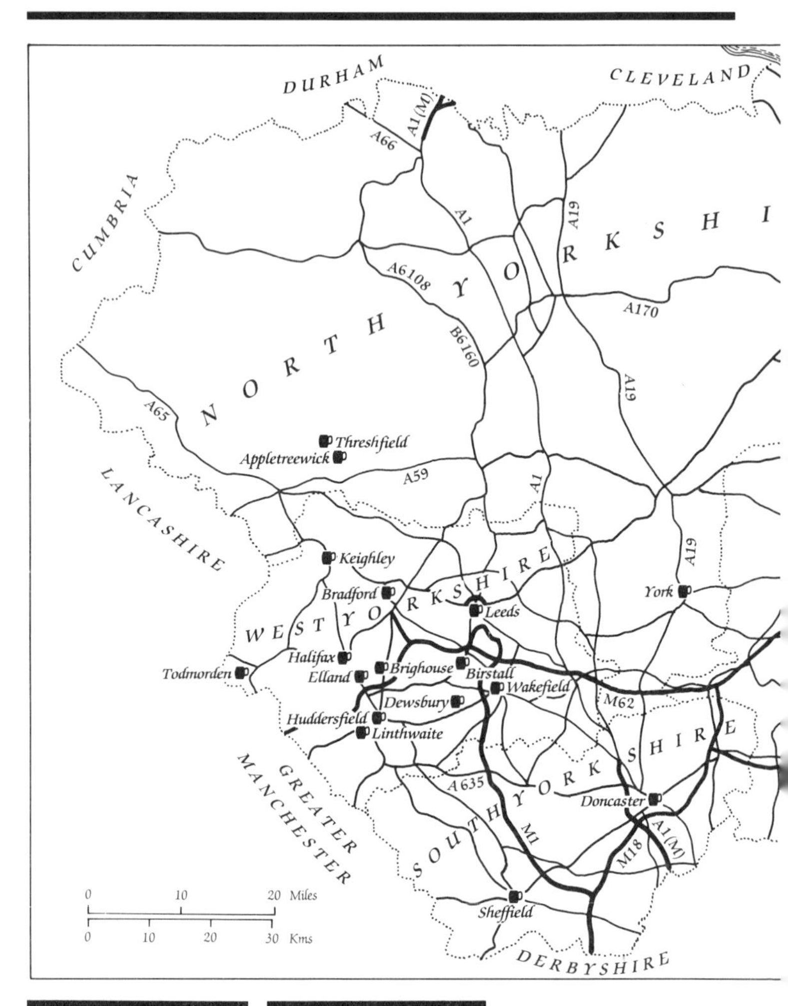

Humberside

Cleethorpes

Small Beer (OL)
199 Grimsby Road
☎ (0472) 699234
Symonds (PC)
Cider Wholesaler with wide range of bottled ciders in stock.

Weekdays: 11–11, Sunday: 12–3; 7–10.30

Willys (P)
17 High Cliff Road
☎ (0472) 602145
Symonds (PC)
Views across Humber estuary to Spurn Head. Meals and snacks 11–3; outdoor drinking area.

Yorkshire

Appletreewick

Weekdays: 11–3; 6.30–11

New Inn (P)
Main Street
☎ (075672) 252
Wilkins (PC)
A pub where drinkers come first. Meals and snacks 12–2.30; outdoor drinking area/garden; camping facilities nearby; large variety of games.

Birstall

Weekdays: 11–3; 5.30–11

Horse & Jockey (P)
Low Lane (near Batley)
☎ (92) 472559
Bulmer (H)

Bradford

Weekdays: 11–2; 5–11

Biko Bar (P)
Bradford University Union, Richmond Road
☎ (0274) 734135 (extension 150)
Taunton (H)
Thatcher (H)
Guest ciders (PC)
The guests include Thatchers perry, Inchs Harvest Scrumpy, Dunkertons, and Westons perry.

Weekdays: 11.30–11, Sunday: 12–3; 7–10.30

Fighting Cock (P)
21–23 Preston Street (off B6145)
☎ (0274) 726967
Guest ciders (PC)
Biddenden Monks Delight (B)
Basic back-street ale and cider house in an industrial area. Chilli and pies at lunchtime, and probably the biggest sandwiches in Bradford. Landlord keen Rugby Union fan.

Brighouse

Monday–Friday: 12–3; 5–11, Saturday: 12–3; 5.30–11

Red Rooster (P)
123 Elland Road (on A6025 ½ mile out of town centre)
☎ (0484) 713737
Westrays (H)
Compact and friendly roadside local. Outdoor drinking area.

Dewsbury

Flying Pig (P)
489 Huddersfield Road
☎ (0924) 461234
Various (PC)
The pub also makes its own, Rooftop, presumably to refresh pigs on the flightpath.

Doncaster

Hallcross (P)
33–34 Hallgate (next to Odeon Cinema)
☎ (0302) 328213
Bulmer (H)
Smartly refurbished home brew pub, using lot of mirrors. Meals and snacks lunchtime; outdoor drinking area. Near Doncaster BR station.

Elland

Barge & Barrell (P)
Park Road
☎ (0422) 73623
Wilkins (PC)
Plush Victorian style pub with polished wood, leaded glass and a fine fireplace in the front room. Lunches and evening meals until 8. Bar billiards. Children's room. Garden.

Halifax

Monday, Tuesday, Thursday: 12–3; 7–11, Wednesday, Friday, Saturday: 7–1 am, Sunday: 7–10.30

Brewers Delight (P)
96 Gibbet Street (third of mile west of town centre)
☎ (0422) 365696
Thatcher (H)
Single large room in Victorian road side hotel. Accommodation; access for disabled.

Monday–Thursday: 11.30–3; 5–11, Friday–Saturday: 11–11.

Woodcock (P)
213 Gibbet Street (½ mile west of town centre)
☎ (0422) 59906
Thatcher (H)
No nonsense local. Meals and snacks lunchtime and evenings; access for disabled.

Huddersfield

Rat & Ratchet (P)
40 Chapel Hill (on A616 near ring road)
☎ (0484) 516734
Thatcher (H)
Students' pub with bare boards, and plusher raised alcoves. Snacks and meals 12–2 – speciality Yorkshire puddings with range of fillings; garden.

Keighley

Monday–Wednesday: 11–3; 6–11, Thursday–Saturday: 11–11, Sunday: 12–3; 7–10.30

Yorkshire & Humberside

Grinning Rat (P)
2 Church Street
☏ (0535) 609747
Various (PC) (H)
Traditional town centre pub. Range of guest ciders and perries include Biddenden, Summers, Thatcher, and Wilkins. Meals and snacks 12–2.30 except Sundays; children's room; access for disabled. Near Keighley BR (and Keighley and Worth Valley Railway) station.

Leeds

Monday–Thursday: 12–10, Friday: 12–10.30, Saturday: 10 am–10.30 pm, Sunday: 7–10

Ale House (OL)
79 Raglan Road (off A660)
☏ (0532) 455447
Westrays Ciders, wide selection (H)

Weekdays: 11–11, Sunday: 12–3; 7–10.30

Crown Hotel (P)
Crown Point Road (adjoining Tetley's brewery)
☏ (0532) 451901
Bulmer (H)
Meals and snacks 12–2; 5–7; pool table.

Weekdays: 11–3; 5.30–11, Sunday: 12–3; 7–10.30

Duck & Drake (P)
43 Kirkgate (near St. Peters Church and market area)
☏ (0532) 465806
Westrays Scrumpy (PC) (H)
Two room city pub. Bar snacks all times; meals 12–2 on weekdays; live music.

Weekdays: 11.30–3; 5.30–11, Sunday: 12–3; 7–10.30

Eagle Tavern (P)
North Street, Leeds 7
☏ (0532) 457146
Various (H)
One of the oldest pubs in the city: only 5 minutes walk from city centre. Meals and snacks 12–2; outdoor drinking area; accommodation. Near Leeds City BR station.

Weekdays: 8 am–10 pm.30

J & V Stannard (OL)
265 Dewsbury Road, Leeds 11 (on A653)
☏ (0532) 705738
Thatcher (PC)

Linthwaite

Weekdays: 7–11, Saturday: 12–3; 7–11 (closed Monday–Friday lunchtimes)

Sair (P)
Lane Top, Hoyle Ing (4 miles south west of Huddersfield on A62, Old Ham road)
☏ (0484) 842370
Causeway (H)
At top of steep hill overlooking Colne valley. The cider is home-made. Children's room; garden.

Sheffield

Weekdays: 11–3; 5.30–11

Fat Cat (P)
23 Alma Street (off A61 northbound)
☏ (0742) 728195
Various (PC)
Real ale freehouse, with one non smoking bar. Meals and snacks lunchtime; snacks evenings to 7; outdoor drinking area.

Weekdays: 11–11, Sunday: 7–10.30

Frog & Parrot (P)
Division Street
☏ (0742) 721280
Bulmer (H)
Rogers Still Life (still)
Rogers Leg Platter (dry)
Rogers Hammerhead (medium sweet)
Rogers Gut Rotter (*very* dry)
A home brew pub with no juke box: Rogers ciders are specially made for the pub. Snacks and full meals weekday lunchtimes – specialises in fish (30–40 types available); separate restaurant; live music Monday evenings.

Monday–Friday: 12–10.30, Saturday: 10.30–10.30, Sunday: 12–2; 7–10.30

Small Beer (OL)
57 Archer Road
☏ (0742) 551356
Symonds (PC)

Thresfield

Old Hall Inn (P)
Side of B6265 at junction with Grassington road
☏ (0756) 752441
Various (PC)
Popular roadside Dales inn with fine wood panelling. Meals lunchtime and evenings; children's room; garden; accommodation; access for disabled; camping facilities nearby.

Todmorden

Weekdays: 12–3; 7–11

Staff of Life (P)
550 Burnley Road, Knotts (on A646 2 miles from town centre)
☏ (0706) 812169
Guest ciders (PC)
Freehouse in atmospheric gorge, with stone walls and floors. Small seafood restaurant, for which booking is advised. Meals lunch and evenings; garden; accommodation; camping facilities nearby.

Wakefield

Monday–Friday: 12–3; 5–11, Saturday: 12–11

Beer Engine (P)
77 Westgate End (5 minutes walk from Westgate station)
☏ (0924) 375887
Guest ciders (PC)
Stone flagged floor, gas lighting, brewery memorabilia. Lunchtime snacks (try the spicy sausage casserole) except Sundays; outdoor drinking area. Near Wakefield Westgate BR station.

York

Monday–Friday: 11–3; 5.30–11, Saturday: 11–11, Sunday: 12–3; 7–10.30

John Bull (P)
Layerthorpe
☏ (0904) 621593
Bulmer (H)
Thatcher (PC)
Thirties pub with colourful collection of enamel advertising signs and authetic decor. Bar snacks lunchtime; outdoor drinking area; regular live music.

Weekdays: 11–11, Sunday: 12–11

Oscars Wine Bar (P)
8 Little Stonegate
☏ (0904) 652002
Guest ciders (B)

Weekdays: 11–11, Sunday: 12–3; 7–10.30

Spread Eagle (P)
98 Walmgate
☏ (0904) 35868
Bulmer (H)
Popular three roomed free house. Substantial and good

value bar snacks 12–7; outdoor drinking area.

Monday: 4.15–10, Tuesday–Friday: 11–10, Saturday: 10–10, Sunday 12–2; 7–10

York Beer Shop (OL)
28 Sandringham Street
(off Fishergate)
☏ (0904) 647136
Thatcher (PC)
Westrays Gloucestershire Farmhouse Scrumpy (PC)
Westons Perry (PC)
Also sells English fruit wines and regional cheeses.

WHAT'S BREWING? What's Brewing, that's what

When those 4 founder members of CAMRA first kicked around the idea of a Campaign for the Revitalisation of Ale in 1971, they hardly expected it to amount to anything, let alone become the most successful consumer organisation in Europe.

But such is the way of things. Their idea, harnessed to the massive well-spring of dissatisfaction with the then trend to keg beer wrought a massive change in the attitudes of drinkers.

Gaining support for the cause is usually the greatest problem and when small minority interest groups begin life one of the first indications of their existence is the newsletter. CAMRA was no exception.

What's Brewing first appeared in 1972 as a single photostated sheet of A4: from these humble beginnings it has mirrored the success and influence of the Campaign and become a professionally produced and printed 16 to 24 page tabloid newspaper.

It is also one of the principal benefits of CAMRA membership. Every month What's Brewing's rich brew of news and views of all things to do with real beer hits the front doormat of each and every member.

Like the Good Beer Guide, What's Brewing is an independent voice among the vested concerns of the brewing industry and the publications that surround it. The aim is to criticise when necessary and give praise when it is due.

But What's Brewing is much more than a campaigning voice against the excesses of the big (and sometimes small) brewers, it is also a darned good read, with features and articles which appeal to all members regardless of whether they are at the front of the fight to protect real ale or not.

Regular features on breweries and their beers; in-depth looks at the brewing process and what goes in to your pint; cartoons, including the infamous Bill Tidy Kegbuster strip; P.A. Newton's savagely humorous Diary . . . there's an awful lot in it.

What's Brewing doesn't just concentrate on the British beer scene either. Information from all over the world is regularly relayed to its readers through renowned beer writer Michael Jackson's World of Beer column, a regular international flavour.

What's Brewing has come a long way since that first issue in 1972, and there is still much for CAMRA and its members to do.

What's Brewing and its readers will be around for a long time yet.

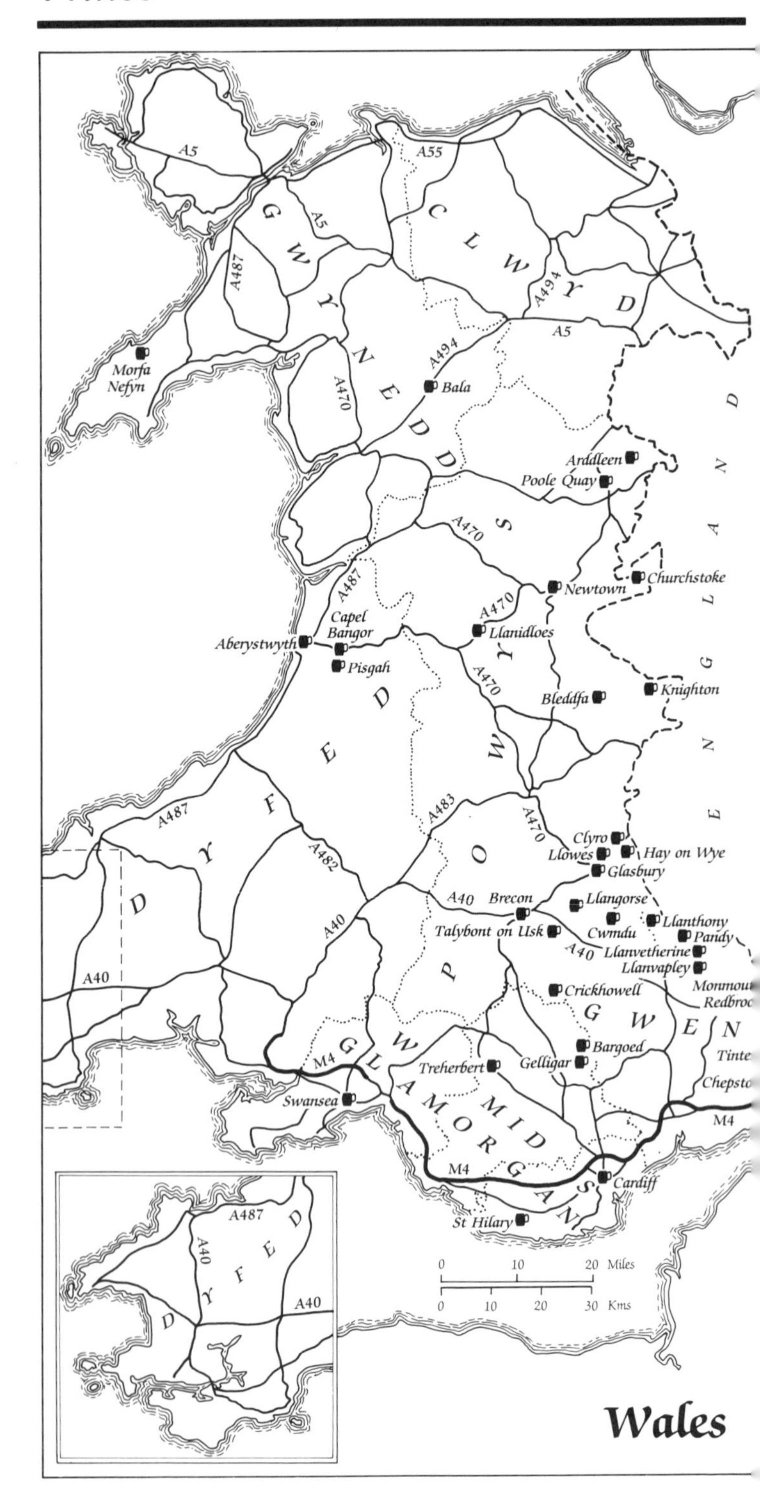

A5
A55
GWYNEDD
CLWYD
A487
A494
A5
Morfa Nefyn
A470
Bala
Arddleen
Poole Quay
A470
POWYS
ENGLAND
Newtown
Churchstoke
A487
Capel Bangor
Aberystwyth
Pisgah
A470
Llanidloes
Bleddfa
Knighton
DYFED
A487
A483
A470
A482
Clyro
Llowes
Hay on Wye
Glasbury
A40
Brecon
Llangorse
Llanthony
Talybont on Usk
Cwmdu
Pandy
A40
Llanvetherine
Llanvapley
A40
Crickhowell
GWENT
M4
MID GLAMORGAN
Treherbert
Gelligar
Bargoed
Swansea
M4
M4
Cardiff
St Hilary
0 10 20 Miles
0 10 20 30 Kms
A487
A40
A40
Wales

Dyfed

Aberystwyth

Weekdays: 7–12

Rummers (P)
Trefechan Bridge
☎ (0970) 625177
Westons Old Rosie (PC)
18th century warehouse on harbourside, previously used by smugglers: many original features. Meals and snacks to 10; outdoor drinking area; camping facilities nearby. 100 yards from Aberystwyth BR station.

Capel Bangor

Weekdays: 11–11 (summer); 11–2.30; 5.30–11 (winter)

Tynllidiart Arms (P)
On A44
☎ (0970) 84248
Bulmer (H)
300 year old coaching inn. Meals lunchtime and evenings; access for disabled.

Pisgah

Weekdays: 12–3; 6–11 (closed on Sundays)

Halfway Inn (P)
Devils Bridge Road (A4120)
☎ (097084) 631
Symonds (PC)
Unusual self service system for draught beers and ciders, from casks on stillage in beamed stone walled room. Near Devils Bridge Falls, and Vale of Rheidol narrow gauge steam railway. Meals and snacks 12–2; 6–10; garden; camping facilities nearby. Near Nantyrowen station on Vale of Rheidol line – summer only.

Glamorgan

Bargoed

Weekdays: 11–11, Sunday: 12–3; 7–10.30

Hanbury Arms (P)
Hanbury Road
☎ (0443) 830136
Bulmer (H)
Large Victorian local. Snacks.

Cardiff

Huxleys (OL)
37–39 Birchgrove Road, Birchgrove
☎ (0222) 692295
James White (PP)

Gelligaer

Harp Inn (P)
2 St. Calwgs Avenue
☎ (0443) 830496
Bulmer (H)

St. Hilary

Weekdays: 11–11 (12 midnight for restaurant customers), Sunday: 12–3; 7–10.30.

Bush Inn (P)
½ mile off A48 between Cardiff and Cowbridge
☎ (04463) 2745
Bulmer (H)
A thatched 16th century inn, in one of the Vale of Glamorgan's most beautiful villages: bare stone walls, stone flagged floors, oak beams, and plenty of atmosphere. High quality catering: meals and bar food 12–2; 7–10 (no bar food Saturday evening); restaurant; garden.

Swansea

Monday–Wednesday: 11–7, Thursday–Saturday: 9–7

Oddbins (OL)
233 Oxford Street
☎ (0792) 642196
Weston (full range)

Treherbert

Weekdays: 11–4.30; 6.30–11

Dunraven Hotel (P)
Dunraven Street
☎ (0443) 775070
Bulmer (H)
A Rhondda valley local.

Gwent

Chepstow

Monday, Tuesday, Thursday: 12–3; 6–11, Wednesday: 6–11, Friday–Saturday: 11–11, Sunday: 12–3; 7–10.30

Berkeley Arms (P)
Station Road
☎ (02912) 3216
Bulmer (H)
Bar snacks 12–2.30; 6–9; outdoor drinking area/ garden; children's play area with slides, swings and seesaw. Near Chepstow BR station.

Weekdays: 11–3; 6–11

Three Tuns (P)
Bridge Street
☎ (02912) 3497
Bulmer (H)
Near castle, museum and River Wye. Snacks 12–2; pool table. Within ½ mile of Chepstow BR station.

Llanthony

Monday–Friday: 11.30–3; 6–11, Saturday: 11–11, Sunday: 12–3; 7–10.30

Abbey Hotel (P)
☎ (0873) 890487
Knights Crumpton Oaks (PC) cider and perry
In a quiet valley in the Black Mountains: a small pub in the cellar of the famous abbey. Snacks lunchtime; meals 7–8.30; restaurant; garden; accommodation.

Llanvapley

Red Hart Inn (P)
On B4233
☎ (060085) 227
Bulmer (H)
Comfortable country pub. Meals and snacks; garden.

Llanvetherine

Kings Arms (P)
☎ (087386) 221
Bulmer (H)

Monmouth

Weekdays: 9.30–5.30

Irma Fingal-Rock (OL)
64 Monnow Street
☎ (0600) 2372
Dunkerton full range (J)
Delicatessen shop; also sells French farm cider.

Pandy

Weekdays: 11–2.30; 6–11

Pandy Inn (P)
On A465
☎ (0873) 890206
Bulmer (H)
In small village in Monnow Valley, close to Black Mountains: Offa's Dyke

passes one mile to the west. Meals and snacks lunchtime and evenings; restaurant.

Redbrook

Bell Inn (P)
☏ (0600) 3137
Weston (PC)
In Wye Valley.

Tintern

Weekdays: 11–3; 6–11

Cherry Tree Inn (P)
Devauden Road (off A466)
☏ (0291) 689292
Bulmer (W)
In Wye Valley, near Tintern Abbey: railway enthusiasts will welcome the preserved station, now a picnic area with displays of the former line. The pub boasts a forty year old 4 pin bar billiard table. The cider comes direct from a wooden cask.

Gwynedd

Bala

Weekdays: 11–11, Sunday: 12–3; 7–10.30

White Lion (P)
61 High Street (in town centre)
☏ (0678) 520314
Weston (PL)
Half timbered coaching inn dating from 1759. Meals 12–2; 7–8.30; snacks 12–2; 6–9; separate restaurant; children's room; outdoor drinking area; accommodation.

Morfa Nefyn

Tycoch (P)
Bulmer (PC)

Powys

Arddlîn

Monday–Friday: 12–3; 5.30–11, Saturday: 12–11

Horseshoe (P)
North of Welshpool
☏ (093875) 318
Weston (H)
Old fashioned pub in small village on Shropshire Union Canal. Meals and snacks lunchtime and evenings; restaurant; children's room; garden; accommodation.

Bleddfa

Weekdays: 11–11 (Easter–October: 11–3; 6–11 (November–Easter)

Hundred House (P)
On A488
☏ (054781) 225
Bulmer (H) – summer only
Comfortable and attractive country pub on edge of Radnor Forest. Meals and snacks lunchtime and evenings; children's room; garden; accommodation; access for disabled.

Brecon

Camden Arms (P)
The Watton
Bulmer (H)
Small busy local. Snacks.

Churchstoke

Weekdays: 8–6 all week.

Harry Toffin Ltd (OL)
☏ (05885) 226
Westons Old Rosie (J) (DJ)
Westons Vintage (J) (DJ)
Large supermarket in rural surroundings. Separate restaurant.

Clyro

Weekdays: 11–11

Baskerville Arms Hotel (P)
☏ (0497) 820670
Weston (J) (DJ)
Modernised Georgian hotel in Kilvert country; oak beams and open fires. Snacks 11–10; meals 12–3; 6–10; restaurant; garden; accommodation; camping facilities nearby.

Crickhowell

Britannia (P)
High Street
☏ (0873) 810553
Bulmer (H)
Town local. Snacks.

Cwmdu

Weekdays: 11–3; 6–11

Farmers Arms (P)
On A479 six miles south of Talgarth
☏ (0874) 730464
Bulmer (PC)
Large wholesome meals a speciality: lunchtime and evenings; garden; accommodation; camping facilities nearby.

Glasbury

Harp (P)
Hay Road (off A438)
☏ (04974) 373
Dunkerton (B)
Weston (PC)
Overlooking River Wye. Snacks lunchtime and evenings; children's room; garden; accommodation; access for disabled.

Llynau Bach Lodge Hotel (P)
☏ (04974) 473
Dunkerton (B)

Maesllwch Arms Hotel (P)
☏ (04974) 226
Dunkerton (B) (PC)
Snacks; evening meals; garden; accommodation.

Three Cocks (P)
☏ (04974) 215
Dunkerton (B)

Hay on Wye

Weekdays: 11–3; 5.30–11

Blue Boar (P)
Castle Street
☏ (0497) 820884
Bulmer (H)
Town centre pub. Meals lunchtime and evenings.

Granary (P)
Broad Street
☏ (0497) 820790
Dunkerton (B)
Small intimate bar attached to a busy tea shop and restaurant. Garden.

Monday–Saturday: 9.30–5.30

Hay Wholefoods & Delicatessen (OL)
Lion Street
☏ (0497) 820708
Dunkerton (B)
Dunkerton Perry (B)
Full range of wholefoods and delicatessen items, many locally made; yummy foods; real dairy ice cream; exotic

sandwiches; organically produced vegetables, bread, wine and lager (as is the cider and perry of course!)

Oscars Restaurant (P)
Scotland House, High Town
☏ (0497) 821193
Dunkerton (B)

Knighton

George & Dragon (P)
Broad Street (A488)
☏ (0547) 532
Bulmer (H)
Small town centre pub. Meals lunchtime and evenings; outdoor drinking area; accommodation.

Red Lion (P)
West Street
☏ (0547) 528231
Bulmer (H)
Lively town local. Meals lunchtime and evenings; accommodation.

Llangorse

Weekdays: 11–3; 6.30–11

Red Lion Hotel (P)
☏ (087484) 238
Bulmer (PC)
Very popular pub in a picturesque area. Bar snacks 12–2; 7–9.30; full meals 7–9.30; restaurant; outdoor drinking area; camping facilities nearby.

Llanidloes

Unicorn Hotel (P)
Longbridge Street
☏ (05512) 3167 or 3516
Weston (J)
Plush, well kept, one bar town pub with small games room. Accommodation and meals.

Llowes

Tuesday–Saturday: 11.30–2.30; 6.30–12, Sunday: 11.30–2.30 (open Sunday evening and Mondays on Bank Holidays)

Radnor Arms (P)
☏ (04974) 460
Weston (H)
Village pub near 11th century castle. Meals and snacks lunchtime and evenings; children's room; accommodation.

Newtown

Weekdays: 11–11

Elephant & Castle (P)
Broad Street
☏ (0886) 626271
Weston (PC)
Large town centre hotel with excellent, good value meals.

Poole Quay

Weekdays: 11–11

Powis Arms (P)
☏ (0938) 75253
Weston (PC)

Talybont on Usk

Monday–Wednesday and Friday: 11–3; 6–11, Thursday and Saturday: 11–11, Sunday: 12–3; 7–10.30

Star Inn (P)
On road through village (B4558); ¾ mile from A40
☏ (087487) 635
Bulmer (H)
Wilkins (PC)
Useful refreshment break if walking or navigating the Brecon Canal. Meals and snacks, with extensive vegetarian menu, lunchtime and evenings; large outdoor drinking area; pool table.

Scotland

Glasgow

Weekdays: 11–12, Sunday: 12–3; 7–10.30

Babbity Bowsters (P)
16–18 Blackfriars Street
☏ (041) 552 5055
Bulmer (H)
Converted building in revitalised merchant city area. Excellent food, lunchtime and evenings; outdoor drinking area; accommodation. Near High Street, Argyle Street BR stations; St. Enoch Underground station.

ABOUT THE EDITOR...

David Kitton's involvement with cider began at a tender age, when he experienced a cloudy yellow liquid in a back street South London pub – long since demolished on health and safety grounds – and realised there was more to life than fizzy bottles with colourful birds on the label. A walking holiday in the West Country in the long hot summers of the mid-1970s introduced him to countless unspoilt hostelries serving the real thing straight from the cask, and he began compiling a list of these outlets, initially for his own benefit: this "research" led to the first national guide to traditional cider in 1984, and subsequently the Good Cider Guide.

Apart from this "consuming interest" he practises as an architect; is trustee of a charity advising churches on the use of their resources; and produces weekly news programmes for hospital radio. His other interests include all forms of transport other than the motor car, which he regards as a "bad thing"; he is part owner of an Edwardian steam locomotive on the Bluebell Line in East Sussex; and his home is dominated by sundry railway relics. He broadcasts on radio; follows the canal system by boat and on foot; and makes his own brand of cider – Gibbon Strangler – which he claims is the only way to remain sane in suburban Bromley.

ABOUT APPLE....

APPLE is the Apple and Pear Produce Liaison Executive, a national sub-committee of CAMRA for the promotion of traditional cider and perry. These most traditional of British drinks, which predate that hoppy upstart, real ale, are now under threat (see the articles on pages 7 and 14). Small cider and perry makers are disappearing fast. If you really care about the cider *you* drink, then join CAMRA and help support the cause. Application form on page 242.

THE A–Z GUIDE TO CIDER AND PERRY

A: Apples: *the only ingredient necessary for making real cider.*

Additives: *ingredients unnecessary for making real cider. Some, such as sulphur dioxide, are used for chemical control; others, such as tartrazine, a colouring agent, are more likely to produce lack of control among allergic consumers.*

B: Bittersweets: *apples low in acid but high in tannin, and rich in sugar which ferments to alcohol: much used by cider makers, with many varieties, allowing choice of blending ad infinitum.*

Bittersharps: *further cider apple category – high in both acid and tannin.*

Beer: *alcoholic beverage best avoided in close proximity to cider. If you must drink both in one session, remember the golden rule – "Beer on cider is a good rider, but cider on beer makes you feel queer".*

C: Carbonation: *the artificial introduction of carbon dioxide to keg and bottled ciders, which renders them quite unrecognisable as a natural product: a process for which the consumer pays extra to cover the cost of equipment and material!*

Crab apples: *the great granddaddy of the cider apple, from whose fermenting juice the first prehistoric man got the first prehistoric hangover.*

D: Designer cider: *new brands dreamed up by bright-eyed bushy-tailed advertising men and executives to appeal to bright-eyed, bushy-tailed yuppies – usually thereby exhausting all the firm's budget to the total exclusion of promoting its established and traditional brands.*

E: Eccentric: *often found behind the cider bar at most beer festivals, with many more in front. In the view of most "progressive" commercial cider makers, anyone reading this book!*

F: Fermentation: *the natural process by which all the sugars present in the fruit are transformed into alcohol.*

G: Gravity: *the surest method of serving cider and perry – in former times direct from wooden casks behind the bar, now from plastic barrels, demijohns or jars.*

H: Hand pump: *the recognised means of drawing cider from the cask in the cellar to the bar, as with real ale. Now, however, being exploited by certain firms as a consumer image to convey authenticity to their pressurised products. Beware! If it is held down and not pumped it is purely a tap, allowing pressure dispense.*

Horse: *often employed in former times to draw a large stone wheel round and round and round and round a stone trough to crush the apples. It didn't do the horse much good either.*

Horse hair: *often employed in former times as the material for the cloths between the layers of pulp in the press. By this stage there clearly was not much left of the horse!*

I: Ice: *and why not? Assuming your cider has not been watered down, a nob or two in the drink on a hot day will work wonders. Remember to take a long swig of the cider* before *asking for the ice, or you will be paying for the ice cubes as part of your pint.*

J: Juice: *the outcoming of the pressed pulp. Now often evaporated down to a concentrated form of treacle by the larger firms, for ease of storage and transport, and later reconstituted by adding back water – fine if you can trust the local water supply and its composition, but not possible to return to its original state, except perhaps if using an artesian well in the orchard where the apples grew.*

K: Keg: *a metal container of cider, highly pressurised with carbon dioxide; with only one opening, controlled by a valve – the cider, usually filtered and pasteurised, is forced into the glass by opening a tap on the bar and letting the gas push it through the pipes.*

L: Libation: *an ancient custom, by which the cider drinker deliberately (or so he claimed) spilt a few drops of the liquid on the floor as an offering to the Goddess Pomona. Non-believers found it still worth practising, as an excuse for an unsteady hand at the start of a drink, and a way of getting rid of the dregs at the end. A habit ready for revival.*

M: Mug: *a china vessel traditionally used for drinking cider: probably adopted so as to avoid seeing the curious objects floating in the drink. Often two and sometimes even three handed. Or a person paying inflated prices for keg cider when a real version is available at 20p less on the same bar.*

N: Nature *the force which "makes" real cider.*

O: Oak: *claimed by many to be the finest material in which to ferment and mature cider and perry. Even many commercial ciders, which subsequently meet a fizzy end, begin their life in oak vats.*

Organic: *at one time all cider and perry was, of course, before the days of sprays and artificial fertilisers. A number of small apple grower/cider makers are now going back to no chemical treatment of the trees and their crops, and the cider and perry from these sources is much sought after.*

P: Promotion: *a multi-million pound advertising campaign to persuade people to buy a product they do not want or need – constantly used by the largest cider makers.*

Publicans: *(in the Bible always linked with sinners). They come in two types:– those who welcome real cider in their pubs as an acceptable alternative drink, and enthusiastically promote it, without a multi-million pound advertising campaign, to customers who've never tried it:– those who loathe it, and on moving into a new pub, which they do at three-monthly intervals, throw all vestige of it and its customers out of the door, even if the pub was previously a cider house.*

Q: Quiet pubs: *the most relaxing atmosphere in which to enjoy your drink – you can actually hear yourself speak! A number of such establishments are listed in this Guide – most in the London area, which perhaps is more urgently in need of them.*

R: Racking off: *the original, and natural, means of controlling the degree of sweetness and strength of a cider, by draining the liquid off the lees (the yeast deposits) at a stage before fermentation is complete, thus obviating the need for adding any additional sweeteners.*

S: Sugar: *naturally present in the fruit, and ferments to alcohol: makers often add more sugar to boost the strength of the fermenting juice. Sugar is also used as a sweetener, but has the drawback of encouraging secondary fermentation.*

Saccharine: *intensely sweet substance obtained from coal tar, often used to sweeten cider, and favoured because it is inert, and thus causes no secondary fermentation: has the drawback of leaving a nasty taste in the mouth.*

Sharps: *category of cider apples, high in acidity, and low in tannin: Bramley culinary apples also fall into this type.*

Sweets: *category of cider apples, used mostly for blending with more assertive fruit.*

T: Tartrazine: *an artificial colouring agent, much used by the larger manufacturers: of suspect safety, and known to cause hyperactivity in children, who should not be drinking cider anyway.*

Television: *an artificial communication medium, much used by the larger manufacturers for invading our homes to persuade us to buy cider which we would never drink otherwise, and known to cause inactivity in children. The cost of such television advertising probably adds at least 10p to the cost of every pint of commercial cider.*

U: Undesirable: *to cider enthusiasts, anyone who gives cider a bad name, by treating it, and himself, irresponsibly. To grumpy landlords (see Publican) anyone who dares ask for real cider or scrumpy.*

V: Vimto: *much used by cider drinkers in the Yeovil, Crewkerne and Taunton areas of Somerset to mix with their drink. It sounds horrible, but it happens.*

W: Water: *used by some cider makers (but never the one you are talking to) to dilute over-strong cider and bring it below the legal limit, over which it would be taxed as wine: used by the more unscrupulous to "stretch" their supplies further.*

X: Extra Dry: *(yes we know it is cheating, but you try to find an "X"!) cider fermented to its fullest extent, crisp, tart, but too demanding for the mass market (hence the Vimto).*

Y: Yeast: *naturally present on the fruit: in fully traditional cider and perry it is retained for the fermentation process: in commercial products, where the maker wishes to ensure a more predictable result every time than the wild yeast would guarantee, the natural yeast is killed off with sulphur dioxide, and replaced with a wine yeast.*

Z: Zider: *Mummersetshire jargon, often heard, and seen, in the cider-type town of Cheddar.*

Cider makers and distributors

★ denotes Category A cider maker

★ **ABBEYGATE CIDER**, Abbeygate Farm, Musbury Road, Axminster, Devon. Contact in firm: Roy Mear, ☏ (0297) 33541, Opening hours; any reasonable time: if coming a long distance please phone first. Type of cider: medium; dry, Containers: litre bottles: or customers may provide their own. Customers may sample before purchasing. Other items on sale: eggs; vegetables. Facilities: caravan and camping site. Directions for finding: on A358 Axminster to Musbury road, about 1 mile south of Axminster.

This is a cider well placed for the holiday maker, being only a few miles from the Devon resort of Seaton. It is also readily accessible for those without private transport – unlike so many – for the BR station at Axminster, on the Salisbury to Exeter line, is within easy walking distance. Should you wish to pay more than a passing visit, there is a camping and caravan site on the farm, open all the year: highly to be recommended in preference to the crowded acres down on the coast, and an excellent centre for a week or fortnight's holiday. Roy makes only about 1,000 gallons of cider each year, using only cider fruit, from neighbouring orchards, so you are advised to come and fill up as early in the season as possible.

★ **APPLE BLOSSOM CIDER**, The Cornish Cider Company, Trevean Farm, Coombe Lea, near Truro, Cornwall, Contact in firm: John Watt, ☏ (0872) 77177. Not sold from the premises. Type of cider: medium sweet; medium; scrumpy. Containers: bottles; plastic 2 pt; 4 pt; 1 gal containers; 5 gal polycasks; stone 2 oz; ½ pt; 1 pt; 3 pt pots.

In Cornwall Apple Blossom time lasts all year round, though most is sold in the summer, when it makes a welcome appearance at many caravan sites, holiday parks, and at several local National Trust properties. There are a number of off-licences which stock it: even one chemist, which gives official credence to the old "apple a day" theory. The cider is fully traditional, and is mainly a blend of the famous Kingston Black cider apples and Bramleys: the result is a good well balanced drink.

ARTS SOMERSET SCRUMPY, Lillypool Farm, Shipham, Cheddar, Somerset, Contact in firm: Arthur David, ☏ (0934) 743994. Opening hours: all week throughout the year. Type of cider: sweet, medium; dry – Somerset Scrumpy Virgins Ruin; Triple Vintage. Containers: bottles from 1 pt upwards; or customers may provide their own. Customers may sample before purchasing. Other items on sale: apple juice; farm produce; cheeses; soft drinks; ploughman's lunches; cream teas; souvenirs. Facilities: large car and coach park; toilets; camp site. Directions for finding: on road from Cheddar to Shipham, about 1 mile south of Shipham village.

Passports are not required for entry to Art's Kingdom, though plenty of time would be an advantage! The place is a rich experience – a ranch-style cider world set high in the Mendip Hills, and well geared to the holiday visitor. Many will find it a welcome alternative to the traffic queues of nearby Cheddar, for here there is plenty of space: some may feel like staying – visas are only needed after six months. Art's Scrumpy puts you in that sort of laid back mood: it is naturally made, and mastered in the wood: it goes by names such as Kate Mary Special, and Claire Diana Special – whether the other brand, Virgins Ruin, has any connection is something no one has ever dared ask. If you are one of those who noted the demise of Broad Oak Cider some while ago, you may be pleased to learn that their products are still available from Art's, in addition to his own range.

★ **ASHWOOD CIDER AND PERRY**, "Ashwood", Shipham Hill, Cheddar, Somerset, Contact in firm: Philip Ford, ☏ (0934) 742393. Opening hours: 9–9 Monday to Saturday; 12 noon–3; 7–11 Sundays and Bank Holidays. Type of cider: sweet; medium; dry. Type of perry: sweet; medium; dry Containers: ½ gal; 1 gal plastic; 2 gal; 5 gal polycasks: or customers may provide their own. Customers may sample before purchasing. Other items on sale: eggs; cheese; three-handled cider mugs. Directions from finding: 100 yards north of junction with A371 Weston Super Mare to Wells road, 1 mile west of Cheddar, on road to Shipham.

The Fords only began cider making in 1986, after dabbling with it as a hobby. They must have learnt fast, for they are now making a very presentable cider and perry. They have acquired an ancient mill, made by A. Day of Mark in 1868, but now belt driven, and a two screw wood press. Apples come from orchards at Wookey and Street. Here cider is made wholly traditionally – pressing with barley straw, and adding no foreign yeast, or sulphur dioxide. The sweet variety does not have any sweetener added either, but is from selected sweeter apples. The final classifying of each barrel into sweet, medium or dry is decided most democratically, at a family conference.

★ **ASHILL CIDER**, Ashtons Farm, Ashill, near Ilminster, Somerset, Contact in firm: C. House, ☏ (0823) 480513. Opening hours: 10–6 Monday–Saturday; 12 noon–1.30 Sunday. Type of cider: sweet; dry. Containers: ½ gal; 1 gal; or customers may provide their own. Customers may sample before purchasing. Directions for finding: on the main A358 Taunton to Chard road in the village of Ashill.

The labels for Ashill Cider are striking, to say the least: a delightful young lady in tights, clutching a glass, and high kicking – she assures us that it is "cider with a real kick"! With that in mind the motorist might be well advised not to go much further after sampling it: camping facilities are available nearby for those who wish to enjoy the cider to the full, and call a halt for the day. Pitch the tent, *then* drink the cider! This is a genuine Somerset cider, made from local cider apples, strong and very pleasant. However, if you want to enjoy this taste of Somerset, you would be wise to visit early in the season: supplies are limited, and you will not get much of a kick out of discovering it's sold out!

★ **ASPALL CYDER**, The Cyder House, Aspall Hall, Debenham, Stowmarket, Suffolk. IP14 6PD. Contact in firm: John Chevallier Guild. ☏ (0728) 860510, Opening hours: weekdays only: 9–12.30; 1.30–3.30 (not open Bank Holidays) Type of cider: medium sweet; dry; extra dry. Containers: 1 litre bottle. Directions for finding: about 1 mile north of Debenham on road to Eye.

The Chevalliers have been growing apples in Suffolk ever since they settled there some 250 years ago: the first cyder was made at Aspall in 1728. The Hall is an elegant moated country mansion dating back over five centuries, and owned by only two families in that time: it was the birthplace of Ann

Chevallier, the mother of Kitchener of Khartoum. The cyder is distinctive in several ways: first it is spelt the Suffolk way, with a "y" rather than an "i"; secondly it does *not* follow the Eastern counties tradition of using only culinary and dessert fruit – it contains the same varieties of Bittersweets that are found in the West Country, with, as there, a proportion of eating apples added. Thirdly it is an "organic" cyder: the apples are entirely free of any artificial fertilisers or chemicals, and the end product has no preservatives added. The cyder has a good pronounced apple taste and aftertaste, with the body of a light wine. Sadly it is only made in small quantities, and indeed John Chevallier Guild is reticent to publicise it too widely for this reason. You will *not* find it outside its native heath, except for very occasional outlets, and even there it is best to check before setting out. The only certain venue is the Hall itself, a splendid setting for an excellent high quality drink.

★ **AVALON CIDER**, Avalon Vineyard, The Drove, East Pennard, near Shepton Mallet, Somerset. BA4 6UA. Contact in firm: Dr. Howard Tripp, ☏ (074986) 393. Opening hours: reasonable times, but please phone first to avoid disappointment. Type of cider: natural still dry: natural sparkling dry, Containers: 75 cl bottles. Customers may sample before purchasing. Directions for finding: turn west off A37 Ilchester to Shepton Mallet road at Wraxall, towards West Bradley; ignore right turn to East Pennard, and after a further mile turn right down a rough track to the Drove.

Dr. Howard Tripp poured some of his cider into wine glasses, an indication of his attitude towards his creation. "We hope to make our cider to a standard which deserves to be treated as wine," he declared, "the bottle looks presentable enough for anyone's dinner table, and it's certainly not the sort of cider one could quaff by the pint. It deserves a gentle appreciation". Avalon is certainly different, not only from the mass market cider, but also from most of the traditional Somerset farm makes. It is, firstly, made entirely from organically grown fruit, so contains no pesticide residues; it is made from selected cider apples, freshly pressed through straw; and the pressing is done on an ancient hand turned press, which squeezes slowly, and so extracts the maximum flavour and colour. Add to that the slow fermenting, with no sugar added to boost the juice, and several months maturing in oak rum barrels, each barrel being kept separate with no attempt to blend to blandness, and you have what Dr. Tripp believes is a cider worth treating with respect. It comes in two forms. The first is fermented to a natural still dry; the other is naturally sparkling, produced by secondary fermentation in the bottle – one of the few examples on the market of a bottle-conditioned cider. For once we can recommend a "real" sparkling cider!

BATTLE VINTAGE CYDER, Garnett Brothers, Oaklands Farm, Moat Lane, Sedlescombe, East Sussex. TN33 0RY, Contact in firm: Bob Garnett ☏ (0424) 751680, Opening hours: any reasonable time daily – please phone if coming long distance to avoid disappointment. Type of cider: vintage. Containers: 1 litre bottle, Customers may sample before purchasing. Other items on sale: wine. Directions for finding: on A21 Tonbridge road about 4 miles north of Hastings, and 1 mile north of junction with A28, turn north east into Moat Lane: Oaklands Farm will be found about ¾ mile along on the right.

Bob and Alan Garnett began making Battle Vintage Cyder in about 1984, following in the steps of those earlier brothers, the monks at nearby Battle Abbey, who used to make and sell a mean drop of cider in their time. The cider is strong and still – about 7½% alcohol content, and this factor, and its marketing in bottles, makes it an ideal alternative to a table wine: culinary apples are used, and this gives the drink a refreshing crispness – Somerset cider makers ought to be sent a bottle as an education into the traditions of the Eastern half of the country.

BIDDENDEN CIDER, Biddenden Vineyards Ltd., "Little Whatmans", Biddenden, near Ashford, Kent. TN27 8DH. Contact in firm: Richard J. Barnes. ☏ (0580) 291726. Opening hours: 11–5 Monday–Saturday; 12–5 Sunday (May–October): 11–2 Monday–Saturday only (November–April). Type of cider: medium; dry. Containers: 1 litre bottles. Customers may sample before purchasing. Other items on sale: apple wines; apple juice; range of table wines. Directions for finding: from north, branch right off A274 1 mile south of Biddenden, and in 1 mile turn left to Vineyard: from Tenterden, take Cranbrook road to Castletons Oak PH, turn right at crossroads, and right again in few hundred yards to Vineyard.

It is true to say that not many years ago Kentish cider was in a poor way: the old established firm of Bob Luck had closed down, and the future looked bleak. But happily just at that time the Barnes family were introducing a new, and distinctive, cider, which has quickly re-established the county as a major cider producing area. "Little Whatmans" began as a vineyard, in 1969, and the Barnes' original third of an acre gradually grew to the present eighteen. The cider followed as a natural adjunct. It is based on culinary rather than cider fruit, as is the custom in Kent, and the resulting strong still drink is crisp and refreshingly tangy. It is also strong, with good body, and as such could easily pass for a light table wine: try it as an accompaniment to a meal, and you will soon realise its potential. You will find that some pubs sell it only in half pints, with a healthy respect for its powers, and it is perhaps best for sipping, rather than downing by the pint, though several glasses will do wonders for you! Besides the normal brand, the firm sells "Monks Delight", a tasty cider blended with honey and spices, delicious either mulled or chilled. Besides sampling the range of wines and ciders at the shop, visitors may also stroll around the vineyard. Guided tours are offered during June to August, at lunchtime or evening, for parties of 25 or more: the visit includes a vineyard walk, a talk on wine making, a light meal, and of course some suitable liquid refreshment. Biddenden Cider may be found in many free houses and off licences throughout Kent and East Sussex, and will add greatly to your enjoyment of the other attractions of the Garden of England.

BLACK BULL CIDER, Norbury's Cider Company, Crowcroft, Leigh Sinton, near Malvern, Worcestershire. WR13 5ED Contact in firm: T. P. Norbury, ☏ (0886) 32206. Opening hours: normal licensing hours, Type of cider: medium sweet; medium dry. Type of perry: medium dry. Containers: ½ gal; 1 gal; 5 gal plastic; bottles and jars. Customers may sample before purchasing. Other items on sale: cherry wine; apple wine. Directions for finding: on A4103 Worcester to Hereford road just west of Leigh Sinton.

Black Bull Cider came into being thanks to the Common Market; perhaps one of the few good consequences of that controversial union! The Norbury family are fruit growers, and with the trade in the doldrums since joining the EEC they needed an outlet for their culinary apples, which otherwise tended to finish up as jam. They began experimenting with cider in 1979, with the farm's old scratter and hand press, and that year made about 1,200 gallons. The result was *not* encouraging – a sour, cloudy, variable, and usually disagreeable product. It took them several years to live it down. Just then a local highly-esteemed cider maker, Mr. Lanchbury, sold up, and the Norburys took the plunge and bought his equipment. Their early experiences had taught them that there was a world of difference between making a few gallons in the back yard, and selling to the general public. Tom Norbury recalls when part of the farm workers wage had been paid in cider, and his father gave them the choice of cash instead: they took the money to a man. With such memories of "traditional" cider in his mind, Tom became convinced of the necessity of firm control during the whole cider-making process, to produce an attractive and consistent drink. Thus the natural yeasts are killed off and replaced by a champagne yeast, and the cider is filtered to give a clear pint; saccharine is added to the sweet variety. The apples are a blend of culinary and cider varieties, the latter including Yarlington Mill, Sweet Coppin, Dabinett, Kingston Black, and Medaille d'Or, grown on the farm. Over 50,000 gallons can be made annually. The result is highly satisfactory: the cider is extremely palatable, with good aroma, a clear light orange colour, a full bodied and almost wine like consistency, and a subtle apple flavour – distinctive and enjoyable. It is worth mentioning that most of Mr. Lanchbury's former outlets still remain firm customers, which must prove something. Even more gratifying though must be the firm's recent success in competition with its older rivals: for several years they have taken on the cider makers of Somerset at the

Mid Somerset Agricultural Show at Shepton Mallet, and beaten them on their own ground, fending off the challenge of 35 other firms to take the championship.

★ **BRIMBLECOMBE'S DEVON FARMHOUSE CIDER**, Farrant's Farm, Dunsford, Devon. Contact in firm: Cliff Brimblecombe, ☏ (039281) 456. Opening hours: all reasonable times – please check first if coming on Sunday or evenings. Type of cider: sweet; medium; dry. Containers: 1; 2; 4 litre plastic; or customers may provide their own. Customers may sample before purchasing. Other items for sale: mulling spices; free range eggs; traditional honey from August onwards. Directions for finding: on the B3212 Dunsford to Exeter road about 1 mile east of Dunsford.

In a changing world it is good to know that some things remain the same. At Farrant's Farm the scene has altered little over the centuries – it is almost like experiencing a time warp. In the farmyard and cats and hens wander happily, while beyond is the ancient cider barn, built of Devon cob. Up a flight of timber steps you are plunged into a cool dark atmosphere; cobwebs hang from the vast oak beams, and gradually you will make out the rows of wooden barrels which line the walls. The barn saw its first barrel well over 400 years ago: up to then it had been the farmhouse, but then a "modern" house was built, and the barn became the cider store. The cider press dates, too, from that time. Cider making here owes nothing to recent innovation; nylon "cloths" are unheard of, the cider cheese being built up with straw, as it always has been. The cider is cloudy, orange in colour, and has considerable strength, with a good apple flavour. The sweet is very sweet, and most people opt for the medium or the dry. Many of the apples used are grown on the farm: 120 new trees have been planted to ensure future supplies. Most are Bittersweets: Hang Me Down, Slap Me Girls, Sweet Alford, Tom Putt, and some newer varieties. Cliff keep bees in the orchard: a meal of bread, butter, honey and cider takes a lot of beating. But the bees are there for other reasons too – to fertilise the trees. The temperature in the barn remains constant, winter and summer, and Cliff maintains that the cool and the dark keep his cider in first-class condition. For those of us not fortunate to have a Devon cob barn in the back garden, a refrigerator is an acceptable, though less roomy, alternative. The quality of the cider, and the magic of the place, guarantee a constant stream of callers, all delighted to find an impressive difference from the ciders they are used to in the shops. People come from far and wide: Yorkshire, the south east, and even Northern Spain. Join them and find out why.

★ **BROMELL'S DEVON FARM CIDER**, Lower Uppercott, Tedburn St. Mary, near Exeter, Devon. Contact in firm: Eric Bromell, ☏ (06476) 294. Opening hours: all reasonable times – if coming a long distance please phone first to avoid disappointment. Type of cider: sweet; medium sweet; medium; dry. Containers: $\frac{1}{2}$ gal plastic; 5 gal polypins; 1 pt stone jars; or customers may provide their own. Customers may sample before purchasing. Other items on sale: farm vegetables; milk. Directions for finding: on Whitestone road just east of Tedburn St. Mary.

Lower Uppercott is first and foremost a working farm, situated on the edge of Dartmoor, and a visit there is a pre-requisite to any walking tour of the National Park. Eric Bromell seemingly combines farming and cider making with no apparent effort, though he produces some 30,000 gallons per year. All the apples used come from within ten miles of the farm. The cider is pleasant and powerful, cloudy yellow in colour, strong and full bodied, with a flavour that gives a slight suggestion of peach. However, everybody's idea of taste varies, and Mr. Bromell will encourage all the members of your party to sample the different barrels: this is finds usually results in complete disagreement within the group, and means he sells a container of cider to everyone to suit their preferred choice, which makes for excellent business. On the subject of containers, Eric is often fearful of the holiday maker who loads up the car boot with plastic carry kegs – he would rather see such visitors at the very end of their break, so that they can take the cider straight home and put it in the fridge. He regards his cider like any other dairy product, and is concerned that his customers treat it with the same respect: after all a plastic tub of butter would be less than appetising after a fortnight in a hot car, and unless you intend to stock up with vinegar the same is true of farmhouse cider. If you have to travel far with it, he recommends using glass, bottles or demijohns. But for your day on the Moors he has no such qualms: a plastic container will be fine – easy to carry, and likely to be empty by the middle of the afternoon. There are also some strategically placed outlets, notably in National Trust restaurants, also several pubs and off licences, should you become desperate before you can make it back to Lower Uppercott.

BROOM FARM CIDER, Broome Farm, Peterstow, Ross on Wye, Herefordshire. HR9 9QG. Contact in firm: John Draper, ☏ (0989) 62824. Opening hours: 9–7 daily. Type of cider: dry. Containers: ½ gal; 1 gal plastic: or customers may provide their own. Customers may sample before purchase. Other items on sale: soft fruit. Facilities: cream teas; bed and breakfast. Directions for finding: on A49 Ross on Wye to Hereford road, turn north just west of Peterstow, past church, and Broome Farm will be found about 1 mile along on the right.

The main business of Broome Farm is to produce apples for H. P. Bulmer. However in 1988 it was decided to use fruit from the old orchards, and in the locality, to make their own cider. A local agricultural engineer built a mill and press, harnessed to a tractor, which can press up to 24 gallons at a time, with a slide system, so that while one cheese is being pressed another can be built up on the side, and slid into position when ready. The apple juice is treated with metabisulphate to destroy the wild yeasts, and a cultured yeast is substituted to give a consistent product. The juice ferments in old whisky barrels. Only unsprayed fruit is used: the apples are traditional varieties – Foxwhelp, Yarlington Mill, Bulmers Norman, and Kingston Black. The verdict on the drink so far is that it is "remarkably smooth", and all have found it suitably strong. Now it is your turn to try.

BRYMPTON D'EVERCY CIDER, Brympton D'Evercy House, near Yeovil, Somerset. BA22 8TD. Contact: Charles Clive Ponsonby-Fane. ☏ (0935) 862528. Opening hours: 2–6 except Thursday and Friday (May–end of September and over Easter). Type of cider: medium. Containers: 2½ litre bottles. Other items on sale: cream teas; produce from the estate. Facilities: gift and plant shop; museum; vineyard; gardens. Directions for finding: off old A3088 west of Yeovil: follow the signs from the A303 and A30.

Brympton is the family home of Charles and Judy Clive-Ponsonby-Fane. It has been owned by only three families during its long 750 year history, and each has added to the buildings, which now make up a veritable architectural history lesson. The place is the epitome of all that is English, with its beautiful peaceful gardens, its elegant rooms, steeped in heritage, and its beguiling atmosphere of unhurried pleasure. The state rooms and extensive grounds are open to the public, and a series of photographic and art exhibitions is staged here every year. The old 14th-century priest house contains a collection of domestic appliances, and an exhibition of cider making through the ages. This latter would be excuse enough for a family excursion, but the fact that cider is still produced here makes it a must. It is made from Kingston Blacks and other Bittersweet apples, and enables you to take away with you some of the tranquility of this splendid country house.

BULMER'S TRADITIONAL DRAUGHT CIDERS, H. P. Bulmer Drinks Limited, The Cider Mills, Plough Lane, Hereford. HR4 0LE. Contact in firm: A. J. Hill, Sales Planning Manager. ☏ (0432) 352000. Type of cider: Traditional Draught – sweet; medium; dry: West Country Traditional Draught – sweet; medium; extra dry.

Leaders for many years of the "Big Three", Bulmer's began in a small way, in 1887. The Rev Charles Bulmer, rector of Credenhill, near Hereford, was greatly interested in anything to do with the land, and wrote much of a study on local apples and pears, the "Herefordshire Pomona". His son, Percy, was a sickly child, and suffered so badly from asthma that he was not expected to grow up, and did not go to school. When he started to look for work in his teens he found no one would employ a lad with no education, and so he decided to start his

own business. His parents influenced him to choose cider making: his father already made a small amount from the rectory orchard, and his mother felt any firm dealing in food or drink must be successful: "these things do not go out of fashion", she declared. Percy began by pressing the family crop, but the following year rented a warehouse in Hereford, bought apples from local farmers, and made 4,000 gallons. Encouraged by his success he moved to larger premises, and was joined by his brother Fred, who took charge of sales. Since then the firm has never looked back. In 1911 it was granted the Royal Warrant, which it has held ever since. The now famous "Woodpecker" brand appeared as early as 1896. In 1936 the company bought further land, and over the years much further development has taken place. Everything at Bulmer's is on a vast scale: it houses the largest alcoholic drinks container in the world, a 1,650,000 gallon tank named "Strongbow", which many local people take to be a gasholder! Over 15 million gallons of cider are stored in huge oak vats, in an enormous underground room which resembles a vast forest. Bulmer's is responsible for around half of the nation's annual consumption of cider, about 30 million gallons. As long ago as 1923 it was realised that the supply of cider apples was not keeping pace with increasing demand, and it was decided to establish a seven acre nursery to supply young trees to local growers at low cost. From this has developed the Bulmer orcharding division, whose task it is to see that enough of the right varieties of apple will always by available to keep pace with growing output. Help is given to local farmers, and advisory staff visit orchards to advise on planting, pruning, spraying and harvesting. The company has about 2,000 acres of its own trees, and buys in supplies from a wide area. Most of the promotion of Bulmer's ciders has been in the field of keg and bottled brands. But from the earliest days the firm has also made a traditional draught cider, which though less advertised, has become increasingly popular in recent years, and may be found all over the country on handpump and in polycask. There are two versions: Traditional Draught: a cask conditioned cider, where a pinch of yeast is added at the casking stage to allow secondary fermentation within the cask, thus giving a slight lift to the drink, and inducing subtle taste changes to enhance the natural flavour – it is slightly cloudy, and should be drunk at room temperature. The other version, West Country Traditional Draught, is less well known, and not so widespread: this again is a hazy cider, but with no secondary fermentation or conditioning, and thus completely still. Both brands are made from cider fruit, with a small proportion of culinary apples blended in, and have a good apple flavour: they are ideal for drinking by the pint. These are the only truly traditional brands, though the bottled Number 7, extra dry and strong, is acknowledged to be a connoisseur's cider. It is the oldest of the Bulmer range, being introduced in 1890, and with all the sugars fermented out may be recommended for diabetics, or indeed anyone who is seeking an acceptable alternative to wine. The drinker should beware of what, at first glance, might appear to be a traditional brand, "Original"; sometimes confused in people's minds with "Traditional". Appearing in pubs with a bar cowl in the form of a small cask, or costrel, it depicts Percy Bulmer, and the date 1887: but one doubts if Percy would recognise it as his early attempt those many years ago in his father's orchard! It is in fact carbonated, and can scarcely be "original" even on Bulmer's own admission, for Number 7 is publicised as the *oldest* brand, and that did not see the light of day for three more years. The mystery deepens!

★ **BURROW HILL SOMERSET CIDER**, Pass Vale Farm, Burrow Hill, Kingsbury Episcopi, Martock, Somerset. Contact in firm: Julian Temperley. ☏ (0460) 40782. Opening hours: weekdays to 6 – please phone to avoid disappointment. Type of cider: dry. Containers: 1 gal; 5 gal plastic; or customers may provide their own. Customers may sample before purchasing. Other items on sale: mulling spices. Directions for finding: off B3168 Curry Rivel to Ilminster road at Hambridge, 2 miles west of Kingsbury Episcopi, on an isolated hill rising 200 ft above the Somerset Levels.

Julian Temperley is something of a politician in the world of traditional cider: As Burrow Hill is a prominent local landmark, so both he and his cider are high profile. He is an enthusiastic advocate for the supremacy of Somerset, stoutly maintaining that his county grows the finest apples, and consequently produces the best results. His haul of awards in national tastings and regional shows over recent years are convincing evidence of his case. He will have no truck with other counties, and talks even more disparagingly when it comes to discussion of foreign apples and the chemical concoctions of the mass producers. His is a philosophy of perfection, and his cider is for the few who can appreciate a good thing when they taste one. The acknowledged quality of Burrow Hill cider is down to the apples, says Julian. Getting the cider right means getting the orchard right, and his 40 acres are a careful selection of some 5000 trees, mostly Somerset varieties such as Dabinetts, Porters Perfection, Yarlington Mill, Chisel Jersey, Somerset Red Streak, and of course the famous Kingston Black, all noted for their cider making potential. Tradition, and no compromise, is the order of the day at Pass Vale Farm. Cider has been made in the cider house for over a hundred years, fermented in oak vats, and sold from wooden barrels. Most of the cider sold is dry, the only way, according to Julian, properly to appreciate the full subtleties of flavour and character. Sweeter brands *are* available, but if you are wise you will heed the expert, and enjoy the "cleverness of the Somerset apples".

SOMERSET ROYAL CIDER BRANDY. This is the fulfilment of a dream that Julian Temperley has had for ten years. Cider brandy has not been distilled in England for several hundred years, and drinkers with a taste for the stuff have been forced to cross the Channel, where the French enjoy less of a nanny state. But in the mid 1980s two "museum licences" were granted, first to the Cider Museum in Hereford, and shortly afterwards to Brympton d'Evercy near Yeovil in Somerset. These permissions were however only for a strictly limited quantity, basically for instructional purposes. In 1989 came the breakthrough, when Julian was awarded a licence to distil his Burrow Hill cider on a commercial scale, producing brandy from cider on the lines of a French Calvados distillery. The distillery is *not* at Pass Vale Farm though: the curious rules of HM Customs and Excise decreed that it should be at least two miles away, so a former milk factory in Kingsbury Episcopi has been converted, and is now in full production. The venture is a partnership with six other local cider makers, including the Taunton Cider Company, whose laboratory facilities should prove invaluable. Julian sees the project as a shot in the arm, or rather the orchard, for the Somerset apple growers, and believes it will reverse the sad decline in recent years, to which Tony Gibson refers in his article elsewhere in the Guide. The name has been chosen to reflect the apples used – Royal Somerset is a cider apple variety; and it also reflects the county. As one might imagine, the technique has had to be acquired from scratch: there is no tradition in this country to draw from. Julian learnt the art in Normandy, from skilled Calvados makers, and it was there too that he obtained his still. With the equipment, the know how, and a ready supply of prime cider apples, the future for drinkers and growers alike shows signs of western promise. The drinker must however exercise patience – it takes three years to mature the spirit in oak vats. If you want to experience the first Somerset Royal, you may reserve up to twelve bottles by sending a deposit, of £2 per bottle, to the Somerset Cider Brandy Company Ltd., at Pass Vale Farm. The final price is likely to be similar to that for single malt whisky.

★ **CHURCHWARD'S CIDER**, M. & V. O. Churchward, Yalbeton Farm, Paignton, Devon. Contact in firm: Vic Churchward. ☏ (0803) 558157. Opening hours: normal times throughout week. Type of cider: sweet; medium; Devon mix; dry. Containers: 3 pt; 1 gal glass; 1 litre – 5 gal plastic; ½ gal; 5 litre stone; or customers may provide their own. Customers may sample before purchasing. Directions for finding: off A3022 Brixham to Newton Abbot road (via A385 Totnes road from Paignton); turn right down Yalberton Road.

This is a prize winning cider, temptingly placed within easy reach of the many thirsty holiday makers of Torbay: the premises are only a mile or so inland from the beach at Paignton, just past the Zoo – perhaps an excuse to visit the latter might lead on to a call at the former? Churchward's Cider has become more prominent in recent years, partly due to the disappearance from the Devon cider scene of Hill's, which previously dominated the market: Churchward now finds its way into some of that firm's outlets. Much of the annual output however is sold straight from the farm, for come rain or shine Vic has a captive audience every summer.

★ **CLARK'S FARMHOUSE CIDER**, Shortridge Hill, Seven Crosses, Tiverton, Devon. EX16 8HH. Contact in firm: Lawrence Clark. ☏ (0884) 252632. Opening hours: always open. Type of cider: medium; dry. Containers: ½ gal; 1 gal plastic: or customers may provide their own. Customers are encouraged to sample before purchasing. Directions for finding: from Bickleigh, on A396 Exeter to Tiverton road, turn west ¼ mile north of Trout Inn, and follow road uphill for 2 miles: at junction turn sharp left, and Clark's Cider will be seen ¾ mile on the right.

Lawrence Clark was an early developer: he began collecting farm implements as soon as he could talk, and started making cider at the age of five! He now farms 40 acres, with sheep and poultry, the latter for the Christmas trade. You will be greeted on arrival by a reception committee of several hundred geese, no doubt lobbying to be saved from the ovens on December 25. Cider is Lawrence's hobby: he makes what he likes, a not too dry blend, and argues that if he did not like it he could never expect other people to. Every cheese is slightly different, so the distinction between medium and dry tends to get a trifle blurred. Only cider apples are used, from local farms, some of uncertain variety, though among them are Woodbine, Sweet Alford, and Chisel Jersey. The press was originally a wooden screw type, but has now been adapted to twin metal screws. The mill is about 100 years old. Needless to say, the method of production is of similar age, and entirely unchanged.

COATES FARMHOUSE CIDER, Showerings Ltd., Kilver Street, Shepton Mallet, Somerset. BA4 5ND. Contact in firm: Jan Carruthers. ☏ (0749) 3333. The cider is not sold from the premises.

R. N. Coates Cider Company was founded at Nailsea in 1925, and bought by

Showerings in 1956. In 1968 it was joined by the old established William Gaymers, of Attleborough, Norfolk, together with Whiteways of Whimple in East Devon. Whiteways has now ceased production, Gaymers concentrates on its well known Old English brand in bottled and keg form, while the Shepton Mallet plant makes Babycham, and traditional draught cider. The firm now forms part of the Allied-Lyons Group. In May 1989 Showerings merged with another Allied-Lyons subsidiary, Goldwell, to create an organisation better able to compete with its rivals Bulmer and Taunton for the static cider market. Unlike the other members of the "Big Three", Showerings have not appeared in the past to be overtly enthusiastic towards traditional cider, being more concerned to rid the drink of its old fashioned and rural image. In the mid 1980s, Shepton Mallet was treated to what could have been interpreted as an indication of the firm's philosophy, when the citizens were confronted with the sight of their streets lined with decorative flower tubs, made by cutting up vast numbers of 5 gallon polycasks, many with their cider labels still in place, and filling them with earth! But perhaps this cask re-conditioning was a mere blip, for in 1986 a new era for traditional cider was proclaimed, with the advent of 'Addlestones', intended "for the serious cider drinker". The subsequent sage of that brand is discussed elsewhere: suffice it to say here that at that stage Showerings pledged continuing commitment to "the very important area of traditional ciders" through both the new brand *and* Coates Farmhouse. But realistically there must be fears for the survival of Coates Farmhouse, now heavily overshadowed by Addlestones, into which all the efforts of the firm seem to be directed, and which has already supplanted it in some pubs. Palmers Brewery, of Bridport, can hardly have helped when they removed Coates from their pub estate in preference to Taunton. Only four or so batches of Coates Farmhouse are made each year, and at that rate its consistency at point of sale must become a problem. In fact if you are lucky enough to track it down, it is surprisingly good: most of the pubs that sell it seem to shift a fair amount, and it has a good local following: at only around two-thirds the price of Addlestones, and with its excellent flavour and body, it represents splendid value. Support it wherever, and whenever you can! It seems odd, does it not, that Showerings, who have openly stated that they want a "traditional and real draught cider" to give them a comprehensive draught cider range, cannot develop and promote the real cider that already have, rather that struggle on with the technical and ethical problems set them by their new creation?

★ **COOMBES TRADITIONAL FARMHOUSE CIDER**, Japonica Farm, Mark, near Highbridge, Somerset, TA9 4QP. Contact in firm: Chris Coombes. ☏ (027864) 265. Opening hours: reasonable hours – please phone first if intending to visit in evening or Sunday. Type of cider: sweet; medium sweet; dry; vintage. Containers: bottles; 1 gal plastic; ½ gal stone; or customers may provide their own. Customers may sample before purchasing. Other items on sale: pure apple juice; sparking perry; souvenirs. Directions for finding: on B3139 Highbridge to Wedmore road between Watchfield and Mark.

The labels promise that "Coombes Cider will make your smile grow wider and wider": but even if you don't need cheering up, a trip to Japonica Farm is recommended. The family has been making cider since 1919 – Chris is the third generation – and they reckon to have perfected the process by now. The varieties of cider apple used include Morgan Sweet, Brown Snout, Breakwell's Seedling, Somerset Red Streak, Taylor's, Yarlington Mill, Chisel Jersey, Dabinett, and Kingston Black. You will know most if not all of these, and recognise them as excellent performers. Chris is keen that visitors see all that is going on; he encourages you to inspect the antique and modern equipment – some dates back to the 1880s – wander round the pressing room, and linger in the cellar while trying the various brands for yourselves. He believes that seeing all the stages of cider making from start to finish will help people to appreciate the drink more, and he specially invites families to look around – cider is, after all, an essential part of the "core" curriculum for today's kids: they are the customers of tomorrow. The farm is ideally situated near the popular Somerset coast, and the nearby caravan site is a tempting venue for any cider enthusiast – especially if it rains for the whole fortnight. It is then, surely, that Coombes Cider will keep you smiling when all else fails.

CORNISH SCRUMPY, Cornish Scrumpy Company Ltd., Callestock Cider Farm, Penhallow, Truro, Cornwall, TR4 9LW. Contact in firm: David Healey. ☏ (0872) 573356. Opening hours: weekdays 9–6. Type of cider: medium sweet; medium dry; dry. Containers: 1 gal glass jars: 2½; 5 litre plastic; 5 gal polycasks; stone jars. Customers may sample before purchasing. Other items on sale: sparkling scrumpy; gooseberry and recurrent wines. Directions for finding: branch off A30 at junction with A390 onto A3075 Newquay road, and turn right at Penhallow (follow the signs).

One does not automatically think of west Cornwall as an apple growing, or cider making, area. But here at Callestock Farm is the exception that proves the rule: a large range of traditional stone barns around an attractive courtyard, well over twenty acres of orchards, and modern equipment, combine to produce a strong, natural, Cornish scrumpy. Though only established here in recent years, the cider farm is well on the way to becoming a fully self sufficient cider producer. Five acres of standard, traditional orchards have been planted, which allow a cycle of three crops: grass, where the sheep can graze while the trees are growing in the early years; fruit when the orchard matures; and finally, a hundred years ahead, the trees themselves, which have been selected for the high quality of their wood for turning and carving. They have an eye to the future in these parts! A further twenty five acres are being converted to bush orchards, which will have a productive life of up to thirty years. The varieties have been selected not only for their juice and natural balance of sugar, but equally importantly their ability to thrive in the unique Cornish climate. The apples include Yarlington Mill, a mild Bittersweet, Dabinett, a full Bittersweet, and sweet varieties such as Harry Masters Jersey, Sweet Coppin, Sweet Alford, and Northwood. For the lower parts of the valley where spring frosts could affect the blossom, they have chosen late flowering varieties: Ashton Brown Jersey, and Dunkerton Late. There is much to see at the farm: from displays on the history of cider making to a trip round the present plant. You will be fascinated by the Round Barn, where you can see a large horse drawn granite mill with its original granite press – unique to Cornwall and the Channel Islands – and the Traditional Cider House, with its collection of hand pressures and mills through the ages. The difference from the modern technology used today will be impressive: in the Pounding House up to four tons of fruit are handled at a time, with as many apples crushed in one hour as the old stone mills could cope with in a day. The double action hydraulic press, with two base trays, which allow one cheese to be dealt with while another is built up, produces 160 gallons of juice an hour, in effortless contrast to those presses you will have just admired! The size of the fermenting tanks, each holding 23,000 litres, will also amaze you. Despite the greater scale and efficiency, the final product is much as it has always been, save for two processes. The first is the replacing of the apple's natural yeast with a champagne yeast, to ensure consistency, and the second the addition of further sugar to the juice to increase the alcohol content to 8% – it is not for nothing that the posters proclaim "Cornish Scrumpy, Legless but Smiling"!

COTSWOLD CIDER, Bottle Green Drinks Company, Spring Mills Estate, Avening Road, Nailsworth, Gloucestershire. Contact in firm: Dr. Kit Morris. ☏ (045383) 4050. Opening hours: 9–5 weekdays. Type of cider: medium dry; dry – still and lightly sparkling. Containers: 1 litre bottle. Customers may sample before purchase. Other items on sale: preservative free citrus cordials; elderflower cordial; sparkling spring water; wines and wine style products. Directions for finding: on A434 Nailsworth to Tetbury road on edge of town.

Dr. Morris is a wine maker by profession, having made "Three Choirs" English Wine for the past 10 years, besides wine for numerous vineyards in the Gloucestershire and South Wales region. It was at Three Choirs that his interest in cider began, and in 1985 he and his wife started making "Cotswold Cider", solely from traditional varieties and from undiluted juice. Initially they experimented with single variety ciders. They wanted to capture the traditional flavours in a clean and balanced drink: by careful blending and handling they believe they now have a product which will be appreciated by the wine drinker. The apples used are Dabinett, Yarlington Mill, Brown Snout, Balls Bitter Sweet, and Kingston Black. The juice is settled, allowed to oxidise for 24 hours, and then fermented on its own and an added champagne yeast. After fermentation containers are kept full, and sulphur dioxide added to prevent acidification. The cider is then balanced by the addition of a small amount of sugar, to bring out the fruit flavours, and filtered into bottles: ideally this is done with chilled cider, to retain a slight prickle of dissolved CO2. The cider is a pleasant and sophisticated drink: smooth, mature and clean. With a strength of about 6.5% alcohol content, it should not perhaps be encouraged as a "session cider", but for sipping by the half pint, and most certainly for use at the table, where it will complement many dishes.

CRIPPLE COCK FARMYARD SCRUMPY, Business Centre, Barn Lane, St. Columb, Cornwall. Contact in firm: Keith Fowler. ☏ (0637) 880992.

Cider drinkers of several years standing will surely recognise the name. It was, of course, the brand purveyed by the scourge of the Big Three, John Dix, alias "Dixie".

Sadly, Dixie fell on hard times, and the name has now passed into fresh hands, where the cider is building itself a new reputation.

★ **CROSSMAN'S PRIME FARMHOUSE CIDER**, Mayfield Farm, Hewish, near Weston Super Mare, Avon. BS24 6RQ. Contact in firm: Ben Crossman. ☏ (0934) 833174. Opening hours: 8.30–7.30 on weekdays, extended to 9 during summer months; 12 noon–2 on Sundays. Type of cider: sweet; medium; dry. Containers ½ gal; 1 gal; 5 gal: or customers may provide their own. Customers may sample before purchasing. Other items on sale: fresh farm eggs; general farm produce. Directions for finding: on south side of A370 Bristol to Weston road at Hewish.

Mayfield Farm is conveniently situated in holiday country. If you are staying in Weston, it is only a short trip out to get supplies sufficient to face the purgatory of crowded beaches and screaming kids – though you may need to come out every day to ensure you make it through the week! If you are travelling from Bristol, you need go no further. Campers and caravanners may start looking for a nearby site, for with good cider and real food available at the farm you will want for nothing. The cider is made from a number of varieties, including Bulmers Norman, Yarlington Mill, Dabinett, Chisel Jersey, and the legendary Kingston Black: the dry is entirely traditional, while the sweet has added sweetener.

COUNTRY FAYRE CIDER, Kneecracker Cider Ltd., Country Fayre, Wedmore, Somerset. Contact in firm: J. J. ☏ (0934) 712801. Not sold from the premises. Type of cider: Kneecracker – strong raw farmhouse; Merry Legs – vintage rough farmhouse; Zummerset Scrumpy – medium dry farmhouse; West Country Nectar – sweet farmhouse. Just a Swallow – dry farmhouse. Containers: 1 litre bottles; plastic; stone jars from 5 oz to 1 gal.

Do not let the funny names mislead you – this is a natural farmhouse cider, made from Somerset cider apples: no pasteurising, no apple concentrate; no dilution with water. Though it is geared for the tourist market, as is clearly evident, it is a popular and good range, and passes the critical palate of the experts. "Just a Swallow" is a miniature, and means just that: you will be wise to aim for somewhat larger quantities, for surely *many* swallows make a summer!

COUNTRYMAN CIDER, Felldownhead, Milton Abbot, Tavistock, Devon. PL19 0QR. Contact in firm: Bob Bunker. ☏ (082287) 226. Opening hours: 9–5 Monday to Friday throughout the year, also weekends between May and September. Type of cider: sweet, medium; dry. Containers: 75 cl bottles; PET bottles; plastic carry kegs; stoneware jars; or customers may provide their own. Customers may sample before purchasing. Directions for finding: to north of A384 Tavistock to Launceston road about 2 miles west of Milton Abbot.

"Lancaster's Countryman Cider" was for many years well known in South Devon. Over five generations its popularity grew, to such an extent that by the early 1970s Horace Lancaster decided to give up farming altogether, and concentrate on making cider. He retired in 1978, and the new owner changed the name to just "Countryman Cider". At the beginning of 1989 Bob Bunker purchased the business, and with past experience in brewing with Guinness, and advice from Horace Lancaster, is building on the good name of Countryman. The cider is widely available in Devon and Cornwall in pubs, restaurants and off licences. Although the firm may have grown the quality has remained the same. Although Felldownhead is over 500 ft up in the hills between Dartmoor and Bodmin Moor, and therefore too high to achieve optimum apple crops, Bob is establishing a small demonstration orchard containing selected cider varieties. For the main production however the best of local apples are brought in. Apart from filtration the cider is completely traditional, and most of the sales remain as still, natural farm cider; light amber colour, full bodied, and with a wine like consistency – an ideal complement to a meal. Visitors are very welcome to the farm, where all the cider making processes may be seen, and a number of pieces of equipment are on display. The dual attractions of the scenery and the cider ensure a steady stream of callers.

★ **COWHILL CIDER**, Fishermans Cottage, Cowhill, near Oldbury on Severn, Avon. Contact in firm: John Tymko. ☏ (0454) 412157. Opening hours: reasonable times – please phone first to avoid disappointment. Type of cider: dry to medium sweet, depending on apple variety and nature! Containers: plastic; or customers may provide their own. Customers may sample before purchasing. Directions for finding: 1 mile south of Oldbury (Cowhill is a local landmark, a church on top of a hill in the otherwise flat expanse of the Severn estuary: the farm is on the south side).

Until a few years ago, the local cider was made by a well-known and much loved character, Tommy Jones. So often, when such folk give up, there is no one to take over, and the cider vanishes, to everyone's loss. In this case however, on Tommy's death his son in law, John Tymko, decided to keep the firm going, and the tradition continues unaltered to this day. This is arguably one of the most traditional ciders in the Guide: a simple timber shed in the orchard gives token protection to the ancient press, which elsewhere you would see only in a museum: here it is in regular use. At Cowhill, time has stood still for a hundred years! John enjoys his cider making: not for him the chemicals, and the adjustments of the bigger firms, who sometimes seem to be set on creating a house trained appleade. Here in the windswept orchard John lets Nature decide. That, for him, is part of the pleasure, never quite knowing till you taste it what the result will be. His is a cider for the enthusiast, who like him is prepared to be adventurous. The adventure starts in the first week of September, when John starts pressing an old variety called Morgan Sweet. This produces a fruity, light, medium sweet cider, ready to drink in six weeks, and very popular with the locals. As the apples ripen and fall John carries on pressing, and waits to see what happens. Around him are some well established trees, such as Bulmers Norman and Tom Putt, but also many new standards like Yarlington Mill, Dabinett, and Tremletts Bitter. It is here, in the orchard, that John does his blending, before any crushing or pressing: after that, it's in the lap of the gods. Here you will find cider as it used to be in the "good old days", but now so seldom is. No addition, no subtraction, and above all no interference. When John taps a barrel in the orchard he is often surprised, for Nature works to her own rules. If like John you have a thirst for the genuine article, make for the church on the hill, and join him in a spot of cider serendipidy.

★ **TONY CULLIMORE'S GENUINE FARMHOUSE CIDER**, Berkeley Heath Farm, Berkeley, Gloucestershire. Contact in firm: Tony Cullimore. ☏ (0453) 810220. Opening hours: 8.30–5.30 Monday to Friday; 9–1 Saturday (open Saturday afternoon and Sunday on occasions – please phone first to check). Type of cider: sweet; medium; dry. Containers: 1 gal; or customers may provide their own. Customers may sample before purchasing. Other items on sale: country wines when available; local honey; general agricultural goods. Directions for finding: off A38, on B4066 just before Berkeley.

You will not, at first glance, recognise this as a farm cider outlet, rather a store for general agricultural requirements, from decoy pigeons to a roll of wire fencing. But in these parts agricultural requirements are deemed to include a regular supply of good honest cider – perhaps to see *twice* the number of decoy pigeons? The cider is a no nonsense, traditional blend of cider apples and culinary fruit, with some sugar added to the sweet variety. Very nearby is the 12th century Berekely Castle, where King Edward II was murdered: it is open to the public, and a visit is highly recommended.

★ **DEAD DICKS SCRUMPY**, Dead Dicks Cider Company, The Smugglers Lair, 32a Fore Street, Buckfastleigh, Devon TQ11 0AA. Contact in firm: Voldis Kudliskis. ☏ (0364) 43095. Wholesale Distributor: does not sell to public from premises. Type of cider: Dead Dicks Scrumpy – medium sweet; dry: Bosun Willies – medium sweet; dry. Containers: bottles; plastic flagons; novelty. Other items on sale: mead.

This is clearly a cider aimed at the holiday market, and it can be found at a number of off licences along the Devon and Cornish coast. One hopes that the "grockles" take it seriously, for despite the quirky titles it is an entirely traditional Devon cider, made from Sweet Alford, Dabinett, and Somerset Red Streak cider apples.

★ **DERRICK'S CIDER**, Cheddar Valley Cheese Depot, the Gorge, Cheddar, Somerset. Contact in firm: Tony Derrick. ☏ (0934) 743113. Opening hours: normal off licence hours. Type of cider: Country Bumpkin – sweet; dry: Tanglefoot – medium sweet. Containers: bottles; plastic from ½ litre–1 gal; stone flagons: customers may sample before purchasing. Other items on sale: English wines; mead; cheese. Directions for finding: from the village, up the Gorge on the right.

It is uncertain whether "Cheddar Gorge" is something people do, or somewhere people go. A dispassionate glance at the hordes of grockles sweeping up and down the street at Cheddar like a human tide suggests that it is probably both. Cheddar is not the best advertisement for persuading anyone that cider is a mature and responsible drink. Youths, and even many old enough to know better, clutch their plastic carry kegs and make Mummersetshire noises that would put Eddie Grundy to shame. It is easy to be carried along by the hype, and find yourself buying before engaging the brain. But in the midst, like a light in the darkness, is Tony Derrick's shop. There you will find good value in a selection of ciders with rustic names, but reliable pedigree. The dry cider is completely traditional, the sweet has sugar added. You will find a drink with a clear orange colour, a good apple aroma, strong tangy apple flavour, and pleasing aftertaste. The best advice, after completing your transaction, is to escape to the hills, complete with some decent cheese, and indulge in your *own* Cheddar gorge.

★ **DUNKERTON'S CIDER**, Dunkertons Cider Co, Hays Head, Luntley, Pembridge, Leominster, Herefordshire. HR6 9ED. Contact in firm: Ivor or Susie Dunkerton. ☏ (05447) 653. Opening hours: 10–6 Monday–Saturday (all year): 12 noon–3 Sunday (summer only). Types of cider and perry: Blended Ciders (6.3% ABV): traditional dry – crisp and unsweetened; medium dry – rounded and mellow; medium sweet – sweeter and fruity; sweet – rich and full bodied. Single Variety Ciders (8% ABV): Breakwells Seedling – fresh fruity medium dry; Court Royal – naturally medium dry; Kingston Black – strong dry. Perry (7% ABV): medium dry; dry. Containers: Blended Ciders: 1 litre bottles; 1 gal jars; 1 pt stone jars; 5 gal polycasks. Single Variety Ciders and Perry: 1 litre bottles. Customers may sample before purchasing. Directions for finding: turn south off A44 Leominster to Kington road in centre of Pembridge, follow road for about a mile over cross roads, Hays Head will be on your left.

The Dunkertons' logo depicts a naked couple in a sunlit orchard: it could be early morning at Hays Head Farm, but we rather think it is symbolic – all about the Garden of Eden, and original purity. For purity, and indeed perfection, is what Susie and Ivor's cider and perry are all about. They specialise in high quality brands, with full flavour and good strength, and take infinite care over the whole process. Most of their cider production is a blend of several varieties, from such apples as Foxwhelp, Binet Rouge, Yarlington Mill, Brown Snout, Strawberry Norman, Cider Ladies Finger, Tremletts Bitter, Frequin and Roi de Pomme. Each of these apple types is pressed and fermented separately, and then blended according to the degree of tannin, sharpness, and sugar content, to give

a still aromatic cider. But in their search for high performance fruit the Dunkertons have discovered some apples which make an excellent cider on their own, and they now offer several single variety ciders also. There is too a perry, made from the increasingly rare Herefordshire perry pears, such as Moorcroft, Blakeney Red, Barland, Butt, and Red Horse. Ivor and Susie are greatly concerned at the rapid disappearance of many of the old and unusual varieties of both apples and pears, and are determined to fight for their survival. At the farm they have established bush orchards of some of the apples which may be on the verge of extinction; such names as Bloody Turk, Kingston Black (only about 60 acres left in the whole country so it is said), Sheeps Nose, White Norman, and Herefordshire Redstreak. The position with perry pears is even more desperate, and with many of the trees almost 300 years old, and not being replaced, the Dunkertons have planted an avenue of Moorcroft and Thorne. All the perrys made at Hays Head, and some of the ciders, comply with the Soil Association standard – a symbol of organic purity. No chemical sprays are allowed on the fruit used, and no water, colourings, flavouring or preservatives are added. The Dunkertons handle their cider and perry with the same care as a wine, and indeed they do have much of the character of a light wine about them. You are encouraged to chill the bottles before drinking, to bring out the full flavour. With the emphasis on organic purity, you may imagine that there is a great demand for Ivor and Susie's products from health food stores and restaurants, and you will find Dunkertons' cider and perry over a wide area.

DYMOCK FARMHOUSE, Three Choirs Vineyards Ltd., Rhyle House, Welsh House Lane, Newent, Gloucestershire. GL11 1LR. Contact in firm: T. W. Day. ☎ (0531) 85555. Opening hours: 9–5 Monday to Friday; 10–5 weekends (except Christmas to Easter). Type of cider: medium; vintage. Containers: $1\frac{1}{2}$ litre bottles. Other items on sale: perry; white English wine; elderflower cordial; apple juices. Directions for finding: 2 miles north of Newent on B4215 Gloucester to Dymock road turn right into Welsh House Lane: Three Choirs Vineyards will be found 1 mile down the lane.

Dymock Farmhouse is a much sought after cider: while it is probably true to say that Three Choirs Vineyards are better known for their wines, it is good to report that they are not neglecting the other traditional English drinks. This is a cider which would be an excellent accompaniment to a meal – a "table cider" to coin a phrase. It has the natural yeast replaced by a wine yeast, and is filtered clear: a strong and palatable alternative to wine. The firm also sells a perry, which you should try.

★ **FARMER JOHN'S DEVONSHIRE FARMHOUSE CIDER**, Parsons Farm, Newton Poppleford, near Sidmouth, Devon. Contact in firm: John Cligg. ☏ (0395) 68152. Opening hours: reasonable hours, but phone first to be certain. Type of cider: Original – vintage cider; Old Rascal – scrumpy. Containers: bottles: or customers may provide their own. Customers may sample before purchasing. Other items on sale: ice cream. Facilities: childrens' play area. Directions for finding: on A3052 Lyme Regis to Exeter road at west end of Newton Poppleford.

Farmer John's cider is produced by the traditional and well tried methods employed by Devon farmers for generations. John Cligg's father, himself a farmer, used to make cider like this as a young man, as did his father before him. John holds that the quality and success of his cider is as much due to the soil in which the apple trees are grown as to the varieties used. The rich red Devon soil is renowned for producing good fruit, and John ensures that all his apples are from local farms. He makes a clean still cider, using only cider varieties; the Old Rascal, a scrumpy, he describes as "a robust 'man's' drink", while the Original, a high quality vintage, is likely to find favour with those who enjoy wine, and may wish to use it as a palatable alternative for dinner parties and special occasions. Parson's Farm is a place for the whole family: John also makes ice cream, which he keeps quite separate from the Old Rascal, and the children may safely play outside, while sampling the products of the ice cream parlour, while their parents get down to more "pressing" matters.

★ **FORGE FARM FAMOUS CIDERS**, The Forge, Richards Castle, near Ludlow, Shropshire. Contact in firm: Tom Evans. ☏ (058474) 672. Opening hours: all reasonable times. Type of cider: medium; dry. Containers; can be supplied, or customers may provide their own. Customers are encouraged to sample before, during and after purchase. Other items on sale: free range eggs; potatoes; tomatoes, vegetables; apples; country wines. Directions for finding: on B4361 secondary road from Leominster to Ludlow, at east side of road on south end of village.

Tom has been making cider here for well over 15 years, and the custom goes back at least as far as great granddad's day. Then the family went round with a horse and cart, selling to local pubs. Nowadays the customers beat a path to Tom's door: a procession of locals, and not so locals, appears, and there is usually a merry party in the old barn – some people are regular callers from Birmingham and the Black Country, 40 miles away: their plans of "having to be back for lunch" are very soon swept aside, and forgotten, in the warmth of the good company! One wonders how Tom ever gets any farm work done, as he acts the genial host to his visitors. He will from time to time encourage you to blend your sample of cider with some of his country wines, with interesting results. By then time will have ceased to matter. Amid the hens, the dogs (4), the cats (9), and the remains of farm implements is the scratter mill and press. Tom makes only about 1,500 gallons a year, which as the press is still worked by hand is probably quite enough. The ingredients are all cider apples, whatever can be had locally; but Tom is planting a new orchard, which will make him become independent in time. Forge Farm is not a shop, it is a way of life: allow plenty of time on your visit, and cancel all future engagements. Then step back half a century, nurse a cat, make a fuss of a dog (there are enough for everyone), and enjoy a small country living. By the end of the day you will want to move out there yourself.

FRAMPTON CIDER, Frampton Village Cider Company, Bridge Road, Frampton on Severn, Gloucestershire. CL2 7HE. Contact in firm: John Doherty, production manager. ☏ (0452) 741094. Do not sell to the public from the premises.

In the early 1980s, there was a cider company based in Oldbury on Severn named Bland's Cider. The firm is no longer there, but its mantle seems to have rested on the Frampton Cider Company. The vast majority of the production is processed cider, but we have received reports of outlets serving still cask versions, and for this reason we include the firm in the Guide. In one or two cases the name "Bland" is still mentioned – we trust it does not describe the character of the cider, merely its antecedent!

★ **FRANKLINS CIDER AND PERRY**, The Cliffs, Little Hereford, near Tenbury Wells, Herefordshire (postal address, Ludlow, Shropshire. SY8 4LW). Contact in firm: Jim and Richard Franklin. ☏ (0584) 810488. Opening hours: 9–8 Monday to Saturday: 12 noon–2 Sunday. Type of cider: medium; dry: Perry: medium; dry. Containers: ½ gal; 1 gal plastic: or customers may provide their own. Customers may sample before purchasing. Facilities: for clubs or organisations guided tours including an orchard walk; a talk on cider making; refreshments. Directions for finding: east off A49 Leominster to Ludlow road at Wooferton onto A456 Tenbury Wells and Bewdley road: the Cliffs will be found 2 miles west of Tenbury Wells on the south side of the road.

The Franklins own six acres of orchards, and used to sell all the fruit on contract, while Jim taught bakery at the local technical college. But one day he decided to exchange one type of yeast for another, and use some of the apples to make his own cider. He now concentrates full time on his orchards, and has no regrets, either about changing his career, or making use of his own fruit, which he is convinced makes better economic sense than contract growing. The apple varieties in the orchards, which include Michelin, Dabinett and Kingston Black, were chosen for maximum juice extraction and flavour: careful fermenting in oak, and no artificial additives, produce a satisfying mellow and clean drink. There is also a perry, made mainly from Worcester Blacks. You will be welcome to inspect the equipment in the old stone barn: the mill is an antique scratter, and the screw press is 85 years old. But though production methods are slow, Jim and his son Richard take great care in their making: the results are the proof.

★ **FRIAR'S CIDER**, Woolvens Farm, Billingshurst Lane, Ashington, West Sussex. RH20 3BB. Contact in firm; John Friar. ☏ (0903) 892273. Opening hours: any time of day or night! Type of cider; medium; dry. Containers: 4 pt cartons; 4½ gal; 9 gal; 15 gal barrels; bag in box: or customers may provide their own. Customers are *obliged* to sample before purchasing! Directions for finding: on B2133 Ashington to Billingshurst road about 1½ mile north east of Ashington.

John Friar is more interested in turning other people's apples and pears into juice and advising them how to make their own cider and perry, than in producing cider himself. He is a travelling cider maker, and can visit people at their home or farm with his mill and press on a trailer. He also tours the local shows to demonstrate to the public how excellent true draught cider really is, and using their own apples, how cheap it can be to make. He regards himself as something of a "cider missionary". However, he does also make about 1,000 gallons each year, to prove he knows what he is talking about. He uses only dessert and culinary fruit, and employs only the natural methods. He finds there is a great interest from parents in apple juice, as a wholesome drink for their children, and advises on the best combinations of apples to achieve the best results.

GODSHILL FARMHOUSE CIDER, The Cider Barn, Godshill, Isle of Wight. Contact in firm: Peter Cramp. ☏ (0983) 840680. Opening hours: 10–6 daily from April to end of September (cider may not be sold on Sundays). Type of cider: medium sweet; medium; dry. Containers: 1; 2 litre bottles; ¼ gal; 1 gal plastic; 2 oz; ½pt; 1 pt stone flagons. Customers may sample before purchasing. Other items on sale: apple wine; mead; cider mugs; sweatshirts, tee shirts; badges; jam; mustard; general produce. Directions for finding: on A3020 Shanklin to Newport road in centre of Godshill village.

Godshill is one of the jewels in the Island's crown: a much visited and photographed village of thatched cottages, dominated by a fine 14th century church. It is, of course, just possible that the crowds which swarm there every day throughout the holiday season have come for quite other motives than admiring the scenery, for here is one of the few opportunities since leaving the mainland of obtaining "proper" liquid refreshment. Godshill Farmhouse cider is made mostly from cider apple varieties, such as Yarlington Mill, Chisel Jersey, and Dabinett. The sweeter type has added sugar, but none is pasteurised, and most is unfiltered. It should not be difficult to persuade your friends or family, cider enthusiasts or not, to pay a visit to this delightful spot.

GRANGE FARM CIDER, Grange Farm, Ambridge, near Felpersham, Borcetshire. Contact in firm: Eddie Grundy. ☏ 021 4725141. Opening hours: 1.40–1.55; 7.05–7.20 Monday to Friday: 10.15–11.15 Sunday. Type of cider: rough. Containers: you are advised to bring your own. Customers should sample before purchasing. Other items on sale: cream teas. Directions for finding: on B4140 Felpersham to Penny Hassett road 1½ miles west of Ambridge turn right down unmade track: Grange Farm will be found after ¼ mile on the left.

You are advised to leave your car in the road, and walk up to the farm: the Grundys have promised to fill the holes before this Guide is published, but they said that last time. Joe used to make the cider single-handed for years, but with his farmer's lung he now has to take things easy, and so lets his son Eddie do most of the work. "We still turns the mill with a crank", Joe declares, staring meaningfully at Eddie, "but I likes to lend a hand when it comes to the tasting". Unlike a dented tractor in the yard, the 20th century has made little impact on the farm, where cobwebs hang thick in the ancient cider barn, a cat dives for something in the straw, and old machinery rusts in pieces in the corner. "Tis all natural", declares Joe, "we don't have no truck with new fangled ways, especially when they costs money. We don't let anything interfere with our cider". This principle extends to the amount made, which is 1,499 gallons, to avoid having to pay duty; also to the strict exclusion from the barn of Eddie's wife, Clarrie, and the two children, Edward and William, following an unfortunate incident when William was small, and he removed the bung from Joe's prize cask: he was found some hours later wobbling uncertainly through the village in his birthday suit, announcing he was a spring chicken. The apples all come from the farm, and are local varieties now no longer found elsewhere: Walters Special, Perkins Pride, and Snells Glory. We wondered if there were any additives. "Rats!" exclaimed Joe, placing a well-timed boot as Eddie nodded vigorously. Our fears were somewhat increased when the cider emerged with a curious reddish tinge. Joe could not understand it – "Tis almost like rust", he mused, "I'm sure we didn't leave anything in there". But just then Eddie reminded him he'd lost his prize ferret at the time they were filling the vat. Joe's face brightened. "Ah", he beamed, "that's what it must be then–ferret's oxide". Grange Farm Cider, though made in limited quantities, is sent all over the country by distributors in Birmingham, and may be enjoyed – if that is the right word – in the privacy of your own home.

★ **GRAY'S FARM CIDER**, Halstow, Tedburn St. Mary, near Exeter, Devon. EX6 6AN. Contact in firm: Tom Gray. ☏ (0647) 61236. Opening hours: 7.30–7.30 Monday to Saturday (closed Sunday). Type of cider: sweet, medium; dry; or a blend of any kind to suit your taste. Containers: plastic carry keg: or customers may provide their own. Customers may sample before purchasing. Directions for finding: south off old main road at Tedburn St. Mary, over A30 bridge, turn left, and in one mile right, thence follow road south towards Dunsford: Halstow is down a drive to the right.

The Grays have been making cider at the Domesday Manor of Halstow for 300 years; they may confidently claim to be the oldest cider makers in Devon. Each generation plants a new orchard, to hand on to the succeeding members of the family, and so it goes on. There are twenty acres of apples on the farm, with a new six acre orchard as the latest addition; facing north, it produces later blossom, but often misses the frosts. The modern bush trees look regimented compared to the rustic older trees. The area immediately around Tedburn is blessed with thick yellow clay, Culm measures, the best soil type for heavy gravity slow fermenting cider. All the apples Tom uses come from this tight knit region – go further afield, he insists, and the *same* variety, on different soil, will give an inferior result. Most of the apples, which are all cider fruit, are Sweets and Bittersweets, with some Sharps, and possess splendid names such as Fair Maid of Devon, Hangy Down Clusters, Sweet Alford, Johnny Andrews, and Slap Me Girl: this last should really be called Slack My Girdle, due to the gassy nature of the apple, which tended to bloat you! Tom will have no truck with cooking and eating apples, which do not press well, and contribute little to the flavour. Besides the soil, the Grays are fortunate in having a cellar, built of stone and Devonshire cob, which is custom made for cider making and storage; the temperature changes little throughout the year, giving ideal conditions for fermenting and maturing. The Grays make about 20,000 gallons of cider each year, and it is a strong and palatable drink. The family drink it themselves every evening, which ensures that the quality is constantly monitored – at least that is the excuse that Tom gives us!

★ **GREAT OAK CIDER**, Great Oak Cider & Honey Company, Roughmoor, Eardisley, Herefordshire. HR3 6PR. Contact in firm: Brian Jones. ☏ (05446) 400. Opening hours: by arrangement: please phone. Type of cider: medium; dry. Containers: 4 litre; 1 gal: or customers may provide their own. Customers may sample before purchasing. Other items on sale: honey; bees wax. Directions for finding: on A4111 Eardisley to Kington road.

The Great Oak, after which Brian's cider is named, is a local attraction: it is said to have stood in the village for 1,000 years, before Eardisley was in the Domesday Book – the tree is 33 ft around, and once housed 24 children for tea and buns. Brian's local beverage is for the more mature: his cider is an alternative to wine, and is generally drunk as such accompanying a meal. He has a mobile press, acquired from Normandy, and makes around 1,500 gallons each year. The cider is fermented in 300 gallon plastic vats, and whichever is ready first is used first, then each in its turn. The apples used are all high quality fruit from the old orchard. The Welsh border country attracts many visitors, and they welcome the opportunity of returning home with a liquid souvenir of their stay.

★ **HANCOCK'S DEVON CIDER**, Hancock's Cider and Mineral Waters, Clapworthy Mill, South Molton, North Devon. Contact in firm: N. W. Hancock. ☏ (07695) 2678. Opening hours: 9–1; 2–5.30 Monday to Saturday: 10.30–1 Sunday. Type of cider: Devon Cider – medium sweet; medium dry; scrumpy: Farm Scrumpy – sweet; medium dry; dry; extra dry. Containers: Devon Cider – 2 litre bottles: Farm Scrumpy – 1 gal jars: or customers may provide their own. Customers may sample before purchasing. Other items on sale: honey; Devon clotted cream; craft centre. Directions for finding: 3 miles west of South Molton on B3226 road to Exeter (via A377)

The Hancocks have been making cider with skills handed down from father to son for five generations, and such is their expertise that they have over the years won more than forty prizes. They started using the old style press with straw, but have been employing hydraulic presses for over fifty years, so can claim to be an early example of hi-tec. That apart, all is as nature intended; apples are bought locally, Bitter Sweets blended with others to achieve the right aroma. The family are rightly proud of their cider: they have invented an acronym for it – doubtless after a few pints to give them inspiration: Have A Noggin Cause Ours Can Kick Some! This says something for their cider's strength, not to mention their own ingenuity. There is plenty to see at Clapworthy Mill. It is situated in the beautiful Bray Valley, and includes a display showing the processes of cider making, also a craft centre with a range of high quality goods.

★ **HARTLAND'S FARMHOUSE CIDER AND PERRY**, Flat Farm, Eldersfield, Gloucestershire. Contact in firm: Dereck Hartland. ☏ Staunton Court (045284) 213. Opening hours: all reasonable times – if coming from a distance please phone first. Type of cider: sweet; medium; dry. Perry: dry. Containers: 1 gal; 5 litres plastic; or customers may provide their own. Customers may sample before purchasing – allow a full day for this procedure! Directions for finding: leave M50 at junction 2; take A417 south east to Staunton, continue east onto B4213, left onto B4211, and in ½ mile right into B4213 – Flat Farm is almost immediately on the left. From Tewkesbury take A438 Hereford road, thence via B4211.

Yes, Flat Farm *is* rather remote: in a peaceful part of Gloucestershire, with fine views across to the Malvern Hills in the west. Here the Hartlands tend fifty two acres: father Ray runs the farm, his wife sees to the hens that live in the old railway wagon, and son Dereck lives on the cider and perry – though it hasn't started to show yet! The Hartlands could have been dreamt up by the writers of the Archers: for this is an escape hatch from the real world. There is a marvellous fruity tang in the air, bits of farm machinery lie rusting in peace in the yard, unused but not unloved, for nothing ever gets thrown away. The farm's original apple barn is still however in use, for this is where it all happens. You will at once be made welcome, and probably invited to drink a cow's horn of perry: this is how business is conducted in these parts. If you are lucky you may be offered a tot from a specially selected cider, maturing gently in an old whisky vat. Then the party will move into the parlour, more cider and perry will be produced, and anyone looking at their watch will be told there's time enough. Ray will by now have burst into song, and the country tales and memorable ditties, fuelled by just another drop, will see the hours slip effortlessly away. Should the conviviality get too out of hand – you'll probably be on the snuff as well by that time – you will be offered a bed for the night in the caravan, kept for the purpose! Before things go too far, get Dereck to show you the works: despite the rustic air, the Hartlands have a mechanical press, though Dereck admits it was more fun doing the job by hand, even if harder. There is also a machine for picking the apples off the ground. But all else is down to nature, as it always has been. You will have gathered from your extended sampling that at Flat Farm, although the cider is delicious, the perry is even better. In fact, the Hartlands are one of the very few surviving firms still growing perry pear trees, and making farmhouse perry from them. Many of the trees are now over 200 years old, and they know of nobody who has planted any new ones within living memory. Flat Farm perry is made from Moorcrofts and Malvern Hills, some of the best varieties, though as Dereck admits, nowadays, one cannot be choosy. One day, perhaps, we shall be able to persuade farmers to plant perry seedlings again, but it will be a long haul before perry such as that at Hartlands becomes widespread. So for the real thing, and of course for their excellent cider too, set aside a day or three and set out for deepest Gloucestershire. We promise you won't be disappointed! If you cannot get to the farm, you may be fortunate to find Hartlands ciders and perry at various CAMRA Beer Festivals: ignore the beer, and head straight for the hard stuff! Hartlands is distributed to certain parts of the country, albeit in fairly small quantities, by WESTRAYS of Endon in Staffordshire, and JON HALLAM from Windsor in Berkshire, both of whom you will find in the County Section of the Guide.

Hartland's were joint winners at the Perry of the Year title in 1989 *at the* Great British Beer Festival

---

★ **HAYE FARM CIDER**, Haye Farm, St. Veep, near Lostwithiel, Cornwall. Contact in firm: Colin Vincent. ☏ (0208) 872250. Opening hours: 9–10 daily. Type of cider: medium sweet; medium. Containers: 2 litres; 5 litres plastic; 1 litre; 1½ litre; 2 litre bottles; 5 gal polycasks: or customers may provide their own. Customers may sample before purchasing. Directions for finding: from Lostwithiel (A390) take road south east to Lerryn, thence continue south past Wooda Cross, over another cross roads, and after ¼ mile turn right down farm track; Haye Farm will be found about ½ mile along on the left.

South of Lostwithiel is a cluster of small cider makers, more in keeping with Devon than Cornwall. Some make only for their own consumption, but others, such as Colin Vincent, produce a commercial quantity. His cider is well known in these parts, and any mention of "real" cider, or "scrumpy" in conversation will inevitably lead to a recommendation to seek out Colin. The cider contains an impressive array of apples: Newton Wanderers, John Broad, Lord of the Isles,

Russetts, Alfriston, Golden Noble, Patagonia, Sydenham, Redstreak, American Mother, James Greaves, Tregonna King, and many more. The cider is crisp, well flavoured, and though with good body not too strong for drinking by the pint.

HAYMAKERS SCRUMPY, Haymakers Cider Mill, Taphouse Commercial Units, East Taphouse, near Liskeard, Cornwall. Contact in firm: Robin Sala. ☎ (0579) 45910.

This is a popular cider along the holiday coast from Weymouth to Padstow, and also occurs in a number of inland locations.

★ **HECKS' FARMHOUSE CIDER**, 9 & 11 Middle Leigh, Street, Somerset. Contact in firm: John Hecks. ☎ (0458) 42367. Opening hours: 9–6 Monday to Saturday. Type of cider: sweet; medium; dry. Containers: ½ gal; 1 gal plastic carry kegs: or customers may provide their own. Customers may sample before purchasing. Other items on sale: general farm and garden produce. Directions for finding: In Street, turn from the High Street into Vestry Road, keep straight into Merryman Road, then Oriel Road: at the junction with Middle Leigh you will find Hecks just to the right.

This is a family business, which has been going since 1896, and combines a cider and general produce store, near the centre of the town. Would that every town was so well provided for! Hecks is a prize winning cider: John took the Devon County Championship with it in 1985, and again in 1989, and was runner up in 1986: many of the firms featured in this Guide were taking part, so his victory is something of an achievement, and is a splendid recommendation for his product. The cider is traditionally made, from a number of varieties of cider apples, including Kingston Black, Loyal Drain, Doves, and Dabinett, which are blended together to make a sweet, medium and dry version.

★ **HENRY'S CIDER**, Tanpits Cider Farm, Dyers Lane, Bathpool, near Taunton, Somerset. Contacts in firm: Harold and Dawn Pring. ☎ (0823) 270663. Opening hours: reasonable times – please phone if coming from some way to avoid disappointment. Type of cider: sweet; dry. Containers: selection of plastic and stone jars: or customers may provide their own. Customers may sample before purchasing. Other items on sale: eggs; potatoes; other farm produce according to season. Directions for finding: from A38 Taunton to Bridgwater road just north of canal bridge at Bathpool, west into Dyers Lane; Henry's is a few hundred yards along on the right. By canal footpath from Taunton (by far the best way to come!) cross the canal by the timber swingbridge on the approach to Bathpool, and turn left into Dyers Lane for 100 yards.

Cider has been made here for about a hundred years, started by Harold's grandfather, whose name was Henry. In the very early days Henry would take a cider barrel round the district on a lorry, and fill up the jars of the eager locals: a ciderman rather than a milkman – surely there is room for a revival of this service? The cider is made with local fruit, and as much as possible is matured in the wood. The Prings have an old stone cider mill and wooden twin screw press, which unfortunately are no longer in use, but can still be seen. Nowadays the cider is made with a hydraulic Bucher press and mill, and produces about 50 gallons from each cheese. The dry cider is entirely natural, the sweet has artificial sweetener added. All the old cider making equipment, and some old farm machinery and ornamental birds, may be seen on the farm, where it is hoped to start a museum.

★ **HOME HOUSE CIDER**, Home House, Combeinteignhead, near Newton Abbot, Devon. TQ12 4RE. Contact in firm: David Halpin. ☎ (0626) 872591. Opening hours: reasonable times, but please phone first. Type of cider: medium; dry. Containers: please bring your own if possible. Customers may sample before purchasing. Directions for finding: on left side of road from Stokeinteignhead to Combeinteignhead on approach to the village.

Mr. and Mrs. Halpin are concerned to keep traditional alive, and are doing their bit in this delightful village. David Halpin is in fact an orthopaedic surgeon; the surgery adjoins the house, as too does the cider store. The Halpins bought a press in the early 1980s, and started making a limited amount of cider:

they have orchards on the hill above the house, and they also planted more trees when they moved in. The annual pressing is a village event, everyone joins in and sometimes it can get too crowded, but with a bit of control about 250 gallons are pressed in a day, and the sessions continue for several weeks till the job is complete. Even more of a community event is the wassailing, which takes place on the second weekend in January, a hundred yards down the road: the villagers gather with lighted torches, and process through the orchard to the accompaniment of Morris men. The customary piece of burnt toast is lifted into the branches as a gift to the robins. If the weather is mild the evening turns into an open air party, with as many as 200 people joining in, and the sound of accordians can be heard far down the valley! During the majority of the year the orchard houses a pig, some sheep, and several donkeys, which help keep the grass down: in October they move out – for the apples' sake and their own. What they think about being invaded at wassailing time is not recorded! The combination of surgery and cider appears to work well. Often David Halpin's patients turn out to be his best customers – do they, one wonders, get the cider on prescription?

★ **HOOK'S CIDER PRESS**, Oak Cottage, 15 Hastings Road, Rolvenden, Kent. TN17 4LS. Contact in firm: Michael Hook. Directions for finding: on A28 Hastings to Ashford road

Michael Hook has been cider making in the Weald of Kent for the last 20 years, following in his father's footsteps. At one time, many farmers in the surrounding villages would make a barrel or two to be consumed at harvest time or other social occasions. But with the advent of modern farming methods, many small orchards have disappeared, leaving only a handful of farms still producing cider. Until 1989 Michael was employed in the City with a firm of stockbrokers, but is now self-employed, and able to concentrate on small scale cider making, mainly for family and friends, but also for anyone who cares to contact him. As is the Kentish tradition, Bramley apples are used, and sugar is added to produce a strong, sweet drink. The natural yeasts are retained for fermenting, though Michael admits he cheats by adding an immersion heater to the barrel to start things off! The cider matures in oak for up to three years. Michael is building a mobile tractor powered press plus mill mounted on a trailer in order to provide a service to local villages pressing and selling juice, as well as making about 1,500 gallons of cider annually at Oak Cottage.

★ **HUNT'S DEVON CIDER**, Higher Yalberton Farm, Collaton St. Mary, near Paignton, Devon. Contact in firm: Mr. Hunt. ☏ (0803) 557694. Opening hours: reasonable times – please phone if intending to visit in evening or Sunday to check first. Type of cider: "rough" – medium dry. Containers: plastic carry kegs: or customers may provide their own. Customers may sample before purchasing. Directions for finding: on A3022 Newton Abbot to Brixham road take second turning on right after crossroads with A385 Paignton to Totnes road into Yalberton Road; Hunts will be seen just after crossing stream.

Holiday makers on the Torbay coast are spoilt for choice when it comes to real cider. Behind the beaches in the hills are in fact two cider makers, living side by side, we hope harmoniously, at Yalberton. One you will find elsewhere in the Guide, the other is Farmer Hunt. Hunt's scrumpy is as traditional and natural as you might wish: as with any cider where nothing is done to interfere with the working of the apples' yeast, each barrel is likely to be slightly different. For the town pub, which demands a predictable product for its predictable punters, this is unwelcome; but for those who prefer the authentic and full flavoured cider that once used to be the norm, it is good news indeed. For body and character, a drop of "Hunt's Rough" is hard to beat!

★ **INCH'S CIDER**, Inch's Cider Company, Western Barn, Hatherleigh Road, Winkleigh, North Devon. Contact in firm: Stuart Conway. ☏ (083783) 363 or 560. Opening hours: 9–5.30 Monday to Friday (closed 1–2): 9–1 Saturday. Type of cider: Cider – sweet; medium; dry: Harvest Waeshal – scrumpy: Pipkin Vintage – scrumpy. Containers: 4 litre minicasks – sweet; medium; dry; scrumpy: 2 litre minicasks – medium; scrumpy: 2 litre glass jars – medium; scrumpy: presentation jar – Pipkin: 5 gal polycask – sweet; medium; dry;

scrumpy. Directions for finding: from Exeter – A377 to Morchard Road, thence B3220 to Winkleigh: from Barnstaple – A377 to Eggesford, then follow signs to Winkleigh: from the West – A30 to Okehampton, B3217 to Monkokehampton, and turn east to Winkleigh. Western Barn is at the west end of the village, on the Monkokehampton and Hatherleigh road.

In 1916 young Sam Inch was taken on at one of the local farms, on condition that he would not get paid, but could have the pick of all the apples in the orchard. He began by selling the fruit, but soon turned his hand to cider making, and before long Inch's Cider became the staple diet for Devon folk. Sam became something of a legend in his own lifetime, and ran the firm until his death at a venerable age a few years ago. He made the cider from a recipe he found in a book printed in 1646, and always used local apples, which gave the cider, to say nothing of its drinkers, a characteristic red colour, most noticeable in the sweet varieties; due to the Red Sandstone soils that are a feature of this part of Devon. It possessed a distinctive flavour, and considerable strength – 6% alcohol content for the sweet brands, and up to 8% for the scrumpy. Throughout Sam's life the recipe never changed, and the winning formula was continued by his son Derek, who greatly expanded production, installing modern equipment and a sophisticated bottling plant: by 1989 the firm was producing a million gallons a year, much still in the traditional form, but an increasing amount carbonated in 1 litre bottles. In the autumn of 1989 Derek Inch retired, and the firm passed out of the family's hands, being bought by a management team – Stuart Conway, James McIlwraith, and Richard Jackson. Mr. Jackson is in charge of production, while Messrs. Conway and McIlwraith are joint managing directors, responsible for marketing and sales, and cider making respectively. They intend to retain the firm's name, and further expand and develop production facilities. Stuart Conway claims there is a serious need in the UK cider industry for an independent, quality, volume cider maker: he believes it is a profile that fits Inch's precisely. Let us hope that any changes that may take place do nothing to affect the traditional draught drink which generations of Devonians and visitors have been enjoying for so long.

JAMES WHITE SUFFOLK CIDER, The Suffolk Cider Company Limited, The Cider House, Friday Street, Brandeston, Woodbridge, Suffolk. IP13 7BP. Contact in firm: Michael Hall. ☏ (072882) 537. Opening hours: for tours of the Cider House: on the hour every hour 10–12; 2–4: Shop; 9.30–1; 2–4.30 (Monday to Friday only). No dogs please. Type of cider: James White Suffolk Cider – dry (8% ABV): October Gold Vintage Cider – medium dry (6% ABV). Containers: James White – glass bottles: 330 ml; 1 litre; 2 litre; 20 litre polypin; 9 gal firkin: October Gold – glass bottles 70 ml. Customers may sample before purchasing. Other items on sale: apple juice; cider vinegar; Cider Royale mulled drink. Direction for finding; south off A1120 at Earl Soham to Brandeston, thence right for 1 mile towards Cretingham, and turn left for ½ mile to Friday Street.

The Suffolk Cider Company was established in 1980, and taken over by the current management team in 1986. Since then it has developed greatly in both efficiency and distribution, and taken its place in the market for premium high quality ciders. Michael Hall's philosophy follows the accepted tradition in the Eastern counties. He uses only cooking and eating apples for pressing, never the West Country cider fruit, which he regards as "too bitter". He works on the principle that if an apple cannot be eaten, either cooked or raw, it is no good for his cider. He set out from the beginning to make a strong cider with a distinctive taste, different from the rest of the market, on the theory that if you can't beat your competitors sell something different from the big boys, and form your own niche. This he has successfully done. There are other important differences from many of the commercial sized firms; notably the use of only apples, rather than, as often happens, a proportion of apple concentrate. There are also no artificial additives, save for a small amount of sulphur dioxide for preservative purposes. The cider is made from mainly Cox, Bramley, Worcester, Ida Red, and Crispen, and produced like wine, with a champagne yeast replacing the natural yeasts; maturing takes place in oak vats for a minimum of five months. The James White Suffolk Cider does in fact have more in common with a dry white wine than what the firm call "the brown fizzy stuff that is commonly available"; it is fully fermented out, and thus very dry. October Gold Vintage Cider is matured for at least eight months in oak; it is slightly less dry, but fuller bodied. There are also three varieties of apple juice, Cox, Russet and Original, all naturally sweet, and with no additives: again made purely from apples, and no concentrate. Try also Cider Royale, a mixture for mulling: a blend of apple juice, sugar, lemon juice, ginger, and cloves, each bottle containing a cinnamon stick, this should not be drunk on its own, but mixed with one part Royale to four parts James White Suffolk Cider, and then warmed before serving – a delicious drink for the winter months. James White is now widely available in pubs and off licences: but every November it travels far further. Michael Hall organises an annual Beaujolais Nouveau run in reverse, with a fleet of sponsored drivers taking his cider to Burgundy. Not only does it enable native Burgundians to experience the delight of porc en cidre anglais, but also raises money for charity, for the drivers come back laden with Nouveau, which is auctioned at a local hostelry.

JESSAMINE FARM CIDER, Jessamine Farm, Old Romney, Romney Marsh, Kent. Contact in firm: Anthony Hicks. ☏ (0679) 63850. Opening hours: 11–4 Friday; Saturday; Sunday; Tuesday. Type of cider: sweet; dry; vintage. Containers: sweet and dry – 2 pt; 4 pt; 1 gal plastic: vintage – bottles. Customers may sample before purchasing. Other items on sale: apple juice; range of home made chutney, jam and marmalade; tea cosies; pottery. Directions for finding: on south side of A259 Rye to Folkestone road at Old Romney, just east of junction with B2076 and opposite the church.

Do not let the title "farm cider" mislead you – this is a very strong drink, more of a wine than a cider, and should be taken by the wine glass rather than by the pint. The strength is in fact between that of a table wine and sherry, with a duty of over 50%. The firm is quite recent; it started in May 1987, and has already created a lot of interest, providing for a market not otherwise catered for by other ciders. The apples used are grown locally, and are a blend of dessert and culinary fruit. The cider accommodates all tastes: the vintage is sweet, and sweet and dry brands may be mixed together in any proportions – buy some of each and experiment. Anthony Hicks also specialises in traditional timber framed buildings, and will gladly sell you one in which to enjoy your new found Kentish cider!

JON HALLAM (WHOLESALE DISTRIBUTOR), 34 Devereux Road, Windsor, Berkshire. Contact in firm: Jon Hallam.. ☏ (0753) 852609.

Quaintly titled "compounder of spirits", which smacks more of alchemy than cider, the firm also distributes cider and perry over a wide area; covering 19 counties, from Aberystwyth to Great Yarmouth and the Lake District to the South Coast. 28 different brands are handled, some only to special order. The main lines of cider and perry are Wilkins, Hartland and Franklin. The firm does not sell from the premises, orders may be made by letter or phone. Deliveries are in returnable $2\frac{1}{4}$ gal and 5 gal polycasks. Whisky casks, much used by cider makers for enhancing their products, are also available wholesale to the trade.

★ **KNIGHT'S CIDER AND PERRY**, Crumpton Oaks Farm, Storridge, near Malvern, Herefordshire. WR13 5HP. Contact in firm: Keith Knight. ☏ (0684) 574594. Opening hours: 10–8 in summer; 11–5 in winter, daily. Type of cider: sweet; medium; dry. Containers: $\frac{1}{2}$ gal; 1 gal plastic: or customers may provide their own. Customers may sample before purchasing. Other items on sale: perry; local apple juices; fresh fruit and vegetables; home made honey and jams; bedding plants; alpines; herbs; shrubs; herbaceous plants; local pottery, crafts and dried flowers; pick your own fruit. Facilities: picnic area; toilets. Directions for finding: on B4219 2 miles from Malvern, near junction with A4103 Worcester to Hereford road.

Crumpton Oaks Farm has a spectacular backdrop of the Malvern Hills, in an area of outstanding beauty. Both the Elgar Trail and the local Cider Trail pass the farm. The Knights specialise in growing high quality fruit, and producing fine vintage ciders: local apples are used in the cider making, many being grown on the farm. Keith has planted hundreds of new trees, and now has 40 acres of orchards. He is concerned for the future of cider apples, and is founder of the Herefordshire Cider Fruit Growers Association. The cider is clear and golden, with a strong consistency, good apple taste and aftertaste, and contains no artificial sweeteners or colouring. Also made is a fine perry, the perry pears coming from the small orchards surrounding the farm. Knights Cider has won many awards: in 1987 for example, it was judged Overall and Reserve Champion at the Hereford Museum of Cider Competition, being first in every class. You are warmly invited to spend a day at the farm: there are numerous walks through the nearby woods and fields, and you may leave the car parked safely while you explore the beautiful countryside. You may also pick your own fruit at the farm: strawberries, gooseberries, raspberries, redcurrants, blackcurrants, and tayberries are available in season, please phone for information and details.

★ **LANE'S CIDER**, Overton, West Monkton, near Taunton, Somerset. TA2 8LS. Contact in firm: Gary Lane. ☏ (0823) 412345. Opening hours: reasonable times, but please phone first. Type of cider: medium; dry. Containers: 1 gal; 5 gal plastic: or customers may provide their own. Customers may sample before purchasing. Directions for finding: from Taunton, north off A361 to West Monkton; in village, take the road out towards Coombe, turn left, and left again, and finally left for a third time by Overton House and follow the road along to Lane's.

The Lanes are an example of the new generation of cider makers who are looking to the future. On their hill top farm, overlooking the Vale of Taunton, is an orchard of new trees, planted systematically to ensure a good crop, even in the lean years. The mixture is of Dabinett, Yarlington Mill, Taylor, Chisel Jersey, Court Royal, Michelin and Kingston Black. As the trees have become established over the last few years, Gary and his father have increased production, and Lane's Cider is fast making a reputation for its authenticity and character, and finding favour with the judges in annual competitions. The farm contains some fascinating old cider making equipment; a *sixth* hand cider press, and a cider mill over a hundred years old. But these are now kept purely for interest and nostalgia, for the firm has moved on, and now uses more modern machinery; at the same time, it has installed increased storage capacity, a sign of its success. The cider may be found in many off licences, pubs, and clubs in the Bridgwater and Taunton area.

★ **LANGDON'S WEST COUNTRY CIDER**, The Cider Mill, Hewish, near Weston Super Mare, Avon. BS24 6RR. Contact in firm: Brian Langdon. ☏ (0934) 833433. Opening hours: 9–6.30 on weekdays; 12 noon–2 on Sundays. Type of cider: sweet; medium; dry; vintage. Containers: ½ gal; 1 gal plastic carry kegs; 5 gal polycasks; 2 litre PET bottles: or customers may provide their own. Customers may sample before purchasing. Other items on sale: country produce, including free range eggs, cheese and tomatoes; mulling spices; tea towels, pottery mugs. Directions for finding; turn west off A370 Weston to Bristol road at Hewish (Wick St. Lawrence road), over railway bridge, and Langdons is on the left.

Langdons is conveniently placed to cater for the holiday trade, being near Weston Super Mare, and locals and tourists alike beat a path to Brian's door. He makes an increasing amount of high quality cider, which has won many awards, and though some is sold carbonated, to please all tastes, the majority is traditional draught, with no additions, and retaining the natural yeasts: in the sweeter brands a sweetener is added. A recent addition to the range is Kingston Black, the King of ciders. This is especially to be welcomed, as 1989 saw the closure of Williams Brothers, just down the road at Backwell, who for many years used to keep the area nourished with Kingston Black cider. It is good that Brian is keeping the tradition going, for this is a unique single variety cider, and a rarity much sought after.

LAZY DAISY QUALITY CIDER, Tumblefirkin, Umbers Hill, Shaftesbury, Dorset. Contact in firm: Mykal Donovan. ☏ (0747) 54890: answerphone during daytime. Does not sell direct from premises. Type of cider: medium sweet; medium; dry. Facilities: delivers in area – Tuesday and Wednesday evenings.

Mykal's business is quite small: he makes less than 1,500 gallons per year. He uses many different varieties of apple, following the old cider maker's philosophy of "mix the apples", the more the merrier. He tends to fall a little short on Bitter-sharps, so adds a small element of Bramleys to bring the acidity to a sensible level. The clarity is also aided by storing in properly cleaned oak casks. Cider apples used include Yarlington Mill, Brown Snout, Churchill, Porters Perfection, Red Streak, Stoke Red, Kingston Black, and Bulmers Norman. Mykal firmly believes that cider is made "in the orchard" – the quality of the varieties is what makes good or bad cider. He learnt his trade from Julian Temperley of Burrow Hill (qv.) He used to be a travelling story teller in a horse drawn wagon – in fact he still does story telling, but without the horse. One autumn his horse and wagon found their way to Burrow Hill, where Mykal was to work for the season and learn about cider apples. He had just bought all the metal parts for an antique top wheel, centre capstan, twin screw Somerset press (very rare), from a Dorset/Australian roof tiler cum busker called Scrumpy Allard, who had travelled with him through Somerset. Scrumpy had been planning to set up pressing in Australia, but realised the problem of bush fires, to say nothing of getting the press there. So Scrumpy's loss was Mykals gain, and with the equipment, and the knowledge, he began making Lazy Daisy. Mykal still goes story telling – under the name Nathaniel of Wessex – so does not have a shopfront for his cider. His main custom is from private orders, which he delivers, and he also serves some food orientated pubs, where both he and his cider feel at home. He is now searching for somewhere to set up his antique cider press collection, and hold cider making demonstrations during the season. He would be delighted to hear from anyone interested in helping.

LLOYD'S COUNTRY BEERS, John Thompson Inn, Ingleby, Derbyshire. Contact in firm: Chris Voyce. ☏ (0332) 863426. Opening hours: normal licensing hours. Type of cider: Westons Bounds Brand: sweet; medium sweet; medium; dry; vintage. Westons Country Brand: medium. Westons Old Rosie Scrumpy: medium; dry. Containers: 3 pint glass jar; 2 gal and 5 gal polycasks; 1 litre non returnable bottles.

As you travel north through England, the number of outlets selling cider rapidly diminish. There are however one or two missionaries working in these unconverted parts, of which Mr. Voyce is an example. He is a cider enthusiast, who distributes genuine Herefordshire cider from the Westons range around Staffordshire and Derbyshire, besides dispensing it from the inn. Westons Perry may also be obtained. Should you come across Westons in that part of the world, you will probably have Mr. Voyce to thank: the Fox at Marston and the Coach & Horses at Great Heyward are two of his customers. He will be happy to give you more information about his activities.

LONG ASHTON CIDER, Long Ashton Cider Ltd., Long Ashton Research Station, Long Ashton, near Bristol, Avon. BS18 9AE. Contact in firm: Martin Gibson. ☏ (0272) 392181. Opening hours: 8–1; 1.30–5 Monday to Friday: 9–12.30 Saturday. Type of cider: medium sweet; medium dry; dry. Containers: 1 gal glass jars; ½ gal plastic: or customers may provide their own. Other items on sale: sparkling medium sweet cider in ½ pt; 1 pt; 1 litre bottles; champagne perry in corked and wired 70 cl and 1 litre bottles; apple juice in 25 cl and 70 cl bottles. Directions for finding: off A370 Bristol to Weston Super Mare road (signposted to Long Ashton): the Research Station is at the far west end of the main street.

Long Ashton Research Station was formed in 1903 to carry out work into the chemical composition and characteristics of cider fruit for the benefit of the industry. In 1912 it was absorbed into Bristol University's Department of Agriculture and Horticulture, and broadened its activities to include other fields. In recent years the fruit and beverage section has moved to Reading, and fruit research is based at East Malling in Kent – all part of the Government rationalisation plans. Then in 1989 the cider plant itself was bought by Martin Gibson, and the new firm – a little publicised example of privatization – is now entirely independent of the research station, though still resident on the premises. Apart from its new won freedom, Long Ashton Cider continues much as before, with a genial gang of three; Bill Toy, Lee Court, and Dave Siviter, in charge of affairs. The long established service of advice to cider makers remains – answering problems and enquiries from small manufacturers with regard to production techniques, factors more important than ever with the increased attention of public health inspectors to premises and equipment, and public concern over standards of food hygiene and quality. Naturally, the "gang" practice what they preach: strict chemical control to give a consistent product; adding sulphur dioxide to adjust the level of acidity; replacing the natural apple yeasts with a cultured yeast. They do not pasteurise, for this they consider leaves an unpleasant aftertaste, but they do filter. The cider is made from about 15 varieties of cider fruit, and is clear, light amber, strong and almost winelike, with a woody apple taste and aftertaste.

★ **LUSCOMBE CIDER**, Luscombe Farm, Buckfastleigh, Devon, Contact in firm: Jonathan Nance.. ☏ (0364) 42373. Opening hours: due to restricted access to the farm visitors other than on foot are not encouraged: please phone first for an appointment. Type of cider: dry. Containers: ½ gal; 1 gal plastic; 5 gal polycask: visitors are asked to provide their own if possible. Customers may sample before purchasing. Directions for finding: from Buckfastleigh, cross old A38, and take minor road south of river (parallel with Dart Valley Railway); bear south and continue for approx. 1 mile; track to Luscombe Farm will be found on the right.

This cider is a team effort: the farm's owner, Julian David, provides the raw material and equipment; Jonathan Nance contributes the expertise and the manpower. Jonathan has established a well deserved reputation with his cider, and won prizes with it. It is a good traditional "scrumpy", with the cider apples being allowed to work out their own chemistry, but blended and overseen by a master at the art, which results in a more refined drink than the rough throatcatching brew that many might expect whenever "scrumpy" is mentioned. The cider is golden, with a slight haze in the glass, a distinctly woody flavour, strong and smooth. The apples include Sweet Alford, Dabinett, Chisel Jersey, Pigs Snout, and Somerset Red Streak. Until recently Luscombe Cider was only made in small quantities: but with the disappearance from the cider map of the large local producer Hills of Staverton, the operation has considerably expanded, been incorporated and registered, and now makes enough to supply several local outlets, using the mill, press and vats obtained from Mr. Hill. Folk down here are beginning to learn that it is actually possible to drink dry cider *without* a dash of lemonade!

★ **LYNE DOWN CIDER AND PERRY**, Lyne Down Farm, Much Marcle, near Ledbury, Herefordshire. HR8 2NT. Contact in firm: Mr. & Mrs. Terry Nowell. ☏ (053184) 691. Opening hours: reasonable times, but please phone to avoid disappointment. Type of cider: medium; dry: Perry: medium. Containers: ½ gal; 1 gal plastic: or customers may provide their own. Customers may sample before purchasing. Other items on sale: free range eggs; quails eggs; honey. Directions for finding: off A449 Ledbury to Ross on Wye road: turn north west about 2 miles south west of Much Marcle up minor road: in 200 yards turn right, and Lyne Down Farm will be found a short way along on the left. The cider house is to the right of the front door – please ring the bell loudly!

Cider and perry have been made at Lyne Farm for many generations, using traditional equipment and methods. When the Nowells moved in, in 1983, they were confronted by an old stone mill, horse powered and an ancient press. They had never made cider before, but were determined to keep up the tradition: they acquired a scratter mill, rather than a horse, and another press, to keep pace with the more efficient mill, which they had restored with new bearings and a new drum. Since then they have been pressing on, making around 1,500 gallons each year. They inherited an old orchard with the farm, 10 mature trees, of Foxwhelp, Bulmers Norman, Custards, Tremletts Bitter, Court Royal, Yarlington Mill, and Dabinett. They have since added further trees, of these last two, plus some Kingston Black. The apples are pressed as they become ripe, and after fermentation the barrels are blended to enhance the flavour. There is also one perry tree, and with this and other local supplies the Nowells make what has lately become a prize winning perry. The old stone mill may still be seen when you visit, as can the two presses, with their timber beams and stone bases. If you call in the autumn beware – all the Nowell's friends and neighbours get persuaded to help with the cider making, and you too could get "press ganged".

Lyne Down were joint winners of 1989 Perry of the Year award.

★ **MILL HOUSE CIDER**, Millhouse Nurseries, Owermoigne, near Dorchester, Dorset. DT2 8HZ. Contact in firm: D. J. Whatmoor. ☏ (0305) 852220. Opening hours: 9–5 (closed 1–2) daily. Type of cider: sweet; dry. Containers: ½ gal; 1 gal; 1 litre plastic: or customers may provide their own. Customers may sample before purchasing. Other items on sale: mulling spices; bedding plants; fuschias. Directions for finding: north off A352 Wareham to Dorchester road at Owermoigne, south off B3390 Weymouth to Wool road at Crossways.

Mr. Whatmoor, with his wife and two brothers, runs a nursery for bedding plants and fuschias. But a new dimension came into their lives in the late nineteen seventies when Philip Whatmoor bought his first cider press! It was, admittedly only a small one, but it was the start of a passion. Three years later a Dorset farmer alerted him to the sale of a one ton 18th century wood screw press: needless to say he bought this too, and cider making at Millhouse Nurseries began. Just 30 gallons were made that first year, but now annual production is in the thousands of gallons: the collection has grown too, with twenty presses and at least twelve crushers, some now restored to working order. In the autumn the whole family are "pressed" into service: the crusher they use is an 1864 Albert Day, from Mark in Somerset, the Victorian high tec answer to the old stone trough – a mangle followed by two granite wheels. Despite the annual burst of activity Philip says he finds cider making "Marvellously relaxing". Demand goes up all the time, and the Whatmoors hardly need to advertise to sell their product. Mr. Whatmoor describes his cider as "inefficient": this means he does not try to extract the last drop out of the pulp, as he believes going easy on the pressure helps the cider keep its body. Though sugar is added to the sweet variety, the process is otherwise completely traditional; the cider is matured in oak vats, and at about 6% alcohol content is ideal for drinking in a wine glass. It also makes an excellent drink mulled, recommended for parties or cold winter evenings. The Millhouse is an excellent place for holiday makers, who will be fascinated by the impressive museum of equipment. There is also a video showing the whole making process. Thomas Hardy's cottage is nearby, so a combined trip to both venues may be planned. Gardening enthusiasts will of course be attracted by the nursery, and time should be allowed to inspect the large choice – there are 300 varieties of fuschias alone!

★ **NAISH'S CIDER**, Piltown Farm, West Pennard, near Glastonbury, Somerset. BA6 8NQ. Contact in firm: H. & F. Naish. ☏ (07489) 260. Opening hours: reasonable times, but please phone first to check if convenient, and for availability of the cider. Type of cider: dry. Containers: 5 gal minimum: customers may provide their own. Customers may sample before purchasing. Directions for finding: A361 Shepton Mallet to Glastonbury road just east of West Pennard.

In Somerset, even more than in other counties, cider used to be part of the way of life. Every farm had its own press, and many of the villagers helped with the cider making, and later the cider drinking. These days you will be lucky to find one press left in a village, but where you do, you can be sure that the tradition of cider making has gone on unbroken for well over a century, and the farmer is loathe to change old habits, or lose the skills handed down from father to son. The Naish brothers are a good example of the surviving traditions. They have been making cider in the family for over 150 years, and still own nine local orchards. Nowadays they sell most of their crop, but they do make a limited gallonage to keep their hand in. In a good year they sell some of the juice direct from the press, and local people ferment it for themselves. A visit to the Naishes is highly recommended: this is what it used to be like in farms all over the county, not so many years ago. The availability of the cider cannot be guaranteed, but even if you are unlucky you will have had a living history lesson.

NEW FOREST CIDER, B. J. & S. D. Topp, Traditional Farmhouse Cider, Littlemead, Pound Lane, Burley, Ringwood, Hampshire. BH24 4ED. Contact in firm: Barry Topp. ☏ (04253) 3589. Opening hours: 9–dusk daily. Type of cider: sweet; medium; dry. Containers: ½ gal; 1 gal plastic: 2 pt; 1 gal stone (1 gal with tap): or customers may provide their own. Customers may sample before purchasing. Other items on sale: apple juice. Directions for finding: in Burley (south off A31 at Picket Post) take Bransgore/Christchurch road (Pound Lane); after 250 yards turn left at the Forest Tea House: New Forest Cider will be found at the end of the lane to the left of the tea rooms.

Burley, in the heart of the New Forest, is noted for its curio shops, and ponies wandering down the street. Now there is another attraction – New Forest Cider. At "Littlemead", a family forest holding with registered Commoners Rights, the Topps have revived the craft of cider making, which was part of the Commoner's way of life on their holdings earlier this century. The apples are a mixture of cider fruit such as Michelin, Dabinett, Yarlington Mill, and Bulmers Norman, with local orchard apples, mostly Bramleys. The various varieties are pressed as they become ripe, and after fermentation the barrels are blended. The strength is approaching 8% alcohol content. The firm's sign depicts a previous Burley cider maker, Eli Sims, operating his press in about 1900. The Topps are to be congratulated for restoring the tradition.

OLIVERS ORCHARD CIDER, Olivers Orchard Ltd., Olivers Lane, Colchester, Essex. CO2 0HH. Contact in firm: Rupert Knowles. ☏ (0206) 330208. Opening hours: Farm shop: June to August: 9–8 Monday to Thursday; 9–6 Friday to Sunday; September and October: 9–dusk daily: November 9–dusk Saturday and Sunday only: December 9–dusk daily. Cafe and cider bar: June to September: 10.30–5 daily (cider bar 12 noon–3 only on Sundays). Type of cider: scrumpy. Containers: 5 litre demijohns: or customers may provide their own. Customers may sample before purchasing. Other items on sale: PYO fruit; morning coffee; light lunches; cream teas; salad suppers; jams; jelly; chutney; vegetables; wine; apple juice. Directions for finding: from A12 London road take A604 flyover towards Mersea; at roundabout take 2nd exit towards Mersea (London Road); turn right at traffic lights into Straight Road; at far end cross staggered crossroads and continue ahead into Gosbecks Road: Olivers Lane will be found 500 yards along on right. From Colchester take B1022 Maldon Road for 3 miles, and turn left at Leather Bottle PH into Gosbecks Road.

Olivers Orchard is a small fruit farm, planted in the 1930s, and has been in the Knowles family since 1938. They grow 15 acres of apples, and one of their specialities is cider, made from their own fruit: they make about 1,500 gallons each year. The Orchard is in the Roman River Valley, a conservation area, and the shallow gravelly soil adds extra flavour and colour to the fruit. Much of the apple crop is sold in the farm shop, but no apples are ever thrown away, and customers appreciate the strong cheap scrumpy, especially after working up a thirst in the picking season! After some unfortunate experiences in the early days, which proved the variability of natural yeasts, champagne yeast is now used, seeding each fermentation vessel from the last after sulphiting. Rupert and his wife, Jennifer, have developed the farm considerably since 1970: Rupert is involved with the conservation work of the Roman River Society, and there is an Interpretation Centre which is the starting point for country walks in the Valley. Pick Your Own soft fruit and vegetables attracts many visitors from June to October, and makes an excuse for a day out, with refreshments, including a cider bar for the adults, and a commando tent for the children. You may enjoy the Essex countryside while taking a pint or two of scrumpy – an ideal way to pass the summer!

OWLET CIDER, Owl House Fruit Farm, Lamberhurst, near Tunbridge Wells, Kent. TN3 8LY. Contact in firm: Colin Corfield. ☏ (0892) 890553. Opening hours: reasonable times – please phone first. Type of cider: draught: medium; dry: bottled – medium dry. Containers: bottles: customers may provide own containers for the draught. Customers may sample before purchasing. Other items on sale: apple juice; mulling spices. Directions for finding: off A21 Hastings to Tunbridge Wells road west of Lamberhurst.

Colin Corfield became interested in cider in 1979: he spent two years in the West Country, firstly with Julian Temperley in Somerset, and then at Bulmers in Hereford, in their orcharding department. On his return to Kent he attempted to make cider the local way, using culinary fruit. It was, he admits, not entirely successful. At that time his experiments took place on a nearby farm, but in 1985 he bought Owl House Farm, and became equipped to put all he had learnt into practice. He decided on a blend of dessert apples from the farm, and Bittersweet cider apples, imported from the West. This mix goes of course against all local tradition – Kent cider seldom sees a cider apple! But Colin believes the tannin from cider fruit is essential for a balanced product. He uses a forty-year old mobile press, imported from France with the help of John Watt (of Apple Blossom Cider fame). Colin and his wife have spent some enjoyable days demonstrating the press at local fairs. Owlet Cider follows traditional methods as far as possible, though Colin introduces a pure strain of cultured yeast, and sugar is added to make a strong cider of about 7 to 8% alcohol content.

★ **PALMERSHAYES CIDER**, Palmershayes, Calverleigh, near Tiverton, Devon. Contact in firm: John and Aubrey Greenslade. ☏ (0884) 254579 or 252900. Opening hours: reasonable times, but please phone to avoid disappointment. Type of cider: sweet; medium; dry. Containers: ½ gal; 1 gal plastic: or customers may provide their own. Customers may sample before purchasing. Other items on sale: cream; milk. Directions for finding: about 2 miles north west of Tiverton on B3221 Tiverton to Rackenford road, just past the Rose & Crown PH.

There are now not many parts of Devon where you will be far from a cider maker – as Somerset seems to be on the decline, the fortunes of this holiday county appear to be looking up. Palmershayes Farm is a typical farm cider makers, where the tradition runs in the family. Grandfather began it all in 1905, and it is now part of the way of life. There are 4 acres of orchards on the farm, and the Greenslades buy in other local apples as they need them. The cider is satisfyingly traditional, strong and with good body, but not too strong for taking by the pint. The reputation of the cider has spread by word of mouth, by far the best way. The Greenslades get visitors from far and wide: not only the Continent, but even Australia. If they are prepared to come that far, there *must* be something in it.

★ **PARADISE CIDER**, Cherry Tree Farm, Ilketshall St. Lawrence, Suffolk. Contact in firm: H. A. Coules. ☏ (098681) 353. Opening hours: 9–5 daily. Type of cider: sweet; medium sweet; dry; scrumpy; vintage. Containers: 2 litre bottles: or customers may provide their own. Customers may sample before purchasing. Other items on sale: four varieties of apple juice; range of country wines. Directions for finding: on A144 Bungay to Halesworth road.

For anyone who imagines that cider was only found in the West, it may come as a surprise to learn that it was made in Suffolk as long ago as 1300, and was at that time the common drink. It was still being made on farms into the present century, but as in most other parts the practice gradually died out, and by the end of the last War had all but stopped. Now, however, Suffolk is back on the cider map – not only, of course, due to James White at Brandeston, but so far as true tradition is concerned, thanks to the Coules family. At Cherry Tree Farm they are making ciders, and apple juices, using only the original wooden mills and presses, now well over a hundred years old: farmyard cider is back! Most of the work is done on Saturdays during the autumn, a ton of fruit at a time going through the presses. The cider matures in oak vats for two years; no filtration or pasteurisation takes place. The family is proud, too, of its apple juices – here again no additives are used. Also made on site are a selection of about a dozen country wines, using the fruit and flowers which are grown on the farm.

★ **PAWLEY FARM CIDER**, Kimberlea, Pawley Farm, Painters Forstal, near Faversham, Kent. Contact in firm: D. R. Macey. ☏ (0795) 532043. Opening hours: reasonable time, but advisable to phone first. Type of cider: sweet; medium; dry. Containers: bring your own if possible. Customers may sample before purchasing. Other items on sale: apple juice; apple wine. Directions for finding: from A2 Canterbury to Sittingbourne road take turning to south for Ospringe; go past Ospringe church, and in 1 mile turn left over M2, and continue for another mile, when Pawley Farm will be found on the right on the approach to Painters Forstal, about 100 yards before the village green.

The Maceys began making cider in the late 1970s as a hobby, but the last few years has seen it grow into a business. The fruit is mostly Bramleys, with some Coxes, all grown on the farm, which extends to about 50 acres. Recently a new Cox orchard has been planted, and there are plans to add some Discovery, and more Bramleys: there are still 15 acres of standard Bramley trees, which should be grubbed out, but they yield so many apples they are continually reprieved. The blend of culinary and dessert fruit, traditional for Kent, produces a crisp and mature cider, of up to 8% alcohol content – more suitable as a table wine equivalent than for drinking by the pint. The apple juice is sold frozen, as it contains no preservatives, and the Maceys found this was the best way to keep it. You buy it in bottles, and take it home looking like the biggest iced lolly in the world: but it will soon thaw out, and makes a delightful apple drink for the younger members of the family, while you tackle the cider.

★ **PENPOL CIDER**, Middle Penpol Farm, St. Veep, near Lostwithiel, Cornwall. Contact in firm: Keith Langmoide. ☏ (0208) 872017. Opening hours: reasonable times, but please phone first. Containers: please provide your own if possible. Customers may sample before purchasing. Directions for finding: from Lostwithiel (A390) take road south east to Lerryn, thence continue south past Wooda Cross and St. Veep: Penpol Farm will be found near the foot of the hill about ½ mile past the village on the right.

This is one of two cider makers in close proximity, in what one would not automatically regard as cider country. But this part of south Cornwall seems to have more in common with Devon than the harsher and bleaker parts of the county. Keith Langmoide is the smaller of the two makers, being a farmer first and foremost, and producing cider, as once did many, as a side line, mainly for his family and friends. However his fame is such that others promote his cider by word of mouth, and although amounts made are not great there should be a drop for you to share. It is relatively easy to reach Penpol by public transport: a train will take you to Lostwithiel, and it is then a pleasant three mile walk via Lerryn – which provides refreshment – and over the hills to St. Veep.

★ **PERRY'S FARMHOUSE CIDER**, Perry's Cider Mills, Dowlish Wake, near Ilminster, Somerset. Contact in firm: Henry Perry. ☏ (04505) 2681. Opening hours: 9–1; 2–5.30 Monday to Friday: 9.30–1; 2–4.30 Saturday: 9.30–1 Sunday: 9.30–1; 2–4.30 Bank Holidays, spring, summer. Type of cider: medium sweet; medium dry; dry: vintage – sweet; medium dry; dry. Containers: ½ gal; 1 gal plastic; range of stone jars. Customers may sample before purchasing. Other items on sale: country style pottery; stone jars; stone bread bins; corn dollies; terracotta ware; baskets; wooden tubs; garden requisites. Directions for finding: branch off A303 at east end of Ilminster to Kingstone, then continue 1 mile south to Dowlish Wake: Perry's Cider Mill is in centre of village on the right.

This is a well-known cider, which has made many friends over the years. The Perry family has been making cider for many generations, and the methods used have changed little during that time. The cider is pressed in a 16th-century thatched barn, where you may also see an interesting collection of country bygones: the Perrys admit to not liking to throw things away, and in consequence we may admire old cider making equipment, farming tools, horse harness, cider jars, and many other relics of the past, once an essential part of the rural way of life. In a new thatched barn, built as recently as 1984, is a further collection, this time of wagons, farm implements, and the large wooden barrels in which the cider is stored and matured. There is also a display of old

photographs showing views of village life around the turn of the century. The cider is made from apples specially grown in the Perry's own orchards, with further supplies from nearby farms. Among the varieties used are Dabinetts, Bulmers Norman, Brown Snout, Somerset Red Streak, Tremletts Bitter, Yarlington Mill, and Kingston Black, also other apples found in old orchards, which add to the taste and variety of the cider. Because most of the apples are grown by small producers the orchards are nearly all organic. The cider is naturally fermented, no additives are used, and good cellar practices ensure a clean pure drink; it has a subtle taste and good apple aftertaste, and a strong consistency.

★ **PIPPIN CIDER**, Badgers Hill Farm, Chilham, near Canterbury, Kent. CT4 8BW. Contact in firm: Bruce de Courcy ☏ (0227) 730573. Opening hours; reasonable times – please phone first if intending to come late or at weekends to check. Type of cider: Pippin – medium; dry: Pilgrim – medium; dry. Containers: $\frac{1}{2}$ gal; 1 gal plastic: or customers may provide their own. Customers may sample before purchasing. Other items for sale: barrel seats and tables; working water pumps, stone cats. Directions for finding: on north side of Chilham bypass (A28): within easy reach of Chilham BR station.

Not to be confused with Pippins Cider, though no doubt it often is! The firm began some years ago as "Pilgrim Cider", and has been bought from the original owner and been developed by Bruce de Courcy. Two individual brands of cider are made: Pippin, as the name implies, is pressed from Coxes Orange Pippin apples. This is a high gravity cider, and although pale in colour is over 8% alcohol content. It is matured in fresh rum casks, and this imparts a distinct rum flavour to the drink. The rum casks are only used *once*, unlike those in some firms, where you are expected to imagine a rum taste after about ten years! The other brand, Pilgrims Cider, is made from at least 50% Bittersweet cider apples, and in this regard is unlike most Kentish ciders. It has a darker colour then Pippins and a stronger flavour on the initial taste: the strength is about 6 to 7% alcohol content. It is quite *unlike* the original Pilgrim some may remember. All the ciders are pressed traditionally, with ash slats and cheese cloths. Most of the production is sold direct from the farm. However, there is one pub outlet, and you may also come across Pippin and Pilgrim at major county shows.

★ **PIPPINFIELD CIDER**, "Pippinfield", Harepath Hill, Seaton, Devon. Contact in firm: Dennis Hunt. ☏ (0297) 20597. Opening hours: reasonable times, but phone first to avoid disappointment. Type of cider: medium sweet; dry; scrumpy. Containers: 4 pt carry keg; 1 gal plastic: or customers may provide their own. Customers may sample before purchasing. Other items on sale; apple wine; apple sherry; Thatchers perry; apple juice. Directions for finding: on A3052 Lyme Regis to Exeter road about 1 mile west of Colyford.

Dennis Hunt must have been destined for cider and wine making; his first memory is of helping his father make wine on the day that Chamberlain declared war on Germany. He learnt his trade from the late Charles Raymond, a well-respected cider maker from Axminster, and carried out research for Long Ashton. The orchards on the farm, on a hill overlooking Seaton, are devoted to dessert fruit, but cider apples are bought in from local farms, and from as far away as Herefordshire. Dennis still uses an old hand press, which he found in a hedge: he also has a hydraulic one but finds it too noisy. He favours a press with two spindles, to give even pressure. He retains the apples' natural yeasts in the fermentation – "if the vessels are sweet and clean nothing will go wrong", he maintains, "good vigorous fermentation will kill off anything". His cider is a vindication of his beliefs: strong and clean. Besides the standard sweet and dry, he produces a "scrumpy" – a mixture of all types of old varieties of cider apple. Most of his customers appear from recommendation: he claims that since he served a satisfied American visitor some while ago he is continually getting word of mouth promotion over the dinner tables of California!

★ **PIPPINS CIDER**, Pippins Cider Company, Pippins Farm, Stonecourt Lane, Pembury, Near Tunbridge Wells, Kent. TN2 4AB. Contact in firm: D. J. Knight. ☏ (089282) 4624. Opening hours: at Farm Shop: 9–6 daily during soft fruit season; 10–5 at weekends, 2–5 Monday to Friday, during plum and apple season (to end of October): Farm Office (next to Oast): 9–5.30 Monday to Friday. Type of cider: medium dry. Containers: ½ gal plastic: or customers may provide their own. Customers may sample before purchasing. Other items on sale: pick your own and ready picked fruit and apples from mid-June to end of October. Directions for finding: down track off B2015 Maidstone road about 1 mile south of centre of Pembury (for Farm Shop); down right turn several hundred yards nearer Pembury, along Stonecourt Lane (for Oast).

This is a good local cider, with the apples all grown on the farm, and the cider made in an old oast house – not perhaps what it was originally designed for, but at least it still serves to quench Kentish thirsts. They use only sound, undamaged fruit for Pippins Cider, and point out that this is because putting any rotten apples in the mixture produces toxins, which eventually result in the drinker waking up with a sore head: this is a wise word of warning for any home cider makers. A blend of Coxes, Bramleys, and dessert apples is used, and makes a cider of almost winelike quality. Being able to control every stage, from growing to pressing, enables the firm to maintain a consistent standard. As with any Kentish cider, Pippins is clean, crisp and strong.

POTMERE FARM CIDER, Norfolk Cider Company, Potmere Farm, Hargham Road, Attleborough, Norfolk. Contacts in firm: Stephen Fisher; Sandy Holdom. ☏ (0953) 456168. Opening hours: anytime. Type of cider: medium dry. Containers: 5 gal polycask: or customers may provide their own. Customers may sample before purchasing. Directions for finding: A11 Attleborough to Thetford road.

Drink your heart out William Gaymer – little did you think when you began in 1770 that you were going to face serious competition! Yes, a new brand of Norfolk cider has made its debut: partners Stephen Fisher and Sandy Holdom have set up their own company to produce a traditional strong still cider at their Attleborough farm. Market fruit is used, the apples being pressed on a 19th-century Norfolk oak press. The natural yeasts are replaced by a wine yeast, and unrefined cane sugar is added to produce a strength of about 14% alcohol content when fully fermented: the sugar also gives the drink a clear golden colour. The cider is diluted by about 50% water, and finally fortified by back-adding some concentrate. It matures for at least nine months in oak whiskey barrels, and is then racked off for another four weeks until it is ready for sale. Glowing reports have been received as to the cider's strength and flavour –

perhaps Gaymers will now be forced to retaliate by bringing out a *proper* version of Olde English!

PULLEN'S CIDER, Pullens Fruit Farm, Ridgeway Cross, near Malvern, Herefordshire. WR13 5JN. ☏ (088684) 232 or 599. Opening hours: 9–5.30 daily. Type of cider: sweet; medium; dry. Containers: quart; ½ gal; 1 gal plastic; bottles: or customers may provide their own. Customers may sample before purchasing. Other items on sale: apple juice; apple wine; country wines; lemon curd; chutney; fruit and vegetables; ice cream: Weston's and Long Ashton perry. Directions for finding: turn north off A4103 Worcester to Hereford road at Ridgeway Cross: Pullens Fruit Farm will be found about ½ mile along on the right.

The farm produces cider made from its own apples: there are 30 acres of orchard. Both dessert and cider fruit are used. Though you will see an old press in the shop, the firm has a hydraulic press, and is also equipped with a modern juicing room and bottling plant. They are also justly proud of their apple juice, Apple Dew, which has no preservative or colouring; they recommend it for every conceivable occasion, as "an adult soft drink which children will also love". They will encourage you to use it in your cooking, too. During the pressing season, from October to January, there are regular demonstrations of cider making: details and times can be obtained on request.

PURBECK RUIN CIDER, 122 High Street, Swanage, Dorset. Contact in firm: E. Shutler. ☏ (0929) 426376. Does not sell to the public from the premises. Type of cider: Swanage Scrumpy – medium sweet; medium; dry.

Eddie Shutler is a member of the Campaign for Real Ale, and also a cider enthusiast. He has no facilities for pressing in the small warehouse which he uses, so takes the apples down to a farm in Somerset for pressing, and then brings the juice back to ferment at Swanage. The apples used are Dabinetts, with other varieties as available. The cider is traditional, apart from the substitution of a wine yeast for the original yeast on the fruit: the sweet brand is sweetened with saccharine. Though you cannot buy Swanage Scrumpy direct from Eddie, he has a splendid shop window for it at an off-licence in the town, and you need never be short of supplies during your stay in this delightful region; and indeed for the journey home.

REALLY FOWL CORNISH CIDER, Really Fowl Cider Company, Bodmin, Cornwall. ☏ (020882) 431. Do not sell direct to the public.

The name sounds like another title for a company formed by Andrew Lloyd Webber, but does not do justice to the cider, which we understand to be really not at all as it purports. The address is that of the distributors, and we understand they have about 50 outlets. We suggest that you contact them for details of their whereabouts: most are in the holiday regions of the southwest.

★ **REDDAWAY'S FARM CIDER**, Lower Rixdale, Luton, Ideford, near Newton Abbot, Devon. Contact in firm: John Reddaway. ☏ (06267) 75218. Opening hours: all day Monday to Saturday, closed Sunday: please phone first if coming any distance. Type of cider: medium; dry. Containers: ½ gal; 1 gal plastic; 5 gal polycask: or customers may provide their own. Customers may sample before purchasing. Directions for finding: off A380 Newton Abbot to Exeter road at Chudleigh Arch south east through Ideford to Luton. In village turn left and continue ahead up farm road to Lower Rixdale. From Teignmouth turn left off B3192 at Teignmouth Golf Course to Luton, turn right in village, thence as above.

John Reddaway's farm is hidden away in the hills behind Teignmouth and Dawlish, and makes an ideal outing. For the energetic, by far the best way of reaching it is to set out on foot from Dawlish, heading east through to the back of the town through Old Town Street, and take the narrow lane along the east side of Dawlish Water: this turns north, and then swings west, along a peaceful valley, till you finally turn left, cross the stream and climb up to and across the B3192 and drop down into Luton. The walk will take you an hour and a half, and you will enjoy some delightful Devon scenery. However you reach Lower Rixdale, you will once there also enjoy some delightful Devon cider, for this is a prize winning make, totally natural, and dispensed from vast oak barrels, one of which, Old Tom, is 200 years-old. The cider comes out clear and golden, with the strong tang of Bittersweet cider fruit. In fact John uses a blend of apples: three quarters are cider apples, and the rest a mix of culinary to give a good balance. It is a formula which has satisfied the judges in many a competition. John farms 200 acres, but cider making is almost as important. His father and grandfather used to make cider, but then gave up, and it was only in the 1970s that John restarted. By then many of the trees were, to put it mildly, past their best, and he has had to cut down one orchard, and begin replacing trees in the other. There are still plenty of apples left each year for the 1,500 gallons he produces, and John will make sure there always will be.

★ **REED'S CIDER**, Broadhayes, Sawmills, Stockland, near Honiton, Devon. Contact in firm: Bill Reed. ☏ (040488) 366. Opening hours: all day Sundays. Type of cider: medium; vintage. Containers: all sizes: or customers may provide their own. Customers may sample before purchasing. Directions for finding: turn north off A35 Axminster to Honiton road at Wilmington; in 2 miles at top of Stockland Hill turn left at T-junction, then in 1 mile, at 2nd cross roads, turn right: Broadhayes will be found about 1 mile along on the left.

Bill Reed's natural habitat is the King's Arms at Stockland. Not surprisingly it is also one of the locations for his excellent cider, which he describes proudly as "natural fermented apple juice". Bill does *not* agree with Jack Woolacott (qv) that the local clay soil will not produce good cider apples – he says there are still many people who grow apples, and make good cider, in these parts. He certainly practices what he preaches: all his cider apples are obtained from local farms. According to Bill, this largely unknown portion of Devon, away from the main roads, continues to uphold the cider tradition. Wassailing still takes place every year at Dunkeswell, north of Honiton. For his part, Bill also intends to keep the flag flying.

RICH'S SOMERSET FARMHOUSE CIDER, Mill Farm, Watchfield, near Highbridge, Somerset. TA9 4RD. Contact in firm: Gordon Rich. ☏ (0278) 783651. Opening hours: reasonable times, please phone first if coming some way, or at 'unsocial' hours. Type of cider: Golden Demon – sweet: Golden Choice – medium: Golden Harvest – dry. Containers: $\frac{1}{2}$ gal; 1 gal plastic: customers may provide their own. Customers may sample before purchasing. Directions for finding: on B3139 Highbridge to Wedmore and Wells road (turn off A38 at Highbridge), about $1\frac{1}{2}$ miles east of M5 motorway bridge.

Much of Gordon Rich's cider is sold direct from the farm. Its fame has spread by word of mouth, and people keep coming back for more of it all the year round. All the output is sold on draught, as opposed to many makers who market much of their cider in bottles and packs. At times the farm tend to resemble a cider-filling station! Gordon will sell you any amount from $\frac{1}{2}$ gallon upwards, and you will be impressed by the value for money prices. There is a cider for every palate, and, by the descriptions Gordon gives them, for every human condition: Gold Demon – naughty but nice; Golden Choice – for the individual; and Golden Harvest – for the connoisseur. Pressing is so programmed that there are supplies all the year. Cider making begins at the end of August, with Morgan Sweets, and goes on to March, with different varieties of cider apples from all over the West Country arriving, depending on the month. All three brands have a highly distinctive tangy flavour, a good aroma, a cloudy orange colour, and good body. They are however not too strong – just right for drinking by the pint, as Gordon's many satisfied customers have discovered.

RICHARDS' CIDER, The Corner Cottage, Smallway, Congresbury, Avon. Contact in firm: G. Richards. ☏ (0934) 832054. Opening hours: reasonable times, but please phone for details if in evenings or weekends. Type of cider: sweet; medium; dry. Containers: plastic $\frac{1}{2}$ gal; 1 gal: or customers may provide their own. Customers may sample before purchasing. Directions for finding: turn west off A370 just north of river bridge in Congresbury onto B3133 Yatton road; Richards' shop will be found a few hundred yards along on the left.

This is a cider with two distinct categories of customer: firstly the holiday makers, for the premises are well placed to attract the many tourists and campers who frequent this region every summer, and secondly the inhabitants of Greater Bristol, who live on Gerald Richards' cider all the year round. It is a strong and tasty cider, and good value for money: if demand increases the Bristol city fathers might be advised to consider a light railway link to Congresbury as one of their routes for new rapid transit systems.

★ **ROSIES CIDER**, Rose Farm, Lattiford, near Wincanton, Somerset. BA9 8AF. Contacts in firm: Rosie or David Aldrich. ☏ (0963) 33680. Opening hours: 8.30–6.30 Monday to Saturday: 12 noon–3 on Sunday. Type of cider: character depending on apple types. Containers: plastic carry kegs; stone jars: or customers may provide their own. Customers may sample before purchasing. Other items on sale: preserves with cider added; many souvenirs. Directions for finding: about $1\frac{1}{2}$ miles south west of Wincanton on A357 to Blandford Forum, just south of A303: if travelling from London direction, turn off A303 for Wincanton, and immediately after crossing over A303, turn right for Templecombe: from west turn off A303 for Wincanton, and immediately turn left for Templecombe.

Laurie Lee, of "Cider and Rosie" fame, gave his blessing to this venture, when he dedicated the Wishing Well at the farmhouse to the Great Ormond Street Wishing Well Appeal. Rosies is an award winning cider: the Aldrichs won the Bath and West Championship with it in both 1987 and 1988. The cider apples used come from a number of nearby villages, and the varying soils produce a range of distinctive ciders. Those from Horsington Marsh give an earthy taste to the early Morgan Sweets, whereas Yarlington Mill apples from Compton Pauncefoot make for a fruity, nutty, deep-coloured cider. Apples from say Henstridge orchards will make quite a different product from those in Holton, Blackford or North Cheriton. This is a high quality cider: some customers use the dry variety as a substitute for a glass of wine. However you use it, the Aldrichs are concerned that you treat it with care: should you wish to keep it for any length of time they advise that you store it in bottles, full to the top to expel any air. Bag in the box containers are offered for customers requiring large quantities; 2 or 5 gallons. The 5 gallon bag in the box can be despatched for you to collect from main line rail stations. There is a wealth of gifts and souvenirs for sale: all on the farmhouse cider theme of course – jars, sweatshirts and tee shirts, mugs, tea towels, and an incredibly accurate model of the Aldrich's pretty thatched cottage. Railway enthusiasts may wish to make the journey to Rose Farm by train, an easy matter from Templecombe station on the Exeter to Salisbury line. The three mile walk soon passes, and on the return journey you will have supplies to give you a Rosie outlook on everything!

★ **SANDFORD CIDER**, Lower Farm House, Sandford Orcas, near Sherborne, Dorset. DT9 4RP. Contact in firm: Nigel Stewart. ☏ (096322) 363. Opening hours: all reasonable times, but please phone first. Type of cider: medium; dry. Containers: min 5 gal: customers may also provide their own – min 5 gal. Customers may sample before purchasing. Directions for finding: on road into Sandford Orcas from Sherborne, take track to right by bend at start of village.

Nigel Stewart has only recently started cider making, but he has set himself high ambitions – to produce a traditional cider of as fine a quality as possible. To judge by the results so far, he is succeeding in his objective. The cider is cloudy golden, has good body, and smooth consistency: the dry is very dry. Nigel describes the apples as "a glorious mixture": well-known varieties such as Yarlington Mill, Kingston Black, Crimson King, Bulmers Norman and Morgan Sweet predominate, with other obscure types which Nigel has still to identify. He has recently planted 1½ acres of orchard with trees rescued from John Gooden, who some cider fans will remember from Compton Manor nearby in the days when he too made cider. To gauge how his cider compared with others, Nigel entered it in the Devon Show County Show, and was pleasantly surprised to come first in the medium and sweet class: the sweet went on to become Reserve Champion. Most of the production, of about 1,500 gallons a year, finds its way to local pubs: only wholesale amounts are obtainable direct from the farm. But wherever you come across it, you too will be pleasantly surprised by this welcome addition to the ranks of traditional cider.

★ **SELLERS' CIDER**, Sherston Earl Vineyards Ltd., Sherston, Malmesbury, Wiltshire. SN16 0PY. Contact in firm: Norman Sellers. ☏ (0666) 840716. Opening hours: reasonable times; please phone if wishing to visit outside normal retail hours. Type of cider: Sherston Scorcher:- medium: Sellers Cider – medium sweet; medium; dry: Single variety specials. Containers: from 2 pints to 5 gals: or customers may provide their own. Customers may sample before purchasing. Other items on sale: apple juice; oak barrels; garden furniture such as oak tubs, barrel seats, and water butts. Directions for finding: just east of B4040 Old Sodbury to Malmesbury road: leave M4 at junction 18, take A46 north for 2 miles, turn right onto B4040 and fork right off it just after Luckington; Sellers will be found about ½ mile along on the right: from Malmesbury, take minor road from town through Foxley, and continue, avoiding Sherston village, whence Sellers will be on left ½ mile before Luckington.

Sherston Scorcher makes the world go round and round – so say the stickers: they also caution you not to drink Sherston Scorcher and drive. This is Norman

Sellers' secret weapon, his top-of-the-range cider. In fact all the ciders are approaching wine strength, so the warning should apply to them too. Norman specialises in single variety ciders, Yarlington Mill, Brown Snout, Dabinett, and Kingston Black: the natural tannins in the apple produce different flavours in each cider. Apples in the normal range include Porters Perfection, Chisel Jersey, Browns Apple, Michelin, Harry Masters Jersey, and Normans. All his cider is made entirely with cider fruit. Apart from some sweetener to the sweeter end of the range nothing is done to interfere with nature, and no water is added – hence the strength. The ciders are all, of course, "Best Sellers", and Norman needs no other outlet than the farm shop, so you will not find them elsewhere – except, of course, at such events as the Great British Beer Festival.

★ **SHEPPY'S CIDER**, R. J. Sheppy & Son, Three Bridges, Bradford on Tone, near Taunton, Somerset. TA4 1ER. Contact in firm: Richard Sheppy. ☏ (082346) 233. Opening hours: Monday–Saturday: 8.30–6 (October 1st–April 30th); 8.30–7 (May 1st–September 30th): Sunday 12 noon–2 only (Easter–Christmas). Type of cider: Farmhouse Draught – sweet; medium; dry: Oakwood Draught: Gold Medal – sweet; medium; dry. Containers: Farmhouse – ½ gal; 1 gal; 5 gal plastic: Oakwood – 3 pt glass jars: Gold Medal – 1 litre bottles: customers may also bring their own for the draught ciders. Customers may sample before purchasing. Other items on sale: cheese; cream; mugs; other general souvenirs. Directions for finding: on A38 mid-way between Taunton and Wellington.

Sheppys are a small independent family business of farmers and cider makers, who have been making cider for over 200 years. In recent years they have been committed to the production of high quality ciders, both draught and bottled, rather than "rough" farmhouse cider. Since 1925 they have won over 200 awards, and two gold medals. Richard Sheppy is probably the last of the true farm cider makers in the Vale of Taunton Deane, but he believes there is a good future for his quality brands, with much more variety, taste and character than the mass produced commercial makes. There are forty two acres of orchards at the farm, including many new bush trees: varieties include Kingston Black, Yarlington Mill, Dabinett, Stoke Red and Tremletts Bitter. You may inspect the cellar and modern Press Room, also an excellent Farm and Cider Museum, housing agricultural and cider equipment, cooper's tools, and those of allied trades. The three varieties of traditional cider have different characteristics: Farmhouse Draught is a high quality natural brand; Oakwood Draught is more full bodied; and Gold Medal is strong and still, a good alternative to a table wine. Visitors come from far and wide to the farm: pre-booked parties are offered a slide presentation explaining the art of cider making, and a tour round the orchards – plus of course a full range of samples. Such parties, of 20 minimum, are very popular, and you should telephone in advance for details of charges and availability.

★ **SNELL'S FARM CIDER**, Snell Bros., Styles Barton Farm, Whitestone, near Exeter, Devon. Contact in firm: Snell brothers. ☏ (039281) 280.Opening hours: all reasonable hours. Type of cider: sweet; medium; dry. Containers: ½ gal; 1 gal plastic: or customers may provide their own. Directions for finding: on Exeter to Whitestone road; at right of road on approach to the village.

The Snells are a good example of the once numerous small farmers who made cider on the premises: many have now either stopped it, or developed it commercially, as Eric Bromwell, just a few miles further along the same road. With the Snells one suspects it is part of their way of life, rather than their livelihood. They used to live in the farm next to the Brimblescombes at Dunsford (qv) and made cider there for 34 years, before moving to Whitestone 12 years ago. The cider ferments and matures in the traditional Devon stone barn, housed in oak barrels, and guarded by the farm dog – does he get paid, as did the old time farm workers, with a pint or two at every meal? Styles Barton Farm has the unusual advantage of being readily accessible. It is on the bus route from Exeter to Chagford, and is only three miles from the city centre, though if you walk it you will find it is a stiff climb. You will, though, be in the mood for a few pints when you arrive.

★ **SPILLER'S CIDER**, Burscombe Farm, Sidford, near Sidmouth, Devon. Contact in firm: Gordon Spiller. ☏ (03957) 267. Opening hours: all reasonable times, but phone first. Type of cider: medium; dry. Containers: please bring your own if possible. Customers may sample before purchase. Directions for finding: leave A3052 Lyme Regis to Exeter road about ½ mile west of centre of Sidford, and take minor road north for about 1 mile: Burscombe Farm will be found in the valley on the right. From Honiton, turn right off A375 about ½ mile before Sidford, and follow road round to left for about 1½ miles; Burscombe Farm will be on the left.

Burscombe Farm is at the head of a delightfully remote valley, yet only just off the busy holiday route through Sidford. Motorists may blanch at the ever narrowing road and enclosing high banks, but persevere, you *can* get through! The cider is in an old stone barn, which stays the same temperature all the year: it will take you time when you enter to adjust to the darkness, and make out the ancient barrels lining the wall – some date back to 1914, when Gordon's grandfather began cider making here, and they were second hand even then. The secret, says Gordon, is never to allow them to dry out. There is a small orchard on the hill above the farm, with Kingston Black, Sweet Blenheim, Morgan Sweet, and Tom Putt. This last is a local apple, first found between here and Honiton, and named after the Lord of the Manor of Gittisham. Gordon does not hold with meddling with the cider, nature is given full freedom, and the result stands favourable comparison with other local makes. Sunday morning at Burscombe turns into quite a "club"; all Gordon's friends turn up, thatchers, brickies, carpenters, and anyone with a thirst. Once you have tried Gordon's cider you will understand why.

★ **STANCOMBE CYDER**, J & J Levy, Stancombe Farm, Sherford, near Kingsbridge, South Devon. Contacts in firm: John & Jude Levy or Richard Foyle. ☏ (0548) 531634. Opening hours: by arrangement, please phone first. Type of cider: medium; dry; mature 3 year old. Containers: sold in 2 pt; 4 pt; and 1 gal; or customers may provide their own (any quantity). Customers may sample before purchasing. Directions for finding: near Stancombe Cross, just outside Sherford.

Stancombe was on one of the three manors in Sherford, and formed part of a gift to Sir Francis Drake by Queen Elizabeth I in 1592 for his circumnavigation of the world. The farm was mentioned in the Domesday Book. The Levys have carried out a massive restoration programme, culminating in the cob built "pound house", about 500 years old, which houses their twin screw press, probably one of the oldest still working in the area. The restoration has not stopped with the buildings; for the orchard has been restocked with 500 trees: once these come to fruit the farm will be entirely self supporting, but till then supplies of various types of cider apple are obtained locally. The cider – spelt hereabouts with a "y" – is a strong, still, and authentic drink. Visitors are encouraged to try the gold liquid for themselves, and to inspect the restoration work at this holiday retreat, which had gained the English Tourist Board's highest accolade – the England for Excellence Award.

★ **STOTT'S SUPERB CIDER**, Shotts Farm, Wookey, near Wells, Somerset. Contact in firm: C. J. Stott. ☏ (0749) 74731 or 73323. Opening hours: 9–6 Monday to Saturday: 9–1 Sunday. Type of cider: sweet; medium; dry. Containers: 1 gal plastic; or customers may provide their own. Customers may sample before purchasing. Directions for finding: from Wells take B3139 Wedmore road; fork left at Wookey by the Pheasant PH, then bear left at first junction, follow the road round Hembury Hill, ignoring left and right turnings – Shotts Farm will be found about 2 miles along on the left.

Yes, we do mean *Shotts* Farm, it is not a printing mistake! Assuming you have persevered you will find you are on the edge of the Somerset levels, a renowned area for cider fruit and cider making, where small orchards of old trees may still be found huddling round the farms. At Shotts Farm Mr. Stott makes about 1,500 gallons of cider a year. The apples used are various, but the result is very pleasing and refreshing: fairly clear orange in colour, with good body, a fine tangy apple flavour, and excellent aftertaste. Some sweetener is added to the sweet variety, but apart from that all is wholly traditional. This applies also to the price, which seems to represent very good value.

★ **SUMMERS' CIDER AND PERRY**, Slimbridge Lane, Halmore, Berkeley, Gloucestershire. GL13 9HH. Contact in firm: Rodney Summers. ☏ (0453) 811218. Opening hours: 9–8 Monday to Saturday: 9–1 Sunday. Type of cider: medium; dry. Perry: medium; dry. Containers: bottles; ½ gal; 1 gal plastic: or customers may provide their own. Customers may sample before purchasing. Other items on sale: fruit wines. Directions for finding: turn off A38 Gloucester to Bristol road 3 miles south of Cambridge to Breadstone and Halmore: just past left turn to Wanswell and Berkeley before Halmore turn right into Slimbridge Lane (sign for Slimbridge) – Summers barn is on the right, and bungalow just opposite.

Rodney Summers offers you two bits of good news: the first is that all his output is from fruit grown free of artificial fertilisers, pesticides and fungicides – truly organic: the second is that he makes not only cider, but his own perry, a very rare and sought after drink which you will nowadays go far to find. He is in fact one of perhaps a dozen small farmers in the country still producing traditional perry – as opposed to the mass produced Babycham, which is everyones' image of the drink today. Both the cider and the perry are clean and strong, and the wooden barrels from which they are served seems to contribute something to the mellow flavour. If you are feeling adventurous, ask him for a "pider" – a blend of the two: there cannot be many places where you can experience such a combination. While in the district, you should also visit the Slimbridge Wildfowl Trust, just a short distance down the road.

★ **SUSSEX BARN CYDER**. Contact in firm: Alan Darby. ☏ (024363) 762. Opening hours: by arrangement – please phone first. Type of cider: dry. Containers: ½ gal plastic: or customers may provide their own. (min total 5 gals). Customers may sample before purchasing. Other items on sale: apple juice; cider vinegar.

Alan Darby is a wheelwright by trade, and only makes cider in small quantities as a sideline. His annual output amounts to only 200 to 300 gallons. It is therefore something of a rarity, though it may sometimes be found at local events: in the third week of October each year you may see Alan pressing his apples, which he obtains locally, at the Singleton Open Air Museum as a demonstration. Apples used include Bramleys, Granny Smiths, and Coxes: you will gather that this is a traditional Eastern Counties cider, not employing cider varieties. The result is however crisp, dry and clean. Alan attributes his success to the high quality of the fruit; he allows no damaged apples in the mixture. The cider is only available wholesale, which means that it is sold in a minimum of 5 gallons; and the premises are not open to casual callers. However it is worth seeking out this totally natural, and very satisfying cider.

SYMONDS' CIDER AND PERRY, Symonds Cider & English Wine Company, Cider Mills & Winery, Stoke Lacy, near Bromyard, Herefordshire. HR7 4HG. Contact in firm: Charles Lewis. ☏ (08853) 411. Opening hours: 9–7 Monday to Friday: 9–5 Saturday and Sunday. Type of cider: Delicious Sweet; Harvest Vat; Strong Vat; Luncheon Dry; Scrumpy Jack; Drystone: Type of Perry: Old Mill. Containers: all available in 10 litre and 5 gal polycasks; Scrumpy Jack; Harvest Vat and Old Mill also in ½ gal and 5 litres: or customers may provide their own containers. Customers may sample before purchasing. Other items on sale: hats; tea towels; tee shirts; numerous souvenirs. Directions for finding: on A465 Hereford to Bromyard road about ½ mile north east of Stoke Lacy village.

The Symonds family made cider in Herefordshire from 1727, and up to 1984 it remained a small traditional operation, with much of the output being sold on the spot, or from local pubs, mostly in draught form. In that year, however, the firm was bought by Warrington brewers Greenall Whitley, who immediately revolutionised everything. It soon became clear that they had acquired Symonds to introduce it as a house cider into their estate of 2,000 pubs in the North West. They also acquired Jeff Williams, until then Cider House Officer at Long Ashton Research Station, and gave him a free hand to create a completely new plant. When he had finished Stoke Lacy possessed the most

SYMONDS'

SCRUMPY

Registered JACK Brand

Old Fashioned
made
Cider

ESTABLISHED 1727

Produced from Herefordshires' Famous Cider Orchards
SYMONDS' CIDER & ENGLISH WINE CO.
Cider & Perry Mills, Stoke Lacy, Herefordshire, England.
Minimum contents 38 Fl. ozs. (1.08 Litres)

modern cider factory in Europe, capable of producing 2 million gallons of cider a year, up to 20 times the original output. The firm still managed to obtain all its apples from the locality, and may well have helped keep some growers in business. But under Jeff Williams the cider portfolio was reformulated: bringing his technical expertise to bear, he set about "perfecting" the product: this involved pasteurised, chilled and carbonated versions of the old brands, pumped into huge road tankers and transported to Greenall Land. Greenalls had gained a somewhat dubious reputation among beer drinkers for their habit of selling brewery-conditioned keg beer through handpumps: many customers were understandably confused, and when they realised the nature of the misleading dispense, not a little annoyed. It was therefore predictable that soon reports began to come in of Symonds' Scrumpy Jack appearing in Greenall's tenanted and managed houses, and trade accounts, dispensed by handpump, but clearly, when drunk, revealing itself to be a carbonated version. Though under pressure from CAMRA Greenalls eventually pledged to cease the practice with regard to keg beer, they made no such promise in respect to Scrumpy Jack Cider, and more and more sightings of fake hand pumps were recorded. But in the summer of 1988 came the shock news that Greenall Whitley had sold its wholly-owned subsidiary Symonds to H. P. Bulmer. The reasons were hard to fathom: it appeared that Bulmers had paid less than the value of the tangible assets of the firm, but those close to the Symonds management said the offer was "too good to refuse". Cynics suspected that Greenalls had become impatient, or bored with their new toy, which perhaps was not producing quick enough results. Whatever the motive, Bulmers certainly did well from the deal, gaining a modern cider plant, and well known brands such as Scrumpy Jack. Symonds has continued as an independent operation, though closely monitored from Hereford. Cider watchers had hoped that freedom from Greenalls might mean the end of the fake hand pump, but such was not to be. Symonds, under their new masters, still persist in the misleading practice, curiously often in real ale pubs, where one would have thought the last thing customers wanted was a keg cider. Conversely, one almost feels sympathy for keg cider drinkers, searching the bar in vain for a keg fount and giving up in despair. At the same time, it is easy to appreciate Symonds' own dilemma: for although they still produce traditional versions of their brands, including Scrumpy Jack, they must be reluctant to serve it as a handpump cider, where it would come into direct competition from Bulmers Traditional, now of course in the same stable. The politics of cider sometimes leave Westminster standing. However, in fairness to their unwary customers, the present deceit must cease: CAMRA has already banned Symonds products from all beer festivals, and naturally no pubs selling Symonds on fake handpump appear in this Guide. What *does* appear are outlets where we understand the traditional version of Symonds is still dispensed, usually in cask form, but in one case, so we are informed, by a real handpump – could this be the onset of sanity?

★ **SYMONS FARM CIDER**, Borough Farm, Holbeton, near Plymouth, Devon. PL8 1JJ. Contact in firm: John Walters-Symons. ☏ (075530) 247. Opening hours: by arrangement – please phone first. Type of cider: medium; dry. Containers: $\frac{1}{2}$ gal; 1 gal plastic: or customers may provide their own. Customers may sample before purchasing. Directions for finding: south off A379 Kingsbridge to Plymouth road mid way between Modbury and Yealmpton. Opposite second turning into Holbeton turn right: Borough Farm will be found after about 1 mile.

This is a popular and well-known cider, which may be found in several local outlets, as well as at the farm. It is made wholly from cider apples, gathered from long established orchards in the locality, and is entirely natural. It is one of the small cider makers which has benefitted from the disappearance from the scene of Hills, which tended in former years to dominate the market. Symons may now be seen in one of two or Hills erstwhile venues.

TAUNTON TRADITIONAL CIDER, The Taunton Cider Company, Norton Fitzwarren, Taunton, Somerset. TA2 6RD. Contact in firm: Marketing Director.

One of the three largest cider producers in the UK – the other two being H. P. Bulmer and Showerings. It is owned by a consortium of brewers, Bass, Courage, Scottish and Newcastle, and a host of smaller firms. In cider making terms it is a comparative newcomer, being established in 1921. Most of its growth has taken place in recent years, thanks mainly to its well-known keg brands Dry Blackthorn and Autumn Gold. These two brands are so well supported by advertising that many drinkers must imagine they are the sum total of the firm's output, though they will have been made aware of their more recent introductions – Diamond White, and Cool. All the above "benefit" from carbonation, and are purely mass market ciders. Unpromoted, but widely appreciated by West Country cider drinkers, is Taunton Traditional, of which probably about three quarters of a million gallons is made each year. Though not strictly a Category A cider, it is, unusually for a large producer, unpasteurised. This may cheer the purists, but helps to explain why it can seldom be found too far from its native heath. Those who clamour for its appearance further east or north would do well to ask themselves whether they would wish to see it compromised, or prefer it to retain its virginity. Traditional is matured in oak casks, and is a golden colour with a slight haze, and of medium strength, which makes it ideal for drinking by the pint: in good condition, which it generally is, as most pubs which stock it don't need to store it long, it is an excellent cider with a satisfying apple tang to it.

★ **TEIGNHEAD FARM CIDER**, Higher Farm, Stokeinteignhead, near Newton Abbot, Devon. Contact in firm: Thomas and Catherine French. ☏ (0626) 873394. Opening hours: 9–8 Monday to Saturday: 9–12 noon Sunday. Type of cider: medium sweet; medium; dry. Containers: $\frac{1}{2}$ gal; 1 gal plastic: or customers may provide their own. Customers may sample before purchasing. Other item on sale: stone jars; two handled mugs. Directions for finding: off A379 Torquay to Teignmouth road at Maidencombe; or on minor road signed from Shaldon: Higher Farm is in the centre of the village just south of the School.

Thomas's father and grandfather used to make cider until the press house collapsed! The family started up again, and invested in a new horizontal screw press, powered by an electric motor. They have also planted 20 new trees, with Michelin, Dabinett, Chisel Jersey and Harry Masters, so the future looks assured. The additional trees augment the old orchard, which contains varieties such as Somerset Red Streak, Slap Me Girdle and other old types: the Frenches also buy in supplies from local farms. Thomas farms 300 acres, with sheep and beef as his main lines, but finds time to keep up the cider tradition as well. The new site for the operation looks much sturdier than the original location sounded – a fine stone barn, in which the cider gently ferments in oak vats in ideal conditions. Higher Farm is well placed for the holiday maker, being close to the popular Torbay coast. Once off the main road you will find a peaceful world of rolling hills, little known and unfrequented by the tourist. Anyone you may find on the road is likely to be on the same trip as you, visiting Thomas and Catherine!

★ **THATCHER'S CIDER**, Myrtle Farm, Station Road, Sandford, Avon. BS19 5RA. Contact in firm: John Thatcher. ☏ (0934) 822862. Opening hours: 8–6 Monday to Friday: 8–6 Saturday. Type of cider: Draught – sweet; medium; dry: Sandford Superb – sweet; medium; dry. Containers: from 1 litre bottles to 5 gal polycasks: or customers may provide their own. Customers may sample before purchasing. Directions for finding: on A368 Weston Super Mare to Bath road about 1½ miles east of Banwell, and ½ mile west of Sandford Church.

Founded in 1903, Thatcher's is a farm-based cider company, whose products are enjoying increasing popularity, and reaching a wider market. The firm expanded in 1982 with the acquisition of its near neighbour, the Cheddar Valley Cider Company. Orchards of new bush trees have been planted, and the farm now grows a third of all the apples it uses in production; the remainder of the supplies come from as far afield as Herefordshire. The traditional cider is the Draught, or Scrumpy, strong, still and cloudy. Sandford Superb caters for those who drink with their eyes, being filtered clear; it is also pasteurised. The firm also makes a carbonated brand, Mendip Magic. Much of the production is sold direct from the farm: the premises are situated in a favoured holiday region. There are also a good number of pub and off licence outlets, and you may find Thatchers from Hampshire to the Tyne, and Avon to Kent.

THEOBOLDS CIDER, A. Riccini & Sons, Heronsgate Farm, Stourmouth, Canterbury, Kent. CT3 1HZ. Contact in firm: Dave Riccini. ☏ (0227) 722275. Opening hours: 10–5. Type of cider: sweet; medium; dry, extra dry. Containers: 1 litre bottles; 4 pt plastic; 11 litre & 23 litre polycasks. Customers may sample before purchasing. Other items on sale: apple juice; fresh fruit; vegetables. Directions for finding: on B2046 just to north of East Stourmouth, near River Stour.

Heronsgate Farm is a family-run business, which was originally devoted entirely to the production of apples and pears. However, the idea of making cider was conceived some time ago, as an alternative to the mass-produced gassy beverage which most people knew. After three years of experimenting, a clear and still cider was perfected, with a full golden colour. Antero Riccini, his wife Yvonne, and their sons David and William, are all involved in the cider making, and endorse Antero's belief that "Kentish Cider should have a distinctive flavour of Kentish orchards, and is best strong and dry". Theobolds Cider, named after the 400 year-old barn which once housed the cider press, certainly bears this out. It is made from Coxes and Bramleys, and is one of the most highly fruity ciders on the market. The original apple yeast is replaced by a predictable strain, and the cider is filtered for appearance. The flavour benefits considerably by maturing in oak rum barrels. There are no artificial colourings, flavourings, or preservatives. Try also the apple juice: this is also produced on the farm, from Kentish apples, in 1 litre bottles. Like the cider, it has no additives – other than Vitamin C – and unopened will keep for many months.

★ **TILLEY'S CIDER AND PERRY**, Moat Farm, Malleson Road, Gotherington, near Cheltenham, Gloucestershire. Contact in firm: Peter Tilley. ☏ (024267) 6807. Opening hours: 9–9 daily. Type of cider: sweet; medium; dry. Type of perry: medium; dry. Containers: can be provided, or customers may bring their own. Customers may sample before purchasing. Facilities: bed and breakfast accommodation. Directions for finding: 600 yards to east of A435 Cheltenham to Evesham road about 4 miles north of Cheltenham, in the centre of Gotherington village.

The farmhouse and moat, dating from 1700, rest in 30 acres of grounds in a delightful Cotswold village, and offer accommodation for visitors on business engagements or relaxing holiday breaks. There is a swimming pool, extensive gardens, and even a registered riding school. As if this were not enough, Peter Tilley makes a fair drop of cider and perry. The apples and pears are all from nearby fruit farms. The perry is a mixture of perry pears and eating pears, and is very good. The individual barrels are blended together after fermentation if required to enhance the flavour and character of the cider.

★ **TINMINERS CIDER**, Dartmoor Cider Company, Michelcombe Farm, Holne, near Newton Abbot, Devon. Contact in firm: Maggie Dinning. ☏ (03643) 491. Opening hours: any time. Type of cider: dry. Containers: ½ gal plastic: 5 gal polycasks: or customers may provide their own. Customers may sample before purchasing. Directions for finding: at Holne, on Buckfastleigh to Hexworthy road, ignore road ¼ mile south into village, and continue north west for several hundred yards; thence take road south west to Michelcombe.

The name sounds more in tune with Cornwall, but the cider is definitely genuine Devon. It is now being seen in a number of strategic outlets, and is yet another of the rich variety of local ciders on offer to tourists and residents in a county that seems set to rival Somerset for its choice of brands. Cider apples only are used: chief among these are Yarlington Mill, Kingston Black, Slap Me Girdle, and Fair Maid of Devon – whether the last two are connected in any way we leave to your imagination! Certainly the result, when they are all blended, is a satisfying golden cider, strong and tasty.

★ **VICKERY'S CIDER**, Hisbeers Farm, Hare Lane, Buckland St. Mary, Somerset. Contact in firm: Jack Vickery. ☏ (046034) 378. Opening hours: any reasonable time – please phone first if coming some distance. Type of cider: medium; dry. Containers: can be provided, or customers may provide their own. Directions for finding: off A303 or A358 Axminster to Taunton road to Broadway; due west from main village street over crossroads into Hare Lane; gateway to farm drive will be found 1½ miles along on the right.

Jack Vickery is a farmer who still makes cider; once everyone did, now it is the exception rather than the rule. Jack is well-known locally for his cider: most of the population tends to make its way up the hill to the barn, to pass the time of day, and to collect the daily ration: it is like a sort of liquid village stores! Even if there is nobody to talk to you may admire the view while you wait for one of the family to come in from the fields to serve you. But the chances are you will have plenty of good company, and after a few samples you will feel no urgency to leave. Life round here proceeds from pint to pint, not hour to hour!

WEST COUNTRY SCRUMPY, West Country Cider Supplies, 67 Redcliffe Street, Cheddar, Somerset. BS27 3PF. Contact in firm: Paul Lillie. ☏ (0934) 744121. Does not sell to the public from the premises. Type of cider: West Country Scrumpy – sweet; medium; dry: Harvester Scrumpy. Containers: West Country Farmhouse Scrumpy – 5 gal polycasks: Harvester Scrumpy – bottles.

Although Paul Lillie does not produce cider, he worked for some years for Thatchers, at Sandford; in 1983 he left and formed his own distribution company. His market is chiefly those parts of the country untouched by decent farm ciders, but he will deliver to almost all parts of England. Sales amount to about 40,000 gallons a year and are still rising. His ciders are matured in oak vats and are traditional, save for the substitution of a controlled yeast for the wild variety on the apples; also sold is a filtered, pasteurised cider. In addition Paul distributes a draught and bottled perry. For full details of his off licence outlets, please contact him direct.

WESTON'S CIDER AND PERRY, H. Weston & Sons Ltd., Bounds, Much Marcle, near Ledbury, Herefordshire. HR8 2NQ. Contacts in firm: Brian Lewis or Michael Roff. ☏ (053184) 233. Opening hours: normal shop hours during the week. Type of cider: Special Vintage – medium sweet: Old Rosie – strong scrumpy: Scrumpy: Traditional – medium sweet; medium dry; dry: Perry – medium. Containers: Special Vintage – 3 pt glass jars; 1 gal demijohns; 2 gal; 5 gal; 11 gal polycasks: Old Rosie – 3 pt glass jars; 2 gal; 5 gal; 11 gal polycasks: Scrumpy – 1 gal demijohns; 2 gal; 5 gal; 11 gal polycasks: Traditional – 1 gal demijohns; 2 gal; 5 gal polycasks: Perry – 1 gal demijohns; 2 gal; 5 gal polycasks. Customers may sample before purchasing. Facilities: tours of the factory, please phone for details. Directions for finding: A449 Ross on Wye to Worcester road to Much Marcle; take minor road to west in village, and Bounds will be a few hundred yards along on the right.

Weston's is the fourth largest cider maker in the UK, producing well over one million gallons per year. It was founded in 1880 by Henry Weston, and is still owned by the family. Henry had come to farm at Bounds, a splendid 17th-century stone farmhouse, two years before, and began making cider as a matter of course. During the summer of 1879 he realised that he would need another source of income if he were to survive, and encouraged by his near neighbour, MP for Hereford, C. W. Radcliffe Cooke, he decided to market his cider commercially. Supplies of apples were no problem: local farmers were only too glad to sell their crop to Henry, and save themselves the trouble of making their own cider. A newly opened branch of the Great Western Railway enabled him to distribute his cider far and wide, and it soon became well-known and very popular, earning itself the title "The Wine of the West". Henry found he did not need to advertise, instead he relied on recommendation and word of mouth, a policy which the firm has held to throughout its life. Very little has changed over the years at Bounds either: ancient corrugated iron buildings, dating from the firm's formation, still stand alongside the farm house, and even the village garage is made of the same material, and is owned and run by the Westons! There have been alterations, particularly in recent years – not to make the firm bigger but more efficient. The result is a wonderful blend of the old and the new: a modern automatic roller press operates alongside the old style presses, and there are plenty of veteran pieces of machinery still hard at work. Pride of place goes to the massive 200 years-old oak vats, in which the cider ferments and matures – these date back far before the start of the firm of course, and were bought secondhand! It is these vats which Weston's claim is the secret of their fame: 65 of them, all solid oak from top to bottom. Any talk of changing to modern materials such as plastic, is instantly dismissed: in the early 1980s when they needed an additional vat they built a new oak one. The 50 acres of orchards produce only a small proportion of the fruit required, the rest comes from a 10-mile radius, supplied by about 200 growers. Only cider apples are used, about 160 varieties in all. Still grown on the farm are perry pears, the tall trees standing out from the rest; there are more in the village, too, planted to commemorate the coronation of Queen Anne, and still bearing fruit to this day. Weston's are justly proud of their perry: they probably make more than any other firm apart from Showerings. Many people claim Weston's perry is the finest in the country; sadly it is not widely available, due to the relatively small

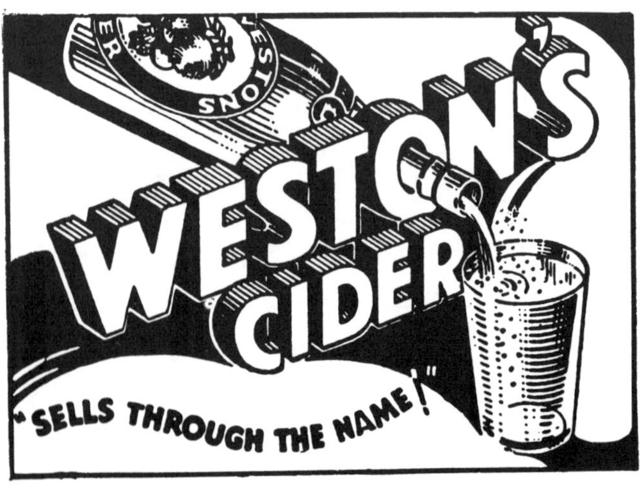

amount made. It is surely time more perry trees were planted at Much Marcle, even if there is nothing special to commemorate! All the draught range of ciders have a distinctive, full fruity flavour quite unlike other makes – this could in part at least be attributable to a small proportion of pears being added to the apples – if so, this is one additive that is definitely a good thing! Old Rosie is a comparative newcomer: named after an ancient steam roller on the farm, depicted on the label, this is a strong scrumpy, of about 7.3% alcohol content – definitely not one for the road. It has fast become extremely popular, and can not be found in many outlets all over the country. The other strong cider, Special Vintage, again 7.3%, is rich and fruity, and makes an ideal accompaniment to a meal. For drinking by the pint the medium strength Scrumpy and Traditional are recommended. The juice is allowed to ferment out to about 12% ABV, and is then diluted by the addition of natural spring water; the natural yeasts are replaced by a champagne yeast – Weston's cannot afford the risk of the natural yeast's behaviour on such a large gallonage – and pasteurisation is practised to allow safe long distance transport and storage in the case of Old Rosie. But these are all minor quibbles! One brand of Weston's cider which is more controversial, however, is "Stowford Press", a keg version which is becoming widely available. This is misleading to the unwary, as it proclaims itself on the bar fount to be "Traditional Draught Cider". To the initiated it is fairly obvious that it is pressure dispensed, for unlike other firm's products which we could – and have – named there is no attempt to disguise the drink with a handpump: whenever you see Weston's on handpump you may be sure it *is* the real thing! However the public description of Stowford Press as "traditional" is unfortunate: let us hope that by the time the next Guide appears Weston's will have thought of something more accurate to call their keg brand.

WESTRAYS CIDERS, 220 Leek Road, Endon, Stoke on Trent, Staffordshire. ST9 9EA. Contact in firm: Kevin Keeling ☏ (0782) 504441.

Kevin Keeling is one of an essential band, dedicated to placing traditional draught ciders in far flung parts of the country. He covers mainly Staffordshire, Manchester and Yorkshire, and is responsible for many of the unexpected ciders which you will find in the County Section of the Guide in those areas. The ciders are mostly listed under their brand names, but in some cases you will discover handpumps labelled "Westrays". Please contact the firm for an update on availability.

★ **WHITEHEAD'S CIDER**, Tootle Bridge Farm, Barton St. David, near Somerton, Somerset. Contact in firm: John Whitehead. ☏ (0458) 50220. Opening hours: all reasonable times. Type of cider: medium; dry. Containers: please bring your own. Customers may sample before purchasing. Directions for finding: Turn west off A37 Yeovil to Shepton Mallet road at junction with B3153: 1 mile along B3153 at Keinton Mandeville turn right in village, and Tootle Bridge Farm will be found about $1\frac{1}{2}$ miles along on the right.

The Whiteheads have farmed here, on the edge of Arthurian Glastonbury, for the last 60 years, and all that time they have made a drop of cider for themselves, their friends and neighbours, and a few favoured customers. Nothing has changed over that time. John makes cider the same way as his father did, and his two sons, Peter and Andrew, have been brought up in the tradition. The only concession to progress is that the 80 year old mill is now belt driven from a tractor. The ancient press, now over a hundred years old, is still used, and you will find no nylon cloths between the layers of pomace as the cheese is built up – just the traditional wheat straw. All the apples come from the farm's six acres of orchard, and the dozen varieties are mixed as they are gathered; each cask is therefore likely to have its own individual character: chief among the fruit are Doves, Yarlington Mill, and Kingston Black. This must be one of the most authentic ciders you will find: it is good to know that here the old standards seem likely to continue for many years to come.

★ **WHITESTONE FARM TRADITIONAL CIDER**, Whitestone Farm, East Cornworthy, Totnes, Devon. Contact in firm: Tom Bertelsen. ☏ (080422) 400. Opening hours: 10–5 most weekdays: please phone beforehand to arrange a visit. Type of cider: Pig Squeal – dry: Adam & Eve – sweet; dry. Containers: ½ gal; 1 gal; or customers may provide their own. Customers are encouraged to sample before purchasing. Other items on sale: organic cooking and dessert apples in season. Directions for finding: turn in off A381 at Harbertonford, through Tuckenhay and Cornworthy – East Cornworthy is between Cornworthy and Dittisham.

Only apples from local cider orchards are used, with the fruit being pressed and fermented separately: natural fermentation takes place in oak casks. This is an organic cider, with nothing added or taken away. The cider is sold by the orchard blend or apple type, all of which will be slightly different, and you will be welcome to wander along the various casks sampling each until you find one to your taste, if you are still capable of decision making by that stage. Beware of "Pig Squeal" – this is alleged to separate the men from the boys, and the tankards from their handles. It obviously has a profound effect on the pigs too! For the technically minded, the press used is made by H. Beare & Sons, Engineers, of Newton Abbot, and is a 70 ton press, dating from the 1930s. It is driven by a 1913 Crossley single cylinder 20 HP gas engine via a line shaft.

★ **WILKINS' FARMHOUSE CIDER AND PERRY**, Lands End Farm, Mudgley, Wedmore, Somerset. Contact in firm: Roger Wilkins. ☏ (0934) 712385. Opening hours: 9–5 Monday to Saturday: 9–1 Sunday. Type of cider: sweet; dry (may be blended to individual taste). Containers: 1 gal plastic; 5 gal polycask: or customers may provide their own. Customers may sample before purchasing. Other items on sale: local fruit and vegetables in season; home made chutney; local cheese; eggs; tee shirts; sweat shirts. Directions for finding: from A3151 Cheddar to Glastonbury road take minor road to east 2 miles south of Wedmore (near foot of Mudgley Hill): Lands End Farm will be found at the far end on the right.

And even then you may need to ask! Not that you will find anyone around, for they will all be "up at Rogers"! Inside the barn you will find a cosmopolitan gathering; some folk from the village, others from as far away as New Zealand – in the midst is Roger, keeping the company topped up with copious samples. They are all there, of course, for the prize winning cider, but the regular visitors

come as much for the relaxed atmosphere, the conversation, and the latest village news. You will be made very welcome. The Wilkins family have been making cider at Mudgley since 1918. It used to be a fairly small scale operation, but once the 1,500 gallon limit was introduced, whereby any maker producing more than that was subject to duty, Roger decided to expand, and make the paperwork worthwhile: many farmers took the opposite course, and elected to call it a day; we must be grateful Roger did not follow them. He now makes an average of 50,000 gallons each year, and besides his home-spun community centre in the barn supplies some thirty pubs and off-licences locally. The most unexpected outlet must be Showerings, the "Big Three" cider maker at Shepton Mallet, where the social club enjoys a drop of real cider, perhaps to remind them what it should taste like. Only cider apples are used; Roger estimates about 200 varieties; the chief ones being Morgans Sweet, Browns Apple, Bulmers Norman, Yarlington Mill, Somerset Red Streak, Vilbre, Tremletts Bitter, and Sheeps Nose. The cider is cloudy yellow, with a smooth consistency and good body, a distinct tang, and a good aftertaste. If you are lucky you may also find Wilkins' Perry, though amounts are limited by the scarcity of the perry pears, and it is not made every year. Roger puts 10% apples with the pears, as they do not have enough natural yeast to ferment well on their own. Roger is known far and wide throughout Somerset, and says he sometimes gets a few black looks from local folk. But then, he claims, he is probably responsible for more marriages, separations, and divorces than most. Yes, Wilkins' Cider is a power in the land! He won the Cider of the Year award in 1988 and 1989 at the Great British Beer Festival.

★ **WOLFETON CIDER**, Wolfeton House, Dorchester, Dorset. Contact in firm: Captain Thimbleby. ☏ (0305) 63500. Opening hours: 2–6 Tuesdays, Fridays, and Bank Holiday Mondays from May to September; also at other times during the year – please phone and enquire. Type of cider: medium dry. Containers: 70 cl bottles; 5 gal polycasks. Customers may sample before purchasing. Facilities: parties by arrangement – ploughman's lunches, teas and evening meals available. Directions for finding: on Dorchester to Yeovil road (A37) 1½ miles north west of Dorchester – indicated by Historic House signs.

Wolfeton House, the home of Captain and Mrs. Thimbleby, is a beautiful and romantic medieval and Elizabethan manor house, with fine stonework and interior woodcarvings, fireplaces, and plaster ceilings. The medieval gatehouse, French in appearance, has two unmatched and far older towers. The main accommodation of note includes the Great Hall and staircase; the parlour; the dining room; the chapel; and the cider house. This last explains why Captain Thimbleby and his magnificent house appear in the Guide, for he makes his own traditional draught cider. He uses only cider apples, such as Golden Ball, Sheeps Nose, Bulmers Norman, and Kingston Black. Many visitors come primarily, of course, to inspect this stately home, and find the cider for sale as an unexpected bonus. But should your chief objective be to purchase the cider, it would be appreciated if you would kindly telephone and make an appointment in advance. In your case, the *house* will prove to be the unexpected and enjoyable bonus!

WONNACOTT'S CIDER, Lansdown Yard, Bude, Cornwall. EX23 8BH. Contact in firm: B. J. Wonnacott. ☏ (0288) 3105. Opening hours: Normal shop times. Type of cider: Scrumpy – medium: Cornish Dry – dry. Containers: ½ litre – 4 litre plastic; 1 litre; 1 gal bottles; 2 gal; 5 gal polycasks: or customers may provide their own. Customers may sample before purchasing. Other items on sale: whole foods; perry; apple wine; mead.

The firm was founded in 1909, and produces an interesting and very tasty cider, which combines culinary and dessert fruit with traditional cider apples: Bramleys, Coxes, with Bulmers Norman and Yarlington Mill. The cider has good aroma, a clear golden yellow colour, and is smooth and clean, with good apple taste and aftertaste. It makes an excellent accompaniment when touring the North Cornish coast.

★ **WOOLACOTTS CIDER**, Bull Farm, Cotleigh, near Honiton, Devon. Contact in firm: Jack Woolacott. ☏ (040483) 255. Opening hours: reasonable times –

but please phone first. Type of cider: medium; dry. Containers: please bring your own if possible. Directions for finding: from A30 Honiton to Chard road, take minor road east 1 mile north of Monkton; go forward over cross road in 1 mile, and in another mile turn left: Bull Farm will be found a few hundred yards along on the left. From A35 Axminster to Honiton road, turn north onto minor road at top of Honiton Hill, $1\frac{1}{2}$ miles east of Honiton: turn right at T junction, proceed for 2 miles, Bull Farm will be on your left.

Jack Woolacott is a splendid example of the old style farmer cum cider maker, who produces a small amount each year mostly for family and friends. However his fame is such that anyone you talk to about cider in these parts will say "you ought to go and see Jack Woolacott". If you take their advice, do *not* invade in hoards: Jack is a farmer first and foremost, and should not be treated like a corner shop. Cider making has been in the family for generations, and the old stone barn, with the scratter mill, and the old screw press with its stone bed, have been in use for many years, though Jack fears his son may not keep the tradition going – a story one hears too often! The farm is on the original Honiton to Chard road, now superseded by the A30, and Jack believes the barn was once a stable for the stage coach horses – there used to be several pubs along the route in the old days. It is delightfully quiet now, and the sight of the old oak barrels in the dim light, with the hot breath of young heifers peering enviously through the door as you take a sample, is like stepping into a time warp. Surprisingly, Jack does not grow the apples he uses: there used to be orchards here, but the clay soil did not make for a good cider – you had to drink it young or it went off. Fellow cider maker Bill Reed, from Stockland, just down the road (qv) would not agree. But the apples that Jack obtains, wherever they come from, make an excellent drop.

YEARLSTONE CYDER, Yearlstone Vineyard, Chilverton, Coldridge, Crediton, Devon. EX17 6BH. Contact in firm: Gillian Pearkes. ☏ (0363) 83302. Opening hours: 9–5 all week. Type of cider: Gold Vintage – dry: Cyder Royale – medium sweet. Containers: 75 cl bottles; $\frac{1}{2}$ gal; 1 gal plastic. Customers may sample before purchasing. Other items on sale: perry (limited quantity); white and red wines, apple juice. Directions for finding: just south of B3220 Morchard Road to Great Torrington road about 5 miles east of Winkleigh.

Miss Pearkes and her brother began with the vineyard, and then went on to cider. Though here you must call it "cyder", the old English spelling, denoting that it is made from undiluted apple juice – "cider" in those days was a weaker product, made by covering the pressed pulp with water, and pressing it out again! Miss Pearkes is something of a perfectionist: she has planted a wide selection of the older varieties of cider apple tree, and spends much time in the orchard: she believes that careful husbandry is essential, to discourage over yield in the so called "on years": sensible pruning, she maintains, is the answer to the problem of biennial fruiting. This is "organic" cyder – the trees are not sprayed with fungicides or pesticides, and the orchards are stock grazed. Only undamaged fruit is permitted. The apples come from the Pearkes' own orchard, and from other ancient orchards in the locality. The care in growing and harvesting continues to the making: the milled apples stand for an hour to extract the flavour and colour from the pulp, and are then pressed slowly and gently, just once, to ensure that no pithy, harsh or bitter flavours escape from the fruit. The juice is fermented and matured in freshly emptied oak spirit barrels, and when still and mature is bottled in Chablis bottles, like a wine. A small amount of perry is also made, though Miss Pearkes does not seem yet to have disabused the perry pear trees of their habit of biennial fruiting, and crops only occur in even years. There are two brands: Yearlstone Gold is crisp and fragrant dry vintage cyder, ideal to accompany ham, gammon, white meat and summer salads; Yearlstone Cyder Royale is a medium sweet vintage cyder, made from selected premium apples from an ancient Exe Valley orchard: it goes well with cheese, most meat and fish, and Italian dishes.

★ **ZUM ZIDER**, West Country Products, Lyon House, 51 Lion Road, Twickenham, Middlesex. Contact in firm: Peter Lyon. ☏ (081) 8924114. Type of cider: Scrumpy – dry: AC/DC – medium: sweet.

West Country Products is a distribution agency for beers and ciders, which though based in the London area covers a wide area of the southeast. The range of ciders handled includes Symonds and Long Ashton, but the main line is Zum, a suitably named West Country brand. It has a very distinctive flavour, and an orange colour, but though you may try to persuade your friends you have gone on to orange squash you will be hard-pressed to maintain the subterfuge beyond a couple of pints – Zum certainly reaches the parts that orange squash never knew existed! Zum is strong, cloudy and still, and after a few pints so will you be, probably in that order.

HOW TO MAKE 'COMPANY CIDER'

1. **Import concentrate apple juice from South Africa & France.**
2. **Buy reject Cox & Bramley from Kent.**
3. **Press out the dessert apples, add Sodium Sulphite to kill off natural yeasts.**
4. **Dilute the concentrate with water.**
5. **Add an Australian wine yeast.**
6. **Four weeks later, fermenting is over.**
7. **Dilute with water to lower alcoholic strength.**
8. **Add sweetener, then Pasteurise it.**
9. **'Fizz' with Co2, add caramel to colour, filter to brightness.**
10. ***Call it 'TRADITIONAL WEST COUNTRY CIDER'***

Issued by the
Save Our Scrumpy
Campaign

ALMA BOOKS

Alma Books Ltd is the publishing company set up by CAMRA (the Campaign for Real Ale) to produce titles of interest to pub-lovers, beer-drinkers, tourists and travellers.

For more information about Alma Books and to obtain the books listed below (which are also available at all good bookshops), write to Alma Books Ltd., 34 Alma Road, St Albans, Herts. AL1 3BW.

Available now:
The Best Pubs in Yorkshire **£4.95**
The Best Pubs in East Anglia **£4.95**
The Best Pubs in Lakeland **£3.95**
The Best Pubs in North Wales **£4.95**
The Best Pubs in London **£4.95**
The Best Pubs in Devon and Cornwall **£4.95**
A series of regional guides offering the reader detailed descriptions of the finest pubs in the area.

Good Pub Food **£5.95**
Over four hundred pubs around the country where good food is as much a priority as good beer and you may find some of the best examples of traditional British cooking, using the finest local produce.

The Best Pubs for Families **£4.95**
Pubs nationwide where children are properly welcomed and catered for, where parents can relax with a pint of decent beer (or cider).

Forthcoming attractions:
A Bedside Book of Beer
The Great British Pub

Join CAMRA

TRIAL MEMBERSHIP OF CAMRA FREE FOR 3 MONTHS!

The GOOD BEER GUIDE could not be produced without painstaking voluntary research by CAMRA members – thousands of them – up and down the country. Our members are even now working on more detailed local Guides, or organising and serving at beer festivals, or going on organised pub crawls, or brewery visits, or trips abroad . . . the list is endless! You can join in.

Why not try out CAMRA membership? It's only £9.00 a year, but you can sample it *free* for 3 months before you commit yourself. Just sign the application form below, and the direct debit form overleaf, and you will become a member of CAMRA absolutely free for the next three months. You will receive:

- ★ the next 3 copies of What's Brewing, CAMRA's monthly newspaper;
- ★ an information packed Member's Handbook;
- ★ a Membership Card, entitling you to free or reduced rate admission to many beer festivals;
- ★ discounts on a range of products and publications.

If after 3 months you do not wish to continue your membership, simply write to us returning your membership card, and you will owe nothing.

If you do not wish to take advantage of this offer, but still want to join CAMRA, *just fill in the application form* (ignore the direct debit overleaf) *and send it together with your first year's subscription of £9.*

Full membership £9; Joint husband/wife membership £9; Life membership £90 Please delete as appropriate: I/We wish to take advantage of the trial membership, and have completed the instructions overleaf. I/We wish to become members of CAMRA. I/We agree to abide by the memorandum and articles of association of the company. I/We enclose a cheque/p.o. for £9/£90 (payable to CAMRA Ltd.)
Name(s)
Address
Signature(s)
CAMRA Ltd, 34 Alma Road, St. Albans, Herts. AL1 3BW.

INSTRUCTION TO YOUR BANK TO PAY DIRECT DEBITS

Please complete parts 1 to 4 to instruct your bank to make payments directly from your account.

Then return the form to Campaign for Real Ale Limited, 34 Alma Road, St. Albans, Herts. AL1 3BW.

To the Manager

Bank ______________________

____

____

1 Please write the full postal address of your bank branch in the box.

2 Name(s) of account-holder(s) ______________________

Address ______________________

____

Post Code ______________________

3 Account number

Banks may refuse to accept instructions to pay direct debits from some types of account

Direct Debit instructions should only be addressed to Banks in the United Kingdom.

CAMRA Computer Membership No. (for office use only)

0	0					

Originators Identification No.

9	2	6	1	2	9

4 Your instruction to the bank, and signature.

* I instruct you to pay direct debits from my account at the request of Campaign for Real Ale Limited.
* The amounts are variable and are to be debited annually.
* I understand that Campaign for Real Ale Limited may change the amount only after giving me prior notice.
* PLEASE CANCEL ALL PREVIOUS STANDING ORDER INSTRUCTIONS IN FAVOUR OF CAMPAIGN FOR REAL ALE LIMITED.
* I will inform the bank in writing if I wish to cancel this instruction.
* I understand that if any direct debit is paid which breaks the terms of this instruction, the bank will make a refund.

Signature(s) ______________________

____

Date ______________________

CORRECTIONS AND AMENDMENTS

Every year sees many pubs change hands. A new licensee can bring improvements or disaster to even the finest establishment. While most details were checked shortly before going to press, errors will inevitably occur and changes come thick and fast.

If you come upon listed pubs which have been ruined or if you find an undiscovered gem on your travels, let me know and I will investigate for the next edition.

Complete the form below or write to: David Kitton, Good Cider Guide, Alma Books, 34 Alma Road, St. Albans, Hertfordshire, AL1 3BW.

County ______________________________

Town or village ______________________________

Name of pub ______________________________

Address ______________________________

Location (A or B road) ______________________________

Tel no. ____________ Name of licensee ______________________________

Description of pub (including bars, food, family room and any special facilities)

____

____

Beers ______________________________

____

____

Reasons for recommendation for inclusion in/deletion from the guide

____

____

____

Your name and address ______________________________

____

____

Postcode ______________________________

County ____________________

Town or village ____________________

Name of pub ____________________

Address ____________________

Location (A or B road) ____________________

Tel no. __________ Name of licensee ____________________

Description of pub (including bars, food, family room and any special facilities)

____

____

Beers ____________________

____

____

Reasons for recommendation for inclusion in/deletion from the guide

____

____

Your name and address ____________________

____

____

Postcode ____________________